The Sound
and the Story

The Sound
and the Story

NPR and the Art of Radio

THOMAS LOOKER

A RICHARD TODD BOOK

Houghton Mifflin Company

BOSTON NEW YORK 1995

For information about permission to reproduce selections from
this book, write to Permissions, Houghton Mifflin Company,
215 Park Avenue South, New York, New York 10003.

Library of Congress Cataloging-in-Publication Data
Looker, Tom.
  The sound and the story : NPR and the art of radio /
Thomas Looker.
     p.   cm.
  "A Richard Todd book."
  ISBN 0-395-67439-5
  1. National Public Radio (U.S.) 2. Public radio —
United States. 3. Radio broadcasters — United States.
I. Title.
HE8697.95.U6L66   1995
384.54'06'573 — dc20   94-45931
                         CIP

Printed in the United States of America
QUM 10 9 8 7 6 5 4 3 2 1

Book design by Melodie Wertelet

To my father
Charles Looker
and the memory of my mother
Jeanette Albert Looker

. . . like . . . heaven's cherubin, hors'd
Upon the sightless couriers of the air,
Shall blow the horrid deed in every eye,
That tears may drown the wind.

Macbeth, I, vii

Contents

SIGN ON

Preface and Acknowledgments

During the late nineteen fifties and early sixties, American radio lost its voice. The once proud medium, the first vehicle of mass communications to reach an audience in the tens of millions, cowered before the face of television, and, mumbling apologetically, shuffled off into the background. An inferiority complex gripped the radio industry. Advertisers, entertainers, and broadcast executives alike started thinking of radio as a second-class citizen — as nothing more than "television without pictures." Increasingly radio was treated as a *background* medium — something for people to turn on when they were too busy to watch TV. Stations carried music, a bit of talk, and a lot of commercials, all designed as aural cushions surrounding people when they got up in the morning or drove their cars to work or did chores around the house. Radio's function became *drowning out* silences, instead of filling them.

In characteristic fashion, commercial broadcasters said *they* were not responsible for the decline of creative radio. Public habits were changing. It was all very well to talk about the potential of radio to stimulate and engage the imagination of an audience, to speak clearly and literately, explain complex issues, to encourage people to think . . . Americans were no longer interested. We had become a nation of viewers not listeners. Radio's proper role was that of a glorified Musak machine. A few critics argued that the commercial networks had given up too easily, had pulled the plug on engaging programs too quickly

and so had actually *encouraged* Americans to stop paying attention —
to stop *listening* — to the medium that had once so absorbed them. But
most broadcast executives ignored such caviling. Conventional wisdom
declared that the wireless had had its day. We lived in the television era.

The creation of National Public Radio in 1971 can be regarded, in part,
as a response to the declining fortunes of American commercial radio
during the previous decade. NPR's initial statement of purpose, written
by one of public radio's visionary founders, Bill Siemering, included the
following appeal: "National Public Radio . . . should lead in revitalizing
the medium of radio so that it may become a first class citizen in the
media community." Many early producers at NPR took on this mission
with an almost crusading zeal. They believed in the creative power of
radio and in the medium's social and cultural importance. They also
believed that while most Americans had fallen out of the habit of
listening to radio, the right kind of programming could bring people
back to the aural medium.

    For the first decade of its existence, NPR pursued its goal of
creating a unique radio voice with considerable critical and creative
success — but without making much of a numerical impression upon
the mass-media audience. Frank Mankiewicz, who became president of
NPR in 1977, often said that National Public Radio was one of the
best kept secrets in American broadcasting. But during the network's
second decade, a variety of circumstances — inside and outside NPR
— led to significant growth in public radio's listenership. By 1994,
during the course of a week, ten million people were tuning in to NPR's
news programming on more than four hundred public radio stations
around the country.

This book discusses the future potential of National Public Radio by
telling stories about the recent past. In the winter of 1993 I spent five
months visiting NPR headquarters, observing the production of a range
of news shows and engaging in many informal conversations with NPR
staff members. I also conducted more than sixty formal interviews.[1]

---

    [1] Though NPR has become predominantly a news organization, the network
still airs a number of excellent arts and cultural programs; regrettably, my reporting
does not encompass this part of the organization, which was housed on a different
floor from NPR News and led a separate existence.

In the pages that follow, I wish to evoke the varieties of creativity involved in the kind of radio that NPR puts on the air. I believe that the expressive and communicative potential of radio has been generally underestimated or misunderstood by commentators on the mass media. I further believe that many of NPR's listeners — and *potential* listeners — may not fully appreciate the enormous, and still often untapped, power of radio to enhance and enrich our lives. Radio encourages those faculties of emotion and intellect that, to a large degree, television dulls or discourages. Thus, an organization like NPR can play a crucial role in our culture and our society *if* it is allowed to fulfill the creative promise of radio, the medium of sound and story.

My account of NPR is intensive rather than all-inclusive: I have not attempted a full history of the organization, nor do I describe every nook and cranny of the news operation. I have included a wealth of detail about some programs in order to conjure in the reader's mind a good deal more than a collection of "facts" that I witnessed behind the microphones. I am interested in invisible processes as much as visible surfaces. For example, though my narrative portrays with some specificity NPR's offices and studios at a particular moment in its history, I suggest that, ironically enough, the physical surroundings where radio "happens" are far less important to the programs we hear than what goes on in the minds and the imaginations of radio producers and their audiences. The "space" that radio inhabits remains paradoxical and ambiguous; it is one of the great mysteries of this most unusual medium.

As a writer and reporter, I believe that we should use the close observation of facts in order to ascend toward more significant truths and understandings. In one of *Walden*'s most evocative metaphors, Henry Thoreau proposes that the elusive sound of a loon is an essential part of the bird's story — in his voice resides his "loonness." So is our own receptivity to sound an essential part of our humanity, and the stories of our lives are more supple and transitory than our mute words on a page may suggest.

This book would not have been possible without the generosity and trust of all the staff members at NPR who tolerated my presence during my weeks of research. A small number of staffers remembered me from "the old days": I worked in public radio from 1975 to 1983 as a freelance writer, reporter, and producer, and a number of my assignments took me to Washington. Following my radio series *New England Almanac*, however, I drifted away from radio into teaching and writing.

For most people currently at NPR, therefore, I was merely a stranger carrying a notepad. Since, over the years, National Public Radio has been exposed to a barrage of incredibly insensitive — not to say crackpot — criticism,[2] some folks at NPR are understandably skittish about being "watched," even though that sense of self-protection is balanced by an even stronger conviction that the organization has nothing to hide . . . *if* observers look with unbiased eyes. Furthermore, radio people tend to be, in Garrison Keillor's phrase, shy folks, and they are not always used to being "seen." For all these reasons, then, I am especially appreciative of the helpfulness shown me by so many at NPR. Certain staffers deserve special mention.

This book would never have been possible without the support of Bill Buzenberg, the vice president in charge of the news division. Bill balanced my needs as a reporter with his desire to protect the privacy of his staff in ways that were fair to all concerned. I am deeply appreciative of his help, as I am of that given by his assistant, Nancy Cohen. My research would not have gotten off the ground without the extraordinary openness of Cindy Carpien, senior producer of *Weekend Edition, Saturday,* the first program I observed. I owe Cindy and her entire staff a great debt of gratitude for their welcoming friendliness. (In addition to Cindy, Marta Haywood and Ken Hom were particularly helpful in ways that do not get expressed in the narrative below.) Even before I contacted Bill Buzenberg, Neal Conan and Bob Malesky — with whom I had worked years ago — eased the awkwardness I felt as something of a "prodigal son" and made a number of practical suggestions that smoothed my reconnection with NPR.

While in Washington, I profited immeasurably from conversations with Ira Glass, Michael Fields, and John Greenberg — more than might be apparent from their appearance in these pages. Ira, one of the most creative reporters at NPR, and Michael, an experienced and gifted editor on the national desk, provided much useful background on many aspects of NPR's evolution. Numerous conversations with John, a talented newcomer to radio, helped clarify my own ideas about aural journalism. I spent a number of informative and enjoyable days observing some NPR News programs that are not profiled below: *Talk*

---

[2] It is not unusual for callers to commercial radio talk shows or Cable TV's C-SPAN to refer to NPR as Radio Havana, Radio Moscow, and so forth—this, in spite of the fact that conservative and moderate commentators regularly appear on NPR's air.

of the Nation (I am grateful to its executive producer and long-time NPR hand, Marc Rosenbaum); *Newscasts* (I must thank executive producer Pete Michaels and also Corey Flintoff, who was extremely generous with his time); and *Weekend All Things Considered.* Staff members of *Weekend ATC* were particularly helpful and friendly. They also demonstrated an admirable professionalism during the coverage of late-breaking weekend news stories which I wish space had permitted me to profile. Conversations with producer Jane Greenhalgh, editor Rob Rand, associate producer Rebecca Davis, directors Rich Dean and Doug Mitchell, and (then) host Katie Davis were most enjoyable and informative.

I am also indebted to (then) news manager John Dinges; Anne Gudenkauf of the science desk; Julie McCarthy, Joyce Davis, and Elizabeth Becker of the foreign desk; national reporters Andy Bowers, Buster Gonzales, Mara Liasson, Brian Naylor, and John Ydstie; Ken Rudin of the Washington desk; John Ogulnik and Jeff Rosenberg of special events; also Bob Boilen, Connie Drummer, Michael Goldfarb, Amy Holmen, Sunni Khalid, Steve Munro, Cathy Raines, Cokie Roberts, Andy Rosenberg, Joan Rubel, Mark Schramm, Michael Skoler, Taki Telonidis, Walter Watson, Ned Wharton, and Fred Wasser.

I received important assistance from several people outside NPR. Jon Solins, a former colleague at WFCR in Amherst, now with WGBH Boston, provided much early help and enthusiasm for the project. Richard Harris, an ex-NPR hand, now with *ABC News Nightline*, generously shared his experiences of the differences between radio and television. Everett Frost, of NYU, has enriched my understanding of European radio and has shown me many professional kindnesses over the years. Alex van Oss, a talented independent radio producer, continually reminded me that public radio consists of far more than *just* National Public Radio. His conversation was always stimulating and helpful. Dale Willman, sometime–NPR newscaster, supported, encouraged, and assisted both my research and my writing in ways too numerous to mention; his good-natured generosity was especially welcome during the book's final stages. I am deeply appreciative of his clear-eyed perspective on NPR, at once insightful and generous.

A number of non-news staff at NPR aided my work. John Sutton graciously provided information about current audiences. Mary Morgan, public relations director, supplied numerous courtesies. Quincey Johnson helped immeasurably in tracking down transcripts and cassettes for programs I had not been able to tape off the air myself.

I am also indebted to a number of friends and colleagues at Amherst College. I am grateful to the American Studies Department, which, for the past nine years, has provided me both comradeship and office space. In addition, my ideas about radio have profited immensely from conversations with a number of individuals. Alan Babb helped clarify my understanding of the physics of radio, as did George Greenstein. Jan Dizard's perspectives and encouragement helped my evolving understandings and spurred along my research. Joel Upton's special passions and convictions, combined with his own love of NPR, energized my enthusiasms in ways that only a good friend, and a great teacher, can. The power of his visual sensitivity continually challenges and enriches my verbal apprehension of the world. I can say the same of Dick Schmalz — painter, neighbor, mentor. Dick has also done much over the years to remind me that "life consists with creativity." Our conversations about radio and about art have sharpened my sensibilities and prodded my ambitions.

The fatigue of spending long weeks away from home were lightened considerably by trips back to Amherst, where I enjoyed the friendship and mealtime conversation of a number of people, including Robin and Jan Dizard; Connie and Bill Gillen; Do and Dick Schmalz; Sara and Joel Upton; and Susan and Geoff Woglom.

The extensive taping I did at NPR required a correspondingly extensive process of transcription. Helen Anglos accomplished the bulk of this with consummate skill, speed, intelligence, and good humor. She did yeoman's work, often at the last minute, and also provided valuable editorial assistance. I am very grateful for all her support. Emily Gillen both typed a number of transcripts and did valuable research and fact-checking. Jennifer Winick and Connie Gillen did some transcribing. I thank Amherst colleagues Duane Bailey and David Cox for their assistance with the section on the mathematician Fermat.

At Houghton Mifflin, Becky Saikia-Wilson was especially inventive at managing the tight production schedule associated with this book. I am also deeply grateful to two other Houghton staffers for their efforts beyond the normal call of duty. Mindy Keskinen was consistently helpful and friendly in guiding me over the various hurdles involved in bringing a book to print; she also proved to be a resourceful fact-checker. Dorothy Henderson, manuscript editor, brought a wonderful disposition and great skill to her arduous and sometimes hectic task.

Richard Todd — editor and friend — played an essential role in the creation of this book. His patience, skill, wit, and insight eased difficulties and stimulated the pursuit of excellence. His connections with this subject matter began in 1979, when I first wrote down some reflections about public radio and sent them to Dick, then executive editor of the *Atlantic Monthly*. Dick's kind note in reply included the following fateful words: "You may have a book here, I'm not sure." I'm delighted finally to have answered Dick's musings in the affirmative, though the full reply has been gestating for some fifteen years.

One final acknowledgment: Dick Todd and I are both products of a particular writing course, English 1, which used to be taught to all freshmen at Amherst College. I first learned about the rich ambiguities of *voice* and language from that strange and challenging class, presided over by a professor whom I might call my first editor, William Coles. "Whom do you *sound* like, Mr. Looker?" Professor Coles would scrawl in the margins of my papers, opposite particularly egregious and cliché-ridden passages. He gave me my first lessons in hearing the voice that my words were creating on the page. I learned a great deal about writing from English 1. Only later did I recognize how much I had also learned about radio.

Pelham, Massachusetts
November 1994

The Sound
and the Story

National Public Radio at Rest

⊂╪

Studio Seven, Two A.M.

In the beginning, silence. And darkness, though not the primordial kind. Small colored lights glimmer through a velvet blackness. The lights illuminate only themselves. Like stars around a new moon, their muted glow suggests the presence of other shapes: the bulk of tape machines, speakers, and audio consoles; the graceful outlines of hanging microphones; the mottled texture of soft, enveloping walls. A large pane of glass looms through the darkness, cutting an opening in one of the walls. You stare through the dark window into another layer of blackness, ambiguously defined by a smaller collection of colored lights. As you look from the sleeping control room into the sleeping studio beyond, the surface of the glass window acts like a prism, echoing the pinpoints of light in each room, refracting and distorting. Three or four red lights seem to be drifting, disconnected, in space; two rows of amber lights line up at impossible angles to each other. It's difficult to make sense of the patterns, to tell which lights are where — but the disorientation is peaceful, a starlit phantasmagoria. Not even the small digital timing clock, which seems to float in the middle of the darkest part of the studio, disturbs the reverie. Its static display adds to the cavelike mood: the crimson digits glow silently, perpetually . . . oo:oo:oo.

The darkness of the control room and the studio is given palpable shape by the cloying softness of the soundproofed walls, whose presence you can feel on your face, against the back of your neck. The sensation is almost like swimming a few feet below water — or perhaps crouching at the back of a dark closet. When the studios are filled with people, you barely notice the deadness of the sounds around you. But when you stand here in silence, in darkness, your whole body responds to the absorptive atmosphere, the unnatural lack of echo. You feel enveloped, protected, isolated — but also nourished. For in the warmly glowing electronic equipment around you reposes extraordinary potential. In a few hours, these dull, mechanical shapes will be called upon to record, mold, and transmit a startling amount of information (sounds and words) to a surprisingly large audience (measured in the millions). These "radio programs" will inform, enlighten, and entertain. The most ambitious of them will attempt to spread what the poets refer to as "truth and beauty," be it in the form of journalism, musical performance, or (on rare occasions these days) spoken-word drama.

In the dark electronic womb of NPR are gathered the creativities of sound and speech: this potential flows as much within every piece of circuitry as through the elaborate physical shell that is built up around the machinery. This fecund environment presents radio producers and reporters with an extraordinary wealth of possibility. In these sleeping studios lives the stuff from which are made the dreams of sound magicians, aural reporters, auditory adventurers, oral storytellers . . .

The control room and the studio are equally immersed in darkness when the overhead lights are turned off and the doors are locked. But the two rooms are not equally quiet. The studio rests in a silence which is absolute — dizzying. Not even the air conditioner makes a sound. The stillness in the control room is less profound. Solid-state electronic equipment contains few mechanical parts, and so though the amplifiers, preamplifiers, and various sound-shaping equipment remain on throughout the night, they do not generate any sound that humans can hear. (It's worth remembering that this equipment is not absolutely "quiet," however. The electrons and other quantum phenomena whizzing through their circuits give off many other emissions aside from audible sound waves — the limited part of the electromagnetic spectrum that our simplistic ears can "hear." These other waves would register on appropriately tuned oscilloscopes . . . sometimes as smooth waves, sometimes as jagged spikes that can be called static — or "noise." So one creature's noise is another creature's silence.)

But the main workhorse machines in the control room — the tape recorders — are not so discrete, so voiceless, as the fully transistorized equipment. Magnetic sound devices marry the brains of electronic circuitry with the muscle and sinew of motors, wheels, and drive pulleys so that miles and miles of recording tape can be pulled past the appropriate electronic sensors and feed the preamps and amps the electronic information that makes them have something to do and to say. If the sophisticated electronic circuitry in the control room looks always forward to the smoothly expansive future of superconducting transistors and turbo-charged computer chips, the tape machines look backward toward the clunky mechanical wonders of the nineteenth century. To the extent that radio stations are still dependent on tape and tape recorders, they employ an *industrial* technology and retain some of the atmosphere of a mechanized factory. And just as some factories run twenty-four-hour shifts, so does all the recording and transmitting equipment at NPR remain constantly on, even when the human technicians have left for home. Here is an irony of radio work, more draconian than anything imagined by Karl Marx: electronic equipment of all kinds suffers so much stress and strain, so much trauma, when electricity first runs through it and "wakes it up," that engineers have decided it's best to leave the machines on all the time. Even the motors in professional tape recorders are built with this principal in mind: they last longer if they never stop turning — if they never are allowed to sleep. So it is that in an otherwise deserted radio control room, a grinding, low-level hum shapes the stillness . . . adds an aural texture to the silence.

Your ears can become accustomed to layers of quiet, just as your eyes can adjust to levels of blackness, and if you listen closely to the darkened room, you can distinguish subtle differences in hums. It turns out that different kinds of tape recorders whir with different voices. The newest, biggest machines, the large Studer reel-to-reel tape recorders — the machines that record and play full-hour and half-hour programs — purr almost noiselessly. Their well-oiled, well-heeled motors and transports demonstrate their advanced technology and perhaps also their European pedigree (Studers are made in Germany). The smaller cassette machines — from Japan — contain proportionately smaller and quieter motors. You have to put your ear right up to them to hear their subtle whine. The noisiest tape players are, technologically speaking, the most regressive pieces of equipment in the room. The American-made tape cartridge machines — cousins to the eight-track stereo cartridges that enjoyed a brief popularity in automobiles thirty years ago — produce a distinct, unending rumble, which sounds like a subterranean heartbeat. "Tape carts" perform a limited yet vital function in radio production these days. Small plastic boxes, four inches wide, five inches long, and about an inch thick, tape cartridges contain a continuous loop of recording tape, from five seconds to five minutes long. The genius of the tape cart is that you can instantly go to a short selection of music or a brief report or announcement without having to waste time searching for the start of the piece: the cart is always "cued up" at the beginning of its run of tape. Yet the sound fidelity of the tape cart is not very good — the technology has changed little over the decades — and the newest electronic technology, *digitally* recorded tape cassettes, is already beginning to replace the analogue cartridge machines. DAT (Digital Audio Tape) tape is as easy to cue up as the venerable cart, and its sound quality equals or surpasses that of analogue reel-to-reel machines, like the Studers.

As the tape cartridges groan into the silence of the darkened control room, you may well imagine that they are complaining against their imminent obsolescence . . . mourning the end of the mechanical age and protesting the juggernaut of the deathly silent digital technology. For it must be said that the ancient rumble of the clunky, old carts does add to the powerful atmosphere of stillness and expectation in the darkened control room. It gives *voice* to the silence, reminding visitors to look to the shadows around them . . . for "Here there be dragons."

PROGRAM ONE

Weekday Mornings

Prospero's Realm

At two o'clock in the morning, on a warm, muggy Wednesday in mid-June, downtown Washington has closed for the night. Dark streets stretch empty and dangerous in front of the blackened windows of locked restaurants and offices. Homeless men and women sleep in doorways or just outside the gates of garages and loading platforms. Taxis occasionally bump along the gray arteries between buildings. Police sirens whine in the distance. No stars are visible overhead: thick, humid clouds cover the sky. Washington sleeps fitfully, and both dreams and nightmares stalk the urban darkness.

In one corner of 2025 M Street, a modest building on the western fringes of the business district, lights burn brightly all night. Most NPR offices are dark and empty and almost as humid as the streets outside — even the air conditioners are dozing. But in a small section of the second floor, along a couple of corridors that spread back from Studios Five, Six, and Seven, the air is cool, computer screens are glowing, and a skeleton staff of producers and editors prepares for NPR's first program of the day: *Morning Edition,* which runs live from six to eight o'clock.

Half a dozen people — production assistants, editors, and producers — sit around tables, reading wire services and newspapers, making telephone calls, listening to tape. They are gathering data — assembling narratives — from different sources about events that have happened (or will happen, or might happen) throughout the country and throughout the world. Slowly, and to an extent unconsciously, these men and women reimagine diverse pieces of information into "the news." They then shape and reconstruct this *news*, using the narrative tools of radio, into reports, interviews, commentaries — *stories* is the best generic term — that will be heard by listeners to NPR later this morning.

Creating a news program for the radio is neither wholly a science nor wholly an art. It is, in essence, an act of the human imagination: separating fantasy from truth, judging what's significant and what's not, deciding what will hold a listener's attention and what will turn it off. The role of the imagination in the life of any news organization is often obscured in the hurly-burly of the daily newsroom, in which reporters and editors race maniacally toward a host of self-imposed deadlines. The inner activity of the mind and the heart — the ultimate "unnamed source" of all reporting — may come closest to being visible in the quiet space defined by the early-morning shift at NPR. Here the most intense news professional seems, in many respects, only half awake, and in the semidreamlike state during which *Morning Edition* begins to take shape, one of Shakespeare's noblest ideas becomes palpable: the news which we reach for each morning when we wake up consists of the same stuff as the dreams we have just left (and our favorite news programs themselves are rounded by a sleep).

Audrey Wynn is sitting at the *Morning Edition* desk, in the producer's chair — she's been at work for a couple of hours. A member of the overnight shift for eight years, Audrey has been the show producer for the past two years. It is a thankless and exhausting job, which has drained a dozen people during the eighteen years that *Morning Edition* has been in existence. Currently, Audrey has a small staff working with her — during the next two hours it will be augmented slightly. Normally, two production assistants arrive at one o'clock to help cut tape and attend to other chores. An editorial assistant comes to work at one-thirty, to handle telephone calls and make final arrangements for interviews, among other duties. The show editor appears at around two o'clock, the director about an hour later. At four o'clock, the backup director arrives, and he or she doubles as a PA.

The host of *Morning Edition*, Bob Edwards, will show up at two-thirty — three and a half hours before the program goes on the air. Bob is one of the most durable and recognizable voices on NPR, and he is ultimately the focus of everyone who works on *Morning Edition.* The "voice of Bob" on the radio is the voice of *the news* — the knowledgeable and comfortable anchorman who sounds as if he knows more than he says and who introduces people who tell us more than we know. It is the responsibility of the staff of *Morning Edition* to help Bob become as comfortable and as knowledgeable as possible, and to assemble around him voices and sounds that engage, interest, and inform listeners. *Morning Edition* is National Public Radio's most listened-to news program. But like all broadcast news, *Morning Edition* is also a stage — in this case an aural stage — whose reporters and anchors must "perform" when they present their news.

At the moment, Audrey is leaning on her elbows and staring at her computer screen. She's wearing a casual white dress with a floral print on it — a tad dressier than the most popular overnight outfit, jeans and T-shirt or sweatshirt. But it's the first day of summer and Audrey is just back from a three-day weekend — a personal holiday. When she arrived at midnight, she seemed refreshed and invigorated. By now, however, familiar anxieties have begun to overtake her. She is scanning blocks of amber letters, which fill half her computer display between bars listing NEWSPRO commands and various identification codes. Audrey reads intently the latest news stories from the Associated Press. Every so often she clicks her keyboard with her index finger and a new block of text crawls down the display, like an old-fashioned electrical sign whose moving letters slither and shift into each other. When she's done with the AP, she will turn to Reuters and perhaps United Press. Audrey glares at the screen through black-rimmed glasses. A woman in her late thirties, wearing her black hair swept firmly back and up on top of her head, Audrey looks calm enough at first glance. Yet the skin around her eyes is drawn tight and she holds her jaw stiffly. Audrey sighs audibly. She is not finding what she needs. As her mood darkens, the flowers in her dress seem to fade. The sleeping tension of the morning coils around the *Morning Edition* desk.

A few yards from Audrey, facing the large windows that look out on M Street, three people sit at the top of the *Newscast* horseshoe, a semicircular arrangement of tables containing several telephones, tape recorders, and computer terminals, as well as a couple of squat, square, tape cartridge machines. The production of newscasts is a separate operation from *Morning Edition.* These shows — from five to eight and a half minutes in length — go on the air first at one minute past five in the morning and continue, each hour, into the late evening.[1] *Newscast* producer Greg Peppers leafs through some first-edition newspapers: *The Washington Post, The Washington Times, USA Today*. A woman to his right is listening to the BBC World Service through a small monitor speaker. Every so often she jots down notes on a yellow pad. Nearby, another woman wears headphones as she auditions a small stack of tape cartridges containing news reports from forty to fifty-five seconds long. These carts have been left by the late-evening newscast unit when it closed down at ten-thirty. Some of these older news spots will be aired during this morning's newscasts.

Greg Peppers and his production staff seem considerably more relaxed than Audrey Wynn. While Audrey must fill two hours with a variety of radio pieces, Greg's primary responsibility is to assemble a collection of news spots that will appear inside newscasts — usually three spots for a five-minute cast, four to five for an eight. The rest of the show is written by the newscasters themselves, and none of them has come to work yet. Carl Kasell, the veteran broadcaster who does the on-the-hour newscasts for *Morning Edition*, will arrive at three o'clock. Jean Cochran, who broadcasts on the half hour, is due in at four. For now the *Newscast* production team is surveying the news of the morning and getting a sense of what reports they might try to solicit from their own correspondents or what audio spots they might pull from other news organizations — United Press International or the British Broadcasting Corporation.

Audrey Wynn's overnight crew is scattered throughout the part of the second floor that's operational at this hour of the morning. The *Morning Edition* desk is more like the capital of a far-flung empire than a compact kingdom. When staff members arrive, they check in with Audrey and then go off to do their work. For example, at the moment, the two on-duty production assistants are preparing tape for the show in Edit Booths One and Two, which are some distance from the main desk, hidden around a quiet corner beyond the *Newscast* horseshoe.

An editing booth is a glorified closet — a small cubicle, heavily soundproofed, containing the paraphernalia needed to cut and splice audiotape. When the doors are closed, people outside can barely hear the sound of voices being slowed down, sliced apart, rearranged, and

---

[1] In late 1993, NPR *Newscasts* began broadcasting twenty-four hours a day, except on weekends.

tightened up. Yet these booths are not well ventilated, and the thick doors are often left slightly ajar, so at any time of day at NPR, you may hear "chipmunk" noises drifting through the hallways — tape being wound quickly forward or backward in a squeal of high-speed babble — followed by voices played at double speed or normal speed or hand-wound at very slow speed, as editors listen over and over again to paragraphs, sentences, phrases. People working on tape struggle to hear the best cuts — to figure out how to prune the often rambling cadences of ordinary speech into cogent, coherent "actualities," those taped excerpts of voices that form a central element of the pieces aired on NPR. For it is the combination of actuality, "natural sound" (also called "ambient sound") and the narrative spoken by a reporter or host (called the "talk tracks") that form NPR's aural signature: the distinctive content, pacing, and rhythm that listeners have grown accustomed to hearing on public radio.

Tape cutters must focus with great intensity on their task, and because of the need for concentrated *listening*, radio newsrooms have always functioned a little differently from those at newspapers or magazines. It is easy to revise written copy in public — neither a red pencil nor a pair of scissors makes much noise. In radio, by contrast, tape editors seldom sit at a table together. Most often they retire into those windowless cubicles where they can focus all their attention on the sounds they manipulate. NPR's offices are honeycombed with at least two dozen editing booths. Should producers have to edit in the presence of other people (usually some final cleanup or tightening), they will put on headphones and withdraw into the comparative privacy created by the cups around their ears.

Within a couple of hours four or five people will be engaged in last-minute editing chores on *Morning Edition*. The noise level of the office will increase with the added activity. The babble of chipmunk and even Donald Duck voices will mix in with the rising tide of story discussion and debate, scriptwriting and revision, as *Morning Edition* and *Newscast* production moves into high gear.

But for now, in spite of the pockets of intense activity around some tape recorders and computer screens, the overall atmosphere of NPR overnight remains surprisingly subdued. Conversations seem slow and relaxed. Considerable coffee is being consumed. There's almost a dreamlike ambiance as the clicking of computer keyboards mixes with the murmur of the air conditioning and the distant whine of chipmunk voices whirring at high speed toward another point of tape.

Flowers Before Dawn

The quiet atmosphere does not signify tranquillity, however, particularly around the *Morning Edition* desk, where Audrey Wynn has just finished scrolling through the Reuters news wire. She leans back in her chair, wraps her arms around her chest, and stares up at the cause of her anxiety — the large white board, four feet high by six and a half feet wide, whose semigloss surface covers the opposite wall like an opaque mirror, a mirror that reflects not the face of the particular viewer but the outlines of the upcoming show. Storyboards are not unique to public radio, but at NPR "the boards" for the various programs have taken on a special character and importance. The *Morning Edition* board shows at a glance the list of reports and features scheduled to be broadcast. A black grid, taped onto the board, divides the surface into the segments of time that make up the two-hour show. Each hour is broken down into five major slots of varying lengths, separated by newscasts, headlines, time-checks, and "cut-aways" — moments during which local stations can identify themselves, give weather and traffic, promote upcoming programs, make pitches for funds.

An empty board looks something like this (times in brackets added):

Open *[:59]* & News *[8:30]*	Open *[:59]* & News *[8:30]*
A *[8:59]*	A *[8:59]*
Billboard & :45 Headlines	Billboard & :45 Headlines
B *[7:59]*	B *[7:59]*
Return [:29] & News [4:59]	Return [:29] & News [4:59]
C *[3:59]*	C *[3:59]*
D *[8:59]*	D *[8:59]*
Billboard & :45 Headlines	Billboard & :45 Headlines
E *[7:29]*	E *[7:29]*
Close & Credits	Close & Credits

Throughout the day, producers and editors, using markers and felt erasers, continually write in and erase the names of reporters, the titles of stories, and the estimated length of time for potential pieces. The inscribing mixes ritual and necessity: slowly, painfully, through the changes and shifts recorded on the opaque white surface, the inchoate "show" takes shape. The ideas of no single producer or editor can control such a drawn-out process, for alone among programs at NPR, the *Morning Edition* desk is staffed by at least one editor or producer twenty-four hours a day. In the course of one program cycle half a dozen hands will mark or erase the board. The board provides a focal point — becomes quite concretely an object of contemplation and reflection — for the entire *Morning Edition* staff. No one walks past without acknowledging it, without noticing changes, problems, and possibilities. *Morning Edition's* board becomes the symbolic center of everyone's hopes and aspirations. If the board is filling up nicely, the *Morning Edition* staff feels good. If the board looks boring or disorganized, gloom and anxiety will spread.

Audrey sees this when she looks up at the board:

Open & News	Open & News
A BE/Zagreb	A BE/Muskie — Vietnam Embargo (Live phoner) Arnold — GOP 3:30
Billboard & :45 Headlines	**Billboard & :45 Headlines**
B Goldman	B Black — Child Abuse Howk — Hickel & Animal Rights
Return & News	Return & News
C Gonyea	C
D Mitchell — Conservative Doctors BE/LaFrance — Smiles	D Kaufman — Vouchers 5:30 Todd — Wrestling Racism 3:50
Billboard & :45 Headlines	**Billboard & :45 Headlines**
E Lawton — Banana Wars	E BE/Waldron — Hodding Carter 7:00
Close & Credits	**Close & Credits**

Even someone who does not understand all the shorthand on the board will notice that only half the opening segment of the show is filled; that the C2 (the C segment of the second hour) is empty; that the B1 or the E1 are long segments that probably need extra pieces in them. When Audrey looks at the board, she sees too many blank white areas staring back at her. But it's not just the number of gaps to be filled that disturbs her. The overnight staff occasionally has to come up with a third of the stories broadcast in the program. What troubles Audrey is the *content* of the holes — that is to say, what's missing in the show. *Morning Edition* is dreadfully short on breaking news, exciting or important events whose contours have changed significantly in the past twelve hours.

Here's a rundown of the pieces Audrey faces this morning:

- Bob Edwards will interview a Bosnian journalist at five o'clock by overseas telephone about political machinations within the Bosnian joint presidency. This "two-way" may provide interesting background, but it strikes Audrey as a weak beginning for the entire program. (Interviews conducted by hosts at NPR are referred to as "host two-ways" or simply "two-ways.")
- The second hour will also start with a two-way; Bob will conduct this one live on the phone (making it a "live phoner") with former senator Ed Muskie, who yesterday released a report encouraging the administration to stop the embargo on trade with Vietnam. While the conversation could generate some news, a diplomatic recommendation does not promise to make an exciting story.
- The second hour continues with a three-and-a-half-minute report from Elizabeth Arnold on attempts by Republicans to stage town meetings around the country like those held by President Clinton.
- Staff reporter Wendy Kaufman has filed a piece outlining an upcoming California vote on school vouchers; a reporter in Dallas has interviewed a number of doctors who oppose the recently released Clinton health plan; from Seattle, Gordon Black discusses a precedent-setting trial of a battered child accused of killing his abusive father; Don Gonyea, in Detroit, has assembled a short piece about General Motors' recent decision to open plants in Mexico. These stories are interesting and contain some news, but they are not *fresh*; listeners may have heard about them before.
- The closest thing to breaking news currently scheduled is a short

report from local station reporter Robert Howk, in Alaska. During a news conference late yesterday, Governor Wally Hickel announced that he plans to sue animal rights groups who are trying to protect the Alaskan timber wolf.

- A couple of extended interviews are scheduled for the program. Bob Edwards will talk for seven minutes with the author of a book about Hodding Carter, Sr., a noted southern journalist, and Tom Goldman will present a six-minute conversation with Kareem Abdul-Jabbar.
- The program contains a few lighter pieces. Bob conducts a discussion with an expert on smiles, and there's a report from Germany about "Banana Wars" — conflicts that have arisen within the Common Market over tariff policies due to Germans' love of bananas.
- Finally, one commentary is scheduled: regular contributor Terry Todd, a weightlifter, will talk about racism in wrestling.

Almost every piece already on the board is a backgrounder or a feature. To Audrey Wynn, the upcoming show looks weak and fluffy.

There was a time, in the not too distant past, when the staff at NPR didn't worry overly much about covering "the news," traditionally defined. Producers thought in looser terms about what made an interesting program. They were reporters and journalists, yes, but they also "made radio," and they enjoyed the offbeat, the playful, the unusual piece as much as the more conventional "acts and tracks" (actualities and talk tracks) report of politics in Washington, diplomacy in the Middle East, and so forth. (Acts and tracks pieces are often described, not entirely accurately, as "newspaper articles read out loud." They consist of the reporter's narration — his or her "talk tracks" — interspersed with short excerpts from recorded interviews — "actualities" or "acts.") In the past, if producers found themselves short of news on a given day, they considered that their creativity was being challenged. The oral history of NPR is filled with stories such as Neal Conan and the Fig Newtons. Once upon a time, during the middle 1970s, the then-producer of *All Things Considered* discovered (at either five o'clock or six o'clock, depending upon the storyteller) that the show was running about two minutes short. What to do: how to fill the gap? Neal had a sudden brainstorm. "I wonder where the name 'Fig Newton' comes from?" he said aloud. Within a few minutes, one of the hosts was talking on the phone with a historian of cookies. Later on that evening, the flagship news program of the young public radio network concluded its ninety-minute broadcast with a conversation about the Fig Newton. (The answer is: Newton, Massachusetts.)

Tales such as this no longer bring smiles to the faces of most people who work at NPR. In recent years, producers on *Morning Edition* (which long ago replaced *All Things Considered* as the most-listened-to NPR program) have developed a strong appetite for hard news — those meat and potato stories of politics, crime, war, and disaster that will grab the attention of listeners who are waking up, or having breakfast, or battling the traffic in their morning commute. When Audrey looks up at this morning's board, she feels a challenge to what NPR staffers now call "journalistic standards." *Morning Edition* is a *news* show first — and to be successful, a news show has got to have news.

From messages she found in her computer when she first came to work, Audrey knows that the problems with this morning's program have been gestating all day. Each group of *Morning Edition* producers and editors leaves an account of itself for successive shifts. These notes, called "pass-offs," used to be compiled on typewriters and paper; now a computer E-mail network connects everyone at NPR, so it's easy to leave a continuing series of electronic lists and messages outlining the evolution of a program. Audrey understands that throughout Tuesday various producers struggled to find reports and stories for the upcoming two-hour program. But the wire services, the newspapers, and NPR's own internal editorial desks all seemed to agree that nothing of any great consequence was happening in the nation or the world. Whatever else might be said about the final day of spring, the run-up to the summer solstice, journalists would think of it primarily as "a slow news day."

With less than four hours before the show goes on the air, Audrey has to start making decisions about how to fill the gaps in the board. She has completed scanning the latest wire service reports, looking for possible stories. It's now time to confer with the overnight foreign editor, Paul Miller, who has recently arrived at work. Given the simple logistics of time zones, late-breaking news on NPR's early-morning programs usually comes from overseas. At six o'clock in the morning, eastern time, most of the U.S. is still asleep. Europe is about to have lunch, the Far East dinner. For a number of years, therefore, NPR's foreign desk — a group of half a dozen people whose job is to keep in touch with correspondents abroad — has supplied an overnight editor to help out *Morning Edition* and the early newscasts. (NPR has five editorial desks: foreign, national, Washington, science, and a combined arts and cultural desk. Their small staffs funnel stories from reporters, freelance producers, and local public radio stations to the various NPR news programs.)

Audrey rises slowly from her chair at the *Morning Edition* desk, takes a final look at the board, then heads back down the corridor, away from the *Newscast* area and around a couple of corners, toward the sleeping studios. Her flowered dress rustles softly, the canvas shoes on her feet gently pad the floor. For all her internal worry about the upcoming show, she almost ambles back down the hallway. There will be plenty of time to run around later; for now, Audrey can afford to act a bit southern.

Paul Miller is sitting just outside the locked doors of Studios Six and Seven, at a corner of the darkened horseshoe of tables and desks inhabited by *All Things Considered* (which everyone at NPR refers to as "*ATC*"). The offices and cubicles for the show's hosts, producers, and staffers stretch back into the unlit gloom. Traditionally, the overnight foreign editor hangs out here, because this area of the second floor is especially quiet early in the morning and the foreign editor usually has to make a lot of overseas phone calls.

Paul has cleared a space for himself at the *ATC* producer's chair, amid the debris of old newspapers, pieces of script, and piles of tape that scatter the surrounding tabletops. He's logged onto the computer terminal and has already made extensive use of the phone lines. He sits with his back to the large console tape recorder on which *ATC* producers audition spots. Paul's work area is lit primarily by the reflected glow of corridor lights that lead back to the main *Morning Edition* desk.

All through NPR, the most lived-in sections are reminiscent of what a school dormitory might look like if there were no summer vacations and a thorough cleaning, with elbow grease and disinfectant, did not take place at least once a year. All manner of odd shapes lurk in the shadows — from dimly visible pictures, press-clippings, pennants, hats, and balloons to vaguer objects, some of which seem to hang downward from the dark ceiling like clumps of moss on the roofs of caves. In fact, something seems to be floating above the console tape recorder at the back of the producer's station: a pink stuffed animal, about a foot long, its arms open wide, hangs from the soundproofed panels. The lumpy figure is hard to identify at first in the half-light;

yet its long tail, "scales," and goofy grin suggest some kind of smiling lizard. Indeed, small and barely noticeable in the darkness, a caricature of a dinosaur — won at a shoreside amusement park — stares down from the ceiling onto the old Scully tape recorder that, even when not in use, hums and growls continually beneath its belly.

Paul Miller is a tall, broad-shouldered man, wearing glasses, who projects an athletic kind of heartiness. His shapely voice and robust manner convey a slightly different aura than what you find typically at National Public Radio. In fact, Paul worked for many years at NBC television news. Paul is now freelancing at NPR, filling in as he can, but he's not been in public radio long enough to have lost the touch of edgy energy that so characterizes voices on American commercial radio and television.[2]

Audrey finds Paul already in conversation with a couple of other *Morning Edition* staffers, reviewing news stories coming out of the former Soviet Union. The "swing shift" editor, who works from four in the afternoon to midnight, left a note in the pass-off that he had discussed with Moscow correspondent Mike Shuster the possibility of doing a spot for the program. Mike proposed a story on political developments in Azerbaijan, but the idea remains tentative enough that it has not yet been added to the board. It will be Paul's responsibility to work with Mike and help determine if the story merits airing. Not everyone on the *Morning Edition* staff is thrilled with the idea of a piece about Azerbaijan. Jim Wallace, this morning's director, has come into work a bit early; he smiles at Paul and shakes his head. "Azerbaijan puts me to sleep," he says in his quiet, crackly voice.

Jim and Paul start discussing the latest events in Estonia, where the government has announced a series of measures against ethnic Russians living in the country. The story is being covered by the BBC as well as various news wires.

Audrey suggests to Paul that when he calls Mike Shuster again he should ask him how interesting he thinks an Estonian story might be.

"Well," Paul says, "Estonia is certainly getting a lot of publicity. It was all over the front page of *The [Washington] Post* yesterday."

"Yeah," says Jim, with a slight drawl. "That was a shock."

---

[2] In 1994, Paul Miller began to report for NPR from the Middle East.

"Especially as there are more people living in 'Southeast' than in Estonia," says Paul, referring to a neighborhood of Washington. Everyone laughs.

Audrey then starts reviewing the other scheduled foreign piece, Bob Edwards's interview with the Bosnian journalist Gordana Knežević. Audrey tells Paul that the editorial assistant, Julia Bailey, has just confirmed that the interview will take place at five o'clock. This leaves less than an hour for someone to prepare the two-way for broadcast.

"You know," says Paul to Audrey, "Gjelten says that Knežević is really well informed about what's going on within the Bosnian presidency." (Paul is referring to NPR's reporter in Central Europe, Tom Gjelten.) "I presume that's what you want her to talk about? I mean, the whole question of the power struggle that's going on within the collective presidency and all that kind of jazz, right?"

Audrey murmurs in assent. "Yes, and the future of Izetbegovic," she adds, referring to the Bosnian president.

Paul brings up a potentially new use for Knežević. "I listened to the interview she did with *WESUN* [*Weekend Edition Sunday*] and read the transcript. And in this interview she came out of nowhere and mentioned a plan which she claims the Bosnian Muslims are thinking about: preparing huge amounts of chlorine gas to unleash on the rest of the former Yugoslavia. They control the area around Tuzla, which is a large chemical-manufacturing area. Knežević says that they have manufactured, or have access to, enormous stocks of poisonous gas. And she said this was dead serious, and I thought, my God . . ."

Audrey speaks in a half sigh. "I hope she's wrong."

"I hope so, too," says Paul, a bit excited. "But she said this is for real."

Audrey murmurs. "It could be like the final step they might take if their backs are against the wall."

Paul has been essentially "pitching a story" to his producer — a frequent occupation of reporters and editors alike — but now he runs into those uncertainties faced by all newspeople who are three thousand miles away from the events they are trying to cover. "We didn't do anything further on her allegations," Paul says. "They're just sitting there in the middle of this *WESUN* interview . . ." His voice trails off. Audrey stares into the middle distance. In the momentary pause, they face, separately and together, the chasm that surrounds National Public Radio in its attempts to make itself a prime source of news. Audrey and

Paul have neither the information nor the expertise nor the resources necessary to judge Knežević's allegations or to pursue them as a line of inquiry.

Audrey resumes talking about the upcoming two-way as a review of politics within the Bosnian presidency — and discussion of chemical warfare comes to a close.

In the "story that never was" lurks one of NPR's deepest dilemmas as a news organization: when covering hard news — breaking events — all the energy, intelligence, and improvisation in the world cannot substitute for people being in the right place at the right time. To have enough reporters, you must be able to hire them, and NPR's "bottom-most line" should be carved below its logo like a fateful epigraph, so fundamental is it to everything that happens in the organization. In 1993, National Public Radio's annual budget for *all* its news coverage — foreign and domestic — was around $16 million . . . less than the amount of money the *Des Moines Register* spends each year to report on Iowa news, less than what the *Los Angeles Times* spends to fill its metropolitan pages.

Given this eternal fact of life in public radio, there are many who say that the true magic of NPR lies in its ability, in spite of scarce resources, to cover the news so well that it has become not a supplement but the main source of news for several million people. *Morning Edition* is proud of ratings numbers that show it to be the most popular radio program for adults in several major markets around the country.

As Audrey Wynn discusses with Paul Miller the questions that Bob Edwards might ask of the Zagreb journalist, she is not feeling particularly magical. The holes still loom on the board down the hall, and she and Paul discuss ways of assuring that the interview about Bosnia will turn out to be interesting. Paul asks how long Audrey thinks the piece should run. "Five-ish . . ." answers Audrey, her voice thoughtful. The final length will depend to an extent on how interesting the conversation seems between Knežević and Edwards. But experienced producers usually don't have to wait to hear an interview to tell how much time *ought* to be spent on a particular story. A three-minute, a four-minute, and a five-minute spot each has a different rhythm, a different cadence. To Audrey, Bosnia "feels" like it's "worth" a five-minute two-way. The precise timing (and when the show goes on the air, all timings have to be precise to the second) will await the actual interview and the final tape cut.

Paul recalls the discussions about Bosnia going on currently within the European Economic Community, and Audrey suggests that they try to find some tape of British prime minister John Major or German chancellor Helmut Kohl to start off the segment with Knežević. She also reminds Paul to keep listening to the BBC so they can pull a story from British radio to fill out the A1. Audrey really does not want the entire segment to be devoted to Bosnia.

When Audrey returns to the desk, she finds that the show editor, Ken Barcus, has arrived and is scanning the pass-off, familiarizing himself with the state of the program. A stocky man with a brown beard, and wearing a green and white striped shirt and greenish tie, Ken smiles pleasantly at Audrey as she resumes her seat.

The *Morning Edition* editor and the producer face each other from opposite sides of the desk. The tabletop between Audrey and Ken is strewn with reels of tape, notepads, piles of computer printouts, stacks of old newspapers. Two sets of the essential tools for creating radio programs rise out of the debris like mushrooms from a forest floor: two computer displays and keyboards, connecting to the central VAX computer, the cerebral cortex of NPR; a pair of multiline digital telephones; and two reel-to-reel tape recorders, mounted in rolling consoles. Both tape recorders have small speakers and headphones, allowing either public or private listening. They also are equipped with splicing blocks, splicing tape, razor blades, grease pencils, and other tools necessary for last-second tape editing.

The producer and editor of a show share the responsibility of listening to every piece of tape before it is broadcast and of reading every piece of copy before it is spoken on the air. Theoretically, the editor focuses on the journalistic and stylistic integrity of each piece, while the producer worries about the overall shape of the show, along with organization and logistics — are the reports coming in on time, are the tape editors working up to speed, does every part of the show have something to fill it? In practice, the roles of producer and editor often become blurred. NPR has a tradition of collegiality rather than bureaucracy. While every piece of written copy will almost always be initialed by the show editor, the producer may wind up auditioning and approving some spots that the editor may not have time to hear. Similarly, while most show producers at NPR don't like to broadcast pieces they have not heard, sometimes, in a crunch, they will defer to ears of their show editors.

The show editor is supposed to be the last person to revise a script before it gets passed to the host, but any number of people contribute to the earlier stages of the copy. Most correspondents in the field will submit suggested "intros" for their stories. The various desk editors — who usually are the conduits to programs for reporters' pieces — may add script suggestions. The production assistants, who make the final edits of taped reports, will often write lead-ins of their own. But it is the host of the program who has the final say about what goes on the air, and no host feels this editorial responsibility more keenly than Bob Edwards. A stickler for making sure the words he reads are clear and concise, Bob spends a good deal of his time, before and during the show, taking pen or pencil to the scripts which are handed to him. Though he may write less original copy than hosts on some other shows, he *edits* with greater care and obsessiveness than many of his colleagues.

Bob has not yet arrived in the building, though he is due shortly. He's been anchoring *Morning Edition* since its creation in 1979 and has kept extremely demanding hours throughout. When *Morning Edition* first went on the air, everyone assumed that the host would come to work at around four o'clock. Such a schedule would be difficult but would permit the host to sleep from mid-evening till two or three in the morning — an hour or two before many farmers get up. Bob Edwards held to that regimen for a while, but then began coming into work earlier and earlier. Since 1989, he has been showing up regularly at *two-thirty* — which means when many people are sitting down to eat dinner, Bob is heading off to bed.

Bob has a small office, across from the show's desk, to the left of the board, at the rear corner of the *Morning Edition* area. Outside Bob's office, silenced Teletype machines (backups, in case the VAX goes down) and a pair of noisy Okidata dot-matrix printers (which connect to all nearby VAX terminals) lead to a glass door that opens out into the rest of NPR. Beyond the door, at two-twenty in the morning, stretches darkness and gathering humidity. This back entrance to *Morning Edition* marks the edge of NPR's overnight civilization. On the other side of the glass lies the still sleeping world of dayside public radio.

Bob Edwards keeps his office locked, and even the senior staff of the program respects his privacy, so after midnight, a small stack of newspapers, notes, wire copy, and scripts starts piling up in front of his door, waiting for his arrival. In addition, this particular morning someone has placed on the floor a small silver vase of red and white flowers, apparently in honor of the first day of summer. But given the odd assortment of objects resting on the gray carpet, these slender blossoms make the detritus outside Bob's office look like a sacramental offering.

When Audrey Wynn has finished briefing Ken Barcus on Bosnia and Estonia, Ken grins and shakes his head. "Pretty slow day," he says. Audrey sighs. She is again staring at the board.

"Shall I listen to 'Smiles,' or shall you?" Ken continues, holding up the usual ten-inch aluminum reel with a very small amount of recording tape wrapped inside. It's the two-way with LaFrance presently scheduled for D1.

"Why don't you," says Audrey. She finds on her desk a reel with excerpts from the news conference held on Monday by John Major. She puts it on her tape recorder and dons her headphones. Ken has already started listening to his tape through his headset. For the next few minutes, they listen intently, staring at the tape timers on their machines, at the wall, at no place in particular — each in a separate world from the other.

The big, Swiss-made Favag clock on the wall above the desk (synchronized with all the other Favag wall clocks in NPR offices and studios) shows two twenty-two. There are a little more than three and a half hours to showtime. At any moment, the man who has been blissfully ignorant of the daylong struggles to fill the program will arrive. With his appearance, the stately, early-morning flow toward broadcast will pick up speed, becoming, eventually, a juggernaut. For a few brief moments, though, the *Morning Edition* area falls quiet — the only sounds the distant voices filtering from beneath Audrey's and Ken's headphones. Audrey is listening to chipmunks. Ken's tape starts with singing, or, more precisely, a disembodied whisper that sounds suspiciously like Johnny Mathis.

For Now We Hear
Through a Glass Dimly

The problems being faced by the overnight shift had begun to take palpable form after lunch on the previous day, when the staff working the dayside shift slowly began to realize that no major news stories were breaking. As the afternoon wore on, the upcoming show looked more and more like a silent, gaping maw.

The board, at two-fifty in the afternoon, told the story:

Open & News	Open & News
A	A Cooper — Somalia (?)
Billboard & :45 Headlines	Billboard & :45 Headlines
B Lawton — Banana Wars	B Black — Child Abuse (5:30)
Return & News	Return & News
C	C
D BE/LaFrance — Smiles (4:30)	D Kaufman — Vouchers 5:30 Todd — Wrestling Racism 3:50
Billboard & :45 Headlines	Billboard & :45 Headlines
E Goldman — Jabbar	E BE/Waldron — Hodding Carter 7:00
Close & Credits	Close & Credits

A1 was a complete blank. The "Lawton — Banana Wars" story was written into the B1. The piece was about to be mixed in Studio Six, according to a clipboard hanging just to the right of the *Morning Edition* board. The C's in both hours were empty. There was a three-minute hole in D1, and the E1 also had a hole in it — the Jabbar piece was not cut to fill the entire seven minutes. The second hour had fewer holes, but they remained significant.

Executive producer Bob Ferrante and senior producer Ellen McDonnell began making the rounds of the various editorial desks after lunch, asking about any news that might be breaking, wondering if stories that had been planned for later in the week might be delivered sooner. As various NPR staffers walked past the *Morning Edition* board, they began noticing how slim it looked, and word spread that the program needed news pieces and needed them badly.

At three o'clock, Ellen McDonnell was sitting by herself at the

Morning Edition desk. She stared at the board, her clear gray eyes wide apart, her blond hair cut short. In her late thirties, Ellen is second only to Bob Ferrante in the *Morning Edition* hierarchy. Wearing pink pumps, an electric blue blouse, and a skirt with a mixed green and purple pattern, Ellen's normally confident, take-charge air seemed frustrated. She sat with her feet curled under her swivel chair, and she jiggled her right leg impatiently as she waited for some *news* to happen.

A few minutes later, Bob Ferrante emerged from his office and sat down in the editor's chair opposite Ellen. In an organization that historically has been staffed by people in their twenties and thirties, Bob stands out as something of an anomaly. A Boston-bred newsman of the old school, Bob's brown hair and handsome, ruddy complexion do not mask his evident maturity so much as they enhance it, almost flaunt it. Nearing sixty, Bob wears stylish suits and shirts — often with suspenders — and broad, colorful ties, which he takes off and puts on at different times of the day. Bob's route to NPR has been quite different from almost everyone else's. He spent most of his journalistic career with commercial television — first on local stations in Boston and other cities, then with CBS in Washington and New York. He wound up with major jobs at CBS, helping to invent, in the early eighties, the network's first late-night news program, with Charlie Rose. Eventually, Bob landed back in Boston, joining public television station WGBH when it started expanding its news division. Bob arrived at NPR in the mid-eighties.

Bob Ferrante leaned back in his chair, the glow of his red suspenders enhancing his infectious, slightly aggressive grin. He looked quizzically at Ellen. She smiled and answered, pointedly, "*Nothing* is happening."

"Well, let me tell you," said Bob. "There's fourteen hours left till the show, and I'd be damn surprised if the world sat on its ass till then. It'd be the first time *that* ever happened." Bob spoke in his distinctive Boston drawl.

At that moment, the glass back door opened up and Neal Conan appeared. A man of medium height, red-haired, blue-eyed, and wearing a trimmed red beard, Neal represents a different generation and a different medium than Bob Ferrante. Barely into his forties, Neal has had a wider range of experience at NPR than almost anyone else in the organization. In his almost twenty years' service, he has done everything from reporting to producing to managing the entire news division. These days Neal floats between assignments as a backup host for a number of shows (including *Morning Edition*), a Washington reporter, and an editor on the foreign desk. You can usually tell what job Neal is filling by observing his clothes. When he's a host, he dresses casually, often wearing a New York Yankee baseball cap around the office. This afternoon he had on a shirt and tie, slightly loosened at the neck: he was helping out as a foreign editor.

After surveying the board, Neal turned to Ellen and Bob. "Looks mighty thin," he said, his eyes darting mischievously from one to the other.

"That's what I like about you guys on the editorial desks," Bob said with mock bonhomie. "You come in here and judge the weight of the board — and then *leave* instead of adding to it!"

"Well, look at it this way," Neal replied. He raised his eyes to the clock. "You have, what . . . over twelve hours . . ."

Bob interrupted: "Fourteen hours to D-day."

Neal looked straight into Bob's face. "There's *hundreds* of aircraft in the air right now. What do you think the chances are of *all* of them landing safely in the next fourteen hours?"

Everyone around the *Morning Edition* desk laughed. Ellen's voice rose above the noise. "Neal! What a thing to say!" But she was smiling too.

At four o'clock, the swing editor, Greg Allen, arrived to hold down the least populated of *Morning Edition*'s three shifts. Once the dayside staff has filtered off home, between five and six o'clock, Greg will sit by himself at the *Morning Edition* desk, doing what he can to prepare material for the upcoming program. The swing shift is a critical time: many a show that looked dull at six o'clock has been turned around by some aggressive and creative activity by the swing editor.

Bob Ferrante yielded his chair to Greg with exaggerated formality. Greg looked at the board and winced. Bob broadened his accent as he teased: "We've left it *all* for you to fix. Don't kid me, Greg, you *love* this kind of challenge." Bob stood straight-backed, between Greg and the board, his gray trousers showing a sharp crease.

"Right," said Greg. "Sure thing." Mild-mannered, with a young-looking face, Greg thinks and talks quickly. He is an idea-man, who seems to enjoy figuring out problems and getting things done efficiently.

Shortly after Greg arrived, Paul Glickman, a thin, dark-faced man with a mustache, appeared and greeted him with a shy, guilty smile. Paul brought more bad news from the foreign desk. "I'm afraid we have to pull Cooper," he said, and took the somewhat unusual step of going over to the board, grabbing an eraser, and wiping off "Cooper — Somalia" from the A2.

"Oh, you've got to be kidding," said Greg, in his crisp, efficient voice. "So we have nothing from you guys tomorrow." Meaning that no new stories were coming from the foreign desk to *Morning Edition*.

Paul spoke softly, nodding. "Nothing. Cooper just got done filing for *ATC* and it's really late for her over there. It would be an invitation to disaster for us to call her up again." Apparently, a range of technical problems with the hookup to Mogadishu had been exacerbated by Ann Cooper's growing fatigue.

Bob Ferrante speaks philosophically. "Look, it probably wouldn't be the best thing to call Cooper in anyway . . ." He taps his foot on the floor as he talks. "It's such a dull fucking story by this point . . ."

Paul left, and in his wake *both* A's were blank holes.

Ellen McDonnell had been conferring at the national desk. When she came back and saw the A's, she dropped into her chair with a look of astonishment. "What happened?" she asked.

Greg described Paul's visit.

"Did he *smile* as he erased Cooper?" asked Ellen, morbidly.

Bob leaned back in his chair, his hands behind his head: "Well, the truth is that story hasn't moved since the day they stopped chasing what's-his-name . . . Adid. You can only sit around for so long saying the same goddamn thing. I thought the piece we had on this morning from Somalia was a waste of time when you get right down to it."

"I think we should get *something* from *someone* in Somalia about the air wars," Ellen said, recalling that air raids were taking place in various parts of the country. "It's what people care about."

Bob threw up his arms in mock exasperation. "Get air wars then. Find a BBC piece. I don't care. I think it sucks. I *don't* think people care about it . . ."

"The problem is," Ellen continued, ignoring Bob's provocative tone, "that a story about the bombing reads better than it works on radio. You know, you have to say, 'They flew to this destination, that destination.' Becomes just a series of names that don't mean anything."

As Ellen stared thoughtfully at the board, she saw the glass door slowly opening and noticed who was about to walk through it. "All right," she said, changing her tone of voice. "Now it's time to get serious. Wanna know the game plan?"

Greg did not look up from the computer screen where he sat scanning the wire service stories. "Yeah, sure," he said.

"Okay. It's about to walk by." Ellen's eyes were twinkling. Bob smiled as Nina Totenberg, NPR's legal affairs correspondent, strode into the *Morning Edition* area. Nina was wearing a beige suit and rocked slightly on her high heels. She carried her glasses and a script in her hands. She was on her way to record a story for *All Things Considered*, but as Nina likes to keep in touch with what's happening on the various programs, she paused briefly before the *Morning Edition* board. She heard Ellen's remark and, smiling, said to the assembled staff, "*What are you planning for me?*"

Ellen waved her hand at the board. "You can have either C or either A! Take your pick. Whatever you want to do."

Nina saw immediately all the problems facing the show. As she smiled more broadly, her narrow eyes took on that glint which can be sweetness or toughness or sarcasm or helpfulness. "I *could* do you another story," Nina said, "but I have to go to some fund-raisers tonight. I have to be their entertainment, I can't be yours."

While Ellen laughed, Nina stared at the board and, trying to be helpful, brought up the possibility of doing a report about the sudden appearance of President Clinton's long-lost brother.

"I *hate* that story," said Ellen, with considerable passion. "Even if Clinton were to say, 'Yes, he's my brother,' I still don't want to do it. It's horrible."

"It is horrible," Nina agreed. "But in my view, it's worth a spot."

"I don't know," said Ellen. "I just don't think I want to use a reporter's time that way."

"What are we going to do," Nina said, "get a new brother every six months?"

"It sounds like, after reading the [*Washington*] *Post* story, that there may be a trail," said Ellen.

"I never read the *Post* story. But you know what?" said Nina, pursuing her point. "You *could* use that story — I'm serious about this. Instead of doing the gossipy number that others are doing, you could do a real 'public broadcasting' thing, but it would actually work: get a *media critic* to talk about the story and how it's being covered and why."

"Andy Bowers," Ellen replied, referring to the NPR staff reporter whose beat is the media.

"Well, Andy could do it," agreed Nina, "but it's a little late for tomorrow morning." Nina mentioned a number of possible people Ellen might call to arrange a two-way with Bob Edwards.

"Ummm," Ellen murmured. She did not sound convinced. Nina did not press the point. After a moment, Nina turned abruptly on her heels. "Go to work, Nina, go to work," she chided herself and walked off down the corridor toward the *All Things Considered* horseshoe and the broadcast studios.

Shortly after Nina's departure, something on the AP wire grabbed Greg's attention. "Here's a possible piece," he said to Ellen and Bob. "Should we talk to Muskie about why he thinks we should give loans to Vietnam?"

Ellen looked up at Greg in disbelief. "*Ed* Muskie?"

Bob, as usual, was more blunt. "Muskie? Is he still alive? I thought he was dead."

"Yeah," Greg said and read from his screen. "A group headed by former U.S. secretary of state Edmund Muskie came out in favor of ending the embargo Monday . . . Took a trip in April . . ."

Ellen said, without a pause, "As long as he doesn't cry on the air we'll take him."

The desk area fell silent. It was possible not everyone in the vicinity was old enough to have remembered how, during the 1972 presidential campaign, Ed Muskie wept in front of the New Hampshire State Legislature and so lost the New Hampshire primary and his chance to run for the presidency. Bob knew what Ellen was talking about. He tapped the table with his open palm twice and said, in a low voice of feigned amazement, "Aw, boy . . . She's tough! She never forgets!"

Greg finished reading the rest of the wire story, then asked, "I don't know, can we do him live on the phone? Tomorrow morning?" Ellen and Bob seemed to treat Greg's question rhetorically.

Suddenly, Ellen's telephone started ringing. She grabbed it and spoke almost before the receiver reached her mouth. "We'll take it!" Everyone laughed, and then waited to hear if someone was offering a piece. No one was.

Bob walked to the board and looked at the blank A1 and the blank A2. Then, picking up the red marker, he wrote in big letters, filling the entire A2, "BE/World" — meaning that Bob Edwards would interview the entire world for eight minutes.

In the meantime, Greg began pursuing the Muskie story, which would eventually wind up in the program.

When Ellen got off the phone, Greg said to her, "Is Audrey coming in tonight? I know she took last night off."

"Yes," said Ellen, "but she wouldn't be if she saw the board."

Sometime after five o'clock, from the *All Things Considered* side of the hall, a thin, angular man emerged — quietly and almost gently. Tom Cole, formerly head of the arts desk, now an editor on the newly reconstituted culture and arts desk, approached the *Morning Edition* area with his usual care and self-control. For eighteen years, the program contained an arts segment — at least one of the E's always had a report or a feature supplied by the arts desk. One month ago, Bob Ferrante eliminated it. He'd been uncomfortable for some time with having any set formulas locking in softer pieces during certain segments. Opinion at NPR was quite divided over this issue.

Tom Cole walked toward the *Morning Edition* desk on narrow, springy legs. He's one of those people who always seems to be smoking, even if he is not. Gaunt, with high cheekbones and a small beard and mustache, Tom seems perpetually busy — yet he rarely raises his voice and keeps his tension coiled tightly inside. He managed a smile as Bob and Ellen greeted him heartily.

"Ah! There's a man bearing gifts," said Bob, grinning. "You could unload one of your real dogs right now!"

"Tom!" exclaimed Ellen. "It's a good day for you!"

"How about that Robert Bly piece," Bob cried, recalling an interview with the prophet of male bonding and drum beating that he had rejected a short time before.

"Oh, no wait . . . Let's do the CEO Rapper," Ellen laughed. "Let's do 'Suck it to the top.' That's a good one!"

"That's a great one. That one's still ready to go," said Bob, chuckling.

Tom Cole smiled at these jibes but didn't reply. He had come by to see the shape of the show, but he could tell at a glance that what *Morning Edition* wanted was more news, not more arts features. So he stayed for a few moments, then, still smiling, glided away.

Just before Tom disappeared, someone asked him quietly what had happened to the CEO Rapper report. Tom seemed to inhale on his invisible cigarette before answering, "I liked it. I might still offer it to one of the weekend shows."

The CEO Rapper piece told the story of a chief executive officer at a corporation in Chicago who liked rap music and had decided to compose a song that would be aimed, not at a black ghetto audience, but at his white suburban neighbors. The radio report — which Tom Cole produced with a reporter from Chicago — began with a description of the record and then played excerpts from the song.

The day that the CEO Rapper feature was auditioned at *Morning Edition* became the stuff of legend. Ellen had cued the tape up on her machine, while Bob sat in the editor's chair. When the music started to play, Ellen, senior editor Vicki O'Hara, and several production assistants stopped work and began paying attention. The lyrics described what a typical white-collar worker had to do to get ahead in an office, but it was the refrain, repeated over and over, that startled the listeners:

> Suck it to the top,
> Suck it to me,
> Suck it to me,
> Suck it to the top.

Bob Ferrante, wearing a striped shirt and a colorful tie, slightly loosened at the neck, was staring off into space as he listened. Those around him began holding their collective breath. The lyrics amused most of the staff members, but everyone knew Bob's vociferous sense of taste concerning what's fit and not fit for broadcast. A generation older than most people at NPR and culturally more conservative, Bob has little tolerance for anything decidedly off-color going out over the air.

When Bob didn't respond to the refrain the first time it was sung, people across the room at the *Newscast* horseshoe stopped work and waited to see what would happen. A few of them exchanged glances. When the refrain started a second time, someone giggled.

Bob Ferrante suddenly stiffened in his chair. He stared at Ellen in disbelief. "What?" he exclaimed, still not fully comprehending. Ellen burst out laughing. "*Suck* it?" Bob cried. "Is that what it is? *Suck* it to the top? . . . *Holy Mother of Jesus!*" Bob's voice boomed while everyone else collapsed in laughter.

"Holy Mother of Jesus," someone echoed in the *Newscast* area, softly enough that Bob would not hear. "I was waiting for that."

Bob kept speaking: "What in God's name does Tom think he's doing, sending me a piece of crap like this. *Holy Mother of Jesus!*" Bob repeated, in amazement and exasperation.

Ellen had stopped laughing and said, "I was wondering why you were sitting there so calmly . . ."

Bob answered in exaggerated cadences. "Because I couldn't believe my ears. I thought it was, 'Sock it to me, sock it to me . . .' I mean, I couldn't believe it. I can't believe it! Jesus, Mary, and Joseph!"

Ellen rewound the tape and took it off her machine. No one at *Morning Edition* ever heard more than the first two and a half minutes of the report.

About a month after *Morning Edition* rejected the CEO Rapper piece, it appeared, unaltered, on *Weekend All Things Considered*. The producer, Jane Greenhalgh, had not heard about Bob's audition of the piece and, when told about it, she looked mildly surprised. "Well, it seemed all right to me," she said in her lilting British accent. "I thought the whole piece was rather amusing."

During the final hour of the dayside shift, the staff discussed a range of possible stories. It was at this point that the foreign desk, in the person of the European editor, Julie McCarthy, came up with the idea of the Knežević interview. Swing editor Greg Allen would have to nail down the two-way, however, later on in the evening. When Bob Ferrante finally had to leave to go to a dinner at the Finnish Embassy, there were still a lot of big news holes in the show. Bob stood up, buttoning his shirt collar and then slinging his coat over his shoulder as he spoke. "Well, let me tell you just how bad it's going to get for us. Tomorrow, *anything* that moves — *any* story at all — we will *pounce* on it."

Amid laughter from his colleagues, Bob gave a wave of his hand and walked gracefully down the corridor, stretching his arms into his suit jacket as he went. Within a few minutes, the rest of the dayside staff had gone and Greg Allen was left alone to work the *Morning Edition* desk, preparing the terrain as best he could for the overnight shift. From the opposite wall, the big, white, opaque piece of plastic continued to stare down at him — silently, dispassionately.

With the fading away of all the chatter and banter of the afternoon, the symbolic, almost metaphysical quality of the board emerges more directly. The wise-alecky, street-smart voices of editors and producers — which sound, on the surface, like the kind of conversation you would find in any newsroom in any medium — should not obscure the ways in which the process of assembling a *radio* news program is different from putting together a TV show, a newspaper, or a magazine. Indeed, the braggadocio demonstrated by the *Morning Edition* staff may be inversely proportional to how clear and concrete "the show" really is in everyone's mind.

The stories these producers and editors discuss among themselves with such confidence have to be far more *imagined* by them than by editors in any other medium. That is to say, print editors can hold a written piece in their hands and see pretty clearly what the finished product will look like when it is published; similarly, they can sketch out a newspaper or magazine page and visualize it fully, long before it is printed up. Television news reports use pictures and graphics that are selected and arranged and framed with copy. Since many different production elements need to be coordinated by many different people, every aspect of the story is worked out to the second. Detailed scripts are also prepared ahead of time for the whole TV program.

By contrast, no one really knows what a radio piece is going to *sound* like until it's almost ready to be broadcast. The final cuts in the tape of a report are made by an individual tape editor, relying on his or her own ears to create the smoothest transitions from section to section. The overall *content* of the piece is decided in consultation with producers and editors and reporters, but the *precise* words and sounds in actualities and the like are not determined until the tape cutter starts working with the tape. So, too, for the entire program: its ultimate aural shape isn't known until the show goes on the air. How well will the host read his or her live introductions to reports? How sensitively will the director mix in the musical bridges between stories? How will the texture of one piece lead into the rhythm and pacing of another? Everyone who works on *Morning Edition* tries to construct an effective and pleasing program, but until the moment of broadcast, the show exists primarily as an idea — or a dimly perceived projection of the collective imagination. There's not even an overall script for the program, only the storyboard, and then, right before airtime, a more detailed reproduction of the board on a sheet of paper, called the "road map," which the director and engineers use to keep track of what gets broadcast when.

Making a radio program like *Morning Edition* is part journalism, part craft, part art, part conjuring trick. The board is the concrete expression of all this creative, imaginative intensity: it mirrors the cacophony of ideas and voices and sounds that flow between the *Morning Edition* staff, through the editing booths and the studios, onto the miles of recording tape. And the board reflects back to the individuals who stare at it a shape, an order — a *hope* of the radio program that is in the process of becoming.

For now we hear through a glass dimly . . .

Swing editor Greg Allen continued to look for stories to fill up the program on this slowest of slow news days. He scanned the news wires, made phone calls to stations, and pursued leads that he imagined might wind up as good hard news stories for *Morning Edition*. But for all his diligent work and clever thinking, when the witching hour struck and Greg passed on proprietorship of the board and the desk to Audrey Wynn, large holes remained in the program, to bedevil Audrey and her staff during their six-hour run-up to broadcast.

"The Radio Friend"

At two twenty-five A.M., at the *Morning Edition* desk, Ken Barcus finishes listening to the piece on smiles and takes off his headphones. He grins at Audrey and compliments the mixing job done at the end of the story, though he obviously finds it a bit campy to be using Johnny Mathis's rendition of the song "A Certain Smile."

Audrey laughs. "I like Johnny Mathis," she says quietly, with a lilt in her voice.

Ken says that he thinks the piece will be fine. Audrey asks him to leave a lot of music at the end, so the director will have some flexibility. "The segment is a bit loose," she concludes, which of course is a comment that could be made about most of the show.

While Ken and Audrey are talking to each other, the glass door behind them suddenly swings open and a large, hulking presence emerges wordlessly from the darkness behind the glass: a tall man, well over six feet, with a tousle of blond and silver hair glimmering like starlight. He moves swiftly, with a certain bulkiness, like some stolid, early-morning ghost. He carries an old leather briefcase under his arm and glides to a halt beside the papers and the flowers on the floor in front of the locked office door. There's a jingle of keys in the muted quiet of the newsroom — the first sound from Bob Edwards. The door swings open. Bob stoops down awkwardly and stuffs the newspapers and the stacks of copy between his left arm and the top of his briefcase. He disappears into his office, leaving the anonymous silver vase on the floor. A few seconds later, Bob reappears and retrieves the flowers.

Broad in face, lanky in bone, Bob Edwards was a tall, wiry youth of twenty-six, vaguely reminiscent of a blond Anthony Perkins, when he started newscasting and then hosting *All Things Considered* in the early 1970s. Twenty years later, there's a slight hint of middle-aged weightiness about him — his face and his midsection droop a bit more. But there's still the look of "a big kid from Louisville" about him as he strides around the corridors of NPR. When he opens his mouth and speaks, however, his voice sounds as resonant, mature, and calming as it always has.

Neither Audrey nor Ken nor anyone else from the *Morning Edition* staff has greeted Bob upon his arrival, nor has he said any audible "good mornings." Arriving through the back door and going swiftly into his office, Bob exudes an aura of privacy and solitude during his first minutes at work. It will be a while before everyone on staff knows for certain that he has arrived. On the other hand, Bob is so regular in his habits, and so reliable in his work, that even people who don't see him will assume, around two-thirty, that he is on the job.

Bob does not turn on the overhead light in his office but prefers the indirect illumination given by a couple of table lamps, and a long, brass banker's lamp with a green glass shade that rests on the back side of his desk. The large windows, fronting on M Street, are not covered with blinds, and as a result the darkness of the street outside flows into the shadows of his office. Bob unpacks his leather briefcase and arranges the newspapers, scripts, and notes in separate piles on his desk. He puts the vase of flowers in the far corner of the windowsill, near a photo of his youngest daughter. Bob's office seems cluttered but orderly. A long tabletop runs the length of the wall opposite his desk — tape recorder, speakers, and amplifier are surrounded by books, papers, empty Styrofoam coffee cups, and trophies of various kinds, for both sports and journalism. On the wall above his desk, rows of photographs and postcards climb toward the ceiling. Prominently visible, toward the top, hangs a picture of Edward R. Murrow.

Bob sits down heavily in a large leather chair and swivels himself toward the computer terminal in front of the windowsill to the left of his desk. Bob is wearing a white dress shirt with thin red stripes, open at the collar, and dark purple Dockers trousers. A black T-shirt is visible at his neck. On his feet he's got a pair of dark, comfortable tennis shoes.

He reaches into his breast pocket and brings out a pair of gold wire-rimmed reading glasses. He puts the black case on his desk in front of the banker's lamp. He logs onto the computer and reads quickly through some messages, beginning to get a sense of the upcoming show. Suddenly he pulls off his glasses, stands up, grabs a large porcelain coffee mug, and lumbers out his door. He strides past the *Morning Edition* desk and heads for the mailboxes and then the coffee machine.

A couple of minutes later, Bob returns to his office, a stack of letters held tightly in one large hand. Steam rises from his coffee mug. Bob puts the letters on his desk in their own pile, leans back in his chair, takes some sips of coffee, and, peering through his gold half-rims, starts reading some of the messages left outside his door. His long legs crossed, he leans his large head against his left fist and breathes deeply. In the subdued light of the office, Bob's thick hair, cut over his ears, seems to shimmer — blond and silver, gold and white . . . the colors merge. Framed by the deep blackness of the city beyond the glass window, Bob looks a little like a golden bear sitting at the mouth of his cave, slowly emerging from hibernation.

As Bob sits reading, Audrey is standing just outside his office, in front of the board. She's holding a black marker in her right hand and she sighs as she stares at the current lineup of stories. Ken Barcus is sitting at the desk reading through the first edition of the *The Washington Post*. Paul Miller is leaning his tall frame against a bookshelf. He has just come back to tell Audrey of his conversation with Mike Shuster in Moscow. They decided to stick with the Azerbaijan story. If Audrey wants to use a piece on Estonia, Paul suggests they pull a spot from the BBC.

At the moment, Audrey is focusing her attention on the A1. "BE/Zagreb" is written in as the program's lead story. Paul feels the piece could be interesting. Audrey is not so sure. She erases the entry, then inscribes "BE/" in the lower half of the A1 box — leaving the lead of the show open.

"Who was the person we've got in Zagreb, Julia?" Audrey asks the editorial assistant, who's coming down the hall from the coffee machine. "Giordano who?"

"Gordana *Knežević*," says Julia slowly from across the room. "She's the editor of *Oslobodenje*."

Audrey begins spelling the woman's name with help from Paul and Julia. The second half of A1 now reads: "BE/Knežević 5:00 A.M. Pretape."

Audrey lowers her hand slowly but keeps her eyes on the board, like a painter critically viewing an evolving canvas. She settles herself on the back of her feet and wraps her arms across her chest. If the interview from Zagreb does not begin the show, what will? Then she walks slowly toward Bob's lair, her arms still wrapped about her. She stands inside the doorway and begins telling Bob about the morning's two-ways: Bosnia and Vietnam, Knežević and Muskie. Bob does not look up as Audrey talks. He's now reading his mail, using a letter opener on the envelopes. Audrey looks sometimes at Bob, sometimes at the deep blackness outside the window.

But Bob is listening. When Audrey finishes her explanations, he mumbles a half-serious complaint about yet another interview he must do later this morning concerning the Balkans: he has read a message that the mayor of Dubrovnik is coming to NPR at ten for a two-way. Bob thinks the conversation will be old news by the time it gets aired tomorrow. Audrey smiles wanly. "He's here in Washington, right? Why not do it at four o'clock instead?"

Bob doesn't smile, but there's humor in his voice. "Guess he's not an early riser." He picks up another envelope. "Let's wake him up," he says dryly.

Bob was not a party to the discussion at the editorial meeting the previous morning during which the decision was made that he should interview the mayor of Dubrovnik. Bob no longer attends the daily meetings that bring together just about everyone else on the staff. While he will occasionally make suggestions about pieces to do or people to interview, in recent years Bob Edwards has let Bob Ferrante, Ellen McDonnell, and the other producers make most decisions about the content of the program. The host's curious passivity in this one area prompts occasional discussion among *Morning Edition* staffers.

At two forty-five, Bob gathers together the letters he has read and puts them, along with some magazines, in a pile on the back table. He arranges the scripts and notes on the desk in front of him. Then he turns again to the back table and stacks the day's newspapers on top of a leather-covered loose-leaf notebook. He adds a magazine or two to the pile and on the very top puts a collection of printouts — notes and script fragments. This is the reading material that he will eventually take with him into the studio.

When the early-morning debris has been ordered and arranged to his satisfaction, Bob swings himself around toward the computer terminal, plants both feet on the floor, enters NEWSPRO, and begins scrolling through the news wires. He taps the keyboard periodically and moves from screen to screen. He stares intently at the terminal, sometimes leaning on his right elbow, sometimes on his left. From time to time he takes a sip of coffee. Once in a while he reaches for a Kleenex box on the windowsill and blows his nose loudly: last week Bob missed several days of work with a touch of the flu and laryngitis. His voice is back, and he does not sound congested, but he still has a slight cold.

On the desk, near his right arm, Bob has placed a clipboard with a yellow pad stuck to it. A series of heavy black lines — crossings out — cover the top third of the pad. Every so often, Bob leans over from the computer screen and writes a few words in pencil below the crossed-out lines. Then he shifts back to his left and continues reading and scrolling, reading and scrolling.

An air of silent intensity envelops Bob Edwards, now deeply enmeshed in the early-morning ritual of order, of routine, and of work that has allowed him to pursue his strange, demanding schedule for fourteen years. He is currently pursuing two parallel tasks. First, he is looking for material to use in the four scripted sections of the show that he alone writes: the "Open" of each hour, in which he greets listeners and previews the day's upcoming news in fifty-nine seconds; and the twenty-nine-second "Returns," light stories which he reads following station breaks on each half-hour. Second, he is putting himself in touch with the news of the morning, preparing himself to be the knowledgeable, comfortable voice of authority that several million Americans will hear when they wake up in a few hours.

Bob begins by looking through the "Daybooks," the wire services' rundowns of upcoming events. He then invokes the NEWSPRO search facility to find stories that have this morning's day of the week in them. He goes through reports that have moved during the past twelve hours. When he finds something important or interesting that will be happening today, Bob writes a slug on the yellow pad in pencil — a word or two that will remind him of the story. He may also print the report on the Okidata outside his office. Meetings, trips, elections, news conferences, congressional hearings or debates — all are candidates for Bob's list. He's also looking for amusing or off-beat stories that he can use in his Returns. When he finds a possible piece, he will print it up.

So, at two fifty-eight, the Okidata spews out an AP feature "Today in History." The top line of the copy is slugged "A.M. — Prep History . . .

User Bedwards." A couple of moments later, the printer whines with a story about Australian emus. The headline reads: "Sexual Loyalty Lands Male Emus in Hot Water." The first paragraph begins: "When is a male's loyalty to his female a problem? When you're an emu farmer." Apparently there's a strong world market for emu meat, and the emu population is not growing fast enough because the males are not promiscuous. This story (slugged "Australia — Emu") may appear in one of Bob's Returns this morning.

Bob retrieves the various print-outs, carefully peals off the rows of holes on each side of the copy, and places the stories in a manila folder next to his yellow pad. He then resumes scanning the news wires.

A little after three o'clock Carl Kasell walks slowly up to Bob's doorway carrying a cup of coffee. Carl arrived at his post at *Newscasts* a few minutes earlier. A tall, portly man in his sixties, with gray, thinning hair and dark-rimmed glasses, Carl has the quiet, friendly manners of someone's southern grandfather. He generates a great deal of affection as well as respect among NPR staff. Carl always wears a jacket and a tie to work; he appears at Bob's doorway in his shirt-sleeves, wearing suspenders and a red tie. Bob pauses in his work to greet Carl, and they exchange pleasantries in low tones. Carl has been broadcasting on *Morning Edition* almost as long as Bob. Many years ago, he even did a short stint as the host of the program. As Carl leans against the doorjamb holding his coffee mug, he and Bob talk about the building that NPR recently bought to be its new headquarters. It's in a much more rundown and dangerous part of town, and many people at NPR have been worried about security in the new site.

Bob and Carl take a light approach to the subject and joke about the amenities in their new home. "No rooftop pool in the new building," says Carl. He's thinking about the swimming pool that is part of the building behind 2025 M Street, but enough NPR offices look down on the pool that it has become one of the famous anomalies of NPR life. In the midst of the various pressures and tensions of their daily work, staff members can look out certain windows in summer and see seminude men and women sunning themselves, splashing around in the blue water, completely oblivious to the deadlines and dramas taking place just a few feet above their heads.

"No rooftop pool," echoes Bob.

Carl laughs slowly. "I haven't checked out the view this year," he says. "Maybe today . . ." Bob smiles broadly — what may be his first

smile of the day. Carl and Bob both speak in lilting, subdued voices —
two southern gentlemen conversing quietly, just out of earshot of the
ladies.

When Carl leaves, Bob goes back to reading the news, taking
notes, and printing out possible Returns. He's now scanning Reuters,
and the printer swings into action again: BRITONS SPEND MORE ON
UNDERWEAR . . . USER BEDWARDS.

While Bob sits at his computer terminal, Audrey has gone back to visit
with Paul Miller and review the possibilities of using BBC pieces
to plug up some of the holes in the show. She's still worried about the
A1, even though sometime during the past half-hour she has erased
"BE/Knežević" from the lower part of the segment and moved it back
to the top.

Audrey and Paul sit side by side on an old gray couch, just outside
Studio Five. On the wall above them hang a couple of Peabody Award
citations. This sitting area, in the middle of the hallway leading to *All
Things Considered*, serves as a kind of green room for guests waiting to
enter the main broadcast studio.

Paul tells Audrey about a piece by Bridgett Kendall of the BBC on
Estonia. Audrey says, "That could be our A1." Paul is noncommittal.
He still thinks the Zagreb interview will be interesting enough to lead
the show. They go on to review what the Shuster piece on Azerbaijan
may contain.

A few minutes later, Audrey has resumed her seat at the desk. "You
thinking of going with Shuster in one of the A's?" asks Ken. Azerbaijan
politics may not be the center of people's attention, but at least Mike's
piece does have some breaking news in it.

"No," says Audrey, her voice low and tired. "It feels like a C."

"Then you're sticking with Zagreb as the lead?"

"Neither one excites me, really. I don't know." She sighs. "I'd like
to find some good stuff. So far the stuff is okay, but it's not . . . well,
it's nothing to pull you into the show."

Audrey now adds the word "Clip?" above the "BE/Knežević" slug
on the board, meaning that she hopes to include a short piece of tape
from the news conferences of either John Major or Helmut Kohl as
part of Bob's introduction. Starting the two-way with some good quotations might help raise audience interest in the rest of the story. She
asks one of the production assistants to search tapes of BBC news
programs for actualities.

"If we find something, that will help a little bit," Audrey explains. "It will help us craft a good lead, even though it's not really a fresh story. I suppose we might still do Shuster. Might do an Estonian thing. But . . . Well, there's still a couple of hours to go." She laughs weakly. "About five-thirty I'll come up with something. Till then I don't have the incentive to put something definite in there."

By five-thirty, as well, Bob will have conducted the two-way with the Bosnian journalist and everyone will have a clearer sense of how the show will sound with that two-way as the lead.

At three-twenty, Bob Edwards emerges from his office holding his coffee mug. He ambles past the desk toward the coffee machine, then disappears back in the other direction, toward the darkened section of NPR. He stretches slightly and yawns as he walks. He says "Hi" to Jean Cochran as she comes off the elevator carrying a brown bag with her breakfast. Jean has been doing the *Morning Edition* newscasts on the half-hour for several years. When she arrives at the *Newscast* area, she takes out her food — some fruit, including a bunch of bananas, and some homemade soup in a plastic container. Jean is a pleasant, quietly friendly woman in her late thirties, thin, with a long face and long, sandy-brown hair that she's wound into one thick braid. She's wearing blue jeans, sneakers, a sleeveless white blouse, and glasses with silver-wire frames.

Carl Kasell greets Jean warmly. She smiles and then frowns a bit as she sits at her computer terminal on the opposite side of the *Newscast* desk from Carl. Jean has surprised herself with her longevity as a *Morning Edition* newscaster. Like many others on the overnight shift, she feels that her schedule has put her out of synch with the regular world of work. When she started the job, in 1989, she didn't intend to stay with it for long; yet, like many others, she has found it hard to break out of the routine.

There is a curious camaraderie among people who work such unusual hours: a camaraderie that is part complaint, part a feeling of "being different" (sometimes from shyness, sometimes from eccentricity, sometimes from genuine creativity), part a strong sense of pride at being associated with such an important NPR program. For the fact is that, unlike television, morning is prime time for radio, and it's also a fact that some of the most famous and inspired radio people — in and out of news — have had to work crazy hours, either early in the morning or late at night. Bob and Ray started as early-morning disc jockeys in Boston. Wolfman Jack became famous in Los Angeles through his late-night broadcasts, as did others as disparate as Jean Shepherd in New York City and Larry King nationally.

What motivates people to take on a job as physically grueling as the overnight shift? For many people at *Morning Edition*, the overnight is boot camp — the way into NPR and more reasonable work hours. Others get used to it and are able to move their schedules around just enough to make the hours tolerable. Carl Kasell seems to have a touch of the Thomas Edison syndrome: he simply does not need a great deal of sleep and finds that quick naps during the day and a few hours in the evening suffice. He likes his hours because he gets to spend a great part of the day with his wife of thirty-five years. Jean Cochran sounds more like an accidental overnighter, yet the reward for her punishing schedule is that, today, she is one of the more recognized voices in public broadcasting.

Of course the main reason people like working overnight at *Morning Edition* is that they put on the air the most popular program that NPR broadcasts, and this inspires an excitement, an adrenaline rush, that partially compensates for the bizarre hours.

By three-thirty Bob Edwards has returned to his office with his second cup of coffee. He is now ready to begin the next part of his morning ritual, writing up the scripts that he has been researching. He rolls his chair beyond his computer terminal and positions himself in front of a Royal Satellite Three electric typewriter that sits on a small table facing the windowsill. He squeezes his knees beneath the low table, inserts a piece of multicopy paper, and starts pounding away at the typewriter's keys, using three fingers on each hand. The Opens and Returns for *Morning Edition* are the only pieces of regular script for an NPR program that are *not* composed on the VAX computer.

Bob types everything in caps and leaves hardly any margins. His fingers move quickly when he is writing, but he stops frequently to stare at the keys and think, or to take a sip of coffee from his brown mug. After writing a few lines, he looks at the yellow sheet of paper with the slugs on it. He crosses out a few words with his pencil, making big black blocks on the page. Occasionally, he picks up the manila folder with loose pieces of copy in it. He leans on his left arm, his face in his hand, as he reads. He grabs a Kleenex and blows his nose loudly. From his pants pocket, he takes a roll of lozenges and pops one in his mouth.

He puts his hands together, elbows out, does a slight stretch, then starts typing again.

The long lines of copy slowly work their way down the page. Bob does not erase or type over his copy much. Apparently he sets his sentences clearly in mind during his pauses and writes them out smoothly and quickly when they are ready.

The anomalous sound of Bob's typewriter helps contribute to a different aural texture, a different atmosphere around the *Morning Edition* desk. The newsroom still seems relatively calm and quiet, especially when contrasted with the activity generated during the dayside shift. But with less than three hours to broadcast, tension is building, and so is the pace of work on the show. The production assistants are busy in their edit booths. The backup director has come in a few minutes early — normally his shift starts at four o'clock — and he is helping out with some editing and mixing. (The backup director assists the main director with odd chores. Today the regular show director, Barry Gordemer, has taken on the backup role so that he will have time later in the morning to run training sessions on radio reporting for a new print reporter who has recently joined the science desk.) The Okidata dot-matrix printers whine and scream more frequently now, as various show elements are written and edited. Draft copies of introductions are handed to Ken or to Audrey, along with the ten-inch reel containing a completed spot. They listen to the tape and make the final edits on the copy. The corrected air script is then printed up, placed on top of the appropriate reel, and added to a growing stack of tape reels on top of a chest-high bookcase that stands against the outer side of the desk.

Meanwhile, the character of the board has changed. Names and check marks in different colors have begun to appear around the familiar slugs of the stories. Audrey has listed which editor is responsible for which story, and when a piece has been completed and handed in to the desk, Audrey puts a check beside it. Most of the longer stories are so marked. Shuster, in C2, hasn't yet been completed — Mike filed the report within the hour, and it is currently being cleaned up. Mike did not include any pieces of tape, so no mixing will be necessary. Paul is constructing a lead-in for the story, which Ken will go over before handing it on to Bob.

Audrey is currently listening to excerpts from a press conference by Helmut Kohl which were found in a BBC broadcast. It looks like she will be able to use an actuality of either Kohl or John Major at the start of the Zagreb two-way. Audrey is wearing headphones as she listens to the tape from the BBC.[3] She taps her white grease pencil on the side of the tape recorder, while holding her chin in her hand. Her demeanor remains calm, but she sits in her chair with a kind of muted tension. Anxiety is more visible in the various production assistants who occasionally walk back and forth between the desk and their edit booths. They move with extra quickness in their steps. It is just after four o'clock, less than two hours before airtime.

Bob usually spends between an hour and a half and two hours gathering material for his scripts and writing them up. By a few minutes after four, he has finished the Open for the second hour of the show.

He pulls the last page from the typewriter, crosses out a couple more words on the yellow sheet, and takes a long drink of coffee. He holds up the two pages of script. "Here's the product of what I've been doin' for the past hour," he says with a wan smile. "These two minutes of copy. Of course, this is really how I find out what's goin' on in the world," he continues. "I sit here reading along, finding out what's happened since I went to bed. It's a useful investment of time because afterwards, if something breaks and I have to go into the studio and talk to somebody, I've got the first five questions in my mind before anyone has to hand me anything. If I have to wing it, I can."

In the days before the computer was installed at NPR, Bob's script-writing took much longer than it does today. Bob would have to read through big, rolled-up scrolls of Teletype copy, looking for what he needed. Doing the Opens and Returns was one reason that Bob began coming in earlier than originally planned, first at three-thirty, then at three o'clock. He started arriving at two-thirty during the Gulf War, because there were many two- and three-way interviews — between Washington, London, and the Middle East — to arrange and pretape. Also, news was breaking so fast that Bob felt he needed extra prep time before each broadcast. Why does he still come in at two-thirty, now that the computer makes his writing so much faster and when there can be very slow news days such as this morning? The answer is habit and routine: when Bob gets used to something he sticks with it.

Take the yellow pad with its lines of pencil markings on it, for

---

[3] NPR can record BBC World Service broadcasts off a digital-encoded fiber optic cable that runs under the Atlantic directly from the BBC in London.

example. Bob keeps the same sheet of yellow paper going for several days until all the lines have been used up and the sheet is a collection of heavy black blobs. In part he does this because once in a while he will hold over a news item from one day to the next, but the pad and the black blobs are also a matter of habit — even a commemorative ritual. "Jay Kernis, who used to produce the program, is something of a graphic artist," Bob explains. He points to a small, mixed-media collage on the wall above his desk. "He did things like that up there. Well, when Jay first saw what I was doing on this yellow pad, he just thought it was amazing. He used to want the pieces of paper when they were finished. So I'd fill the whole page and give it to him."

Habit also partly explains why Bob still uses a typewriter. "I know the computer is much easier, and you can edit better and all of that. But . . ." He pauses, and searches in vain for a clear explanation of his choice. "I don't know. I still prefer the typewriter."

"Of course, you know," he adds dryly, "when the computer goes down, all these people out there are scrambling around looking for typewriters . . . and there's nowhere to find them. They're all gone. But as long as the power's on, I'm in business."

Bob is more articulate about why he uses the typewriter for writing letters and notes to people. "I don't want my personal correspondence in here," he says, tapping the computer. He's speaking in a low clipped voice, which he uses when he is being simultaneously playful and serious. "I don't know who reads this. Does Max Cacas [one of NPR's computer gurus] sit up there in his office and read all this shit?" Bob raises his eyebrows, but he is not smiling. "No . . . I learned from Ollie North. Ollie North didn't know that there were copies made of all E-mail messages down the hall somewhere. No way. And then there was the Bryant Gumbel memo that got out.[4] He had to go around making apologies to everyone in the building."

Bob pauses again and says in his driest voice. "You pay a lot for candor." He reaches for a Kleenex. "No way. So, I just stick with my little typewriter here, which forgets as soon as you type it."

The Opens for *Morning Edition* are a bit unusual for a magazine program, because they do not give a listing (usually called a "billboard")

---

[4] In 1989, Bryant Gumbel, host of NBC's *Today* program, reviewed the performance of a number of his colleagues in a private note that somehow circulated around NBC and eventually hit the media.

of what's going to appear on the show. Since *Morning Edition* is "modularized" — divided into discrete segments so that local stations may cut away and insert their own news and features as they see fit — the producers in Washington do not know what stories will be heard by which stations. So from the inception of the show, the opening minute of each hour was conceived of as a general "Good morning: here's what kind of day this is going to be." Bob Edwards puts it succinctly: "The Opens are not billboards of the show; they're billboards of the day." He says he looks for items that are fresh — something that listeners may not have known before they went to bed.

The style of the Open symbolizes the significant shift in programming that *Morning Edition* represented when it went on the air in the fall of 1979. The first great NPR news program, *All Things Considered*, started in 1971 and was designed as a ninety-minute show, divided into three half-hour sections. Each segment was put together as a whole unit — with stories of varying lengths — and producers tried to think about the ebb, flow, and shape of the entire ninety minutes.

But while the people at NPR in Washington felt quite comfortable with the format of a ninety-minute afternoon program, many local stations took a different view. The structure of *All Things Considered* meant that local stations could talk to their listeners only on the half-hour, during a brief station identification. This emphasis on the network violated some fundamental principals of American radio broadcasting that had developed at commercial stations in the fifties and sixties, following the demise of the great commercial radio networks. Stations had begun to focus on building strong connections with their listeners by using techniques such as constantly repeating the station call letters and frequently interrupting programs with announcements addressed to their local audience. Furthermore, the managers of some public radio stations seemed more concerned than people at NPR in Washington that by not having a national morning program, public radio was missing out on its biggest potential listenership.

So throughout the 1970s, certain voices at "the periphery" of the public radio system asked with increasing stridency that "the center" create a *morning* news *service* with a format that would allow local stations to break in frequently and give their audiences some of what they were used to during "morning drive-time" — reports on local weather, local news, local traffic.

By the end of the decade, NPR was ready to add morning news to its schedule — in part because the organization felt that it could now *afford* such a commitment. (A morning program is far more expensive to produce than an afternoon show, because of the hours its staff has to work.) *Morning Edition* would consist of short segments, and local stations would be given frequent opportunities to cut away if they wished. The show would be more hard-news oriented than *All Things Considered* in deference to audience habits at that time of the day. On the other hand, the production team that eventually got the first *Morning Edition* on the air was led by a young, brilliant producer of *arts* programming, Jay Kernis, and was staffed by producers and reporters who were used to the more flexible format of the afternoon program. From its beginning, then, *Morning Edition* contained behind the scenes certain tensions and even contradictions, which could sometimes lead to creativity, sometimes to less happy results.

As far as audiences were concerned, *Morning Edition* quickly became a hit, with listenership eventually surpassing that of *All Things Considered*. These days, *Morning Edition* has around three quarters of a million more listeners each week than *ATC*.

Bob Edwards encapsulates within his career and his attitudes the shift in programming — and the accompanying ambivalences — that *Morning Edition* brought to NPR. Bob had cohosted the free-wheeling *All Things Considered* with Susan Stamberg for five years before he was tapped for the anchor chair at *Morning Edition*. He understands well the forces that have driven the development of the show. While taking a break between Opens and Returns, Bob talks about the needs of the *Morning Edition* audience with the same deadpan, slightly sardonic tone with which he discusses anything. "Local stations have so many priorities," he says, leaning his head in his hand and tilting back his swivel chair. "They're raising money, they're doing local news, and features and weather . . . They have their own priorities and I made my peace with that the day I took this job. I had all those years on *ATC* where everything we put out went on every station, and that clearly was not meant to be the case with *Morning Edition*. Well, okay. I'm going to do some things that people are not going to hear. That's what this format is all about. And a lot of people here have trouble with that, and they shouldn't — they should understand that at *Morning Edition* we are a network service. But they can't make peace with that. They want their cousin in Moline to hear everything that they do. It's not what a network's about.

"I go out to a station every month somewhere," he says, a touch of pride entering his voice, "and I think it's very important. Not just for the politics, and not just for the fund-raising. But to get me out of here and meet listeners and find out what they're talking about. Find out what they like about this program, what they don't like, find out what *in* the news they're talking about. And that makes me better when I get in there" — he points toward the studio.

"We make assumptions here that such and such is important to them. Certainly some of the things we do we feel *should* be important to them, whether they feel it is or not, you know. I mean, we kind of do 'Eat your spinach' at that point. But it's important to have that feedback. If I just talked with these people every day" — he gestures toward the *Morning Edition* desk — "and I didn't get out and talk with the audience, this wouldn't work. It'd be sitting here talking just to ourselves.

"I really feel badly that the people that produce this program can't have that experience. Because it would *change* them, if they had a sense of that audience. There's a lot going on out there during the show. They're packing school lunches, and they're shaving and showering, and there's breakfast and orange juice, and all kinds of stuff going on. And we should have a clearer sense of what people in the audience took with them to the office — what they remembered after a program was over, what touched them and what didn't."

Yet Bob's attitude toward the local stations is complex. While he clearly sees himself as something of an advocate for "the audience," he disapproves of some of the tilt toward hard news in recent years that has been encouraged by local stations. He remembers with fondness the days when Jay Kernis produced *Morning Edition*, precisely because Jay did not entirely succomb to pressures to turn the program into a "radio service," providing hard news and headlines for local stations.

"I don't think our audience wants only hard news," says Bob. "You've got to have some relief. I mean, look at what we do. Bosnia, Somalia, AIDS. I mean, after the three of those, you need a little Red Barber or something.[5] And that was the relief, we *had* Red Barber. We need Baxter Black [*Morning Edition*'s cowboy commentator], we need something . . ." Bob pauses, looking for the words. He speaks slowly

---

[5] For more than a decade, Bob carried on a weekly conversation with the articulate and charming retired sportscaster Red Barber. Their chat became one of the most popular parts of the program. Red's death in 1992 prompted Bob Edwards to write a book about the man known to generations of baseball fans as "The Old Red-Head."

and with conviction: "Somethin' to make you feel that it's worth going through the rest of the day. I mean, you know, that there's some *light* at the end of the *tunnel*, to use a cliché. That there's something *uplifting* in the world. That it's not just people blowing each other's brains out, and passing disease, and hating one another."

Bob says that Jay used his creativity to bring some relief to the unremitting beat of hard news. "See, what he did was bring creativity *in*to the news," says Bob, speaking with greater animation. "It didn't dilute the news, but made the news more listenable. He didn't water down the ugliness. Sometimes he made the ugliness register more.

"Jay had more ideas before breakfast than most of us come up with in weeks." Bob Edwards sighs heavily. His voice slows: "But back then, we had a broader definition of the news than we have today. It was more than just wars and presidents and news conferences and 'the long green.' It was life.

"Today . . . well . . . there's a much narrower picture of the news here. From the top . . . the people on the top." Bob's voice sounds weary and cynical.

"We used to have built in to the program two sports segments each day and two arts segments. No more. Now we have no designated segments. When they were there, the news could never push them out. Occasionally, they'd push the arts segments out if there was really heavy news. But they'd never push the sports segments." Bob takes a sip of coffee. "Arts: you used to be guaranteed arts pieces. Jay had two arts segments. Recently, we've had one. Now there are none.

"Part of the reason for that was the feeling that if you locked in the arts segments, that gave the stations an easy excuse to drop in their own pieces — I mean some local stations ended their carriage of *Morning Edition* when the arts segment came on, particularly since some of the arts people here were dedicated to the most esoteric performance art pieces. They felt that was being on the cutting edge. It was fine to interview Chick Corea, or someone very established, but they also wanted to find the new talent. And very often they did. People who are now huge, I heard first here, a year or two years before they ever made it big. I mean, someone like Whoopi Goldberg.

"I'm sure the day we put her on, people were going, 'What in the hell was that?'" Bob raises his voice in imitation. "'What the *hell* was that?' And the news people would just be tearing their hair out. And, now look! . . .

"I mean, the news people are always taking about wanting to

break news. Well, we used to break arts — we broke arts news, all the time. But it just didn't matter to them — the news people — because it wasn't Bosnia or Somalia . . . things that get *Washington Post* editors all excited."

Bob looks out the window briefly and then resumes. "Of course, you know, many of us believe that radio itself is an art form, but it never gets any attention as one. When you see discussions of the arts, they might even go into art in television. But they never consider art on radio. And you know, radio is pretty much a cash register now. It's not even a jukebox anymore. It's simply a vehicle for making the station manager wealthy.

"But in public radio we still feel a mission to use the medium. It's a sound . . . I mean it just lends itself to art — to production, to beautiful sounds. It's always been difficult to incorporate that into news, but there used to be more of a premium on it here. Bill [Buzenberg, NPR's vice president in charge of news] and John [Dinges, manager of the daily news operations] come from much more of a news background than a radio background. Now *I've* never seen the two as exclusive, but you have people here who feel they are. That's very unfortunate.

"The sounds can enhance a story. They can eliminate the need for narrative in many cases. If you establish a locale, an activity with sound, you don't have to mention it — it's already there. It takes a real skilled craftsman to do it. But we've had those people. Still do — Neal Conan, Deb Amos, Scott Simon, Tom Gjelten . . ."

Bob stretches and shifts himself in his chair. He speaks slowly, with emphasis. "You've got to use sound to make radio compelling — and if you can make a piece of radio compelling listening, then the audience will be paying attention to all the things that a Buzenberg or a Dinges wants them to pay attention to. You can't just do talk. Well — I mean, sometimes you have to. Nina [Totenberg] did a long story the other day, very important story, with no tape . . . no tape at all. But our listeners will probably take that from Nina. Another reporter doesn't have Nina's credibility and that record for breaking news . . . or the simple storytelling ability. Another reporter would have a very difficult time sustaining two or three minutes without some tape, without some sound.

"I mean, you hear Nina and you pay attention. I can imagine people in the car pool going, 'Shh! It's Nina!'"

Bob is quite conscious that he plays an entirely different role on

Morning Edition from that of reporters like Nina Totenberg. "I'm the companion," he says in a low voice. "I'm the guy who . . ." he pauses and sighs. "Well, look: people want to hear the *familiar* voice, the radio friend, and decide whether they want to get up or not." Bob delivers this line in his deadpan, almost weary way. "And it's a different role than a reporter's. It's all journalism, but it's different kinds. I'm kind of the interlocutor. I'm the guy who says, 'Well, here's Nina, and this is all right . . . The world is not going to hell, even though there's some serious shit over here.' And you'll hear me do — I don't know — eight different styles in the morning, or more maybe. Depending on the material, where it is in the program . . . There are *so* many ways to read something. I mean you don't do murder and mayhem the same way you do the Returns.

"I can't even articulate what I do anymore, I just do it. I use my experience — doing it again and again: what's worked, what's failed, what wears well with a listener. That's what I think about all the time because I'm here for the duration. I want to *be there* for listeners — last week, next week, next year. That's okay because I've got nineteen years left in this business before I retire."

Bob becomes more animated when he discusses how long he has been hosting *Morning Edition*. He has just passed Susan Stamberg as the longest-running host on NPR, since Susan is no longer hosting regularly. "She did fourteen years," says Bob. "I think I've got all the TV people beat too. Pauley did fourteen years on *Today*. And I think that's the record. In two weeks, I'll be into my fifteenth year.

"But I first hosted *All Things Considered* when I was twenty-six. I'm now forty-six. I run into people all the time who heard Susan and me together, from seventy-four to seventy-nine. And still remember bits we did."

Bob blows his nose loudly and looks at his watch. It's about four-thirty, and he has two Returns to write. He turns back to his desk.

"Now comes the frivolity, which is the little piece of business at the bottom of the hour." He takes out of the manila folder the printouts of the stories he has chosen. As if to emphasize his change in tone and focus, he leans back in his chair and puts his feet up on the edge of his desk. He rereads the copy. Then he puts his chin in his head. "I probably put more work into this than I should," he says, "but I'm not entirely happy with one of the stories I've chosen."

He straightens himself and turns back to the computer terminal;

before writing up what he has, Bob takes one more swing through the wire services. He moves the screens of text more quickly than before; his computer beeps every time he presses the scroll button.

"People wouldn't believe what we don't report," he says slowly, while he reads. "Now here's a man who was attacked by a bat as he slept . . ." His voice trails off as he scans the story. His computer beeps. Bob reads another story, then speaks in a flat voice. "People throwing babies out of skyscrapers? I've got my nice little house . . . and my daughters . . . And I'm going to read this shit?"

In his driest, most sardonic tones, Bob speaks for the sensibilities of his sleeping audience, who will shortly be listening to his voice, encouraging them to get out of bed and face another day.

He swings his chair back to his typewriter, glances quickly at the story he has already chosen to be his first Return, and starts pounding the keyboard.

Meanwhile, outside Bob's office, Paul Miller has finished his draft of the script that Bob will use during the Bosnian two-way, and he has sent the copy electronically to the part of the VAX computer that is the general storage area for *Morning Edition* scripts. The show editor, Ken Barcus, has retrieved Paul's script on his own screen; as he reads he begins to type in some changes. Paul happens to walk by the *Morning Edition* desk at this moment and sees Ken's fingers moving on the keyboard.

"So what are you doing?" Paul says in a loud, friendly voice. "Raping my intro?"

"Go away," says Ken quietly, with a small smile. He continues typing.

"Just don't press the delete button," says Paul.

By four fifty-five, Bob has completed the two Returns. He's chosen two reports from Reuters — a frequent source of light pieces, he says, because of the British tolerance of eccentricity.

One story concerns the clothing tastes of Europeans — which country's citizens buy the most of what clothes. The British, it turns out, purchase the most underwear per capita. The other piece comes from Australia and tells of a man who tried to get workers' compensation after being injured on the job; his case was thrown out when he stupidly admitted to a friend that he had been stoned on marijuana at the time.

Even after he's done writing, Bob would like to replace the story from Australia with something else. He scans the wires for a couple of minutes, going back further and further into the previous day's stories. He even double-checks the emu piece that he considered and then rejected. "It didn't produce all that it promised," he explains. "You know, I've only got twenty-three seconds [after theme music and his "hello"]. Some stories just take me longer to draw the picture." Bob stops scrolling. "Here's the emu feature: they want the male emus to be more promiscuous, they don't want them sitting out there on the eggs, which apparently the males do. So they're setting up an emu semen bank so they can impregnate more females to get more emus."

Bob shrugs his shoulders. "Now, I could write that. But it's kind of an *mmmmmmmm*." He makes a face and moves his hand back and forth. "But what I'm after is 'Ah *ha* ha!'" He almost shouts. "See, it's got to be a quick setup, draw 'em a little picture, draw 'em in, and then *zing*. There's a formula to it.

"But that can be said of writing for radio in general. You've got to be short. Now in addition, I speak very slowly compared to a lot of people. But even so, you can't pack in more and more and more. That distracts, that dilutes. Go directly to the points. More is not necessarily better."

Bob scans a couple more stories. "Nope," he says finally, "'fraid not. And there's no news either. Just a real slow night." He clicks another screen, then finally turns away. "That's it! Some days you got it, and some days you don't."

He grabs the four pages of script he has written, stands up, and walks out to the desk. The time is four fifty-eight.

Bob shows the Opens and the Returns to Ken for his perusal. The show editor rarely revises Bob's copy, but once in a while he may catch an inaccuracy or a mistake of some kind. Bob leans against a bookcase while Ken goes through the story. Ken chuckles as he reads. Afterward, Bob returns briefly to his office. He puts his notebook, his newspapers, and various computer printouts under his left arm. He tucks his reading glasses into his shirt pocket, places his coffee mug in his right hand, and heads down the hall toward Studio Five. It is two minutes after five, and Bob is about to record his first tape of the day.

While Audrey and Paul finish work on the script, Julia Bailey, the editorial assistant who has arranged the Bosnian interview, walks quickly to the desk. She's been phoning Zagreb. "I've got Knežević," Julia says. "She's on the line now."

Audrey looks up from her terminal. "Ask her to pronounce her name and the name of her paper," she says to Julia. "Go to the studio and have Bob record her name and the paper's name while she's listening. Also, check with the TD [technical director] and make sure her line is strong enough."

"Where is Bob?" says Julia. "Is he in his office?" It's five minutes after five o'clock and Julia is waiting for the various elements of the two-way to come together. At the moment, the *Morning Edition* staff is acting like a family trying to get itself out the door together and on time.

"No, I think he went into the studio," says Audrey while typing.

"Why don't you say something like this," says Paul, looking over Audrey's shoulder at her computer screen. "'For a critical view of developments in Bosnia, we turn now to Gordana Knežević . . .'"

Julia hurries off to the studio. The two-way cannot start until Audrey and Paul finish writing the introduction, but Julia wants the engineer to start checking the line to Zagreb so he can add whatever electronic filtering and shaping might be needed to make Knežević's voice as clear as possible.

Toward the Far Side of the Moon

A heavy metal door, two and a half inches thick, separates Studio Five from the rest of NPR. The door no longer opens as smoothly as it once did, and its worn hinges exhale a high-pitched, weary squeak. Inside, a curved inner hallway, about twenty feet long, dimly lit and heavily soundproofed, forks in two directions. To the left, a broad passageway slants upward a few yards, then curves sharply to the right until it ends at another metal door — the entrance to the broadcast studio, where the host sits. The other branch of the hall is narrower and shorter: it runs straight from the main door, ramping upward at a steep slope for about ten feet, then it bends slightly to the left till it reaches two small doors set at right angles to each other. The side door opens into the tiny announce booth, where newscasters do their reports. The other door leads to the main control room — the central focus of activity, of behind-the-scenes drama, once a program has gone on the air.

The lighting in the control room is somewhat brighter than the hallway outside, but it remains relatively subdued — track lights and a few strategically placed gooseneck desk lamps provide a quiet illumination. In part this is because the electronic equipment in the room is filled with VU meters and colored lights that need to be read easily. But in part also, as engineer Rich Rarey puts it, "You can't hear as well when the lights are bright." Furthermore, the dimmed lights help people in the control room see without strain into the main studio and the announce booth; both are connected to the control room through large, double-paned windows. The announce booth is lit more softly than the control room, while the studio seems a little brighter; yet here, too, the illumination comes from muted, incandescent lamps, quite different from the fluorescent lights used elsewhere in NPR offices.

While control room, studio, and booth are easily visible to each other (there's a small, separate window between the announce booth and the studio), each area is thoroughly soundproofed — which is to say, cut off and isolated aurally — by means of heavily treated walls and ceilings, and thick doors and windows. People can talk to each other, however, using a variety of technologies. Intercom circuits connect the rooms when the correct buttons are pressed. There's also a "cue system," separate from the main broadcast circuit, which lets the control room listen to any microphone (or tape recorder, or CD, or telephone for that matter) through small, low-quality monitor speakers. Finally, during broadcasts, directors, newscasters, and hosts can use hand signals to exchange simple messages. Yet notwithstanding the various means of communication, each room still feels, in essence, separate and disconnected, for each exists in its own distinct sound-space, which you can feel clearly when you move from room to room . . . a slightly different pressure against your cheek, a different tingle at the back of your neck.

This suite of quietly lit spaces is reminiscent of an aquarium: a group of environments, clearly visible to each other yet profoundly separated — distinct aural worlds, interacting and interdependent, yet removed and tangential . . . each floating in its own private silence.

Studio Five's control room is fully three times the size of the control room for Studio Seven. Five's control room is dominated by the large mixing console, seven feet long by three feet deep, which is filled with buttons, knobs, sliders, VU meters, and glowing lights. Some eighteen different inputs can be mixed together — faded and cross-faded or played simultaneously — while other lines can be equalized and sound-treated . . . a bewildering array of electronic possibility. Engineers who work at NPR must know every adjustment the console can make because it represents the final arbiter — the last gatekeeper — shaping the sound that gets broadcast over the air. There are a dozen more pieces of equipment between this console and the satellite dish on the roof of NPR, which finally shoots the program up to Galaxy IV, NPR's "ear in the sky"; but the various amplifiers and transmitters along the signal path are mere relay messengers whose function is to assure that the strongest possible signal gets sent to the satellite. They do not change the content of the program in any way, but they do perform an extraordinary transmogrification of its form. For by the time an NPR transmission has arrived at the rooftop satellite dish, it is no longer a collection of sounds and voices: it has become instead a silent and invisible stream of electromagnetic energy — a beam of microwave emission, ready to embark upon a fantastic journey into space . . . and perhaps even to the stars.

The jump to satellite transmission represents a jump into science fiction. Once the sounds of a radio program have been translated into microwave signals, the antenna on the roof of NPR aims this stream of energy at a satellite as wide as a couple of buses, floating in space twenty-three thousand miles above the earth — higher than the clouds and the weather, higher than the stratosphere and the ionosphere, beyond air pollution, the ozone layer, the northern lights. The satellite must be placed at that distance so it can float in permanent, geosynchronous orbit, always above exactly the same spot on earth. Galaxy IV moves, in fact, through near space — a region with no air, no gravity, little density . . . a cold, dark vacuum that presents to any travelers from earth who happen by their first intimations of that vast and profound silence which envelops the universe.

Into this dreadful emptiness pours the microwave energy stream that carries NPR programs. The emissions themselves are as mute as the void through which they travel: the voices and sounds of NPR have been translated and stored in electromagnetic waves, in much the way a computer stores information for later retrieval.[6] The microwaves are aimed at antennae on Galaxy IV, and, remarkably, just about all of the emissions reach that comparatively small target. (The image of shooting an eye out of a squirrel at ten miles comes to mind.) The satellite then immediately rebroadcasts these signals, at a different frequency,

---

[6] Technically speaking, NPR programs are "modulated onto" the microwave emissions.

back down toward earth to be picked up by receiving dishes at local NPR stations.

While most of what NPR sends up into space is returned to earth by the satellite, there is always a certain amount of leakage, of spray . . . Small portions of NPR radio programs, then, escape Galaxy's antennae, and continue sailing away from the earth, toward areas of deeper darkness and more profound silence. They propagate through the solar system, through the galaxy, their ultimate destination eternal and unknowable. They may reach the stars, they may reach the dark side of the moon. NPR's diffused signals would become significant — take on added meaning and importance — only if, at some point, somewhere in the vastness of the cosmos, they are ever "heard" — which is to say, "someone" singles out NPR's electromagnetic energy from all the other radiation that fills the galaxy, tunes into it, and decodes it, or at least, interprets it. If that should happen, then this electromagnetic residue from a-day-in-the-broadcast-life of NPR might take on a more resonant importance, indeed.

These incredible journeys — literally across time and space, at speeds faster than that of sound unaided by radio waves — begin with the push of a few buttons on the broadcast console in Studio Five's control room. The engineer who presses the buttons (and who adjusts the knobs and moves the sliders) thus wields a power which earlier generations would have called magical. And yet, today, we call such an individual a "technician" and perceive her or him as but the final link in a chain of rational decisions and explicable events, grounded in science and motivated by a range of self-evident, unremarkable truths, including a simple one, not dreamed of by Thomas Jefferson, that all Americans have an inalienable right to be woken up in the morning, if they so choose, by a news broadcast on their clock radios.

The main console stretches out in front of the huge picture window, twelve feet long, four feet high, made of double-paned glass, which looks into the large studio beyond. Above the window sits a large round Favag clock. To the right of the mixing board, four reel-to-reel tape recorders line up side by side, each built into its own diagonally sloping table mount, each with its own preamplifier and VU meters placed in an overhanging shelf. These machines share with the host the honor of speaking most extensively to the audience; in fact, the vast majority of what listeners hear on NPR comes from these tape recorders, not from the live microphones set up in the studio.

To the left of the main console stands equipment that plays back other media: two cartridge tape players, a professional compact disc player that can be cued up to start playing at any second in any track of a CD, a Digital Audio Tape machine for playing back DAT tapes. Below and behind these rack-mounted players sits an old turntable for phonograph records, almost never used these days.

The console and the row of playback machines form three sides of a small open quadrangle, in the midst of which sit the broadcast engineers, rolling from position to position on swivel chairs. During broadcasts, NPR uses two engineers: primary and backup. The primary engineer sits in front of the console and takes charge of the show's technical aspects. The backup engineer tends the line of reel-to-reel recorders, cueing up tapes (in the right order), announcing when they are ready to go, keeping an eye out for any developing mechanical problems.

For the most part, the backup engineer spends a much more relaxed shift than the primary engineer. There is no hierarchy in this part of the production process, however: the primary and backup engineers usually swap places halfway through a program.

Along the back side of the engineer's quadrangle, parallel to the main console but three or four feet behind it, stretches a long, high counter and desktop, built into the floor. The front of this unit houses the all-important patch panel, a collection of plugs and sockets that looks very much like an old-fashioned telephone operator's board. This panel connects Studio Five's control room with the rest of NPR and with the world beyond. By making the right connections, using single-ended patch cords, an engineer can pipe into the control room a satellite link to the Middle East; or a dedicated line to NPR's Los Angeles bureau; or a connection to an external radio network like the BBC or the CBC; or a telephone call from Bosnia.

If the maze of wires and circuitry connecting all the equipment within the control room itself dazzles the imagination, the brass- and gold-plated sockets in the patch panel explode the imagery a thousand-fold. For these passive receptacles represent but one terminus for thousands of miles of wires and circuits that run all through NPR — in the walls, in the ceilings, in the floors, from the subbasement to the roof. Hidden, enveloping, and omnipresent, the wiring for National Public Radio may be viewed as a metal-plated capillary network within a huge electronic circulatory system.

Technologically, this system seems extremely advanced, but viewed as an organism, it is surprisingly old-fashioned, resembling the amoeba or protozoa, with its endlessly redundant features — or perhaps one of those low-order segmented creatures, capable of moving in many different directions at once. When a program is about to go on the air, however, higher organs are grafted onto this primitive body and the somnolent creature leaps into active, creative life.

Central to this transformation is the woman or man who sits behind the raised countertop, on a high draftsman's chair with a swivel and low back. The director of the program looks down upon the main console and into the studio beyond, where the hosts sit. The director's station is compact and quite low-tech in contrast to everything else in the control room. Two digital timers — and an old analogue timer, rarely used — are built into the desktop along with an array of levers to set, reset, start, stop, count forward, and count backward. The director's intercom system connects to the studio, the announce booth, and a range of other important locations throughout the building, including Record Central, Master Control, Studios Six and Seven, and the *Morning Edition* and *All Things Considered* desks. Next to the intercom's speaker stretch a row of buttons and toggle switches that activate the various options; a silver gooseneck microphone, two feet long, curls upward from the countertop at a gentle angle.

The accoutrements surrounding the director may be modest, but the power she or he yields is extreme. It is the director who tells the engineer what button to press when; who signals the host when it is time to speak; who selects what music to play between stories; who coordinates the announcements; who keeps track of the timing of the program's segments; and who is ultimately responsible for a program beginning exactly on schedule and ending within a fraction of a second of its allotted time. While preparations for broadcast involve considerable collaboration and cooperation among the production staff, once a show is on the air, an almost militarylike structure replaces freewheeling democracy. The director becomes an absolute monarch: engineers are supposed to listen only to the voice of the director and to obey without hesitation. The point of this hierarchy is practical, not ideological: local stations expect NPR programs to begin and end right on time. Within programs like *Morning Edition*, the precision extends to individual segments. If the newscast runs two seconds long, stations coming back to the network after local cut-aways will catch the final words of programming that they were not carrying. If a segment ends early, local stations will face dead air — a few seconds of unexpected silence. The program will then sound choppy to listeners, and the atmosphere of smooth professionalism will be broken.

The psychology of aural communications is unfair and demanding; the fabric of connection and expectation woven between broadcasters and their audience remains extremely fragile. Glitches, bad transitions, unplanned silences, or flubbed entrances can easily distract listeners and even add a touch of doubt and uncertainty to their belief in NPR as a reliable source of information.

There is always "a director" in an NPR control room. Even during a simple mix — when, for example, two or three separate pieces of tape are played back in a particular sequence and recorded on a single master tape that will then be broadcast — the production assistant who has edited and prepared the tape will cue the engineer when to roll which segments. Similarly, during the recording of interviews — either in-studio or by telephone — someone always sits in the director's chair and takes on the formal authority to supervise the flow and shape of the interview. One or two people from the editorial side of the program also regularly come into the control room during a two-way: the producer or production assistant who is responsible for cutting the interview down to time and an editor (or perhaps the show producer) who is listening to hear how the piece will fit into the program as a whole. Depending upon the importance and interest of the two-way, other people may also eavesdrop.

This morning, for the two-way with the Bosnian journalist, a larger number of people than usual will eventually settle into the control room, in part because this interview will lead the program, in part because it is being conducted at the last minute. But though the conversation was scheduled to start at five, people have been slow to gather and Studio Five sustains a brief moment of calm, its three fishbowl compartments staring blankly, quietly, at each other through the large, silent slabs of glass.

Tongue Twisters Before Breakfast

At three minutes after five, Bob Edwards walks into the studio carrying his load of scripts, newspapers, and magazines under his arm. He arranges his reading material on a narrow blue table, shaped like a squared-off kidney, the center of which holds a wooden console inlaid with electronic outlets and switches. Four microphone booms grow out of the console like metal trees. Fat, Neumann U-87 microphones, covered with sponge rubberlike windscreens, are suspended at the ends of these booms like fruit. Headphones of various weights and sizes are plugged into each microphone station. A computer terminal glows on the far side of the desk. Four swivel armchairs are set around the table. Near the far corner of the studio, an old television set squats on a roll-about cart. Above the window into the control room hangs another Favag clock. On the windowsill sit two red digital timers with inch-high displays. Between them is a ten-inch Plexiglas square, split into two signs, each lit by a white light. When "MIC" is on, the studio mikes are live and feeding voices into the control room. "NET" means that the show is on the air — the control room is connected to the network via the satellite.

For the rest, the large room is sparsely and somewhat untidily decorated: some books, random pieces of electronic gear, old reels of tape. Small pieces of debris — assorted pens, a few old coffee cups — cluster on the narrow wooden molding that runs like wainscoting along the wall.

Bob swaps chairs and sits down behind the principal mike, midway along the back of the table. The tallest of all NPR hosts, Bob has adjusted the chair he sits in for broadcasts to be surprisingly low — his knees are noticeably higher than his hips when he puts both feet flat on the floor. He seems not to mind the awkward position but unfolds one of his newspapers, takes a sip of coffee, pops a throat lozenge in his mouth, and starts reading. He can do nothing until the final script arrives from Audrey.

Meanwhile, in the control room, Art Laurent, the technical director for *Morning Edition*, leans back in his swivel chair in front of the mixing console and idly watches a small black and white television, perched unobtrusively on top of a corner shelf. Art is a stocky young man with blond hair and a round face. He's been at work for about an hour and has spent most of that time getting Studio Five ready for broadcast, cleaning all the tape recorders, checking their adjustments, and sending test tones from the main console throughout every piece of equipment — which might be considered analogous to a singer doing warmup scales before a performance.

From about five o'clock on, Studio Five is reserved for recording late-breaking host interviews and random talk-tracks, as needed. The Opens and Returns for the program will also be taped. All NPR news programs try to prerecord the initial minute of their shows. These introductions have music in them and they sometimes mix excerpts from tape in addition to the host's voice. Most important, the entire production *must* conclude in exactly fifty-nine seconds, so that NPR's hourly newscast can begin, after a second of silence, precisely at one minute past the hour. A botched opening can sour the tone of a whole broadcast. *Morning Edition*'s Returns, on the half-hour, are also prerecorded because they include music and must end promptly in twenty-nine seconds.

This morning, production of the Opens and Returns must await the recording of the Bosnian two-way. Julia walks into the control room, sees the hold light blinking on one of the telephone lines, and asks Art if the overseas telephone line has been patched into the mixing board okay. "Yep," says Art, slowly turning his head. He swivels his chair over to the panel that holds all the equalizing equipment — the notch filters and frequency boosters and noise attenuators. Julia picks up the phone and asks Ms. Knežević to talk a bit so the engineer can check the technical quality of the line. Within a few moments, a deep, thickly accented Middle-European voice is crackling over the studio monitors, first describing the weather in Zagreb and then reading a news story she happens to find on her desk: "As far as the G-7 meetings in Tokyo are concerned, Mr. MacKenzie replied that the agenda of items to be discussed in negotiations . . ." Art fiddles with knobs and dials, and the voice in the speaker changes, first subtly, then dramatically, as Art isolates certain frequencies individually to optimize them. Within a few moments he has adjusted the sound — equalized or EQed it — as best he can.

Barry Gordemer walks into the control room carrying a yellow pad and twiddling a pen between his fingers. Since the Knežević interview will be leading the program, Audrey has asked Barry, one of her most experienced tape editors, to "cut the two-way," that is, to reduce the conversation to a length that best sustains audience interest. Barry will have less than an hour to turn out the finished piece. He will make a log of the two-way on his yellow pad, noting what sounds like "good tape" as he goes along. Barry will also be director during the interview, so when he enters the control room he heads for the high chair behind the engineer's quadrangle.

A short, compact man with close-cropped brown hair, Barry speaks in a high, quick voice filled with energy and smile. Of all people working at NPR in positions of great tension and pressure, Barry is simultaneously one of the fastest, most efficient, and most good-natured. He's wearing a purple short-sleeved shirt, gray pants, and sneakers. Barry lifts himself into the director's seat and, with a series of sharp, efficient movements, sets all the timing clocks to zero. He looks into the studio where Bob continues to sit placidly, reading a newspaper.

At twelve minutes past five, Paul Miller enters the control room; he will listen to the interview in his capacity as foreign editor to make sure that the conversation touches salient points. Then, through the window, Audrey can be seen entering the studio and handing Bob the final script for the two-way. Their mouth movements indicate that they exchange some words. Audrey smiles and leaves. Bob starts reading the script. It includes an introduction and series of suggested questions — some of which Bob will use, some of which he will ignore. Within a few seconds of receiving the script, Bob is making changes in it with his pen.

Audrey comes into the control room and hands two more copies of the script to Barry. She then squeezes herself against the back wall in between Paul and Julia. Audrey will hang around for the interview because she needs to know, as soon as possible, exactly how much good material Bob gets from Knežević so that afterward, she can make final decisions about the entire A1 segment.

The door to the control room swings open — squeaking slightly — and the tall, looming figure of Bob Edwards appears. He has come to review pronunciations with Julia. She repeats the reporter's name and the newspaper's name, and Bob scribbles on his script with his pen. He speaks out loud as he writes "Os . . . lo . . ."

Audrey says, encouragingly, "You've heard Gjelten say that before."

". . . bo . . . jane . . ." Bob continues to speak slowly and write phonetically on his script.

"Which means 'something from Liberation,' I think," says Julia, giggling. "Serbian . . . Yugoslavian . . ."

Bob suddenly explodes — his voice walking a tightrope between wry, mock-irritation and genuine testiness. "Oh, for God's sake! What is this?" He points to several lines of script with a slew of Yugoslavian names in them. "You've got another one up here. I can't do all these. Got to do them individually."

"What are you talking about," says Audrey in a high, lilting voice, assuming the role of pacifier. She knows what Bob is concerned about, however. "All right. Here's what I'm thinking," she begins, but he interrupts.

"You guys are putting me on!" Bob says in a clearly exaggerated tone.

Bob is reading through the introductory paragraph on which Paul and Audrey have collaborated. At the end of the passage, the copy reads, "Bosnia's president, Alija Izetbegovic, is in Zagreb for a meeting with other members of the collective government. Joining us now is Gordana Knežević, the editor of the Sarajevo newspaper *Oslobodenje*." Bob is concerned about trying to say all these tongue twisters and then launching into the interview with the journalist. It's usual practice in two-ways for the host to read the introduction and then start the conversation. This makes for the smoothest transition: the host's voice can change naturally from reading to asking questions, and the guest understands better the framework within which the discussion will occur.

Audrey understands what Bob has in mind and agrees with him. "No, no. You don't have to say all that."

"Okay," says Bob in a quiet, professional voice. He's decided what he's going to do.

Audrey continues a discussion she was having with Paul about the script, pointing at Bob's copy. "My contention, anyway, is that this line is in the wrong place. This line should be here."

"Well guess what?" says Bob, speaking with a touch of irony but still calmly and pleasantly. "I'm not going to say it yet. I'm going to ask this person *that* question while we have them on the line" — he points to his script — "and we will fix the rest of *this* later." Bob knows it is getting late, plans to do his own editing of the introduction before he records it, and wants to get into the studio quickly.

"Let's just do 'Joining us now is . . .'" says Audrey in a conciliatory tone. "Good. Thank you."

"I'm not going to do 'joining us now,'" Bob insists. "I can't pronounce that," he says, pointing at the journalist's name.

"Which one can't you pronounce?" says Audrey.

"Nothing. Good morning." Bob speaks abruptly and starts to move toward the control room door. The tone of his final remark slid clearly from sardonic to testy. The shift was not lost on someone in the control room, who whispers, with a touch of irritability: "Come on, Bob! She just gave the pronunciation to you!"

Audrey, however, chooses to ignore Bob's grumpy tone and continues to speak to him in a calm, motherly fashion — albeit a slightly nagging mother. "You should do it while it's fresh in your mind. Next, you won't be able to remember it. You know . . . you're an old biddy, like the rest of us, and you're not going to remember it."

Bob murmurs something at Audrey as he goes out through the

door. He reappears in the studio a few seconds later. Barry senses that showtime is approaching. He straightens himself up in the director's chair, placing his fingers beside the timer.

"You already have a fix on the lines?" Barry asks Art, referring to the filtering and EQing that Art did earlier. The engineer nods. "Got your levels?" Barry says, inquiring whether the engineer has got the telephone and Bob's microphone set at the proper volume. "Yep," Art says.

Bob sits in his low chair, places a pair of black headphones over his ears, puts on his reading glasses, sets his script down in front of him, and almost immediately begins speaking into his microphone. "Hello," he says in his deeply resonant voice. A muffled "Yes?," a tad surprised, comes back across the telephone. "Hi, Bob Edwards, how are you?" Bob says quickly, but with a friendly tone.

"Oh, very well, thank you," the low voice replies over the phone.

"Are you all set to go?" Bob asks pleasantly but with no preamble.

"Yes," comes the reply.

"Okay," Bob says. "Arthur, how about you?" Bob looks up into the control room. Art nods. He started the tape recorder shortly after Bob took his seat in the studio.

Bob looks down at the script and reads his first question without pausing a beat. "Is the pressure on the president to accept partition an attempt by the Croats to take control of the presidency or is it motivated by the feeling that Muslims had better get whatever deal they can get before they lose everything?"

(When Bob finishes his question, Audrey nods approvingly and exclaims, "Yeah." Bob has made a few simple adjustments to the phrasing of the question and clarified one of the points over which Audrey and Paul had been haggling.)

As Bob reads his script, his voice undergoes a subtle but distinct transformation. It is not that he exaggerates any single quality of his normal speaking voice. His cadences are similar to his cadences in normal conversation: his voice has the same resonance, the same dry tone. Yet some indefinable quality of authority has appeared. No longer aided by eye contact or hand gesture, Bob is now communicating totally with verbal inflection, with vocal projection. A close analysis of his speech patterns might indicate that Bob slows down slightly when he speaks on the radio or that he *tends* to *emphasize* certain *words* more when he becomes a broadcaster. But again, what's most remarkable about Bob's delivery — his "vocal technique" — is how closely it mirrors his normal speech patterns.

In fact, one of the most distinctive qualities of most people who broadcast on National Public Radio is that their on-air voice is almost indistinguishable from their normal, conversational voice. Quite apart from commercial broadcasting, where conventions abound and announcers are encouraged to put on one kind of tone or another, at NPR reporters and hosts have always been encouraged to sound as "natural" as possible.

Knežević responds to Bob's question with a little sigh and then starts talking. "The situation is, is very confusing at the moment," she replies. "During last night, ah, session of presidency took place here in Zagreb, Izetbegovic managed to come and, ah, he joined this session. As far as we learned here this meeting was, ah, mainly, the accus . . . accusation . . . the members . . . members of presidency accused each other of, ah, of wrong policy . . ."

In charming but sometimes halting English, Knežević spins out her first response. She tries to describe the complexity of Bosnian president Izetbegovic's position as leader of a multi-ethnic government in Bosnia-Herzegovina. But though she speaks for about a minute, she never articulates clearly the political fault lines between Croats and Muslims, which was the focus of Bob's first question. In other circumstances, Bob might have given Knežević a second chance by rephrasing his question. But Bob is conducting this two-way under severe deadline pressure and he is determined that the interview will run as close to "real time" as possible — no longer than six or seven minutes. So Bob moves forward and picks up on one of Knežević's comments about the influence which the European Community is having on Bosnian politics in general and on Presdient Izetbegovic in particular.

"Has his position been strengthened at all by President Clinton and Chancellor Kohl's . . . ah . . . urging that . . . ah . . . the embargo on arms be lifted for his government?" Bob reads the question, but does so with such a sound of spontaneity that when he hesitates before the word "embargo," Paul Miller, standing in the control room and reading along in the script, instinctively says the word out loud, as though to help Bob through a stumble.

"It is certainly of some influence of mood and atmosphere here," Knežević begins, "and those were only good pieces of news which reach the area, really." Knežević goes on to describe the debates in Zagreb over the current peace plan being discussed at Geneva, which envisions the partition of Bosnia-Herzegovina. Her English continues to sound somewhat tortured, yet her voice conveys a strong personality. In the control room, Barry is scribbling notes furiously on his yellow pad, occasionally marking down the elapsed time as displayed on his timer. On the other side of the director's counter, Paul is also taking notes, less extensively than Barry. He has his own personal stopwatch balanced on his notepad. Audrey listens intently with that distracted expression in her eyes of someone who is focusing on voices.

The interview continues for more than five minutes. Sometimes Bob reads questions that Audrey and Paul have written ahead of time. Occasionally he will extemporize. At about five and a half minutes into the two-way, Knežević makes a roundabout comment concerning her own views about the latest peace plan ("She's waltzing the subject," says Paul, as he listens). Bob would like to get the Bosnian reporter to express her criticism more directly. "So . . . it *won't* bring peace then," he says, prompting her, by his own example, to speak bluntly.

Knežević does not respond to Bob's lead. She gives another rambling answer, which would need considerable editing to be effective on the radio. More than six minutes have now elapsed, and Bob wants to wrap things up. He looks down at a final question in his script and instinctively shortens it. "Well, if not partition, then what? Is there a peace plan that would work?"

Knežević sighs again before giving her final answer, which, for all her twisted syntax, emerges rather more clearly than other parts of her conversation. "Even . . . you know, even Vance-Owen plan which is now declared dead was some kind of better solution. At least the idea of the plan was to freeze situation as it is . . . and to let Bosnia chance . . . so in next couple of years it would either slip or survive. But now this new plan doesn't, uh, leave any . . . doesn't leave any chance for Bosnia as a state to survive. And for Izetbegovic to accept this kind of talk it means . . . you know, to, to, to accept willingly to sign death sentence to the country he's the head of."

"Thank you," says Bob abruptly. He senses that her last response will form a reasonable conclusion to the two-way, and the clock shows that six minutes and thirty-two seconds have elapsed. It's time to end the conversation. *Morning Edition* goes on the air in less than forty minutes. Bob has to record an introduction for the piece, Barry has to cut the tape — and, of course, Bob has yet to do the show's Opens and Returns.

Bob leans back from the microphone. The quickness of his ending takes everyone a little by surprise and there's silence in the control room for a moment. Then Art switches Bob's mike and Knežević's phone line out of the main amplifying circuit. He stops the tape machine that has been recording the two-way. The connection to Zagreb returns to that "hold" limbo of telephone technology.

Five seconds after Art has disconnected Bob's mike from the telephone line, Bob's voice is heard through the control room's intercom speakers. "Now I'm going to rehearse these names."

Still wearing his headphones, with his feet flat on the floor, Bob starts going through the introduction, pen in hand. He pops a lozenge into his mouth as he works.

Thirteen seconds elapse between Bob's abrupt "thank you" and the moment that Julia finally picks up the extension phone to say good-bye to Knežević. "Thank you very much for speaking to us," she says, and after a quick reply from the other end of the line, Julia says, "All right. Bye-bye," and hangs up the phone.

For her ten or fifteen minutes on hold and her six and a half minutes of conversation with Bob Edwards, Gordana Knežević will receive a fee of one hundred and fifty dollars from National Public Radio.

Paul brings up the subject of editing the piece. "Audrey, what do you think? We're about six and a half minutes. Do you want to keep that length and do two minutes with something else?"

"She did a lot of stumbling around," says Audrey thoughtfully. If Barry edits out some of the verbal looseness in the Knežević interview, the piece will be more effective but a larger hole will be made in the A1 segment. It will be far easier to find a ninety-second spot on the BBC, and then write a thirty-second lead for it, than to dig up a good two-and-a-half or three-minute piece. "But we *do* have to clean it up a *little*," Audrey says, then walks out of the control room with Paul, while going over a list of possible stories that could fill out the segment. Audrey asks Paul to check the length of the BBC spot on Estonia, by Bridgett Kendall.

Meanwhile, Art is cueing up on the reel-to-reel tape recorder labeled "Tape One" the brief actuality that will be used as part of Bob's introduction to Knežević: an excerpt from a news conference by British prime minister John Major. "I don't believe that lifting the arms embargo and shoving more arms into the area . . ." Art plays the tape, sets the level, checks the quality of the sound, then rewinds the tape to the beginning.

Major's "veddy British" voice inspires Art to start speaking in an English accent. "So good to hear you, John," says Art, as he flips some switches. He then sits back in his chair and waits for Bob to finish editing his copy in the studio.

Barry remains at the director's desk. He will not start cutting the two-way until Bob has recorded its introduction: then he will splice the intro onto the top of the interview and proceed to trim the piece down according to whatever instructions he receives from Audrey. The edit will be quite straightforward; the only difficulty will be not to trim so much from the piece that the A1 segment runs short. Barry looks at the clock. It's five twenty-five. The door to the control room swings open and Bob strides in. He's revising the introduction to Knežević and must listen to the beginning of the two-way. He asks Art, "Can I hear the top so I can write into the answer?"

As Art rewinds the tape of the two-way, Barry says, "I was thinking of starting her off where she says, 'The situation is very confusing.'" He puts on a slight European accent. "You could actually use that line if you wanted."

Bob speaks with a deadpan delivery that could be ironic and could express a genuine surprise. "That was a *she?*"

Barry smiles. Knežević's voice sounded unusually deep. "That was a she, Bob."

Bob is standing beside one of the tall speakers, resting his copy on top. "Marlboros, I'd say," he replies. "Five packs a day."

Art plays back the end of Bob's first question and the entire first answer from Knežević. "Okay, you can stop it," says Bob. He writes some words down on his copy. When he speaks again, he, too, is putting on an Eastern European accent. "European community is 'looking for person to sign treaty' — right?" Bob's accent, it must be said, is not very convincing.

"*Jyess*," says Barry, doing a much better job as a mimic.

Bob has put one foot up on the mixing console as he writes. He works for almost half a minute on his script in silence as Art and Barry wait. "*Oslobodenje*," Bob says out loud, practicing. Then he falls silent again for another thirty seconds. Meanwhile, Art has fast-forwarded the interview to reach the unused portion of the tape. Art will record Bob's introduction here so Barry will have all the elements of the two-way on the same reel.

"All right. I think I got it," Bob says, heading out the door.

"This ought to be good," says Barry, imitating a bit of Bob's own ironic wit.

Bob appears in the studio and sits in front of the microphone.

Though in theory Barry at this point should cue Art to roll tape and Bob to speak, the taping begins wordlessly, at twenty-seven minutes past five. Art presses the button that starts Tape Three running and recording, then turns on Bob's mike. Bob sees the white MIC light and starts talking. He is reading the copy that will bring listeners back from the six o'clock newscast.

"This is *Morning Edition*. I'm Bob Edwards. President Clinton has enlisted the support of German chancellor Helmut Kohl for a proposal to lift the arms embargo on Bosnian Muslims . . ."

As Bob speaks, Art quickly slips Tape Three's playback mode into cue to make sure the machine is recording okay. A half-second delay of Bob's voice echoes briefly up from the cue speaker. Art kills the cue playback, and Bob's voice returns to normal.

". . . Kohl tried unsuccessfully yesterday to sell the proposal to European Community leaders meeting in Copenhagen. Britain and France oppose lifting the arms embargo . . ."

Barry has been following along in the script and sees that Bob is starting his introduction to the brief excerpt from John Major. He warns Art about the coming switch to tape. "Ready on One," Barry says forcefully yet calmly. By "One" he means Tape Recorder One.

". . . in part because they are worried about their peacekeepers in Bosnia. British prime minister John Major says it would be counter-productive."

"Hit-it-mike-out," says Barry, almost as one syllable. "Hit it" means start the tape recorder. "Mike out" means take Bob's mike out of channel while the tape plays. This way Bob can clear his throat or rustle his papers and not interfere with the piece of tape.

"I don't believe that lifting the arms embargo and shoving more arms into the area . . ." John Major begins yet again.

The tape runs about twenty seconds. While it plays, Art asks Barry, "Do you know where this tape comes from?"

Barry has his eye on the clock and the script but he is used to carrying on conversations in the middle of mixes or broadcasts. It seems to be one of the control room traditions at NPR to act, frequently, as though you are not really paying attention to what's happening in the studio or on the air — whereas, in fact, people are keenly aware of what's going on around them. Self-distraction is one way of keeping tension within manageable limits.

"Don't know," says Barry, speaking rapidly. "They didn't say," he continues, putting on a slight British accent.

"Well, find out!" says Art, in cockney dialect.

Meanwhile, Major is coming to the end of his speech. Barry has the "outcue" — Major's final words — in his script, and the end of the piece of tape is also physically marked with several inches of white paper leader tape, spliced onto the end of the recording. ". . . will do anything other than stop any chance of negotiated settlement, add to the fighting, add to the killing, add to the length of the war . . ."

"Open!" says Barry. As he speaks, he raises the palm of his right hand high in the air. Sitting in the studio, Bob could see the director's signal clearly if he were not looking at his script. The white light in the window goes on. Bob's mike is now live, though the host won't speak for a couple of seconds yet.

". . . and open the prospect of it widening. That's not a policy I favor."

Barry's wrist snaps forward, his finger pointing at Bob. Bob still has his eyes on his script but begins speaking as though in response to Barry's signal. Meanwhile, Art presses a button that stops Tape One's playback.

"The Europeans want to preserve territory for the Muslims and not reward Serbian aggression," Bob begins. He reads clearly and simply. There is no hint of the dozens of revisions that have gone into this brief thirty-second script. Bob holds his copy in his right hand and with his left hand he brushes hair from his forehead absent-mindedly. "They call for a continuation of a single Bosnian state. In Bosnia, Serbs and Croats now are working together to carve up the country into three ethnic states and Bosnia's Muslim president is under pressure from within his government to accept the deal.

"The Tanube News Agency says Bosnian Serbs and Croats have agreed to exchange prisoners and to allow the transfer of civilians. Muslim radio says the Croats and Serbs have joined the fight against Muslim troops in the central part of the country."

Like a hurdler approaching his gates after a straight sprint, Bob now faces the three sentences he'd been complaining about earlier. Yet there is no change in his expression or his demeanor: he sits as before, his feet planted solidly on the floor, his head moving ever so slightly as he emphasizes individual words, his mouth managing always to keep exactly the same distance from the microphone.

"Bosnia's president, Alija Izetbegovic . . ." — on this word, Bob indulges in only the slightest hesitation, well masked, given his slow, moderately choppy delivery — "is in Zagreb for a meeting with other members of the collective government. Gordana Knežević is the editor of the Sarajevo newspaper *Oslobodenje* . . ." Bob sails smoothly through the reporter's name, but a slight hesitation creeps into his delivery when he says the newspaper's name. It is similar to his pause around Izetbegovic — more an exaggerated carefulness than a stumble — but there is something about his delivery that he doesn't like; some line of acceptability was crossed. Bob stops himself. "Almost," he says. He pauses for a second or two to give Barry some clear tape to work with (Art keeps the tape rolling throughout), then picks up where he left off. ". . . the Sarajevo newspaper *Oslobodenje*. She describes the pressure on the Bosnian president."

Bob falls silent. Art says, "That's it?" but Barry doesn't have to answer, for Bob starts talking. "Then there's tape, and after it's over I say 'Gordana Knežević is the editor of the Sarajevo newspaper *Oslobodenje*.'"

It's five twenty-nine. Bob has done in one take — with one slight burble — a series of tongue twisters that would have daunted many a seasoned reporter and host.

"Good," says Barry quietly, and Art turns off Bob's mike. Art lets the tape run a bit longer, then rolls his chair over to Tape Recorder Three, cuts the tape with a razor blade, and hands the reel with the interview and the introduction to Barry. "So how long are you supposed to cut it down to?" he asks.

"I have *no* idea," says Barry, putting the ten-inch reel on his yellow pad and preparing to leave for an edit booth.

Meanwhile, in the studio, Bob moves the Bosnian script to one side of his desk, pops another lozenge into his mouth, and assembles the scripts for the Opens and Returns, which will be his next task. He's taken the headphones off his ears and has them circling his neck.

The control room door squeaks open and Audrey walks in.

"He's tracked," Barry says to Audrey, meaning that Bob has recorded his talk tracks for the two-way. Barry stands up and stretches. "Any idea on length?" he continues. "As long as it comes out? If I really clean it up a lot?"

"Umm," says Audrey slowly. "Something like six minutes."

"Total? I think it'll be tough getting it to that length."

"You think it will be longer — will it be longer than that?"

"I think it will be *barely* six minutes." Barry is not only a quick and experienced tape editor, he also maintains high standards about what should be broadcast and what shouldn't. He knows that Audrey has been having a hard time trying to fill up the program, but he also feels keenly that the Knežević interview ought to be cut short. Her accent and her grammar are hard to understand, she repeats herself — as the lead story of the morning, she will lose many listeners if she is not edited down properly.

"Well," says Audrey in an encouraging voice, "try for six first, and if that doesn't work, then we'll come up with Plan B." She and Barry walk out of the control room. It is exactly five-thirty, and Barry has forty minutes before the Knežević interview is scheduled to go on the air.

Live on Tape

As Barry hurries off to an editing booth, Jim Wallace, this morning's director, walks into the control room carrying a stack of CDs and some ten-inch reels of tape. Jim has spent the past hour or so reviewing the tentative rundown of the show and selecting music for the various bridges — the transitions from segment to segment. He's been using the CD library and CD player in Barry Gordemer's office, which is right next to Bob Edwards's. Jim has also copied the latest information from the board and has printed out a penultimate version of the road map using a Macintosh computer, also located in Barry's office. (Like Bob's typewriter, the Mac-produced road map is another eccentricity unique to *Morning Edition*.) The road map isn't final yet because the A1 segment remains tentative.

Jim knows that Art is looking for this rundown of the show, and as he settles himself into the director's chair, he addresses Art's unspoken concern.

"Yes, we ain't got no road map," he says. "I'll make copies for you after we finish tracking."

Art leans back in his chair. "No road map? You don't even have any music to play."

By this Art means that Jim hasn't yet handed him the compact disc upon which is recorded the *Morning Edition* theme music. Jim grunts as he passes over the CD and also a ten-inch reel of tape that contains the promos — advertisements — for a number of programs, including today's edition of *All Things Considered*. Art puts the CD in the player and slaps the promo reel on Tape Three. He's already loaded a large hub of fresh tape on Tape Four and has switched the speed-select knob to fifteen inches per second, twice the normal speed of recording and playback. Art has also placed a thin little red flag, made out of tape, over the knob to remind everyone that this tape machine is now at high speed. (Major program elements like the Opens and Returns are always recorded at high speed because it gives the best possible fidelity.) On this reel of tape Art will record, in order, the Opens, Returns, promos, and most of the music that fills up the time in between segments, when local stations may be identifying themselves or broadcasting their own announcements. The various elements will be played back at the appropriate moments during the show. No one edits this important reel. If anyone makes a mistake during production, Art will rewind the tape and record over the error.

In the studio, Bob has placed his headphones back onto his ears and he's looking over the tops of his glasses into the control room. He's set to begin recording.

"Ready, dude?" Art asks Jim in a Bart Simpson–like voice.

"Ready, dude," Jim replies. Art presses buttons that start Tape Four rolling and recording. Then, after a short pause, the CD begins playing the *Morning Edition* theme.

Five seconds into the theme, Jim raises his hand and says, "Open . . ." Art presses a button, and the light goes on in the studio window. Jim listens for the cymbals in the theme, and as the trumpet trills, he says to Art, "Under . . . ," while simultaneously pointing at Bob. Jim's gestures are clear and distinct but less abrupt and dramatic than Barry's. By "under," Jim instructs Art to fade the theme music under Bob's voice but to keep it audible.

"Good morning," says the familiar voice of Bob Edwards. "Bosnia's leaders meet today to discuss the division of their country along ethnic lines. I'm Bob Edwards. Today is Tuesday, June twenty-second, and this is NPR's *Morning Edition*."

"Up full, mike out," says Jim quickly, but not so rapid-fire as Barry. "Up full" means that the theme swells up and is heard without any voice-over.

The pattern of this opening has been the same ever since *Morning Edition* began thousands of shows ago: eight seconds of theme, ten seconds that begin with Bob saying "Good morning" and end with ". . . NPR's *Morning Edition*"; six seconds of theme; back to Bob reading the full text that "billboards the day"; then, during the final four seconds of the Open, a particularly quick and self-contained swelling of the theme (sometimes called a "stinger"), followed by Bob saying, "The news is next" as the stinger fades away to silence. The music itself contains crescendos and diminuendos, so the engineer does not have to fiddle excessively with levels. In the jargon of sound mixing, the theme contains natural "posts": moments where the music wants to be heard in the clear, unencumbered by a voice. Should Bob write a few too many words in his first, brief segment, for example, the music's natural swell in volume will rise up behind him and start fighting to be heard. The Open will sound jumpy and Bob will seem to be "stepping on" his own theme music.

By this point, of course, Bob must have the rhythm of this opening imprinted in his genes; engineer and director are also so familiar with the routine that the complex series of steps seems to flow easily and without strain. Jim gives oral cues to Art, but, in truth, all staff members could probably do these mixes in their sleep.

"Open," says Jim after six seconds of music. "Under . . ." He points to Bob.

"European Community heads of government wrap up their summit today in Copenhagen. They've been discussing the Bosnian war and the creation of jobs in their respective countries . . ."

As Bob begins reading his Open, Art asks Jim for the outcue, the final words Bob will say with music behind him.

"Ed Bradley; he's fifty-two years old," Jim reads from his script.

"Fifty-two?" says Art, sounding surprised.

"Apparently," Jim says.

Meanwhile, Bob has been continuing. He's sitting with his right hand against his head. "United Nations personnel in Somalia hope to reopen more distribution points today in the capital, Mogadishu. Middle East peace talks resume today here in Washington. Jordan's King Hussein meets today with Defense Secretary Aspin. Today is the birthday of Ed Bradley; he's fifty-two years old."

Bob has seemed to hurry up just a little bit as he read his copy: he knows he must "get out" of his text in time for the swell in the music that occurs at fifty-six seconds.

"Up," says Jim, and as Art moves the slider to increase the volume slightly, the theme's stinger is heard. Then, while the music decays naturally behind him, Bob takes a tad more than a second to say his final words: "The news is next."

The take is perfect . . . no flubs, no miscues. A fairly complex interweaving of music and words has been accomplished with astonishing ease. And yet, in the context of *Morning Edition*, the results are commonplace. Bob flips his page of script, looking as phlegmatic and unemotional as ever.

"Okee-do-kee," says Jim. "We have . . . a rerun," he says to Art, punning on the Return that they record next. Art knows the drill well. The *Morning Edition* CD contains different versions of the theme. Art cues up the disc at the short cut which plays behind Returns. (Not all NPR programs have gone to the expense of putting their music on CD. Some use DAT cartridges. A few still rely on reel-to-reel tape, dubbed at fifteen ips from master recordings.)

Jim says nothing to Bob. Tape Four rolls, Art starts the CD. The shorter version of the theme music begins. Here there are no posts, no back-and-forths, only Bob's straight read-through of his copy and a natural fade-out of the theme.

"Open," Jim says after two seconds of theme music. After four seconds, Bob starts speaking. Jim does not say "Under" to Art because the music naturally fades down to a low level and, after about fifteen seconds, drops out.

"Good morning, I'm Bob Edwards. A market-research firm in London has published a survey of European lifestyles. The firm concluded that the Germans spend the most money on leisure activities, the Belgians spend the most on food, drink, and tobacco — more than the Italians and the French. Italians spend the most on clothes. But the British spend the most on underwear. The report did not reveal which country spends the most on market research." Bob delivers this final line with a great deal of ironic relish, yet he doesn't smile. "You're listening to NPR's *Morning Edition*."

During this Return, Art and Jim have responded to each of Bob's lines with a grunt or a comment. At the end, Jim and Art have a good laugh. This was the Return that most pleased Bob: it has a nice double kick — a punch line about the British from the original Reuters dispatch, and a topper by Bob himself.

Art says to Jim, "Does that mean the British are buying more underwear or that their underwear is more expensive?"

Once again, there is no communication between the studio and the control room. Bob moves on to the second opening and looks it over quickly while Art resets the theme-music CD. It is now twenty-six minutes to six.

"Ready?" asks Art in a thin funny voice.

"Ready," says Jim.

Bob hasn't looked up from his script, but Jim knows from experience that he is simply waiting for the theme music to begin. Bob is holding his copy with both hands now, his feet still solidly planted on the floor.

Again, the six seconds of music, Jim's hand signals and verbal cues to Art, and Bob's voice flows in and out of the music just as it should. "Good morning. The Organization of American States meets today here in Washington to discuss Haiti. I'm Bob Edwards. Today is Tuesday, June twenty-second, and this is NPR's *Morning Edition*."

Bob says *Toos*day, not Tuesday. He hits the music post perfectly, and the second Open is completed in one take. So is the second Return, the story from New Zealand (about the man who lost his workers' compensation) that Bob has been trying to replace all morning. Bob makes the most of this tale, delivering the kicker with an extremely light touch: "But now Simon has been forced to return the money and pay a hundred-eight-dollar fine. Authorities learned that Simon Breeze actually hurt his jaw while yawning widely after smoking *marijuana*." Bob hits the word "marijuana" with a kind of fadeaway twist, very different from any other cadence he's used this morning. He smiles wanly at the end of this Return. In the control room, Art and Jim chuckle a little, but there is no great guffaw as greeted the previous piece. Bob quickly takes off his glasses, puts his headphones down on the desk, stands up, and leaves the studio — saying nothing to the director and hearing nothing back from the control room. It is twenty-two minutes before six.

Jim spends part of the remaining minutes before the show goes on the air checking out a stack of CDs he's brought with him that will supply the music bridges between various stories. He's a bit perplexed about how to end the A segment if Bridgett Kendall's report on Estonia is used following the Bosnian two-way. Jim hands Art a CD of Elvis Costello and the Brodsky Quartet, and tells him what cut to play. The music begins — a minor chord, sustained, on an unidentifiable instrument, followed by a violin that sounds both electronic and gypsylike.

"Does that sound like sad Estonian music?" asks Jim. Art gives him a quizzical look in response. "It has some way to go before we get to where I want the backtime to start."

Directors use a number of tricks when working the musical transitions between show elements. While it's always possible to fade down in the middle of a piece of music, the production sounds cleaner — and listeners get a more satisfying feeling of closure — if the music stops naturally. So directors spend considerable time listening to the endings of various musical compositions. When they find something they like, they work backward from the closing bars and figure out how much music is needed to fill out time between stories, or to bridge from the end of a report to the end of the segment and the break to the local station. The length of music needed is called the "backtime." Usually, however, directors will start the music playing a little before they fade it up (so that the engineer doesn't have to worry about pressing a button and moving a volume slider simultaneously). This maneuver is referred to as a "deadroll" because the CD begins playing with the volume all the way down. Backtiming a segment and choosing where to begin the deadroll are crucial parts of on-the-air production. (The time-remaining display on CD players has become a valuable tool in radio production. In the past, when phonograph records were used, turntables literally had to be played backward for the appropriate length of time to determine the correct place to cue up a record.) If a director calculates correctly and an engineer hits the backtime or the deadroll at the right moment, a musical bridge will fade up, play itself out, and stop, just at the moment that the host begins the next story or gives the time check (or the standard out cue) and sends the show back to the local stations.

Countdown and Blastoff

In the final twenty minutes before airtime, the atmosphere of coiled tension that's lain beneath the somnolent surface of early-morning NPR breaks out into the open. People are walking faster and talking more loudly than before. The shift is not any larger now than it was two hours ago, but suddenly more people seem to be crowding the second floor. In the *Newscast* area, Carl Kasell and Jean Cochran are writing their upcoming newscasts at full speed. Greg Peppers, their producer, is on the phone lining up spots from stations. The production assistants are pulling tape from UPI, BBC, and NPR sources. They are auditioning reports, timing them, and writing intros for Carl and Jean.

Ken Barcus is busy at the *Morning Edition* desk going over late pieces of script that are now being handed in by production assistants who are finishing off the final edits for each spot. Many reels of tape are stacked on the shelf between Audrey and Ken. Audrey is listening through headphones to some reports she hasn't yet had a chance to hear. Paul is off looking for the most recent and longest BBC report on Estonia. On the board, A1 is still not fully filled in, pending the results of Barry's edit and Paul's search.

Barry sits in Edit Booth Five, a short distance from the desk, cutting down the Bosnian two-way. Audrey has asked Barry to keep as much as possible, but at five forty-six he has already made some ruthless decisions about the opening of the interview and has cut out a large chunk of tape.

Here is how Knežević responded to Bob's first question. This transcript includes a few of her stumbles and hesitations, to give a flavor of how difficult the tape would have been for listeners:

> [Sigh] The situation is, is very confusing at the moment. During last night, ah, session of presidency took place here in Zagreb, Izetbegovic managed to come and, ah, he joined this session. As far as we learned here this meeting was, ah, mainly, the . . . accus . . . accusation . . . the members . . . members of presidency accused each other of, ah, of wrong policy. But, ah, it looks that Izetbegovic is not to be, ah, pushed down and nobody thinks that he is weaker after this meeting which took place here in Zagreb. But the pressure is obvious and it looks like European Community is looking for a fellow who would sign partition.

In the control room, Barry assumed he would keep the first sentence. Knežević's line seemed interesting, and her small sigh gave a subtle but palpable sense of the weariness enveloping both participants and reporters of the Balkan civil war.

Yet Bob wrote into Knežević's comments with a broad enough comment ("She describes the pressure on the Bosnian president") that Barry does not have to keep the initial sentence. And, in fact, in the edit booth, Barry realizes that the pace of the first answer is too slow. If left uncut, the tape will push listeners away instead of drawing them into the two-way. Barry knows he has to leave some loose tape in the interview, but it will be much better if those weaker sections come later in the conversation. So Barry slices into the tape, grabs a blank reel, and begins spooling onto it large chunks of Knežević's opening comments. Within five minutes, he has reduced a tangled response to something direct, and even pithy. The following transcript adds ellipses [. . .] to show where Barry made the major cut:

During last night, ah, session of presidency, [. . .] members of
presidency accused each other of, ah, of wrong policy. But, ah,
it looks that Izetbegovic is not to be, ah, pushed down and
nobody thinks that he is weaker after this meeting which took
place here in Zagreb. But the pressure is obvious and it looks
like European Community is looking for a fellow who would
sign partition.

By shortening Knežević's overall answer, Barry has made the remaining
stumbles easier to listen to — they now sound personable and spontaneous rather than tedious. Interestingly, he has also clarified her broken
English, even rendered it charming. "Members of presidency accused
each other of wrong policy." "European Community is looking for a
fellow . . ." These phrases are more comprehensible aurally because
the previous thicket of tangled verbiage has been pruned away.

With less than twenty minutes to complete his edits, Barry does
not articulate consciously what he is doing: he follows his ear and his
instincts, listening his way toward clearer, more engaging tape. Like all
editors, though, he is keenly aware of the passage of time — in two
contexts. As he sits at his machine, stretching himself tall to press the
buttons, move the reels, and swing his razor blade, he frequently looks
down at his wrist to see how much time is left before the show begins.
And he keeps an eye on the round cylinder in the middle of the tape
recorder — a tape counter that measures, in minutes and seconds, the
amount of tape that passes around it. Barry knows that the *improvements*
he has made to the Knežević two-way have already reduced the length
of the spot by fifteen seconds — and he has several more chunks of
tape that he wants to extract.

At ten minutes before six, Bob Edwards appears in his office: he is
examining his bookshelves. He hasn't said anything to anyone, but it
turns out that as he was reading the script for one of the long pieces
in the show — an interview he conducted with writer Ann Waldron,
about her biography of southern newspaper publisher Hodding Carter,
Sr. — Bob ran across a piece of information that he believes to be
wrong. He finds Waldron's book, leafs through it, and then changes
the script. The production assistant who wrote the introduction confused a subtle historical point and misnamed the newspaper for which
Carter was most famous. Bob's editing work at NPR is filled with such
obsessive attention to detail.

At eight minutes to six, Ken Barcus is beginning to organize the elements for the first hour of the show. Each story is on its separate reel, and on top of each reel is a multicopied script, which will be broken down and passed round to the host and the director, who gets two copies. Paul Miller suddenly arrives with some bad news for Audrey. He has been checking out Bridgett Kendall's report on Estonia, and it has come up thirty seconds short. "I can't understand it," he says. "We heard it on the Beebe's [BBC's] *Newshour* at three o'clock, and I swear it was longer."

"It *was* a minute thirty — it *had* to be," says Audrey.

"But now it's not," says Paul. Audrey sighs. The A1 has been a problem all morning and with less than ten minutes to showtime it begins to seem that this nine-minute slot will never be filled.

Paul goes off to see if there is another tape of Kendall lying around somewhere. Perhaps she produced two versions of the story, a short spot for the BBC on-the-hour newscast and a longer version that he and Julia heard on the hour-long newsmagazine program.

Six minutes to six. Barry walks out of his booth.

"I didn't take out much at all and I got five-nineteen," says Barry. "With a button." A button is a short piece of music or sound — no longer than five or ten seconds — that separates two related stories. "I just cut it for clarity. The longest chunk I took was like that." He holds up his hands to show a short length of tape. "I was worried that this would happen."

Audrey retains her taciturn look, but the news is getting worse and worse. One minute forty for Estonia (unless Paul finds the longer report) plus five minutes nineteen seconds for Bosnia makes a grand total of six minutes, fifty-nine seconds for a segment that is supposed to run a little under nine minutes. That leaves almost two minutes to fill.

At that moment Paul reappears. "Kendall is one-thirty!" he exclaims happily.

"Oh, you found the other spot," says Audrey with a slow smile.

Paul nods. "You need the vindication this morning."

"But Bosnia is only five-thirty . . . five nineteen, actually," Audrey says with a curious calmness.

"Oh dear," he says, his smile evaporating. He scribbles on a piece of paper the timings for the various A intros and stories and sees how short the segment has become. "What do we do now, Mom?" he says at last.

"Can you write a long lead for Estonia?"

"I guess you want a *really* long lead," Paul says, nodding.

At one minute to six, Carl Kasell leaves the news horseshoe and heads down to Studio Five carrying many pages of copy and a handful of tape cartridges. He will be live on NPR's air before Bob Edwards. He goes into the control room and hands Jim a carbon of the newscast script along with five tape carts containing spots that Carl will use during his broadcast: two during the first segment, which lasts two minutes and fifty-nine seconds; one during the second segment, which lasts one minute and fifty-nine seconds; and two during the third segment, which contains mostly economic news and runs three minutes and thirty seconds. (Many stations will break away for local news during the third segment; a few will even drop the network at the start of the second segment.) Carl then goes into the small, dark announce booth, turns on the desk lamp, puts the pair of headphones across his silvery hair, and readies himself for the broadcast.

Five fifty-nine and thirty seconds. Bob Edwards enters Studio Five. He sits down in his low chair and reaches over to the far left-hand side of the desk, near the computer display. He picks up a small, flat black object with buttons on it. He presses some of them, and the television in the corner comes to life. He adjusts the volume to zero, takes a quick look at the screen, then turns his attention to the computer terminal. He begins scanning the news wires while sipping his mug of coffee.

In the control room, Jim and Art are watching the second hand on the Favag above the window. This clock is so accurate that it has spawned a verb at NPR: to "Favag" a tape means to time it by one of the big clocks. All the Favags are connected to a single "master clock driver" that periodically calls into a dataport at the U.S. Naval Observatory to get the official time. The clocks are dead accurate to within a few percentage points of a second.

Two minutes before the broadcast starts, Art sends out a minute of tone from the control room board to all the tape recorders in other parts of NPR that will make copies of the upcoming *Morning Edition* broadcast. At five fifty-nine, the tone stops. At five fifty-nine and twenty seconds, an entirely different section of NPR, one that handles satellite communications, sends up a tone to Galaxy VI. This note can be heard by all stations that are preparing to broadcast *Morning Edition*. It may be considered the wake-up call to the network. But then, at five fifty-nine and fifty seconds, the tone is turned off. The silence of the next ten seconds gives the final, eloquent cue that National Public Radio is about to broadcast its first major program of the day.

"Ready Tape Four," says Jim, his eyes on the Favag. The big red hand moves discretely from second to second. When it clunks onto the twelve, Jim says, "Hit it!" The *Morning Edition* theme begins; then, after six seconds, Bob Edwards says "Good morning" and starts introducing the program. Several million listeners hear Bob's voice resonating through their bedside radios or their car stereos. But as Bob-on-tape speaks through the airwaves, Bob-in-the-flesh is scrolling through the latest newswires on the studio's computer terminal and popping a throat lozenge into his mouth.

At just about six o'clock, Audrey receives the final timings for the Bosnian and Estonian pieces. They will leave the segment one minute twenty seconds short, but it is simply too late to add a new story or to lengthen the pieces they already have. Over the intercom, she tells director Jim Wallace to do the best he can to stretch the music. Jim decides to drop the Elvis Costello piece and use instead the Brodsky Quartet, alone, playing a version of Ravel's "Pavane for Sleeping Beauty," from the ballet *Mother Goose*. In the context of a series of Eastern European reports, this French music will acquire a certain "Slavic" tone . . . it is also a strong enough work to hold the audience's attention through an unusually long musical interlude at the conclusion of the segment.

At one minute after six, Carl Kasell begins broadcasting the news from the small announce booth. As Carl starts reading his first story, Jim hands Art the Ravel CD and asks him to backtime the cut he is going to use at the conclusion of A1. Before Art can complete the backtime, he must hit a newscart — cued by Jim — and then, after fifty seconds, reopen Carl's microphone. There's considerable activity in the control room as *Morning Edition* gets under way.

Meanwhile, Bob is sitting quietly in the studio. At two minutes after six, Barry brings in a script, an introduction for the A2 segment by Bridgett Kendall. This will be the first live radio from Bob this morning. Barry leaves the script on the desk without a word. Bob looks up only briefly from the computer screen.

Scanning the wires, Bob has come across a story that he wants to check out. At three minutes after six, he leaves the studio, walks quickly out to the printer behind the *Morning Edition* desk, picks up his copy, and returns to the studio. He gets back to his desk a little before five minutes after six. Carl is now into the second section of his news report. Bob looks quickly at the TV set, then, pen in hand, he starts going over the script that Barry left. At that moment, Julia walks in carrying more copy. She does not announce what the scripts are (most of the B and C segments) because the pages are clearly marked. In fact, like Barry, she doesn't say anything at all. But when Bob looks up from his editing and takes the copy from her hand, he says a brief, professional "Thank you."

Bob takes a quick glance into the control room before he returns the scripts. He also checks the time — on three different clocks. The Favag above the window shows him the official time throughout NPR. Below the window, the two digital timers, with their big red numbers, are connected to the timers in front of the director. One clock counts down the number of minutes and seconds left in the current segment (in this case, Carl's newscast); the other clock shows the time remaining in the particular spot now being aired (a review of current economic indicators).

Time for NPR programs is thus measured in several different ways simultaneously. Each is essential to keep in mind if host, director, and producer are to know the "position" of the show at any given moment.

The newscast concludes at nine minutes and twenty seconds after six. It's followed by an underwriting credit and twenty-nine seconds of music called "the beeble." Then, at ten minutes after six, Art Laurent presses a button, and Tape One starts playing. The first part of the A1 — the Bosnian two-way, complete with its prerecorded introduction — goes on the air. In the studio, Bob Edwards blows his nose. He's sitting calmly and somewhat lumpily in his low-slung chair, editing his up-coming scripts. He brushes his hair with his right hand from time to time. His coffee mug steams beside him.

At thirteen minutes past six, Bob puts his scripts together in a neat pile and then leans in the opposite direction and picks up a newspaper from his stack of reading material. He starts glancing through the paper, opening it out to its full size. After a while he puts on his headphones. At six-fourteen and fifty seconds, Bob folds up his paper and puts both wrists on the table. He holds a pen in his right hand.

The digital clock to the right of the window reads 00:35, the remaining time in the Bosnia piece. Bob is sucking on a lozenge. He leans his face in his right hand. At six-fifteen and twenty-five seconds, the Bosnian story ends and the ten-second "button" which Barry inserted at the end of the tape starts playing. Jim lets the music decay for a long while — adding as much time as he can to the segment — before he points to Bob through the glass. The two white lights, NET and MIC, are now on simultaneously, and Bob speaks live to his listeners for the first time this morning, though no one outside the NPR studio has any way of knowing this. His script lies flat on the table, his hands are folded together, his pen still stuck between two of his right fingers:

The Baltic republic of Estonia is making a successful economic transition from Soviet-occupied state to a free-market economy. It's having more of a problem in its relations with the leading Soviet-successor state. Russia has warned Estonia of serious consequences if it goes ahead with a new law which could classify Russians living there as illegal immigrants. Yesterday, Estonia's parliament approved the law, which requires all non-Estonians who have been living in the country for more than three years to apply for residents' permits or be deported. Almost six hundred thousand Russian-speakers still live in Estonia, making up a third of the population. More from the BBC's Bridgett Kendall.

Bob pulls his head back from the mike and purses his lips slightly as he concludes his reading. He has sounded authoritative, informed — and smooth. He puts the copy he just read in a discard pile, leans back in his chair, and picks up the newspaper again. He leaves his headphones on as he begins reading.

So the A segment winds down: eighteen hours of concern and three or four hours of acute anxiety end with Bob reading forty seconds of copy and then perusing the early edition of *The Washington Post*. It is not clear how much of the drama surrounding the A1 filtered through to Bob. No one sought his opinion about the various stories under consideration, no one discussed with him how much Knežević should be cut and whether another story should be substituted for Kendall's report on Estonia. Bob learned of the Bosnian two-way when he arrived and he conducted the interview with his usual skill; he was handed the various scripts and he added his final editorial touches to them. That appears to be the extent of his connectedness to the angst experienced by Audrey, Paul, Barry, and the rest of the staff.

Yet Bob is not oblivious to all the hard work going on around him and he pays attention to the consequences of that effort. For example, even as he is scanning the newspaper with his eyes, his ears are taking in the gist of Kendall's story. The British reporter concludes her report with these words:

> But already Russia has declared the treatment of minorities will have a bearing on the speed of Russian troop withdrawals from both Estonia and Latvia. And what must concern the governments in Tallinn and Riga still more is the possibility of economic sanctions. Both republics rely on Russia for crucial energy supplies and without them they might find it hard to survive. Bridgett Kendall, BBC, Moscow.

Jim cues Art to fade up the Ravel, which will play for almost fifty seconds; as the music starts Bob puts down his newspaper and positions himself in front of his microphone, ready to do the time check at the end of the segment. He also presses the intercom button on his console and speaks to the control room about Kendall's piece. "More alphabet soup," he says, sardonically — meaning that listeners will be confused by the many unfamiliar names in the BBC report.

As the Ravel draws to a close, Jim says to Art, "Ready on Bob. Open his mike." Bob says, "The time is nineteen minutes past the hour," and Jim says, "Mike out. Hit Four." Tape Four contains a fifty-nine-second continuation of the Ravel music for local stations to play behind whatever kind of break they wish to do. Or they can simply "dump it out" (fade down the music) and come back to the network in sixty seconds.

When the program resumes after the first break, Bob normally reads a fifteen-second billboard that gives a taste of an upcoming report in the B segment. Then Carl Kasell delivers thirty-five seconds of headlines. This morning, Tom Goldman, the producer of the Abdul-Jabbar segment, has decided to do something different. As the Ravel music plays in the background, Jim alerts Art to what's coming up. "Let me hear Three," says Jim, meaning he wants Art to play what's cued up on Tape Three. A short cut from Kareem begins the tape: "A lot of time I'm mistaken for Michael Jordan. Of course I'm flattered to be mistaken for Michael Jordan . . ."

"What is this?" Art exclaims.

". . . but you talk about sixteen years and about eight inches in height, and sixty pounds . . . I don't know about that." The tape ends with a chuckle.

"Don't tell me — it goes with the billboard!" Art continues.

"Well, that *starts* the billboard," Jim explains.

"Starts the billboard?"

"Yeah, we hit that, come out of it to Bob, go to Carl."

"Okay. Gotcha," says Art.

Art recues the tape. "Does Bob know it starts with tape?" Art asks with about five seconds left in the Ravel.

"He'll find out soon," says Jim in a slow voice. "Ready . . . on the tape."

"Um-hmm," Art answers.

"Hit it."

The Jabbar tape starts playing. Bob has his copy of the script and so follows along with no problem. When Jabbar says, "sixty pounds," Jim says abruptly "Open!" and raises his hand for Bob to see. He points at Bob when the chuckle starts, but in spite of the fact that Bob did not look up from his copy, he comes in perfectly, speaking in a wry tone that perfectly compliments Jabbar's shy playfulness.

"He is *not* like Mike. If anything, it's the other way around! First headlines . . ."

"Open, Carl," Jim exclaims.

". . . with Carl Kasell."

"Good morning," says Carl, and begins his stately read through the top of the news.

Following the headlines, Bob returns, live, to read an introduction to the Jabbar interview, which, at almost seven and a half minutes, will fill the B segment and carry the program to the six-thirty break.

Out around the *Morning Edition* desk, the last pieces of tape for the upcoming half-hour are being checked over by Audrey, while Ken puts the finishing touches on the scripts shortly to be carried into the studio and the control room. While everything is proceeding smoothly enough, last-minute details occasionally need to be worked out. For example, at one point the intercom box on Audrey's desk squawks and Jim Wallace calls in from the control room, a little concerned about the music that will end the final piece of the half-hour, the spot slugged

"Banana Wars." The story comes from Michael Lawton in Germany and he has sent along an oompa-oompa version of "Yes, We Have No Bananas," sung in German. (*"Ausgerechnet Bananen."*) Jim worries that there's too much of the same music at the beginning and end of the report. Does anyone have any ideas of other banana music that they might use?

A few people around the desk make suggestions; most of the proposals are impractical. Then someone else in the control room calls out on the intercom in a self-consciously impertinent tone: "There must be a copy of Belafonte's 'Banana Boat Song' around somewhere." The significance of the suggestion is not lost on Audrey, an African-American. She replies in a deeply ironic voice, "Yes, it's in the trash." Everyone laughs. Audrey shakes her head. Jim winds up sticking with the German song he has at hand.

The parts of the show to be broadcast during the second hour also seem to be coming along without too much trouble. Many of these remaining pieces have been completed for some time. The big exception, of course, is something that no one has had much time to think about so far — the live two-way that Bob will be conducting with former senator Edmund Muskie at the start of the A2. As this two-way was arranged by Greg Allen on the overnight shift, a script has been available for several hours.

The rest is up to Bob. He must handle the conversation skillfully enough so that it will finish exactly on time or a few seconds early, for Elizabeth Arnold's three-minute thirty-second report must start precisely as scheduled if the segment is to end properly. Since the success of the A2 rests so squarely with Bob, there is nothing that anyone else can do or say.

The second half-hour of the show continues without a hitch. Jean Cochran does her five-minute newscast. Bob makes small changes in each of the brief introductions he reads for pieces broadcast in the C and D segments. An editor at the science desk wrote the original lead for the report about doctors in Texas who disagree with the Clinton health reform proposal. The copy refers to these physicians as "conservative doctors." Bob shakes his head and grunts as he crosses out "conservative." He takes a sip of coffee just before the white light goes on and he bobs his head a little as he reads the short introduction that he's made one word shorter. Afterward, he pops a lozenge in his mouth and starts looking over another newspaper.

The second part of the D segment consists of a two-way between Bob and a professor of social psychology, MaryAnn LaFrance, who has studied how people respond to smiles. The piece holds few surprises, though the end contains a moderately amusing moment: right after LaFrance quizzes Bob about *his* smile, Johnny Mathis begins singing "A Certain Smile."

Following a break and thirty-five seconds of headlines from Jean, Bob reads a live introduction to the final story of the hour: the "Banana Wars" piece from British correspondent Michael Lawton. The report begins and ends with music, which allows what is essentially a six-minute spot to fill the entire seven-and-a-half-minute segment.

The report itself may be taken as a good example of a "typically offbeat" NPR report in these days of hard-news emphasis. A well written script is delivered in an engaging style by Lawton — whose British voice, combined with the various German accents in his actualities, seems to augment the sense of whimsy that pervades the piece.

MUSIC: One full chorus of *"Ausgerechnet Bananen."*

LAWTON: It seems as if everyone in Germany is quoting the title of this old hit these days. In the song the young man complains that his girlfriend doesn't want anything else — no roses, just, of all things, bananas. Well, that's not unusual for the Germans. They eat more bananas than anyone else in the world — an average of forty pounds a year each. And in one of the most vivid images of the fall of the Berlin Wall, the West Germans welcomed the East Germans into freedom with bunches of bananas.

Now once more bananas have taken political center stage.
GERMAN MAN: I personally like bananas and I eat, well, more or less, I would say one to two each day.
LAWTON: Bruno Hofstadt is one of Germany's banana negotiators, fighting for the right of the Germans to keep eating bananas the way they've been used to: without quotas and without customs duties — in other words, cheap. Like most of the banana bureaucrats, Hofstadt is an enthusiast. Banana-shaped lamps grace the desks of his department and soft toy bananas with funny faces hang in the offices.
But peel away the fun and the talk turns serious.

HOFSTADT: Well, we expect that the effect on the price for the consumer would be that he would have to pay about seventy to eighty percent more than he does now . . .

Spending several minutes discussing Germany's fight to preserve cheap bananas resonates with some of the old traditions of NPR, suggesting the broader definition of "news" to which Bob Edwards referred earlier. But the whimsical charm of the opening is not sustained. The report quickly turns into an account of tariffs and trade wars. The "love of bananas" becomes a colorful oddity decorating the edges of an economics piece. The softer story about the *origins* of the German taste for bananas remains untold. (Some roots go back to deprivations suffered after the Second World War.) The hard-news slant also draws the reporter away from *sound*. In the entire six-minute story, there is one clip of natural sound: fifteen seconds recorded in a market. Yet the subject matter seems rich with aural possibility: Germans eating bananas or talking about them at home, or in restaurants, at work, on picnics . . . or why not take listeners to the former site of the Berlin Wall, where bananas played such a symbolic role? The sound potential includes the humorous and the serious. Yet the reporter was not encouraged to think with his *ears* as well as with his mind. The result is a clever and informative story rather than a memorable moment of radio.

Sitting in the studio, Bob Edwards still looks occasionally at his newspaper, but he also laughs at the banana story from time to time. In the control room, Jim smiles and shakes his head: "Two goofy music pieces in a row." He's watching his timings carefully so that he'll cue Art to start the deadroll of *"Ausgerechnet Bananen"* at the right moment, which will close out the report.

This bit of live production is complicated because Art will be fading up a *song* behind Michael Lawton's final talk tracks. The engineer will have to watch his levels carefully so that the words of the singer do not interfere with the words of the reporter. Also, it's very easy to fade up on a song in a way that sounds awkward and disjointed — as, for instance, if the singer is in midline or midword when he or she comes up into the clear.

"Okay. Let's hear it in cue, Art," says Jim, as the Lawton report draws to a close. The music is instrumental at this point. "Sneak it!" says Jim, and Art slowly inches the volume slide higher. The oompa-oompa band becomes audible behind Lawton. Then the singing resumes, but Art keeps the volume very low so there is no conflict. Lawton's final words are heard clearly. After his sign-off, Jim says, "Up full!" This is the moment of truth. A half second of instrumental phrasing fades up into the clear, and then the singer enters, cleanly, at the start of a new line. "*Sie möcht' dabei essen . . .*" Art says "Oh!" approvingly. Jim says, "Ah!" in relief, then lets out a long sigh. The cross-fade could not have been better.

Art asks how the hour will end. "Pick up on Bob under the music or what?"

"No," Jim says, "the music ends. Bob talks. Then transcript cart [a familiar, generic announcement from NPR about how to order transcripts and tapes of programs]."

As the music begins to wind down, Bob's voice suddenly comes in over the intercom. "This is where I used to do the German Marshall Fund credit."

Everyone laughs. The German Marshall Fund was one of the first charitable organizations to underwrite a portion of NPR's news coverage. It supports stories from Europe and receives periodic on-air credit from hosts.

Bob continues, "One day I did it over '*Deutschland Uber Alles.*'" He pauses. "Mankiewicz loved it." The crackling intercom speaker makes Bob's tone sound even drier than usual.

"Ready on the host," says Jim. There are five seconds to the end of the song.

"Open!"

"This is NPR's *Morning Edition.* I'm Bob Edwards." Bob's voice returns to its nonsardonic, resonant fullness, even though he leans his head against his right hand as he speaks.

"Hit it," says Jim, referring to the announcement cued up in the tape cartridge machine. "Mike out."

"If you'd like to order a transcript or tape of this program . . ." the transcript cart begins.

Bob takes off his glasses and his headphones and collects the first hour's scripts together in a pile on one side of his desk. He stretches himself, stands, and strides out of the studio for a short break before the second hour begins.

In the control room, Jim reaches both hands above his head and leans back in his chair. "Well, it ended perfectly, to the extent that it could," he says.

"As *perrfect* as *posssible,*" says Art in a slightly German accent. For the next few moments, the banter in the control room takes on a Teutonic tone.

Bob Edwards returns to the studio just before Carl Kasell begins his newscast at one minute after seven. Something catches Bob's eye on the television set, and he raises the volume momentarily. Then he picks up another newspaper, takes a sip of coffee, puts his feet up on the edge of the table, and yawns. In nine minutes, Bob will be conducting a live interview with former secretary of state Ed Muskie about his recent trip to Vietnam. Bob has already read over the script; he has also found a story or two in the newspapers and on the wires about Muskie's trip. If he feels any nervousness about the upcoming two-way, such jitters are locked deep within his large frame.

At four minutes past seven, editorial assistant Julia Bailey telephones Senator Muskie at his home in Maine. After a quick good morning, she explains that he will be speaking to Bob Edwards in about four minutes. The backup engineer, Tom Carpenter, has switched places with Art Laurent and Tom begins setting up proper connections so that the senator can hear not just Bob Edwards but the entire program. Art helps out, working on the patch panel. Their technical adjustments occur in the middle of Carl's newscast, which means that Tom must frequently start and stop news carts and turn Carl's microphone on and off. Tom must also be careful that none of the conversations with Maine accidentally get sent over the air.

At eight and a half minutes after seven, Bob pops a lozenge into his mouth and puts on his headphones, stretching his arms and yawning once again. He then sits quite still, looking at his script as the newscast runs its course. Bob does not speak to Senator Muskie ahead of time. He takes a straightforward approach to live interviews and seems to see no purpose in extra chitchat or warm-up.

During the music bridge following the newscast, Jim directs a message to Muskie through an intercom-telephone hookup. "About thirty seconds, Mr. Secretary."

"All right," comes the reply over the intercom speakers.

Jim looks over the copy accompanying Elizabeth Arnold's report that will follow Bob's two-way. He thinks out loud. "Arnold is three and a half . . . So Bob's got five minutes." Jim presses the intercom button connecting to the studio. Bob will hear Jim's voice through his headphones. "You've got five minutes, chief," he says to the host.

Bob nods, but says nothing. His eyes are fixed on the Muskie script.

A live two-way always triggers some excitement, and a number of staff members have already come into the control room to watch what happens. Audrey is the last to arrive. She stands in the back, near Ken and Julia.

"Okay," says Jim. He presses the intercom button again. "Stand by the host." Then, as the music bridge ends, he tells Tom to open Bob's mike. When Bob starts talking, Jim presses the timer button, and red digits start counting down from 5:00. 4:59, 4:58, 4:57 . . .

"This is *Morning Edition*, I'm Bob Edwards. Secretary of State Warren Christopher says he expects to have a decision in the near future on whether the United States will drop its opposition to international loans for Vietnam . . ." Bob reads a brief introduction which Muskie can hear over the phone, even though he cannot yet speak with Bob. The incoming telephone line will be kept off the air until the last moment so that coughs or even simple breathing from Muskie won't distract listeners from Bob's script. Jim waits for Bob to mention Muskie's name before he says, "Bring in the senator," The volume on Muskie's line is turned up. The senator is now live on *Morning Edition*.

Bob briefly mentions Muskie's recent trip and says, "Senator Muskie now joins me from his home in Maine. Good morning."

"Good morning," replies Muskie.

Bob sits with both his elbows on the table, his hands up near the sides of his head. The introduction ran forty-five seconds, so Bob now has four minutes to work with Muskie. Bob reads the short first question, which gets right down to basics: "What did you see during your visit to Vietnam that convinced you that the embargo should be lifted?"

"Well, of course we saw a great deal of Vietnam," Muskie begins. "We met with many of the Vietnamese leaders, we saw something of Cambodia . . ." He propels himself into a smoothly delivered answer that presses on for more than a minute and a half. A couple of times an attentive listener can hear some quiet rustlings from Bob that indicate he has considered intervening to help shape the senator's responses. But Muskie moves so gracefully and inexorably from point to point that he leaves little room for Bob to interrupt.

Interviews over the phone pose special difficulties for a radio host because it's easy for a guest to lapse into long, rambling, self-directed speech as he or she stares into the faceless anonymity of "telephone space." Some hosts, like Susan Stamberg, will make a certain amount of noise on their end of the line in order to establish an audible connection with their interviewees. (During taped two-ways, these grunts and giggles and *uh-huhs* can make the task of the tape cutter difficult, however, so even more voluble hosts try to keep their reponses to a bare minimum.) Bob Edwards's style is altogether cleaner and more formal — he does not intrude quite as much as some interviewers into the space of the person with whom he's speaking (just as he does not push himself into the space of listeners who are overhearing the conversation).

So like many politicians, Muskie talks longer than he should without letting Bob pose another question. Eventually, the senator brings up the subject of missing Americans:

> Following the points set forth by the Bush administration, in its road map policy of 1991, the Vietnamese government has released South Vietnamese reeducation-camp detainees and has given us more information pertaining to the fate of Americans listed as missing in action . . . and . . .

Bob has been sitting quietly, staring down at the table. Hearing Muskie take a breath after the word "action," Bob pounces, even as Muskie begins moving on to the next sentence. "You said there is some improvement, but are they fully cooperating?"

With this question, Bob hopes to focus Muskie's attention on something listeners are especially concerned about. Enough of diplomatic niceties. Are the Vietnamese helping us account for MIAs? The question is also designed to prod the senator into a more give-and-take manner of speech.

Bob's intervention throws Muskie off-stride, which means his words do not come as smoothly as they did before. Yet his answer is to the point:

> That was our impression. We met with the Americans involved in . . . in running down . . . ah . . . stories of live-sitings, stories about additional information that's available. And the level of cooperation has been distinctly better than it was the last time I was in . . . in Vietnam three years ago.

Bob jumps in again. There are less than two minutes left in the segment. Bob reads from his script at a surprisingly rapid clip, with considerable animation in his voice. It almost seems that the slow pace of Muskie's speech has triggered an oppositional response from the usually measured Bob Edwards:

Much of the pressure to *lift* the trade embargo comes from
U.S. *business* interests that would like access to a market *closed*
to them for nearly thirty years — is that the main motivation
here, to put American businesses on an equal footing with
Japanese and French companies?

Even with his sped-up delivery, Bob manages to make his question
seem spontaneous: it sounds passionate, but it does not sound "read."

Well, that is a motivation, [Muskie replies,] but let me put the
other side to that. The other side to that is that the Vietnamese
are interested in normalizing relations, and as a result their
attitude toward American interests, including the MIA issue,
has improved from our perception. And we had long talks with
all of the key Vietnamese leaders while we were there.

Muskie is now giving answers that last about thirty seconds, a good
length for this kind of conversation. Bob has a minute and fifteen
seconds remaining on the digital timer, and he decides to frame a
distinctly political question. He does not look down at his script but
stares into a middle distance.

President Clinton has had . . . ah . . . his share of political
struggles in his first few months in office. Wouldn't there be a
risk here that he might have to use up some political capital
on a fight that he really doesn't need at this point in his term?"

Bob's question inadvertently allows Muskie to slip back into a more
cautious, rambling response:

Well, the key issues in any presidency carry precarious political
risks, and I suspect there may be political risks here and indeed
in all frankness it is the MIA–POW issue and the pressure of
the families of those Americans who died and are missing in
Vietnam that has influenced our policies there more than any
other. So it has been that very political risk that you describe
that has delayed normalization . . .

There are now forty-five seconds left, and Muskie is still talking.
Everyone begins to wonder if he is going to wind down in time.

But we see here, in the attitude — or . . . we saw here . . . in
our visit, in the attitude of Vietnamese leaders, the Vietnamese
people — a desire to improve relations from their point of

view. So there is an interest now, I think, in moving on both sides to normalization . . . [fifteen seconds left — and a reasonable place for the senator to stop, but his cadence carries him forward, and there is no way for Bob to give him the "cutoff" sign] . . . and that . . . I say, if there is that kind of movement, if there is that kind of improvement, then it should mean an improvement in business relations as well as in others.

The segment clock shows no time left.
"Senator, thank you very much." Bob says quickly.
"Thank you very much," Muskie answers.
"Edmund Muskie served as secretary of state in the Carter administration." About eight seconds have now elapsed beyond the allotted time of the Muskie interview: Bob continues immediately with his introduction to Elizabeth Arnold's report. "The Republican National Committee is forming a new foundation designed to give rank-and-file voters more voice in making policy . . ." Without sounding rushed, Bob nonetheless subtly speeds up the rhythm of his normal read and concludes an introduction that editors had timed out at thirty seconds in something between twenty and twenty-five seconds. The result is that though Muskie ran a tad long, Elizabeth Arnold's piece starts right on time and the A2 segment concludes on schedule. The thirty-second cushion of music, included in the show's road map at the end of Arnold's report, plays out fully, adding a relaxed feeling to the end of the first block of this hour's show.

Bob takes a sip of coffee after his talk with Muskie, turns to the computer screen, and reads the latest news bulletins. Then he starts looking through other pieces of script on his desk, making a few revisions as he goes along. At seven-eighteen, he leans far to his right and retrieves the TV remote control. He raises the volume and listens to a little bit of a network news program. An interview with Clinton's newly found half-brother has caught Bob's attention. Just before seven-nineteen, he mutes the TV and broadcasts the live time-check. Then he goes back to watching the television for half a minute. He returns to radio at seven-twenty, doing a billboard for the B2 and introducing Carl Kasell's headlines. At seven-twenty-one, he reads the lead-in for the report about Wally Hickel and animal rights. As he concludes, he pulls his head back slightly from the microphone, his lips pursed. The white MIC light goes out; the NET light stays on. Bob leans back in his chair, takes off his glasses, and rubs his eyes. Then he opens another newspaper. The fingers of his free hand curl around his coffee cup.

In the quiet light of the studio, nearing seven-twenty-five in the morning, following a taped interview with a reporter halfway around the world and a live two-way with an ex-politician about to have breakfast; after many minutes of script-reading using a variety of deliveries; and after several tongue-twister names, spoken with hardly a stumble . . . Bob Edwards, the silver-golden bear of public radio, sits comfortably in a chair that is far too low for him, sipping his coffee, reading his newspaper, watching his television. Take away the microphones, the computer terminal, the white lights and the big clocks, and you would be looking at a familiar sight: one of many millions of ordinary Americans starting their day . . . with coffee, the newspaper, TV — and the radio.

Bob Edwards identifies deeply with those who listen to him each morning. If he compartmentalizes his work at NPR, separating himself in many ways from the complex process by which *Morning Edition* is put on the air, his studied distance does allow him to think about, to worry over — even to commune with — a vast radio audience that stretches out, vague and invisible yet powerfully imagined . . . beyond the grasp of inessential technology, where "the dark fields of the republic" roll on under the dawn.

Compartmental Stumbles

Morning Edition has entered its last half-hour, and everything appears to be falling into place nicely. Bob has a stack of scripts on his desk to introduce the final set of stories. The tapes for each segment are being cleaned up and brought to the control room with plenty of time before they go on the air.

Jean Cochran begins her second newscast following Bob's Return about marijuana. Bob is reading his newspaper. In the control room, the two-and-a-half-minute report from Mike Shuster about politics in Azerbaijan is ready to go on Tape Two: it will form the C segment, following the newscast.

What happens next is unclear. The control room has the Shuster tape and its introductory script almost five minutes before the C segment starts. But when Jean Cochran ends her newscast, and Jim Wallace says, "Ready host . . . Open . . ." Bob Edwards looks down at the script before him — and sees it is slugged D, not C. The copy introduces the five-minute piece by Wendy Kaufman from Los Angeles. C segment stories can be no longer than three minutes. Where is the *host's* copy of the Shuster script?

Bob looks up at the control room, opens his arms wide, and shrugs his shoulders. Jim says suddenly, "Where is Bob's script?" then quickly starts making decisions. Jim has in front of him the script that Bob needs, but it's too late to run his copy into the studio. Wendy Kaufman's report from Los Angeles is the only other piece of tape cued up on a machine, but Jim checks the length of the report and confirms that it's far too long. He sees on the road map that the second story scheduled for the D — Todd's commentary about racism in wrestling — *would* fit the allotted time. But this piece of tape has not yet been delivered to the control room.

There have already been ten seconds of dead air — an unnatural silence. Jim tells Tom Carpenter to hit Tape Two and roll Shuster without an introduction. The report from Azerbaijan starts up.

Jim looks around the control room. "What the hell happened?" he asks. The production staff exchange silent glances. The intercom beeps and Audrey's voice comes on the line. "Where was Bob's script?" she asks simply and without recrimination.

The mishap is unfortunate, but not a major disaster. Everyone feels funny about it. People in the control room grumble about the production assistant who (it is assumed) neglected to take in the script, but at first there's no time to do anything but make sure that C ends properly. New music has to be cued up to end the segment, which will run very short, given the lack of an introduction. Jim has to choose something that will be easy to fade down during the second feed of the program — for everyone knows that when it is time to retransmit the second hour of the program at nine o'clock, Bob's intro to Shuster will be spliced into the master tape.

"Oh, man!" says Jim with a delayed reaction to the stumble.

Art says, "We should have had Bob say, 'And now . . . Miiiike Shuster!'"

No one laughs much. Barry Gordemer walks into the control room smiling. He knows everyone is upset, and he hits just the right tone. "You know, I stop directing the show for one day, and *you* guys want to change the format."

Some people laugh. Jim, as the man with official responsibility, shakes his head. "What a fucking disaster."

Barry keeps wanting to minimize the incident. "There's no good way out of it, and I think you played it as good as you can do."

Barry continues his subtle investigation. "So you had the tape and script."

"I had my script. But somebody left Bob's copy in here . . . Nobody took his script into the studio. And Bob didn't tell me."

Barry cannot hold a serious expression for long. "It's *sort of* important that Bob gets a copy," he says wryly.

Jim says, "I'd have held mine up, but I didn't think he could see it."

"I've actually read back-announces through the mike before," Barry recollects. The "back-announce" is the tag line from the host that identifies the previous reporter or story. Barry is saying that he has acted like a prompter on stage, feeding lines to the host through the intercom system.

"Now that would have been something," says Jim. "There you go!"

"I did that with a billboard once with Neal [Conan]," Barry continues. "I read the whole billboard to him like a second before he started."

Jim is looking down at the "lost" script. He starts reading it. "'There is an increasingly dangerous and convoluted political conflict . . .' Yeah, right!" Everyone laughs, imagining the complex language filtering into Bob's headphones through the intercom. "That would have been great! I'd loved to have seen that."

"You could have just announced it yourself," says Art.

Jim puts on a Bob Edwards–like radio voice. "Mike Shuster has this report on Russia."

Some people laugh. Slowly the matter drops. The rest of the program starts to demand attention.

Bob himself doesn't say much about the incident, but what he does say is acerbic. "Outrageous," he comments later. "That was just outrageous. First I knew there was a problem was when I looked down at the script in front of me and realized it was the wrong copy for the segment. That *should not happen* in a professional organization," he says slowly. "But it did."

Perhaps what's most remarkable about the mistake is what people do *not* say about it. No one wonders why Bob waited until the last minute before noticing that he had the wrong script. Compartmentalization. Everyone knows that Bob defines his job precisely — and narrowly — and that he expects other people to fulfill their jobs as intensely and competently as he fulfills his. It is *not* Bob's job to check up on the scripts. Besides, copy is often rushed into him at the last second. If he were to ask after every script that he did not have in hand at any given moment, he'd have little time to think about anything else. So Bob has learned to wait.

For its part, the staff takes a calm and professional approach to the incident. While a few discreet inquiries are made in an attempt to discover the chain of events that led to the error, Audrey conducts no inquisition nor does the senior staff make a big deal about the glitch when they arrive in the office following the close of the program at eight o'clock.

Listeners across the country have noticed the lack of an introduction, of course. Most of them probably have blamed their own local stations for pressing the wrong button at the wrong time. Perhaps some of the more sophisticated thought to themselves, "Sun spots," deciding that a few seconds of the program had been lost to the vagaries of satellite technology.

The majority of stations in the public radio system will not *receive* the mistake in any case, for a fix will be made in the master tape of the program, scheduled to be refed to the satellite from eight to ten, and from ten to noon. It's common for Bob to have to record a couple of small changes in the program and then for these changes to either be physically spliced back into the master or to be remixed during the second feed. "Fixes" may correct flubs, or they may update stories that change during the time *Morning Edition* is being sent to stations.

The rest of the second hour proceeds without incident. The final piece of the day is an extended interview with Ann Waldron, the biographer of Hodding Carter, Sr. Bob pays some attention to this two-way, sometimes closing his eyes to concentrate on the tape. But then as the piece winds down, he stretches himself and prepares for his final live broadcasting of the day. He places his pen in his shirt pocket, puts on his glasses, and settles himself squarely in front of the microphone. He looks down at his script — the back-announce for the two-way — and waits, listening to the tape and watching the two red digital clocks on the windowsill together count down toward 00:00. The clock on the right will get there thirty seconds faster than the clock on the left, and that's the clock Bob watches most closely. At 00:05 the MIC light between the clocks goes on and the Waldron interview is no longer heard through the studio speakers, only through the headphones that Bob is wearing. In the sudden silence of the soundproofed space, Bob's voice seems like a shout through the heavy atmosphere. "Ann Waldron is author of *Hodding Carter: The Reconstruction of a Racist.* This is NPR's *Morning Edition.* I'm Bob Edwards." The silence descends again around Bob for a split second, as he leans back in his chair, but then the white light on the windowsill goes off and the jaunty Dixieland music that Jim had snuck up behind the book's title fills the studio with its happy sound. The music plays for twenty seconds, stops, and one of the standard NPR ID and funding carts begins.

Bob is arranging the script pages on his desk and gathering his belongings together. He does not stand up because he knows he has a few retakes to do. In addition to the Shuster introduction, the lead-in for the Bosnian two-way has been revised, due to some late-breaking news from the meeting of European Community leaders. (Bob makes a face when told about this retake, but Jim assures him that he will not need to redo any of the difficult names. Only the copy before the John Major actuality has been changed.)

While Bob is recording the new introduction to A1, the control room receives a call from Audrey about one more possible fix. Jim warily passes the message to Bob.

"Audrey says we got a call from our friends in the science unit who say that the word 'conservative' has to be reinserted into the Mitchell lead because it's only the conservative doctors, I guess, who are complaining about the Clinton program."

Bob stares at Jim and barely moves his head. Bob speaks in a low, deceptively calm voice. "How can you have a *conservative* doctor?"

"I don't know," says Jim a bit defensively.

"We never say *liberal* doctor," Bob says in a flat, reasonable tone. But a steely will stretches tightly beneath that dry reasonableness. Jim hears in Bob's voice a silent but adamant rejection of any further changes in the script.

Bob does a clean read of the "lost" introduction to the Shuster piece, then immediately takes off his headphones and puts his glasses in his breast pocket. He turns off the television set with the remote control and logs off the computer. He gathers together all his scripts and arranges them on top of his newspapers, which he then piles on top of his leather satchel. At five minutes past eight, Bob Edwards leaves Studio Five as he entered three hours earlier — with his satchel stuffed under his arm and his coffee mug in his hand.

A large crowd has gathered around the *Morning Edition* desk. The early arrivals for the day shift are mixing with the survivors of the overnight. The sun shines brightly through the window facing the *Newscast* horseshoe. The newsroom is filled with conversation, laughter, and the smell of coffee and doughnuts. Elsewhere on the second floor, the air conditioning is back on and individual offices are slowly filling up. Within an hour, NPR will be fully staffed and back at work.

As Bob approaches the desk, the first person to greet him is Ellen McDonnell. She has just arrived and looks fresh and buoyant in a light blue dress with floral decoration. "Morning, Bob!" she says in a cheerful voice.

"How are you?" says Bob quietly.

"I *loved* Waldron!" Ellen continues enthusiastically. "Wonderful interview!"

Bob acknowledges the compliment, but then he sees Audrey and stops to speak with her. "What is a conservative doctor?" he asks in his familiar deadpan. "One who doesn't charge much?"

Audrey does not disagree with Bob. She had merely passed on the message from the science editor. Bob shakes his head and starts moving toward his office again. "Conservative doctors," he repeats. "They're the ones who wait before they do the C-section . . ."

Bob enters his office and deposits his satchel, newspapers, and books on the back table. He sits down again in his leather chair. He sighs, yawns, and rubs his eyes. He stares for a few moments through the window at the waking world outside. In a couple of hours he will tape an interview with the mayor of Dubrovnik. Otherwise, he'll do odds and ends around the office till eleven or twelve o'clock. Primarily Bob keeps himself available in case a major news story breaks and the West Coast feed of *Morning Edition* needs to be updated.

The phrase "conservative doctors" continues to linger in his mind, and he starts discussing the importance of good writing — something he picked up from his teacher and mentor, Edward Bliss, a colleague of Ed Murrow's and now a journalism professor. Bliss has trained a number of NPR staffers.

"We're in the business of clear expression," Bob says. "There's accuracy in that as well as in journalism. Now the writing here at NPR is probably better than elsewhere, and yet it's horrible. I hear trash every day. I see trash every day, and sometimes I speak trash. Because it gets by me. I'm just mortified when that happens. Some of the worst offenders here are editors . . . desk editors, who are editing the reporters. It's bad enough that reporters write that way, but the editors can be even worse. I've seen editors take good copy and make it bad — I've seen it happen.

"Now Ed Bliss wanted to make us believe that good writing *matters*. People screw up the language, people take liberties with it. They feel it doesn't matter — it's more important to be cute, clever, timely, or hip." Bob stares at the desktop. "But they're wrong. For Ed, it was more important to be accurate . . ." Bob searches for the right word. "Accurate . . . and *timeless*."

Leaning his large face in his hand, Bob begins to reflect upon the use to which he puts his words in his function as host of NPR's *Morning Edition*. In typical fashion, he thinks first about his audience. "Part of my job is to relax. It's to be cool and calm when there's chaos around. The listener doesn't care about chaos. Doesn't care about whether Audrey is fighting with one of the production assistants who isn't doing his job. Or if tempers are flaring with deadlines approaching . . . The listener shouldn't have to bother with that. There's enough tension in their lives. They don't tune us in to get more tension."

But is it important that Bob not only *sound* relaxed but be relaxed, within himself? He straightens himself in his chair and speaks more quickly.

"Well, there isn't anything I can do about it anyway. I feel a lot of tension . . . They've carted me out of here to the hospital once — that's how much tension I've felt. I thought I was having a heart attack. I didn't know it was tension. But . . ." He nods to himself, remembering the episode from a few years earlier. "Now I don't feel the tension in my chest anymore. It's in my throat." He pauses. "Yes. So now I have myself regularly checked for throat cancer. Stress, you know . . ."

He slouches back down in his chair. "But, see, once again: the listener doesn't care anything about that. It's not important. It's my job to keep all of that out. And just focus on communicating with the listener. That's all I'm supposed to do.

"Of course, I'm also reading the paper and watching television, even during the broadcast. I'm still trying to absorb more information — that's important, too. To prepare for whatever story might break.

"'Cause, you know, there's another big part of my job: not to fuck up." And he smiles. "It was Cagney who said, 'Know your lines, don't bump into the furniture.' That's what I do. Don't embarrass yourself and fuck up. That's really all it is — aside from live interviews . . . and being *ready* for one, if they drop one on you." Bob's voice falls to almost a whisper. Then he exhales deeply, remembering. "I had a morning once where I did thirty live interviews. This was the day after Reagan was first elected. Got me boom, boom, boom, boom, boom." He snaps his fingers as he speaks. "They'd tell me who they had next and I had to wing most of it.

"Now there are some newsrooms I'm told — say in all-news stations and in places on television — where the person on the air writes nothing and says nothing that isn't written for him. His questions come up on a monitor." Bob's voice drops low again, and he almost murmurs: "Well, I think it's *dangerous* for that to be called news. You could hire Vanna White to do that."

Out at the desk, Ellen McDonnell stands at the board, holding an eraser in her hand, looking for the last time at the outline of the just completed program. "You know what?" she says, addressing no one person in particular. "There was no way of knowing this until you heard the show as a whole — and I'm not sure there was anything we could have done about it anyway — but we wound up having two back-to-back pieces with music at top and bottom. Lawton had banana music top and bottom, and LaFrance opened and closed with music. It was such a flukie thing anyway to run pieces with music at the top and bottom, that to have *two* pieces like that and then play them back to back . . ."

Ellen has heard something that Jim and the engineers noticed in the control room and commented about. It speaks to the overall flow of the program, the inchoate aural shape in which form and content intermingle and influence each other. She has pointed to something that, a few years ago, people at NPR might have avoided at all costs — for, in fact, while using music to make humorous commentary can be extremely effective, the trick can become repetitive and clichéd if done too often. To have two musical jokes side by side reduces the effectiveness of each.

Yet as quickly as Ellen notes the problem, she puts the matter to one side. "But there was nothing we could have done . . . and anyway, you wouldn't get this *unless* you were listening to the show as a whole."

Audrey says quietly, "I didn't think about it."

"You don't," Ellen says sympathetically, "because you listen differently. As *I* listen differently." Ellen's ambivalence about her own critique of the show reflects conflicting currents at NPR and at *Morning Edition.* Certain research about audience habits reports that listeners do not turn on a radio program like *Morning Edition* when it *starts* and listen through consistently to when it *ends.* People tune in and out of the segments all the time. Therefore, the argument goes, producers needn't concern themselves with "overall design." Yet there is another tradition among some public radio producers to care about such matters.

Ellen continues to stare at the board as Bob Ferrante appears wearing a dapper, lightweight summer suit, a broad tie, and suspenders. He's ebullient.

"You did a *terrific* job," says Bob to everyone. "No one would ever know how desperate yesterday was. You know what Zorba the Greek once said? 'You can knock forever on the door of a dead man and you'll never get an answer.' Ellen and I knocked all fuckin' day yesterday and didn't get one goddamn answer.

"In other words," Bob concludes, "congratulations!"

"There were moments," Ellen agrees with him, laughing. "We did what we could."

"We filled two hours," says Audrey simply.

Ellen approaches the board with her eraser poised. "Now we'll do it again."

BREAK ONE

The Alternative Institution

Learning to Listen

Before the creation of *Morning Edition*, the late evening and overnight hours were an especially fertile time at National Public Radio. In the early 1970s, the first generation of NPR reporters, editors, producers, and engineers often found the stillness of the evening conducive to intense, obsessive *listening*, as they sought to rediscover the sound medium, which had fallen into such disuse during the 1950s and '60s. When NPR was established in 1971, longer forms of creative radio — essentially anything lasting more than two minutes — had just about dried up in America and a whole range of basic radio techniques — from simple tape editing to complicated mixing — had to be reinvented as much as learned. Some producers at NPR turned to Canada and Europe for instruction and inspiration — programs on the CBC like *Sunday Morning* and *As It Happens*, and in Europe legendary "feature" producers like Peter Leonhard Braun at *Sender Freies Berlin*.[1] Many

---

[1] The feature is a form of radio documentary developed in Europe that blends sound and narration in a particularly creative way. In Germany features are usually an hour long; in France they can run even longer. By contrast, the BBC does not have the same tradition of feature production, having emphasized talk more than sound in its radio production for many years. (In recent years the BBC has begun

NPR producers and engineers came back from visits to these countries inspired to the point of fanaticism with the aural possibilities that had opened up to them. Working together — often late into the night along these same corridors and within these same recording studios at 2025 M Street — a few dozen men and women at National Public Radio developed new kinds of radio programs for American audiences that broke fresh ground and revealed possibilities latent in the medium of sound.

The key to the creative work evolving at NPR was learning to *listen* — an apparently simple act that many Americans were neglecting in their gathering mania for the visual media of television and the movies. The first generations of NPR producers and reporters learned to use their ears in addition to their voices as they painted pictures, evoked moods, and told stories. These new radio artisans were reviving one of the most ancient means of communication (long before the written word, oral traditions defined a people's history and shaped their identity) and at the same time they were creating an entirely new form of expression.

Bob Malesky is one of the few producers still at NPR whose career goes back to the earliest years of the organization. Now senior producer of *Weekend Edition Sunday*, this "old-timer" is still only in his mid-forties. "Back in seventy-three, seventy-four, seventy-five," Bob remembers, "everyone, arts and news, were all on the same floor. And as you walked down the hall if you heard something interesting in someone's office or edit booth, you'd stop in the doorway and listen — and comment. You'd get arts people hanging out with news producers, offering suggestions, and vice versa. And you would get arguments about audio philosophy. And it was great because everyone was learning, doing something new, experimenting with what you could do with sound to tell stories. We were small enough that everyone knew what everyone else was doing. If you were working on something great, everyone in the building knew about it."

Jay Kernis, one of the principal architects of *Morning Edition*, also

---

to do more "sound portraits," in part, it seems, because of influence filtering over the Atlantic from NPR.)

Leo Braun's beautifully evocative features, such as *Bells in Europe* and *Hyenas*, were perhaps the single most important influence on early documentary producers at NPR, and his production center in Berlin took on almost mythic overtones for a host of young international radio producers.

vividly remembers the listening sessions at NPR from which so much of his own appreciation and understanding of the creative potential of radio evolved. He derived some inspiration about how to *use* radio's power from an original statement of purpose for public radio, drawn up in the late 1960s by Bill Siemering, one of the early visionaries at NPR. Jay recalls: "Bill wrote that public radio will speak in many voices and will hold up this mirror to America and say, 'Here's what you did today, here's what you thought about, here's what you sounded like.' It wasn't simply, 'Here are today's top stories from around the world,' though there always were newscasts, so the news was always a part of this vision. But beyond that, it was 'Here's what we thought about, as a nation.'

"There's one phrase I remember especially," Jay continues. "Siemering wrote, 'Public radio will reflect the joy of human experience.' Siemering felt that radio was uniquely able, as a medium, to reflect this inner life of people. He said, essentially, that public radio will have a heart."

In the early years, NPR producers and executives recognized that they were attempting to create programming which, at first, might have only limited appeal in a culture so increasingly dominated by television and the movies. NPR was not oblivious to the small size of its audience, but neither were people in Washington obsessed with enlarging their listenership. Many reporters and producers focused their energies on developing new and original aural styles and techniques and assumed that audiences would follow eventually. These were the days when Robert Krulwich worked with a variety of invented voices (including, occasionally, his famous mice)[2] to help him explain economic stories; when Mike Waters, one of the first hosts of *All Things Considered*, once concluded a program by "directing" a sunset in the voice of the Angel

---

[2] Robert would play back his recorded voice at high speed to create the mice — a kind of radio cartoon. He also developed a range of other vocal characters, including professors with foreign accents and schoolchildren. This one-man stock company staged aural dramas to illustrate his reports. Robert Krulwich moved to CBS television in the early eighties, where he met a fate similar to radio talents such as monologist Jean Shepherd and comedians Bob and Ray when they tried to transfer their essentially aural humor to TV. Robert has done a good job for CBS, but his star has not risen as high as it did at NPR, in part because the medium seems to dull the edge of his originality. He has yet to find the visual correlatives for his witty, sound-oriented sensibility. While Robert comes across as intelligent and amusing on TV, his work does not always exhibit the same spark of genius that pervaded so much of what he did on the radio.

Gabriel; when Ira Flatow used a variety of aural tricks to discuss science and scientific phenomena. At the same time, Josh Darsa and Keith Talbot were producing audio documentaries filled with layers of sound, on subjects like cowboys, attics, and oceans. Robert Montiegel was developing groundbreaking hourlong "portraits in sound" (like *Sea Island Sketches*, a visit to the unique geography and culture of the chain of islands off the Carolina coast) that demonstrated just how *visual* a medium radio could be. The work of these and other producers was made possible by the innovative technical collaboration of young engineers and aural designers such as Jim Anderson, Skip Pizzi, and John Widoff, who were discovering the magic potential latent in high-quality stereo sound.

These were also the days when a number of Washington reporters (most famous among them Linda Wertheimer, Nina Totenberg, and later Cokie Roberts, but also newsmen like Ted Clark and William Drummond) began developing distinctive techniques of narrative journalism for radio. Not so self-consciously *aural* as producers who were working with longer forms of radio, these correspondents nevertheless began to steer *oral* reporting away from the minute-long spots that had become the standard on commercial radio toward the four-, five-, or seven-minute "story" — a spoken narration, interspersed with excerpts from taped interviews, which led listeners, step by step, through a particular event or a particular set of ideas. The oral reporters who worked at NPR in the early years had far more of a tradition to draw upon than the aural producers. In the forties and early fifties, a number of radio correspondents had set high standards for on-the-air storytelling. Edward R. Murrow is the best remembered, but there were many others. These early broadcasters would sometimes speak their reports for fifteen minutes without interruption from a taped sound bite since the technology for such production did not yet exist. (In the earliest days, newscasts were never interrupted by commercials either; Murrow was quite upset when commercials were first inserted into the middle of on-the-hour newscasts.)[3] Writing was the key to holding the atten-

---

[3] In October 1958 Murrow addressed a convention of radio and television news directors in Chicago. The following comments seem particularly important in light of the direction taken by the commercial networks in recent years and the emergence of NPR as a force in news broadcasting:

"So far as radio — that most satisfying and rewarding instrument — is concerned, the diagnosis of its difficulties is rather easy. And obviously I speak only of

tion of listeners and conveying the ideas and information surrounding a story — writing and the way the words were said into the microphone. The new generation of storytelling reporters at NPR partly reinvented the wheel, figuring out oral techniques for themselves and their new technology, but partly they learned from examples and exemplars of the past.

During the seventies, then, sharp divisions did not exist at National Public Radio between reporters, pursuing the craft of journalism in a new medium, and producers, developing new aesthetics and techniques for a new genre — the public radio broadcast. Listeners to *All Things Considered*, NPR's first foray into daily news, heard a variety of different audio styles — a range of radio journalism — in each program. Linda Wertheimer would report from Capitol Hill about budget battles and intersperse her narration with clips from various senators and members of Congress; Susan Stamberg would do an interview in the studio with a famous author or artist or talk by telephone with people around the world; Bob Edwards would introduce a short "sound portrait" or "sound experience" produced by Keith Talbot or even Robert Montiegel himself. Not everything that went on the air during the early years was polished and professional. NPR's sound could be as crude and unvarnished as the medium-fidelity land lines used to connect stations to NPR and the early generation of cassette recorders on which reporters relied. And while NPR producers knew they wanted to establish a different kind of pace, a different rhythm from commercial radio, they sometimes pushed the envelope too far. Tedious, long-winded stories could challenge the attention span of even the most devoted listener. There were plenty of mistakes and inappropriate judgments, many

news and information. In order to progress, it need only go backward. To the time when singing commercials were not allowed on news reports, when there was no middle commercial in a 15-minute news report, when radio was rather proud, alert, and fast. I recently asked a network official, 'Why this great rash of five-minute news reports (including three commercials) on weekends?' He replied, 'Because that seems to be the only thing we can sell.'

"In this kind of complex and confusing world, you can't tell very much about the why of the news in broadcasts where only three minutes is available for news . . . If radio news is to be regarded as a commodity, only acceptable when salable, then I don't care what you call it — I say it isn't news."

From *In Search of Light: The Broadcasts of Edward R. Murrow, 1938–1961*, edited by Edward Bliss, Jr. (New York, Knopf, 1967), p. 357.

instances of what Noah Adams calls "ear candy," in place of genuinely inspiring or informative pieces; but the fact is that new styles of production and new approaches to radio journalism *did* emerge and begin to flower during this period. Different news would often elicit different audio styles. Typically, the daily life of Washington politics fit more easily into an acts and tracks report rather than into a piece in which sound was used to establish "scenes" out of which narration and interviews would emerge. Yet a correspondent with sensitive ears and a creative tongue, like the young Scott Simon, could give even minute-long spots for hourly newscasts the flavor of a portrait in sound.

Connections between reporters and producers were heightened during NPR's early years in part because National Public Radio produced a wide variety of programs in addition to its daily magazine shows. The news division was only one part of a large organization that was also devoted to arts and cultural programs. NPR distributed to its local stations the documentary series *Options*, which broadcast a potpourri of hourlong programs each week, produced in this country and abroad. *Options in Education* provided a weekly hour of educational news. Each show was devoted to a single issue, discussed in a variety of reports and interviews from around the country. During the 1970s, "Ops in Ed" was second only to *All Things Considered* in popularity and name recognition among NPR listeners.

NPR also distributed concerts and recitals and kept trying to bring back radio drama. It also produced a number of limited-run, special series. *The World of F. Scott Fitzgerald* combined half-hour documentaries with dramatizations of several Fitzgerald short stories. *Faces, Mirrors, Masks* presented portraits of Latin American authors. A series on Andrés Segovia brought listeners into an intimate relationship with the great Spanish guitarist five years before his death.

Few of these programs gained large audiences, but in those days NPR's finances depended more on critical response than on Arbitron ratings. This was one of the major justifications for "public" radio: programming decisions were supposed to be removed from the marketplace that ran commercial broadcasting. So NPR got significant underwriting support from agencies like the National Endowment for the Humanities for a number of extremely ambitious documentary projects. The biggest and most expensive series consisted of thirteen highly produced hourlong programs, introducing some of the major humanists of the twentieth century — such as Simone de Beauvoir,

Sigmund Freud, William Faulkner, Igor Stravinsky, and W.E.B. Dubois. *A Question of Place* put sound in the service of literature and philosophy, cultural criticism, and discussion. Producers developed aural metaphors to help convey complex ideas such as Claude Lévi-Strauss's theories of structuralism or Michel Foucault's perspectives on history. They hired talented actors to dramatize excerpts from texts: members of the RTE Repertoire Company, Dublin, performed pages from James Joyce's *Ulysses* and *Dubliners* as part of a sound portrait of the Irish writer's linguistic sensibility. Scholar Hugh Kenner helped write the script for this program.

A Question of Place represented a high-water mark in NPR's era of experimentation. There had been nothing like it on American radio before; there has been nothing like it since. *A Question of Place* was one of the most expensive documentary projects ever launched at NPR. Scripts were meticulously researched and endlessly refined. Producers and engineers traveled around the world collecting tape and then spent hours and hours assembling their complex, aurally stunning mixes. While the creativity and ambition of the series seemed appropriate for public radio, the costs were embarrassingly high. Broadcast in 1980, *A Question of Place* effectively signaled the beginning and the end of NPR's association with such ambitious and expensive ventures.[4]

The news division also attempted some unusual documentaries during this period, including a four-night series on the arms race. But the most famous news documentary of all is surely *Father Cares: The Last of Jonestown*, an account of the Reverend Jim Jones's religious cult that culminated in a mass suicide at the settlement of Jonestown, Guyana, in 1978. *Father Cares* captured the fanaticism, the madness, of Jonestown by broadcasting some of the original tape recordings made by Jones and his followers, including cassettes recorded right before the suicide order was given.

Father Cares won many awards and got more public notoriety than most NPR documentaries of the period. Like everything produced at

---

[4] To be fair to the producers at NPR, some of that cost was prompted by the requirements of the NEH grant — the need for panels of reviewers, endless streams of reports, and expensive publications and publicity. The results are certainly some of the most beautiful-sounding and intellectually challenging programs ever produced anywhere. And yet, it might be argued that CBC Radio, in its daily program *Ideas*, provides as much of an educational wallop as *A Question of Place* and does so at a fraction of the cost, per program.

NPR during its first decade of existence, the program taught a great deal about radio to staff members, as well as to a public that was slowly becoming more aware of this new radio network.

During the first decade of NPR's existence, then, 2025 M Street was filled with a burgeoning creativity that was sometimes successful and sometimes wayward. These were years of experimentation, when producers and reporters pushed the envelope of aural possibility. Everyone at NPR was sharing in the excitement of discovering a new medium — a new set of aural aesthetics with which to engage, to inspire, and to enlighten an audience.

Jay Kernis remembers those early days when few Americans had ever heard of National Public Radio: "I would always say to people I'd meet, 'Give me three chances. Don't judge public radio on your first listening. Give it a second shot. And *then* give it a third shot. If you give it that *third* shot, I'll guarantee you'll be hooked.'

"Because NPR was something you sort of had to '*get* . . .'" Jay continues. "You had to learn what it was about. An announcer was not going to just read from a piece of paper with a couple of actualities thrown in. We were going to tell you *stories*. We were going to tell stories in such an interesting way that you would not be able to turn us off, but you had to first open yourself up and start *listening*."

According to Jay, people on both sides of the microphone had to be sensitive to the innovative quality of public radio and to the need for a kind of aural public education. "In the early days," Jay explains, "I was always saying to reporters and other producers, 'We must be aware of having to *teach* the audience how to listen to this programming.' Because either the audience had not listened to anything like this for two or three decades, or they had no memory of it, or we were really doing something new — depending upon what we happened to be producing. The visual metaphors listeners were used to, from television and the movies, didn't translate immediately into sound for them. So I would always say that the audience needed help — listeners needed to be brought along with us." For Jay this meant that producers and reporters had to maintain a delicate balance between sound and words. Too much reliance on sound, and the audience would get lost. Too little use of sound, and the power of radio to affect people would be diminished. But Jay also believed that NPR listeners could learn to enjoy more creative forms of radio so long as producers kept challenging them, kept trying to stretch their attentiveness.

Jay Kernis and other producers like him found themselves in a bind when it came to their audience. By the 1970s, Americans had gotten used to the pace and the content of commercial radio, where the basic pulse was set by the minute-long commercial. Americans had fallen out of the habit of *paying attention* to the radio for long periods of time, yet the kind of reports, features, and programs that people at NPR wished to make *demanded* longer attention spans. Time is not the only factor that makes for creative radio, but there are many things you cannot do with sound, and there are many stories you cannot tell in words, if you must constrict yourself always to sixty-second spots.[5] The thorniest problem, the biggest uncertainty, facing NPR centers always on this question of attention span: to what extent should NPR go along with the foreshortened attention span of the American radio audience, and to what extent should NPR push against it? How is an NPR producer, reporter, or tape cutter to determine if a program, a report, or a piece of tape is *interesting* or *boring*? By whose standards should these judgments be made?

This question runs through NPR like a spinal nerve, just beneath the surface — from the simplest edit in a three-minute acts and tracks spot to fundamental programming decisions made at the highest levels of management. In the seventies, generally speaking, NPR leaned more toward being different and challenging than toward being familiar and easily accessible. Producers tended to trust their own ears, to heed their own rhythms, and had faith that the public would follow them instinctively — or would learn to do so.

"We assumed that our listeners were curious about a lot of things and also that they had a certain patience, and we programmed to that assumption," remembers Joe Gwathmey, who held a number of key executive programming positions at NPR from its initial years through the late eighties. Joe now lives in San Antonio, Texas, where he heads

---

[5] In the years since NPR first began broadcasting, the attention span in commercial broadcasting has continued to shrink. Commercials are now typically thirty seconds, or even twenty seconds, and standard news spots can now run between twenty and forty seconds. Commercial television broadcasts slightly longer reports — since it's assumed that moving pictures can hold audience attention longer than unadorned sound or speech — but here, too, the standard report has shrunk by as much as a minute or two since the early seventies. Recently, the pace of TV news reports has become positively frantic, as rapid jump-cutting of images is combined with increasingly truncated, nonlinear scripts.

a small network of public radio stations. "Part of our thinking grew out of what Bill Siemering wrote in his original paper about what public radio ought to be," Joe continues. "In part, NPR was a missionary enterprise whose role was to broadcast programs which would *not* be commercially viable. I still like this notion that we should put our listeners in a position to learn about things that they wouldn't have thought they were interested in, and that they wouldn't have sought out on their own. I like the idea of surprising them. I think it's okay to assume a curiosity that may transcend any number of formats and to try to find the ways artfully to carry people through those. I mean, that's the challenge that makes this all worth doing."

A tall, gentle man with a neatly trimmed black and gray beard, Joe Gwathmey speaks slowly — very slowly — in a deep, chesty voice. A certain stiff elegance has always surrounded him, suggesting (as with so many radio people) a touch of shyness within. Throughout his long tenure at NPR, Joe always seemed to be among the "older" generation, even when not so many years separated him from members of the production staff. Yet Joe's kindness and decency easily penetrated his occasionally phlegmatic exterior. One of the "founding fathers" of NPR, he was a favorite executive of many of the youngest and most creative reporters and producers, whose talents he nurtured, as best he could, in an environment that began changing dramatically during his later years in Washington.

"In Siemering's paper he talked about giving voice to people and ideas that didn't have much opportunity to be heard," Joe recalls. "The point was not that we just satisfy some kind of intellectual curiosity: our mission was to equip people to be better citizens, better consumers, better voters — to help them be better at inquiring. Those were the values that really sang for me. And they still do."

Public radio has always been engaged in a delicate balancing act when it comes to thinking about how to enlarge its audience, according to Joe. "There's never been any mystery about what you would do to get the biggest audience numbers," he explains. "You would do what commercial broadcasters do. They shoot for the lowest common denominator in their programming decisions — always have. Nothing wrong with that . . . it's what they must do to be commercially viable. But I used to say in my speeches at public radio conferences that what distinguished us in public radio, I thought, was that we were shooting for the *highest* common denominator in our programming decisions."

The early attempts by NPR to choose its programs on the basis of noncommercial criteria has led to a lot of misunderstanding by critics both inside and outside the organization. NPR has often been attacked by political conservatives for being "left-wing" and "elitist." It has also been attacked by liberals and radicals for being "predictable," "establishment," and "elitist." News organizations that try to be nonideological are always lambasted for their political bias, real or imaginary — little more can be added to this familiar, and tedious, debate between left and right. The charge of elitism, on the other hand, raises some interesting issues: it is a criticism that some current NPR staffers level at their predecessors and in one fashion or another it is one of the concerns that has propelled NPR along its present, hard-news trajectory.[6]

National Public Radio was created as part of the Public Broadcasting Act of 1967. Originally, the bill was called the Public Television Act and was drawn up in response to a Carnegie Commission report encouraging federal support for a noncommercial, national television network. Intense lobbying by a group of radio broadcasters, in particular an organization called the National Association of Educational Broadcasters, got Congress, as Joe Gwathmey puts it, "to add the words 'and radio' just about everywhere that the word 'television' appeared in the original bill." To the extent that National Public Radio was created to be different from commercial radio, it was, from the start, an "alternative" institution. But just what *kind* of an alternative it turned out to be has been widely misinterpreted, particularly in recent years.

NPR sprang into existence in 1971, quite literally out of the head of "educational radio" — a phenomenon that had grown up during the sixties at low-powered FM stations usually associated with universities and colleges. NPR's roots were thus in *academic* radio, which is not the

---

[6] For example, former NPR president Doug Bennet is quoted as rejecting the old NPR approach to programming (which he calls "precious, self-indulgent, and cutesy") in the following way: "When you hear some white male saying [the news programs] aren't as good as they were in the old days, they really mean they're not the same, and that's good." (Mary Collins, *National Public Radio: The Cast of Characters.* Seven Locks Press, Washington, D.C., 1993, p. 94.)

Bennet can certainly take pride in increasing the diversity of NPR's staff during his tenure (1983–93), though the organization was never quite as male-dominated and "lily white" as other segments of the American media of the same period (which, admittedly, is not to say very much). His judgments about *radio* have been far more controversial within the corridors of NPR.

same as elite or intellectual radio. The typical educational radio station in the early seventies was located at a small Midwestern university and broadcast to a mixed audience of students, farmers, teachers, and small-town professionals. Except for a handful of unusual urban stations like WGBH, Boston, few people who lived in big cities knew that something called educational radio existed. This strongly rural profile continued during the first few years of NPR's existence. Thus, it's the height of intellectual snobbery for some critics of public radio to assume that since educational radio typically broadcast a lot of lectures, debates, and symposiums, therefore NPR's origins are "intellectual and snobby." In fact, NPR's roots are *populist*, growing out of the same rural, self-reliant, self-improving soil as the Chautauqua Movement or the Grange. Not only pointy-headed, eastern intellectuals are interested in educating themselves.

It is true that many of the people who came to *work* at NPR in the early years did not fit the profile of the average NPR *listener.* For example, a number of early reporters who rose to prominence were graduates of prestigious colleges and universities. Another group of reporters and producers drifted over to NPR from Pacifica Radio, whose origins were West Coast, urban, and left-wing. (Interestingly, the radical orientation of Pacifica, which led it to scorn commercial sponsorship by capitalist enterprises, also prompted its stations to inaugurate the first on-the-air fund drives. "Power to the people" meant badgering the people, periodically, to share some of their power with the station. Educational radio stations, at first, did not engage in such undignified hoopla.) But though a number of important people at NPR came from the urban intelligentsia, the majority of the staff did not. A great number climbed the ladder of educational/public radio, from small stations at the periphery to the center in Washington. Similarly, many of the executives who created NPR in the first place came from small towns or second-tier cities. Bill Siemering, in many respects the spiritual godfather of public radio, was running a station in Buffalo, New York, while helping to sire NPR. He had begun his radio work at WHA, the station of the University of Wisconsin. Joe Gwathmey was working at a small station in Austin, Texas. These people, and many others, did not come to Washington from "alternative institutions" associated with the counterculture of the period, but neither did they espouse establishment thinking when it came to the broadcast media. They were innovators — even revolutionaries — not because of their politics but because of their aesthetics. They assaulted the status quo not with ideology but with electronics. They were guerrillas fighting in the media wasteland created by television against the tyranny of the visual. They were subversives who were asking Americans to close their eyes and open their ears.

This is what many critics — and supporters — of National Public Radio have ignored over the years: NPR's "different sound" during the seventies and early eighties did not originate in any hidden (or not so hidden) political agenda, nor did it derive from the countercultural milieu that a few of its staff members inhabited. Such a view of NPR trivializes the institution and its purposes, ignoring what is truly "dangerous" about public radio — its capacity to offer profound, intimate, and sometimes even transforming experiences to listeners through the intelligent and sensitive use of language and sound. These experiences represent a clear alternative to norms that have developed in American broadcasting since the advent of television. NPR's most creative programming challenges habits of passivity and verbal dullness among people who have stared at too many frenetically flashy TV images and been assaulted by too much glib TV babble-talk. Because of the medium in which it operates, public radio can cajole, prod, stimulate, and inspire listeners to respond more creatively to their surroundings and to understand themselves and others more articulately and with greater compassion. If the typical television viewer is a quiescent observer, staring vacantly at dancing images on the TV screen, the typical listener to creative radio is an engaged participant, whose imagination is constantly responding to the shifting sounds and voices that pour out of the loudspeaker. Look at the eyes of people watching TV: the inner picture-making process of the imagination has surrendered control to whatever appears on the surface of the cathode tube. Look into the eyes of people listening to a stimulating radio piece: private imagery flickers across their gaze at a level deeper than simple sight. Received language and sound mingle with inner speech; each individual consciousness tumbles through pirouettes of metaphor and meaning while on its way to making connections and achieving a special kind of intimate knowledge.

Commercial radio in this country hasn't aspired to its full potential as a vehicle of communication for many decades. Regarded as a handicapped medium — as *only* "television without pictures" — it has been treated by broadcasters as a second-class citizen and audiences have responded by relegating the sound medium to the backgrounds of their lives.[7] Commercial broadcasters assume that their audience is always "doing something else" while they have the radio on — for what contemporary American would ever sit down for half an hour and simply *listen?* So commercial radio programs are chopped up into short, flashy segments (bracketed by commercials) in such a way that listeners are actually encouraged to "tune in" and "tune out." The basic rhythm is repetitive, predictable, and unchallenging. Commercial radio engages

---

[7] Apologists for the path American radio has taken will argue that audience habits were changed by television, not by any shifts that radio broadcasters made; but then commercial broadcasters always insist that they merely reflect the choices and tastes of their listeners and viewers. Time and again, network executives have denied any responsibility for the effects of their technology on the minds and emotions of the people who tune them in. This is not the place for a full discussion of such a complex "chicken or egg" question. But it seems at least plausible to argue that the American commercial broadcast news media are in a sorry state today in large measure because of their irresponsible disregard of the effects their technology has upon their audience. One example of many that could be cited: the mindless and uncritical pursuit of "live coverage" by the current generation of television news editors, in stories as diverse as the bombing of Baghdad, the siege of the religious sect at Waco, Texas, and O.J. Simpson's prime-time freeway car chase. In each case, the craft of journalism became perverted into something resembling a peep show, whose main consequence (whatever the high-minded intent) was to turn stories of death and destruction into trivial visual thrills and occasions for irresponsible rumor-mongering and ambulance chasing. (The sight of half a dozen Eye-in-the-Sky helicopters fighting for position over O.J. Simpson's house surely marks one of the low points in the history of American TV news.) Each of these stories was put on the air instantaneously *because the technology permitted it*, with little regard for the complex relationship between those "live pictures" and the fully nuanced, human reality unfolding during each set of events. When "news" comes to be defined as "live, unedited pictures," the craft of journalism has been radically altered, with the most profound of consequences for our society, our culture, and our selves. Throughout human history, *storytellers* have told the events of the day, and, in the describing, they have helped construct a sense of history, a sense of community. When storytellers abdicate their role and substitute technologically generated imagery that has not been significantly shaped and reconstructed by a human imagination, one of our society's — one of *our* — fundamental connections with human experience has been altered. "The news" has *never* consisted solely of data which could be measured and recorded by instruments of science and technology without the intervention of human consciousness and understanding. Yet ratings-driven and picture-driven TV news falls increasingly into the trap of allowing machines — and the products they generate — to dominate human intelligence, human language, and *humane* insight.

    Yet did anyone in commercial TV news ever discuss these issues before they began their live coverage? Have there been any serious attempts to take control of

in a balancing act; while it is fine for the attention of audiences to wander a little, listeners are never allowed to get *bored* to the extent that they will change stations. Programs must include elements that audiences want to *hear* but not material that audiences must actively *listen to.* "Radio-as-wallpaper" means radio that you enjoy having on but that is neither too distracting nor demanding.

In the early years of public radio, NPR heard the rumors about Americans' listening habits — but most producers at the network felt a touch of "missionary zeal," to borrow Joe Gwathmey's phrase, and tried to pursue, with sensitivity and thoughtfulness, the unusual aural potential of the medium. They hoped an audience would learn to listen.

Changing Formats

When *Morning Edition* went on the air in November 1979, the show marked a turning point in NPR's evolution. While the program grew out of the fecund, slightly eccentric environment that had flourished at 2025 M Street during public radio's first decade, *Morning Edition* also represented the first major attempt by NPR to respond to the preferences and pressures of local stations — and, by extension, local listeners. And sure enough, within a few months of the program's debut, its ratings were spiraling upward. The show was very popular on those stations that broadcast it; ironically, the only impediment to overall ratings growth was the reluctance of a few larger stations to abandon local programming (quite often, classical music shows) which had been on the air for many years and had developed small but extremely loyal audiences. *Morning Edition's* popularity was irresistible, however. Within a very few years, its national audience was close to that of the venerable *All Things Considered,* even though the older program was being carried

television technology and turn it into a storytelling tool that enhances our humanity, our capacity to understand the world in which we find ourselves? Beyond ABC's *Nightline* (run by public radio aficionados and increasingly staffed by ex-NPR producers and reporters), CBS's *Sunday Morning* (until recently a vehicle for perhaps the only two truly literate reporters left on Ed Murrow's network, Charles Kuralt and Charles Osgood — and now Kuralt has retired), and various offerings on public television (such as those by MacNeil-Lehrer and Bill Moyers), American TV news shows every sign of falling deeper and deeper into the morass of mindless mediocrity that it has constructed for itself.

by more stations. In 1989, *Morning Edition* finally surged past *ATC* (4.9 million to 4.6 listeners weekly) and the afternoon program has never caught up.

Initially, the most obvious difference between *Morning Edition* and *All Things Considered* was its structure. *ATC* consisted of three free-form, half-hour segments within which radio reports could grow to whatever length seemed appropriate. *Morning Edition* imposed the rigid discipline of the clock, familiar in commercial broadcasting but relatively new to noncommercial radio.[8] As discussed earlier, this segmentation allowed local stations to break in and out of the show, making *Morning Edition* the first two-hour news *service* that NPR produced.

In the first year of its existence, *Morning Edition* reported stories that were not all that different from those on *All Things Considered* since many of the people who worked on the morning program came over from the afternoon show, including, of course, Bob Edwards.[9] But right from the start, *Morning Edition* laid the groundwork for a different kind of radio production and, eventually, for a different kind of programming focus. *Morning Edition* had to be a faster-paced show than *All Things Considered* — after all, it was supposed to be an "aural cup of coffee" for listeners. *Morning Edition* assumed that its audience could be only moderately reflective about what it heard on the radio; in the battle over attention span, *Morning Edition* marked the first clear retreat from the goal of trying to enlarge significantly the focus and concentration of listeners. Compromise underlay many programming choices made for the morning program.

The initial results did not seem promising. Two weeks before the scheduled premiere, a pilot program was sent out for stations to audition. It was a disaster. NPR management hated it, local stations hated it. The committee that created this radio-version-of-the-camel had consulted with psychologists and pollsters and had brought in people

---

[8] Neal Conan tells the story about the first time he was asked to do a spot for an hourly newscast, sometime in the mid-seventies. The report would be sixty seconds long, the editor said. *"Exactly* sixty seconds?" Neal replied, incredulous. When working for Pacifica's New York station, WBAI, he had never worried about such precise timings.

[9] The first Open for *Morning Edition*'s first broadcast began, "Good morning. Today is Guy Fawkes Day. Guy's plot to blow up the parliament was discovered on this day in 1605. Today is the beginning of National Split Pea Soup Week and the debut of this program. I'm Bob Edwards." *Morning Edition* did not become a straight-ahead news program overnight. Quoted in Collins, p. 48.

from outside public radio to produce and host the show. The results sounded fluffy, inconsequential — and in many ways, too much like commercial radio. When NPR president Frank Mankiewicz heard the pilot, he didn't need media experts to tell him what to do. He fired the top *Morning Edition* staffers who were new to NPR and asked the rump of public radio veterans, which included the young Jay Kernis, to rework the program.

Many reviewers of the pilot expressed satisfaction with the new *structure* of *Morning Edition* and only complained about what had been done inside it. But a few skeptics at NPR worried that the whole project was off base. It seemed to these critics that *Morning Edition's* form and function were skewed and could never result in good *public* radio. Wasn't the program envisioned as a disjointed smorgasbord around which local stations could drape their local news, traffic, and weather reports? No segment would be longer than nine minutes, which meant, effectively, that no single piece could run more than seven or eight minutes. Most reports would be three to five minutes long. Each segment would open and close the same way each morning, so that local stations would get used to their incues and outcues. How could such a rigid, predictable, and *repetitive* structure ever hope to carry the creative punch of *All Things Considered*, or a program like the award-winning weekly arts magazine *Voices in the Wind?* (Unkindest cut of all: *Voices* and a number of other arts and performance programs had been dropped in order to make room in the budget for the new morning experiment.) Critics doubted that *Morning Edition* could ever transcend its *Good Morning America*–like theme music and create a *public radio* style of morning wake-up show consistent with the traditions of the programs that were being cast aside in its wake.

But Mankiewicz chose well when he tapped Jay Kernis to supervise the reimaging and rebuilding of *Morning Edition*. Still in his late twenties, Jay was nonetheless one of the major creative talents at NPR, a man of principle, intelligence, and vision who was not prepared to give up on the ideals of public radio and yet who was ready to work creatively within the structural requirements of *Morning Edition*. It was Jay, the collage artist, who had created the original "program wheel" for the show. This conceptual tool allowed producers physically to slice up a *Morning Edition* hour into segments of different sizes and then to argue over the best shape for the pie. In the final two weeks before *Morning Edition* first broadcast, Jay worked with his colleagues to revise the wheel yet again, making its components more substantive and at the same time more creative. He persuaded a number of former arts and performance producers to join the morning show and got these audio producers talking with the show's news producers about ideas and approaches appropriate for *Morning Edition*'s new format.

A key member of the new *Morning Edition* team was reporter and producer Alex Chadwick. In the early seventies, Alex had studied journalism and news writing with Edward Bliss at American University in Washington, before moving to Maine where he became a lobster fisherman for a time. In 1976 Alex joined NPR as host-producer of a nine-minute morning news feature, *A Closer Look*. Here, Alex combined his training in news with a deepening appreciation for the aural side of radio. Alex had collaborated closely with Jay in the initial conceptualization of *Morning Edition* before outsiders had been brought in to create the show. Now, during the reconstruction of the program, Alex became the first dayside producer. He assumed particular responsibility for news coverage, while Jay took on the job of overnight producer.

The show still needed hosts. With only a few days to go before the network premiere, Jay wanted to find at least one experienced voice deeply anchored in NPR tradition. He asked Bob Edwards if he would come over from *All Things Considered* temporarily — for perhaps a month — and team up with relative newcomer Barbara Hochter. Bob agreed, and *Morning Edition* was born.

Bob Edwards recalls that he and his *ATC* cohost Susan Stamberg had laughed when they heard the original *Morning Edition* pilot — *this* was the show that was supposed to compete for resources with *All Things Considered?*[10] The two figured that *Morning Edition* wouldn't last long. But after a few weeks working with Jay, Alex, and the rest of the production team, Bob became hooked on the potential of the morning program. Barbara Hochter left the show after a few months, and from then on Bob was content to perform solo. Many at NPR believe that *Morning Edition* was the making of Bob Edwards. Good as he was on *All Things Considered*, he tended always to be the foil for the dynamic, ebullient Susan Stamberg. On the morning program, Bob's star rose high — solitary and unencumbered.

The revamped *Morning Edition* proved to be a great success with listeners. The new production team put together a program that seemed

---

[10] Collins, p. 54.

to take NPR's creative strengths and merge them with the demands of a new format and a new time slot. When Jay talks about the compromises that went into creating *Morning Edition*, he does not make them sound like a surrender by audio artists to the pressures of the public radio marketplace.

"*All Things Considered* was always a program with a beginning, a middle, and an end," Jay explains. "In those days *ATC* began with the hosts' 'hello' and ended with their 'good-bye.' *Morning Edition* was created to be a *service* — and that's a big difference. But the segmented structure did not have to be seen as a constriction, as a problem. It all depends on your perspective.

"Here's how I looked at it — and it was Fred Calland [who used to produce and host NPR concert programs] who taught me this.[11] Not only did *All Things Considered* have to create a new program every night, but it had to create its own *architecture*, its own rhythms and pacings, every single night. And on nights where it failed, the program could fail. For example, if one piece went on too long, listeners wouldn't want to hear anything else. Or if there were three phone pieces back to back — well, after the second phoner, everything would start sounding like a blur of mush. If the producers didn't get the rhythm of the pieces, the pacing, right, the audience instinctively *knew* that something was wrong . . . and they would stop listening.

"By contrast, *Morning Edition* has this structure that's the same every day — the same architecture is there. And so, what Fred Calland said to me was, 'Since the architecture is given to you, therefore you are *free* to experiment with it. You are free to play with it. You are free to have *fun* with it. The audience will eventually learn what it is, so you can then be creative through it.' And I took this advice very much to heart and always said to the staff, 'Be *liberated* by the clock. Don't be trapped by the clock.'"

Any art, says Jay, embraces structure — and then transforms it and transcends it. The *Morning Edition* format was not so rigid that it did not allow for a great deal of invention. Even the conception of the show

---

[11] Fred Calland began his broadcasting career in educational radio at WFCR, a small station in rural Massachusetts, long before NPR was founded. In the seventies, Fred moved to Washington, where he became one of the mainstays of NPR's arts and performance division. (His wife, Diana, held administrative posts at NPR and CPB.) Fred's graciously professional on-air manner became well known to NPR's classical music audience.

as a service, as something that most listeners would not listen to from start to finish, could be regarded as a challenge to a producer's creativity. "I always knew that this program was designed to be something that a listener could tune in to at any time," Jay explains. "So as producer, I tried to make sure that no matter which twenty minutes of the program you listened to, you would get an arts piece, a news piece, and a feature piece. That's what was in my mind when I worked up the show clock. I wanted all our listeners to get hard-news emotion and then real-people emotion, and then imagination. I was always trying to build in those different textures, those different experiences. It was difficult to do, but if you listen to some of the old programs, you can hear when we are making the format really sing. They still do it today, too, every now and then. The structure — the possibility — remains in place.

"When I was producing the show, I figured it was my job to pay specific attention to the overall flow of the program because I had other people who paid attention to the news. I knew that every piece had to have a beginning and a middle and an end . . . and that each segment had to have the same kind of flow — a beginning, a middle, and an end . . . and that each half-hour should also have an overall structure — that it should build to something. I mean, that's what the storytelling tradition is: using narrative blocks and creating larger structures with them.

"And, remember, in the beginning we were teaching the audience how to listen to the program. This kind of show had not existed before. So I was trying to make the program as accessible — as *listenable* — as possible . . . to give it a flow which would carry people through it, even with all the interruptions — the local breaks, the headlines, and so on."

So Jay Kernis imagined a program that would allow an audience to dip in and out — in typical "morning listening" style — and yet would also reward those who could tune in for longer stretches. He also envisioned training part of the audience to listen longer than they might have thought they wanted to, and he tried to promise unexpected rewards if they did.

For Jay, every part of the *Morning Edition* structure held creative possibility, and he encouraged his staff to be inventive. Jay paid particular attention to the music that was used at the end of a story, and he would sometimes huddle with his staff looking for just the right piece to set a mood or prepare a transition or make a subtle joke. Even something as short and apparently routine as the billboards — the ten seconds of copy that Bob reads just before the headlines — could be punched up and made into something interesting.

"You could always have fun with the billboards," Jay remembers. "My favorite example concerns a time when we were doing a story about a poet who lived in New Jersey. He was very well known for his haiku, and as I was putting the segment together, I thought to myself, 'What if I write the billboard that precedes the piece in haiku form?' So I came up with the following:

> Some words hit, some hurt
> Jersey poet writes haiku.
> News from Jean Cochran.

And that's what Bob read on the air. It scans to perfect haiku meter. And I just thought it was one of the best things I'd ever done on radio because it encapsulated the whole piece. It told the audience: 'This is the poetry you will be hearing about, stay tuned — it will be fun.'

"That's a very simple illustration of the kind of things we tried to do throughout the program, whenever we could. Once you establish a format, you can start working *with* and sometimes *against* that format to create an effect. If the audience always expects a piece of music in a particular place, what happens when you don't put the music there? If the audience expects Bob to introduce himself and then continue reading, what happens when Bob says, 'This is *Morning Edition*. I'm Bob Edwards' — and then you hear sound? So every part of the format could be manipulated *for meaning* . . . when you thought about it, when you experimented with it."

Crucial to Jay Kernis's aesthetic, of course, is the phrase "for meaning." Jay's work in radio would never be different just for the sake of being different or clever just to call attention to his own cleverness. The haiku billboard provides an excellent example — a perfect merging of innovation and originality with content and purpose. Many listeners might not have noticed Bob's verse. For them the billboard would have been simply informative, if a tad cryptic. Yet the ten seconds of copy also worked on a different level, providing a satisfying and stimulating moment for those in the audience who heard Bob speaking haiku.

Greg Smith first worked on *Morning Edition* in 1980; in 1985 he left NPR to began a career in film, though he has moved back and forth between jobs in film sound and stints at NPR ever since. (His wife, Margaret, has worked as a producer on *All Things Considered* for many years.) Greg has maintained close friendships with a number of colleagues and often becomes the "designated" editor or producer, pinch-hitting when certain programs are temporarily short-staffed. A man of medium height, solidly built, with a quick smile and a rapid, frank way of speaking, Greg recalls his early days on *Morning Edition*: "It was clear from the start that Bob was going to be one of the keys to the whole program. And in the years that I was first here, Bob was very much an *activist* host. When Jay was producing the show, Bob was always very excited about the program. And we'd do crazy things, we'd go nuts. I remember once, when I was directing the program, there was a Return that we did, during the Falklands War. Wasn't it young Prince Andrew who was a marine helicopter pilot? And I think his mother, the Queen, had sent him a letter, which got onto the wires. Bob read the story and said something like, 'Wouldn't it be funny if we had an English accent to read some of this?' I said, 'Great, I'll do an outrageous British voice.' So I went in and read a section of the letter with Bob, as part of the Return, you know.

"But see, we were all producing Bob. Jay, me, Cindy Carpien [now producer of *Weekend Edition Saturday*] — we were all doing 'Bob pieces' and having a ball. 'Bob, try this,' we'd say — and he'd usually go along. We would take him out of the building, we would go and do things. He *loved* road trips, you know, and it was the rare week that we didn't have three or four production pieces with Bob involved. I don't mean two-ways — I mean produced spots.

"And even two-ways wouldn't always just be simple conversations. 'Okay, what else can we do?' we'd say to ourselves. 'Let's get a little bit of music or add some sound effects.' Say, for example, that Bob had done an interview with an author about Thomas Jefferson. Okay. Now let's go to Monticello . . . let's do a walking tour. Either do it with Bob, or maybe a reporter can go and record the tour. And then we might mix the two pieces of tape together — the two-way and the tour . . . something like that. There are a million and one things you can do. But that was always the thought, you know, how can we make interesting host pieces? How can we make a two-way more than just a two-way?"

During the first five years of *Morning Edition*, when Jay Kernis was one of the principal producers, there were many tensions and conflicts within the staff, often precipitated by the different perspectives of those whose backgrounds were in hard news and those who came from the arts or aural documentary side of radio. (Alex Chadwick, whose own work increasingly became an amalgam of these points of view, left *Morning Edition* early on to produce, and then host, *Weekend All Things*

Considered.) The lore of *Morning Edition* is sprinkled with tales of shouting matches, temper tantrums, and wounded feelings. But radio broadcasting always contains a strong element of *performance*, and performers — behind as well as in front of the microphone — use their egos heavily in their work. The atmosphere at *Morning Edition* was no more contentious than backstage at a play or on a movie set, and none of the *Sturm und Drang* leaked over onto the air — where Bob Edwards began to build an aura of calm confidence and professionalism that drew larger and larger audiences.

Hardening the News

The great success of *Morning Edition* had ripple effects throughout National Public Radio. NPR began to devote a larger share of its resources to hard news and provided less support for creative radio production. This change occurred gradually, and it was not simply the product of *Morning Edition*. But the advent of the morning program reflected certain attitudes that had been growing within public radio, and the show's success further spread this news orientation.

In practical terms, the scope of *Morning Edition* required a significant increase in the size of NPR's news division. The early broadcast time of the program necessitated a round-the-clock staff. Furthermore, now that NPR was broadcasting two separate, major newsmagazines, some kind of supra-program organization was needed to coordinate news coverage — to determine which reporters would follow what stories for whose program. The creation of *Morning Edition* thus led inevitably to the creation of the editorial desk system.

Where was all this additional staff to come from? While NPR management looked within the public radio system for some of its new personnel, increasingly, as the eighties progressed, new editors and reporters were hired from newspapers and magazines. Part of the reason for this was simply the weak tradition of radio news in this country: not that many topnotch reporters were being trained either at local public stations or at commercial stations. While some attention was paid to a few of the better television journalists (NPR nabbed one or two, most notably Daniel Schorr and Anne Garrels), in fact, the meager wages that NPR offered could not compete with the six-figure salaries paid as a matter of course by TV news organizations. By far the largest and most promising pool of editorial and reportorial talent was located at the nation's newspapers and magazines.

The move to hire print people was not just motivated by logistics, however. For all the expertise that NPR's own reporters had developed during the brief history of the network, senior management continued to share the bias — traditionally a part of all American broadcast news organizations — that the print media remained the best training ground for reporters. (During the Golden Age of television news — the sixties and early seventies, when Huntley-Brinkley were at NBC and Cronkite was at CBS — you could not get a job in TV news unless you had first been trained on a newspaper or magazine. Only in recent years have networks started hiring reporters straight out of journalism school.)

Bob Ferrante — whose experience in broadcast news ranges from CBS-TV, to public television, to NPR — sums up the attitude toward print reporting that became canonical at public radio during the eighties: "When I was in television, and I was hiring a reporter, if I had two people of identical skills and one had newspaper, magazine, or wire training, I would hire that person before I'd hire the one who only had worked in TV. Print is still the best training — that's the only thing I didn't have and I've always missed it. But I've always hired only the print person.

"Because anybody can learn the technology. If you can turn on a TV set, if you can turn on an automobile, if you can change a flat tire — it's not a big deal to learn to do sound. You don't have to go to MIT to learn how to use the equipment we have here. But nobody can learn to write unless they *write* — and that's part of what you get from beginning in print. That, and fundamental skills as a reporter. And, anyway, the best radio is really the best written. The basic skill should be the writing. That's the base of it. If you don't start with the writing there's nothing there."

Ferrante touches on another, more general reason why NPR turned naturally to print reporters to fill many of the new editorial positions. As the *literate electronic medium*, radio news both benefits from good writing and rewards reporters who write well. While not all print reporters can develop the ear necessary to become good oral reporters, the transition from print to radio is often a smooth and natural one.

The influx of new editors and reporters from newspapers and magazines created some problems within NPR. While many of the newer members of the NPR team were curious about the audio side of radio, most were apt to be skeptical about some of the habits they found in place at the organization. Siemering's softer aesthetics of "curiosity and evocation" did not have much appeal to hard-edged newshounds from the city desk or correspondents who had been working in foreign war zones. In general, the newcomers from print liked the faster pace, the newsy focus of *Morning Edition*'s prime segments. They were not quite sure what to make of "aural reporting." When they thought about journalism, they thought about getting the facts straight, about telling a clear, intelligible story, about presenting a balanced, objective point of view. Print people often saw the concerns of the audio producers as ephemeral — "matters of aesthetics," not matters of fact . . . and *facts* to well-trained print reporters are coin of the realm.

Meanwhile, on the other side of the office, some NPR veterans treated "print people" with a certain standoffishness. They would complain about the prosaic quality that had entered public radio with all the new editors, who thought on their typewriters and not in their ears. They were bored by acts and tracks reports, which they said sounded more like magazine articles read aloud than like radio stories.

The "radio people" were not always diplomatic in their handling of the newcomers from print, but, then, the office culture at NPR had not always been open and welcoming to outsiders. Throughout the seventies, visitors to NPR had often noted a certain cliquishness among the staff of shows like *All Things Considered* — a certain inbred, clannish feeling. This slightly defensive atmosphere had its origins partly in NPR's curious position vis-à-vis the rest of American broadcasting. Public radio was very much out on its own limb, isolated and ignored by mainstream media. NPR folks had learned to look out for each other and to protect themselves against the slights and criticisms from more established organizations. When the audio cliques at NPR began being invaded by a trickle and then a stream of people from print, tensions were inevitable. Throughout the eighties, the two groups inflicted subtle — and not so subtle — wounds on each other. Scars from these skirmishes remain visible to this day. The discussions and debates were usually joined under the generalized heading of "journalistic standards," but what the two camps were often arguing about was the relative importance of the story and the sound in public radio.

During the years that Jay Kernis worked on *Morning Edition*, the struggles between print and radio people remained in a kind of balance, and it could be argued that during this period the tensions between the groups remained creative — leading to the expansion and improvement of NPR news coverage; the growth of audiences for both *Morning Edition* and *All Things Considered;* and the development of creative aural approaches to the radio magazine format. Had NPR been able to evolve smoothly and naturally throughout the 1980s, who knows what kinds of diverse and varied programs the network might now be offering to who knows how large a public radio audience? The great tragedy of National Public Radio is that such a steady creative development did not happen. A mixture of politics and personality resulted in a massive financial meltdown of the organization in the midst of the Reagan presidency — and this led to the end of the period of creative ferment. In the climate of retrenchment and reevaluation, based on bare-knuckled principles of survival, the hard-nosed, hard-news voices at NPR effectively took charge of the organization. The implications of this shift in power and attitude have only slowly become apparent. NPR is a small bureaucracy, but it is still a bureaucracy, and even dramatic changes happen gradually. But the NPR that currently enjoys the greatest financial security and the largest listening audience in its history is a significantly different organization from the one that launched *Morning Edition* in 1979.

It has been a long time since Bob Edwards read haiku before headlines from Jean Cochran.

Soft Finances

It is part of current mythology at NPR today to assume that the network's hard-news focus is a relatively new phenomenon, stimulated especially by the success of NPR's coverage of the Gulf War in 1991. Some staffers with longer memories look back to the financial crisis of 1983 and see that debacle as the push that propelled NPR toward the grail of hard news. Both points of view implicitly assume that "news" at NPR only really became polished and professional when a critical mass of ex-print people joined the organization and outnumbered the radio reporters. This perspective oversimplifies NPR's complex history. Joe Gwathmey remembers, for example, that as early as 1974, NPR executives expressed an interest in strengthening the journalistic side of the network and started hiring some hard-nosed editors to help train the young and enthusiastic talent on *All Things Considered.* And certainly it was Frank Mankiewicz, when he became president of NPR in 1977, who first articulated the goal of making NPR the *"New York Times* of radio." By the late seventies, Mankiewicz was already proud of NPR's journalistic accomplishments, including its early coverage of the Watergate hearings and its historic first live broadcast from Congress of the Panama Canal Treaty debate in 1978. Mankiewicz was also one of the first to say that NPR was "the best-kept secret in American broadcasting," and he was determined to get the story out. *Morning Edition* came into existence in part because of Mankiewicz's commitment to improving the quality of NPR's journalism, to expanding its production schedule, and to enlarging the size of its audience.[12]

Son and nephew of Hollywood's famous Mankiewicz brothers, writer Herman J. and director Joseph L., Frank Mankiewicz brought a unique mix of experience and perspective to NPR. He was a man of the establishment and the counterestablishment, a journalist and a public relations man, who kept one foot in the Washington corridors of power (he'd worked on Senator Robert Kennedy's staff), one foot with the generations of antiwar protesters (he'd been press secretary for George McGovern's presidential campaign), and yet another foot in the world of art, literature, and film that had been a part of his childhood in Los Angeles and New York. Straddling many worlds and many aesthetics, Mankiewicz was in certain respects a perfect man to come to NPR during these early years, for he crystallized within his personality and his aspirations the conflicting and sometimes contradictory tensions that drove the young, evolving phenomenon of public radio. While Mankiewicz clearly wished to strengthen the news side of NPR (he brought over Cokie Roberts to be congressional correspondent and hired the managing editor of *The Washington Star,* Barbara Cohen, to be news director), he also wanted to keep public radio's cultural programming strong and expanding. One of the last creative projects of the Mankiewicz years was the highly successful, thirteen-part radio adaptation of the movies *Star Wars* and *The Empire Strikes Back,* created in cooperation with filmmaker George Lucas and (to a limited extent) the BBC. Lavishly produced with stunning sound effects and music, these extremely expensive investments in 1981 and 1983

---

[12] The following account of the Mankiewicz years at NPR comes mostly from my own recollections of the period and from conversations with current NPR staffers. Mary Collins's book includes a more detailed discussion of developments at NPR during the seventies and eighties.

paid off handsomely both in terms of raw audience figures (well over a million listeners to *Star Wars* — unprecedented for a radio drama) and general public awareness of NPR.

Meanwhile, Mankiewicz also had the practical political skills to fight many crucial battles on Capitol Hill; he managed to keep funding going for public radio and even expanded it during a time of increased budgetary constraint. (Public funds are funneled to public radio and public television through the Corporation for Public Broadcasting, dimly modeled on the authority in Britain that tries — and usually succeeds — in keeping the BBC surprisingly independent of government interference. Neither PBS nor NPR have ever enjoyed the BBC's degree of political insularity and financial stability.)[13] The total budget for NPR remained extraordinarily small in contrast with public television, and laughably minuscule when compared to what the commercial networks spent on themselves. In the early seventies, public radio received 10 percent of the moneys dispersed by the Corporation for Public Broadcasting. Mankiewicz succeeded in getting this share of the pie increased to 25 percent, so that by the time *Morning Edition* went on the air, NPR was receiving around $20 million from the CPB. But then the Carter administration gave way to the Reagan administration, which slashed funds for public broadcasting by a third, precisely during a period when Mankiewicz wanted to expand NPR. Mankiewicz began trying to invent ways of protecting NPR from new political pressures by eventually withdrawing the organization from all government funding. He and his staff launched an ambitious plan called Project Independence to create a number of commercial ventures (such as renting out satellite time) and new programming initiatives (like "NPR Plus," a twenty-four-hour classical music service) to generate more revenue from underwriters, stations, and the public. But Mankiewicz's dreams of increased independence, expanded programming, and a widening financial horizon abruptly collapsed in the middle of 1983, when a cavernous debt came to light within the fabric of NPR.[14]

---

[13] While the regulatory agency that keeps watch over the BBC is far more independent than the Corporation for Public Broadcasting in this country, the real key to the BBC's success, of course, has been its method of funding: British citizens pay an annual license fee for every radio and TV set they own. Such tithing has often been proposed by public broadcasting enthusiasts in this country, but it has never received a whiff of support on Capitol Hill from voters.

[14] For a vivid account of NPR's financial crisis, see Collins, pp. 65–78.

Most people who have written about the debacle of 1983 attribute the $7-million debt to poor bookkeeping and naive bean counting. Ironically, it was some of the very projects designed to make NPR free of government handouts that helped precipitate the crisis, though the difficulties may have been latent in the careless way in which the Mankiewicz administration handled its finances; it's also possible that subtle political agendas were also at work between Reagan appointees and NPR. During the summer of 1983, estimates of the size of the NPR debt kept changing, ranging from a low of $2 million to a high of $9 million. The board of directors accepted Mankiewicz's resignation and began slashing expenses to keep NPR afloat. When the dust finally settled, the staff had been cut by a third and programming hours by half. The budget for arts and cultural programming had been reduced by 80 percent. Only the news department was spared the most draconian cuts, though drastic economies were instituted and a number of staff members were let go. NPR had come within one day of closing down before the CPB agreed to loan the organization the necessary money, with member stations acting as guarantors. Extremely difficult negotiations had led to this solution, partly due to Washington politics, partly due to simmering resentments within the public radio system itself.

These long-standing tensions between the center and the periphery — between NPR and its member stations — are most poignantly illustrated by what happened following the negotiation of the loan, when NPR tried to launch a national fund-raising appeal in order to demonstrate that it was going to do everything possible to pay off the debt. Executives in Washington devised "The Drive to Survive" campaign, to be aired during a part of *All Things Considered*. But two-thirds of local stations refused to carry this portion of the afternoon program, feeling that it was inappropriate for NPR to "go over their heads" and solicit money directly from their listeners. So, two versions of *All Things Considered* were fed to the network during that week, one with the fund drive and one without. (In spite of the small carriage, *ATC* listeners contributed $2.25 million to help save NPR.)[15]

The fall of Mankiewicz and the implosion of NPR that followed loom large in the history of public radio. The year 1983 marked a watershed in the kind of programming — the varieties of radio — that

---

[15] My account of "The Drive to Survive" derives in part from Collins, pp. 72–73, and in part from amplifications supplied by Joe Gwathmey.

the network would now broadcast. The decade of creative expansiveness at NPR was over. What followed was a period of retrenchment until 1985, when the debt was paid off, and then a second, very different period of growth began, one based on a different orientation toward the medium of radio. During the seventies, on the whole, local stations could depend on grants from private foundations and various state and federal government authorities to cover basic operating expenses — what kept them on the air and broadcasting. Stations turned to their listeners — to contributions from "members" — for the cost of their membership in National Public Radio. Typically, this meant something like one third of their operating expenses. But during the eighties, the percentages reversed. Now stations found that government and foundation moneys were not enough to keep their facilities on the air. If educational radio stations had once looked down their noses at Pacifica stations with their noisy, badgering fund drives, the public radio stations of the 1980s found themselves spending a lot of their time trying to squeeze money from the public which they were trying to serve. On-air membership drives proliferated and became more insistent. Ironically, stations simultaneously had to reach out to a brand-new source of funding that implicitly contradicted the pleas for individual support. Corporate underwriting became an important part of public stations' financial base, and suddenly the public airwaves, which for a couple of decades had provided a haven from the sales pitches of commercial broadcasting, began including a couple of minutes each hour of "business," the euphemism adopted by station managers to mean, essentially, a restricted form of commercial messages.

The new president of NPR, Doug Bennet, epitomized the new direction. Bennet brought to his job no background in the media, no experience in journalism; he was a career public servant and an experienced manager who had had a number of jobs in the Washington bureaucracy. His twin goals were to put NPR on a solid financial footing and to strengthen public radio as a public service. Bennet saw one obvious strategy for achieving both ends: increase the size of NPR's audience. The more listeners, the more contributors, both individual and corporate (in keeping with the new atmosphere in Washington, Bennet saw public radio relying increasingly on private business for support). Also, the bigger an audience NPR had, the more it would be fulfilling its mandate to be a *public* radio service.

Bennet was not just a number cruncher when it came to ratings. He believed deeply in broadening NPR's base, picking up on that part of public radio's original mandate that said the network should reach out to communities not well served by commercial radio. Bennet was convinced that NPR's audience as well as its staff were too white, too middle-class, and too male. He vigorously pursued a policy of hiring minorities at NPR and he supported efforts by executives like Joe Gwathmey to diversify public radio's programming in similar directions.

Bennet's focus on audience *ratings*, however, were not coupled with any special insights into the medium of radio itself — its history or its current practice. The laudable desire to serve as many people as possible thereby fell into the trap that had bedeviled NPR programmers right from the start: if public radio had to be *different* in order to fulfill radio's creative potential, how could NPR also be *popular*, in order to disseminate that potential to as wide a public as possible? Bennet — and the majority of other public radio managers in the eighties — overlooked this contradiction or simply didn't believe it existed. The creative radio experiments of the past decade were dismissed as "precious, self-indulgent, and cutesy" — or simply "old-fashioned."[16] Public radio programmers — in Washington and then at the local level — turned increasingly to professional pollsters and media surveys to discover how Americans used radio so that NPR could better serve their needs and attract more listeners. The message came back, loud and strong: what audiences wanted was more news, quicker news, harder news.

Bennet threw his support behind those people at NPR who wanted a stronger, more traditional journalistic orientation, and by the time he left NPR in 1993, the majority of people working for NPR News had backgrounds in print journalism or came from the hard-news side of broadcasting.

NPR's renewed concern with ratings and its decisive shift toward hard news under Bennet's administration were not simply the product of internal discussion and review in Washington following the events of 1983. They came about in large measure due to a change in the essential power structure within public radio nationally. Part of the reason for Mankiewicz's fall lay in moves he had made to make NPR more independent of cuts in government funding. His Project Independence had envisioned that NPR would operate without any federal support by 1987. Bennet's administration took a different tack toward the problem of federal funding. To insulate itself as much as possible

---

[16] According to Mary Collins, Bennet still finds "nostalgia for the old style" of radio programs at NPR "rather ridiculous." Collins, p. 94.

from potential political tinkering from Capitol Hill, NPR supported a change in how the Corporation for Public Broadcasting funneled federal money to public radio: CPB would cease to give any funds directly to National Public Radio. Instead, *all* of its support would go to local stations, which would then finance NPR through increased yearly membership fees. So today NPR receives virtually no direct subsidy from taxpayers; almost all public moneys go straight to local public stations. While this change has offered some measure of protection from Washington politics, it has left NPR more dependent on the good will of local stations — and its national programming decisions are more susceptible to pressures from local programming directors. In the seventies, NPR was an organization that produced programs for broadcast by its member stations. By the end of the eighties, NPR was a programming service owned by local public radio stations.

NPR continues to exercise its own professional judgment as much as it can; the organization is far from a rubber stamp carrying out the wishes of local station managers. For example, for many years most local stations have been trying to get *All Things Considered* to break itself up into segments like *Morning Edition*. Strong objections by the show's producers, supported by the vice president in charge of news, Bill Buzenberg, have consistently staved off this change. Some stations would like NPR to offer an all-news-all-the-time service and become something like a radio CNN. This, too, has been strenuously resisted (even though, in late 1993, NPR did install a microphone in its newsroom so that it can now feed to local stations any breaking news stories with just a few moments notice).

Yet over the past decade the needs of local stations have decisively changed what public radio audiences hear over the air, and just as the style of local television news has peculated upward to shape how the commercial networks present their evening newscasts, so has the changed style of local public radio influenced aspects of NPR's basic sound.

During the eighties, the relaxation of Federal Communication Commission rules about the language and length of underwriting credits opened up vast new potential for funding to public radio stations, increasingly strapped for money. But the sound of public radio was being forever altered. By 1994 "taking care of business" might consume as much as three or four minutes out of every half hour on some local stations. It's instructive to remember that commercial television news broadcasts typically have twenty-two minutes of news and seven minutes of commercials. Furthermore, the distinction between *underwrit-*

ing and *sponsorship* was becoming increasingly blurred. Originally, public broadcasting offered businesses a chance to associate themselves with a public service and build goodwill among potential customers by helping to pay the costs of particular programming. The underwriting credit was designed to announce this financial connection — period. But once the FCC began allowing some identification of the products or services supplied by the business underwriter, the door was opened for credits to start sounding more and more like advertisements, especially when stations began substituting the phrase "brought to you by" or even "sponsored by," instead of keeping to the original language "is made possible by a grant from." The change in wording is significant, because it confuses the different *purposes* between sponsor's messages in the commercial media and underwriting announcements in noncommercial broadcasting.

For its part, during the eighties, NPR's news programs began including underwriting credits, at first merely identifying grant authorities that were funding various kinds of special coverage or special projects. By the nineties, these "funders" were being squeezed into thirty-second spots, spoken at an extraordinarily rapid pace by the ex-director of specialized audience programming, Frank Tavares. Frank's machine-gun delivery somehow manages not to sound like a hard sell, even though he's clearly working in the tradition of such thoroughly commercial voices as the Veg-O-Matic announcer and a thousand used-car ads on late-night television. At first NPR only included funders on the half-hour, though a couple of years ago it started throwing in a ten-second credit at the conclusion of some of its newscasts — which means, effectively, in the middle of *Morning Edition* and *All Things Considered.*

Many people who work in public radio, particularly at the local level, bristle at criticism of "the business" that keeps them on the air. People who object are thought to be hopelessly idealistic or too concerned about "aesthetics." If public radio is to survive, surely it must raise adequate funding; furthermore, listeners do not mind the occasional breaks for underwriting credits, as the interruptions are far less irritating than those on commercial broadcasts. This eminently practical point of view ignores the long-term effects of these "noncommercial commercials" on the listening habits of the public radio audience. For the first decade of its existence, NPR tried to get listeners to pay closer attention than they ever had before to what they heard on the radio. Producers on public radio — either implicitly or explicitly — knew they had to change the habits of their audience, if only just a little, in order to broadcast the kinds of programs that realized the full promise of radio. As NPR enters its third decade, more and more of the public radio air is being filled with dull, lifeless moments from which listeners disconnect — just as they do when listening to commercial broadcasting. Increasingly, the public radio audience is being allowed to listen with half an ear, which is to say, it is being allowed to return to the very habits that permitted the commercial networks to kill off creative radio in this country in the first place several decades ago.

Furthermore, though sponsorship plays an increasingly large part in public radio's financing, the most stable source of a station's revenue remains individual contributions from station listeners: the membership rolls. Since surveys can show that donations to a station are directly related to (a) size of audience and (b) *faithfulness* of that audience, local stations will start to think a great deal about their ratings. They will want to carry only programs that can "pay their own way" — that will generate income from listeners. They will therefore pressure NPR for programs which their audiences *are used* to, with which they are *familiar*, and which fulfill clearly perceived needs — such as hard news, weather, and traffic. Shows that are more difficult to listen to or that might surprise listeners with their quirkiness and unpredictability tend to be excluded from such lists.

Many people in public radio — at the local as well as the national level — articulate their fears of all this "creeping commercialization," this movement toward a lowest common denominator in programming form and content. Some station managers, such as Joe Gwathmey, continue to air programs that may not be widely popular because they feel this is part of public radio's reason for being. Some stations, like WGBH in Boston, continue to go against the advice of media experts and refuse to adopt a *single format*, demonstrably the best way to increase audience and increase revenues. WGBH used to plug its quirkiness on the air, celebrating itself as "a world of choice." Meanwhile, Boston is home to one of the biggest success stories in public radio, along one scale of measurement at least. WBUR — which broadcasts mostly news and talk — receives the top ratings of any FM station in its market, which include several dozen commercial stations. WBUR leapfrogged into the lead shortly after it dropped its old-style eclectic programming and went with essentially a single format.

Local stations have always been more susceptible to marketplace pressures than people in Washington since they come in daily contact with their listeners and with their payrolls and expense sheets. Local station managers do not always have — they cannot always *afford* to have — the driving idealistic fervor that may propel some decision-makers (and producers) working at the center. Yet before the mid-eighties, National Public Radio in Washington strongly advocated an approach to public broadcasting that served either as a model, a gadfly, or an irritant to local stations, depending upon the perspective of the particular organization. After 1983 the kind of leadership NPR offered the public radio system began to change. Financial power became more decentralized, and so did influence on programming content. To over-simplify a complex picture, it could be argued that once Doug Bennet and others at NPR announced the goal of doubling NPR's audience within five years and thereby affirmed the goal of increasing listenership as a valid and noble purpose for public radio, the genie that some have called "creeping commercialism" popped out of its bottle and made a home for itself in public radio's air. The genie is subtle and friendly and seems able to grant more than just three wishes.

It does not appear that this particular spirit will be soon exorcised.

The New York Times of the Air?

By the mid-nineties, NPR had become a highly successful organization by many measures. Its audience had been growing at a rapid clip, its programming continued to win journalistic accolades. Yet within the hallways of NPR, discussion and debate continued about the present and future direction of the twenty-year-old organization — most particularly over the role that *sound* should play when reporters on the radio tell their stories. NPR's current management echoes the clear drift away from the perspectives of the older, looser days of public radio.

John Dinges, who was manager of daily news operations at NPR during the last couple of years at 2025 M Street, worked mostly in print before coming to NPR in 1985. His perspective on radio journalism might be taken as a logical extension of forces that were set in motion by the creation of *Morning Edition*. A dark-haired, long-faced man with a small droopy moustache and soft brown eyes, John speaks slowly and quietly, choosing his words carefully. But a gentle smile will often break through his reserve and his earnest eyes will sparkle with amusement or enthusiasm.

"I come at this job from a journalistic perspective," John says. "I don't really distinguish NPR as radio from NPR as journalism . . . any more than I would say that Ed Murrow was a great *radio* journalist. He was a great journalist. He's among the pantheon of great American journalists. The fact that he was a radio journalist and then was in television is not significant — he was great in whatever medium he chose.

"And I like to think that NPR has developed within that tradition, which is to grapple with the task of *reporting*. All the debates over advocacy versus objectivity that went on in all of American journalism were played out at NPR, because the aspiration for what we were trying to accomplish was always very high."

John is convinced that the great increase in NPR's audience in recent years has been caused by what he calls an improvement in the quality of NPR's journalism. He does not share the idea that NPR in any way has to "train" an audience to listen to a particular kind of radio. "I think what we've been doing the past few years has been *attracting* listeners to our kind of radio, not *educating* them to like our kind of radio," John says. "I think people are 'coming home' to NPR. All of a sudden they discover it on the dial, and they say, 'Oh, my God, where have you *been* all my life?' They were always ready to listen to this kind of stuff — they just didn't know where it was."

John leans forward in his chair and picks his words slowly. "Of course, some people here don't like us to talk about the size of our audience. They think it makes us somehow commercial. We have people around here who say we're too big because we are attracting close to ten million, now, in overall listenership," John laughs. "Now five million of those people won't listen to long, elaborate pieces anymore — so folks here who want to make those pieces say we're watering down our product, we're lowering the common denominator. As somebody who was never a great fan of that kind of old-fashioned stuff, I'd say that we haven't attracted those new five million by lowering our standards. We've attracted them by giving them a better journalistic product, something that meets their perceived needs better than what we did before. And it's not just accidental. We've stepped into a vacuum left by newspapers and television across the country. They have lowered their standards and given people less quality journalism. I mean, if TV were providing people with fantastic, intelligent coverage, we probably wouldn't be as successful as we are. Because if people had their druthers, they'd probably prefer to watch television — it's more accessible, it's all over the place. I mean they have a hundred times the budget that we do, you know." John's face darkens. "They could wipe us off the map if they wanted to! But they have chosen not to do the kind of journalism we have chosen to."

John sits back in his chair and his eyes become softer. "I'm overstating my case a little to make a point: I'm not sure how much TV could really compete directly for the audience we now have. Our listeners are loyal. There are a lot of variables, and I'm talking about a pretty hypothetical situation. All I want to say is that I am struck by the fact that *we* have *grown* as television and local newspapers have been perceived as *declining*, all around the country. Remember, our success is in not just the major urban areas, but it's in middle America, geographically, in small towns.

"My personal image — which could be inaccurate, but it's my image, based on who calls me up when I've been on various radio call-in shows — my impression is that our 'average listener' is the Methodist minister in a town of 3,500 in northwest Iowa, or the English teacher, or the town businessman. NPR provides the best news that these people are getting. They are starved for a high level of intellectual give and take, and they're not finding it on commercial television. These are the people that watch C-SPAN. They watch *MacNeil-Lehrer* and *Washington Week in Review* on public television."

John makes a small gesture with his hands and laughs. "I mean, *nobody* in Washington watches *Washington Week!* Or at least people here don't go around discussing it. But when I go out in the midwest, people are always talking about *Washington Week in Review*. And these are the people who are listening, regularly, to *Morning Edition* and *All Things Considered*. These are people who are relying on the high quality of journalism here at NPR."

Alex Chadwick's work as a reporter, producer, and host at NPR has often combined the kind of hard news journalism discussed by John Dinges with the softer, more evocative pieces associated with the older style of NPR. A good example might be his reporting from Czechoslovakia during the fall of communism, which won him an Overseas Press Club award. In addition to the straight-ahead news coverage he provided from Prague, Alex also spent many hours collecting tape among students who were organizing themselves to help precipitate the bloodless revolution. Eventually Alex assembled an eighteen-minute story — filled with aural scene-painting — which brought listeners inside the endless, exhausting student meetings and then told the story of the dramatic moment (announced over the radio of a taxi cab) when the hard-line government fell. Alex also captured the thrilling sound in Wenceslas Square when the crowd jingled hundreds of keys to symbolize the opening of the door to democracy.

Alex shares Jay Kernis's feelings about the latent power of radio in general, and NPR in particular, to do more than duplicate the front page of a newspaper — and to cover stories in a unique way. "I believe that the radio audience wants to know about *the world*, not just the *news* of the world," he says. "Our audience is like us. They are curious people — that's one reason they listen to NPR. They, and we, want to know about the war in Bosnia, certainly. We want to know about the economy. But we also want to know why people are lonely. Why people are going bowling more — or not going bowling more. Why green is the most popular color for a balloon, if it is. We want to know who thought up the idea of striped toothpaste. This is what makes life interesting."

Alex Chadwick might be described as the Charles Kuralt of NPR. In his middle forties, of medium height, and with a receding hairline above his wire-rimmed glasses, Alex exhibits a tendency toward the bulges of middle age, even though he is an enthusiastic, intramural basketball player, like so many of his generation at NPR. Alex's voice — his on-air presence — shares some of the quiet but sophisticated folksiness that Kuralt exhibits on television. Most significantly, though, Alex is regarded by just about all his colleagues as the best *writer* at NPR. If Jay begins his thinking about radio with *sound*, Alex starts with *words*. To him, radio is a special medium for language: "At NPR, we have the opportunity to be writers . . . I don't think very many people think about this, but we have the opportunity to be writers who can talk about *anything* — anything that's kind of interesting or curious or that people can respond to and get something out of. Of course, we are writers who use sound to help us tell our stories — sometimes the sound enhances our words, sometimes it substitutes for words.

"I'm always trying to tell stories — I think people like to hear stories. I know I like to write them." He laughs, then smiles, with a slightly distracted look behind his spectacles.

Bob Ferrante admires Alex Chadwick's work as much as does Alex's old friend and colleague Jay Kernis, though Bob admires it in a different way and in a different context. Bob has been producer of *Morning Edition* during the period when its listenership has climbed from three and a half million to about seven million people weekly. Bob and most of the managers at NPR credit this expanding audience to a shift in emphasis toward hard news — and a conscious move away from the sound-oriented aesthetics articulated by Jay Kernis. In fact Bob Ferrante's ruddy face gets even ruddier whenever the discussion turns to "sound" and "radio production." "These people who argue that great radio production is great radio," he says, "in my opinion, are full of shit. We're not *Masterpiece Theatre*. Good writing is better than good radio production. That's all it takes. Many of the people who complain about the fact that we have so many acts and tracks pieces can't write, and think that by fooling around with pieces of equipment, by adding 'background sounds,' they will achieve the same effect as good writing. They won't.

"Now, Alex is a master storyteller. Alex writes beautifully, and uses the pauses, uses sound — the natural sound — as a *sentence* to go from here to there. That's what sound is — that's a place for sound. Alex can do an emotional piece. Alex can elevate human emotion, paint the picture for you. That's what he does beautifully. That's why, no, we can never get enough pieces from him. But Alex would never just indulge himself in big sound production — a lot of sound for the sake of sound. That's not his shtick.

"Some of the most effective radio has no production at all. What big production was necessary when Nixon resigned? The wise reporter — the great reporter — will just write, 'President Nixon resigned today.' What production do you need? It says it all, in four words."

While the debate between "radio people" and "news people" often becomes polarized, upon reflection many at NPR agree that these different approaches are not necessarily mutually exclusive. Hardly anyone would disagree that the absolute best radio that NPR produces mixes great reporting and great production. Tom Gjelten's work from the former Yugoslavia, reports from Africa filed by Daniel Zwerdling, the stories from the Gulf War produced by Scott Simon, Neal Conan, and Deborah Amos — all are given as examples of this ideal interweaving of sound and story.

And the apparently hard-news-nosed Bob Ferrante is also an impassioned supporter of lighter pieces on *Morning Edition,* or what he calls, in his inimitable Boston accent, "ahhnaments." Bob says that ornaments are vital to the program: "They add spice — they keep us interesting and break up the unremitting rhythm of hard news, hard news, hard news. You can't just live on meat and potatoes — protein and carbohydrates — right? You have to eat a well-balanced meal, including dessert."

In addition to Alex Chadwick, Bob is particularly fond of Ira Glass, a young producer, barely into his thirties, who started working at NPR in 1979, when he was eighteen. Ira felt the influence of sound-oriented producers like Jay Kernis and particularly Keith Talbot, who during that time was one of the most unconventional — even flaky — producers at NPR. Ira has done a wide range of work for NPR — he even helped cover the 1992 election campaign — but he most enjoys producing offbeat pieces that mix music and sound with the voices of people telling stories. He once did a series of six- and seven-minute pieces on the biggest *lies* that people have ever told. (Ira often has to produce these reports on his own time, working late into the evening, editing and mixing.) Ira explains that for a time Bob Ferrante was the only producer on the daily programs who would *always* take his pieces. "I remember playing the first two segments of 'Liars' for just about every person on *All Things Considered*," Ira explains in his thick Baltimore accent. "*Every one* of them turned them down. And these were friends of mine, people I'd worked with. I was an associate producer on *ATC* for a long time. But they just couldn't get it — they couldn't comprehend what was going on in these pieces. 'What's the point?' they said. 'Why should we listen to this? What's it trying to tell me?'

"Essentially, I think some of them were nervous about trying something new. And they've become too obsessed with 'just covering the news' — they do fewer and fewer pieces that are essentially for pleasure . . . things that amuse us.

"Now, I'm not sure Bob Ferrante always understands what I'm doing, but then, *I* don't always understand what I'm doing." Ira laughs. "But Bob has an old broadcasting view of how you put together a radio show. He believes that his radio show can't just be news, news, news. People need something else. Ferrante will say to me, '*Ira! I want you to give me some ahhnaments!*' So that's what I do. I mean, I feel like *Morning Edition* has really been a safe haven for me — it's really been my savior."[17]

·   ·   ·

----

[17] Times and tastes change. In the fall of 1993, Ira contracted with *ATC* to do a year-long series of extended reports on life inside a Chicago high school. Ira's stories were marvelous mixes of sound and narration that evoked the texture of teenage life in an inner-city school.

While Bob Ferrante may like to serve up some variety on *Morning Edition*, the fact remains that he regards as dessert much of what Jay Kernis would regard as the creative core of radio. Greg Smith puts his criticism of NPR's current direction this way: "Let's face it: *Morning Edition* — like so much of NPR programming — has become very *safe*. I think it's partly that everyone's playing it safe for the stations. You know it's ironic that it was Frank Mankiewicz's thinking that got *Morning Edition* on the air. 'Let's get out there, let's take some chances,' was his approach. I think Frank is rightly credited for letting people stretch out a little bit, encouraging people to try anything and see how it goes. Then in 1983 we got the wake-up call — and suddenly we were borrowing Teletype-machine paper from CBS across the street. We literally had to shut down some of the wire machines here because we couldn't afford enough paper. We hit the bottom line — and a lot happened afterwards. But basically NPR is now in the lap of the member stations. It all comes down to accountability. Now we are accountable to them, and they are accountable to their audience. Therefore *Morning Edition* has to be more 'accessible' to a larger group of people. There's the problem — well, *I* call it a problem. Because it can lead to blandness and the lowest common denominator in programming.

"Look. We used to be on the cutting edge of radio — we were covering the news, but we were also doing unusual, interesting things. Then we went through the meat grinder, and when we came out the other end, the member stations started realizing *they* could now say things like, 'We don't want this type of program' or 'We want *Morning Edition* to do this.' They said something, and NPR, the national network, would have to listen. The problem here is one of balance: the point of view of stations can sometimes be exclusively that a program must appeal to as wide an audience as possible. And you're not talking just about an individual station looking at their audience, but you're talking about all the member stations together looking at all the audiences. And if you're talking about everybody's audience research, everybody's audience share and what will appeal to them, you wind up with very white bread — bland, safe programs. Which is what *Morning Edition* sometimes becomes. You have to put on programming that anybody can relate to — that a child can relate to."

Greg Smith describes an old radio piece that he and a group of producers had been listening to earlier in the day. Jay Allison, an independent producer with a strong imaginative flair, had once met a woman who carried on conversations with her horse. Jay interviewed the woman and then reproduced, on tape, the words of the "horse" as *Jay* imagined them. The story was a bit off-the-wall, a bit confusing, but very amusing. It ran on *All Things Considered* at least ten years ago.

"If you took Jay Allison's piece," Greg explains, "and tested it in a focus group, which everybody likes to do these days (it would have to test in regional focus groups around the country and then individual focus groups) . . . if you shopped that piece around, it would *never* go *anywhere* today — it would never be broadcast. And I think the reason is because of the direct feedback that member stations now give the national network. They are calling the shots — and they are more cautious. They have made NPR a safer network.

"I mean it's been interesting to pop in and out of here over the past few years. I can see the difference, not just on *Morning Edition* but on all the shows. People don't want to take the chance to really stretch out. And I think that's disappointing."

Greg takes it as symbolic of the "new NPR" that Bob Edwards no longer gets as involved in produced pieces on *Morning Edition* as he used to — that he no longer attends morning meetings or leaves the building to do reporting. Greg continues to have nothing but admiration for Bob's talents as a host — and his endurance on the air. But he gets the feeling that neither Bob nor the *Morning Edition* producers are pushing against the envelope of creative radio as much as they did in the past.

Yet for all the controversy within NPR, the revolutionary *aural* potential will remain always within NPR's grasp — waiting to be used — because it is an ingredient of all radio, forever separating the medium of sound from certain dominant trends in American culture. And as much as most of NPR news programming may try to "go mainstream," the anarchic, unpredictable magic that lurks within the creativity of radio will keep popping up so long as there is anyone around the network who is sensitive to *the sound* as well as the story. You can see this continuing possibility in the personalities of certain public radio broadcasters and staff members — from reporters and producers through to technicians and engineers — who understand the special qualities of the sound medium. On-the-air personalities like Garrison Keillor, Terry Gross, and Tom and Ray Magliozzi (Click and Clack of the immensely popular program *Car Talk*); hosts and reporters like Scott Simon, Ira Glass, Margo Adler, and Alice Furlaud; and a number of men and women who work behind the scenes — all are a little unusual, a bit to one side of the conventional — a tad eccentric. In part this may be because they are still using their ears while the rest of the culture is not, but, in fact, by its very nature, the medium of radio has always rewarded strands of individuality and quirkiness. The history of radio is filled with examples of nonconformist characters, from comedians like Bob and Ray and Jean Shepherd to talk-show hosts like Long John Nebel, from an interviewer like Studs Terkel to a "newscaster" like Paul Harvey (who for many years was the single most popular radio personality in America).

It is well to remember that even the legendary Edward R. Murrow, who helped define broadcast journalism and is thought of today as one of the pillars of responsibility and steadiness, started his work in radio on the fringes of conventionality. When Murrow stood on a London rooftop, "feeling rather large and lonesome," he was not following the rules of an established form of communication — he was not playing it safe and giving the audience what they knew they wanted to hear. He was breaking new ground and investigating the potential of the new medium. Like other radio pioneers, he followed his ears. The story goes that he once draped a microphone over the edge of the roof to get the sound of bombs falling. He also learned to explore the possibilities of his voice, even though like so many of the best radio reporters after him, Murrow thought of himself as a *listener* and a *writer* before he thought of himself as a *speaker*.

While Murrow was eventually embraced by the commercial broadcasting establishment, a good deal of this veneration developed after he had left CBS in 1961.[18] Though many in Murrow's audience appreciated his talents, CBS executives on the whole had a dimmer view of him, especially toward the end of his career. The organization came to regard Murrow as a bit of a crank — an idealistic gadfly who was out of place in the increasingly commercialized world of American broadcasting.

Murrow expressed deep affection for radio, calling it "that most satisfying and rewarding instrument." His greatest legacy to the sound medium may be a combination of his ear for language, his intuitive sense for oral storytelling, and his boldness in experimenting with the possibilities of the new medium. What better foundation upon which to construct a truly alternative broadcast organization like National Public Radio?

---

[18] Murrow was asked by President Kennedy to head up the United States Information Agency. His tenure there was tragically brief, for within a short time he was diagnosed with lung cancer. Murrow died in 1965.

PROGRAM TWO

Weekday Afternoons

Musical Chairs

If *Morning Edition* is the workhorse of NPR programs, then *All Things Considered* might be viewed as the thoroughbred of the public radio stables. Proud, headstrong, brazen, willful — capable of achieving towering success and crashing failure — *All Things Considered* was the first hit show that NPR produced, winning much critical and audience acclaim during its early years. It's not an exaggeration to say that *All Things Considered* was chiefly responsible for making an audience of several million people aware of National Public Radio. *ATC* also helped define an identity for NPR.

Joe Gwathmey explains that *All Things Considered* initially represented, in part, "the conversion from dull, boring, educational radio" to the kind of creative and innovative medium that was part of NPR's original mission. "Subjects which traditionally would have been approached on educational radio using a half-hour panel discussion were now treated with some artful writing and some imaginative recording in the field," Joe remembers. "The stories were very wide-ranging — news-oriented, certainly, but not news-driven. We assumed that our listeners were curious about a lot of things."

For the first fourteen years of its existence, the "curiosity" that drove *All Things Considered* became personified in its longest-serving host,

Susan Stamberg. A dynamic, quirky, and thoroughly "radio" personality — with a large ego but an even larger sense of professionalism — Susan's warm, chummy, easily recognizable voice reached out over the airwaves like a pair of broad arms and enveloped listeners in an almost tangible embrace. (Barry Gordemer says of Susan's voice: "There are times when you feel like you want to move closer to the radio to hear what she's saying — she draws you in almost in a *physical* sense. It's a strength — a kind of remarkable personality strength — that comes through her voice.")

As *All Things Considered* and NPR struggled to define an identity with a public that had fallen out of the habit of listening to radio, Susan Stamberg's distinctive on-the-air style came to epitomize the panache, the chutzpah, the literateness of the young organization. Susan had become an *ATC* host ten months after the program first went on the air, joining Mike Waters, already a veteran radio broadcaster. Susan was fascinated by the art of conversation and by the medium of sound. She exploited her natural gift of gab and added to it a developing aural sensitivity, along with the elusive air of authority that finally makes or breaks a radio host. While most listeners loved Susan, a few couldn't abide her strong radio presence. Others flipped back and forth in their opinion, feeling about Susan as they might about an eccentric aunt — a "character" who could be endearing one day and irritating another. But whatever emotions Susan Stamberg provoked, the fact was that she was getting many listeners to pay attention to NPR in general and to *All Things Considered* in particular. As longtime staffer John Ydstie puts it, "In the early days of NPR, Susan probably did more than any single individual to create an audience for public radio. For that reason alone, we all owe her a tremendous debt of gratitude."

Though Susan Stamberg brought a great deal to *All Things Considered*, the program was always far more than a showcase for one talent. Many fine hosts shared the microphones with Susan from 1971 to 1986, including Bob Edwards, Sanford Unger (a distinguished print journalist, now an equally distinguished academician), and Noah Adams. Each played a crucial role in the evolving shape of *All Things Considered*, as did the many producers and reporters who together were constructing NPR's distinctive form of radio.

ATC's unique style during those early days — and the pressures that later developed to change it — can be illustrated emblematically by following the evolution of the program's opening and closing, the way hosts greeted listeners at five o'clock and signed off at six-thirty. The original *ATC* theme was recorded on an old-fashioned synthesizer and was referred to by the production team as the *"dink dink dinks."* Though many people felt affection for the perky jingle-jangle, the synthesized theme sounded less polished (and more eccentric?) than the lush music that *Morning Edition* used when it went on the air in 1979. Shortly thereafter, *All Things Considered*'s theme was rerecorded with a piano (or, to be accurate, a synthesizer that reproduced a piano very realistically) and brass instruments, a far less quirky sound.

The original *ATC* opening also included a *greeting* from the hosts, referred to as "the hello." The show started with a few *dink dink dinks,* and then Bob Edwards and Susan Stamberg, for example, would say:

> BOB: Good evening. From National Public Radio in Washington, I'm Bob Edwards.
> SUSAN: And I'm Susan Stamberg, with *All Things Considered.*

The theme swelled up for several seconds, and then the hosts returned and gave a partial billboard for the entire program, that is, they listed some of the stories to be broadcast in the next ninety minutes. They also included a snippet of tape — a "teaser" — from an upcoming story. The *ATC* Open could last as long as a minute and a half and it concluded with the words "That . . . *and more* . . . tonight, on *All Things Considered.*" The scripting implied that a good deal was going to happen on the program: stay tuned and be surprised.

In the original format, *ATC* began its Close somewhere around six twenty-eight, following the final piece, with these words from one of the hosts: "And for this evening, that's *All Things Considered.*" Theme music and credits followed, leading to the final host identifications and SOC (standard outcue): "This is NPR, National Public Radio."

During the mid-seventies, the start of regular newscasts at one minute after the hour reduced the free-flowing feel of the *ATC* Open — suddenly the billboard and the teaser had to fit within a fifty-nine-second format. During the early to middle eighties, other changes were introduced, even though then executive producer Ted Clark and others tried to resist them. Hosts would now list only stories to be aired during the coming half-hour. Further, the billboard was to be complete — no more uncertainties or surprises as implied by the phrase "that and more." Listeners would know exactly what they were going to get during the next thirty minutes. The hosts were still saying "hello" and "good-bye," but pressure was mounting to abandon this format. Stations were becoming more flexible about when they started *All Things*

Considered (some began with the second or third half-hour) and a few local outlets were choosing to fill a *two-hour* slot with the ninety-minute show, so they were airing one of the segments twice. As a result of these scheduling decisions, some listeners heard the "good-bye" of the third half-hour and *then* heard the "hello" of the first third.

Susan Stamberg eventually went along with all the changes in format except the proposals to dump the "hello" and the "good-bye." Susan felt strongly that altering the style of the Open and Close in this manner would add a layer of distance between *ATC* hosts and their listeners. "Here was my rationale for keeping the greeting," Susan remembers, "and I can put it very simply: it was how I was raised! When you're introduced to someone, you say 'Hello,' and when you leave, you say 'Good-bye.' They wanted us to quit saying it. But Noah [Adams] and I fought it. Then I left the program, and soon after Noah did, too . . . for a while. (He came back a couple of years later.) And that's when they disbanded the greeting, because no one else understood that concept. And so now you can't say 'hello' and you can't say 'good-bye' on that program. And to me, that makes no sense."

In 1986 Susan finally left *ATC*, and shortly afterwards a new opening was implemented. The show now started with a few seconds of music and then one of the hosts read a news tease: "Congress nears a vote on the president's budget, on *All Things Considered*, from National Public Radio." The theme music returned, after which the hosts introduced themselves and gave a rundown of stories coming up in the next half-hour. The new conclusion of the show represented a curious compromise. Hosts no longer began the Close: "And for this evening, that's *All Things Considered* . . ." Instead, the show never really *ended*. After the final story, one of the hosts read the credits and then said: "It's *All Things Considered*." Barely grammatical, the phrase did not always flow smoothly off the tongue, and hosts had to use considerable skill to mask the awkwardness. "This is Noah Adams. It's *All Things Considered*." The most natural cadence here might be, "This is Noah Adams and you're listening to *All Things Considered*," or simply, ". . . and this is *All Things Considered*." But both of these alternatives imply that the program will continue. The favored construction creates a vagueness, an uncertainty — the show might be winding up or it might keep going. And this imprecision was exactly what local station managers wanted.

The loss of the "hello, good-bye" format signified a new phase in the history of *All Things Considered*. The revised Open and Close allowed stations more flexibility, but, in quiet yet important ways, it also altered the *feeling* of the program. *ATC* had become a bit more of a service, like *Morning Edition*, and a little less of a program that started and stopped at a specific moment.

The general direction of *All Things Considered* over the next several years can be traced — with only a touch of distortion — in the new lineup of hosts for the show.

The choice of Robert Siegel as a successor to Susan Stamberg signaled the changes in store for *ATC*. A veteran NPR staffer, Robert, like Neal Conan, has held an astonishing variety of posts in the organization, from editorial to reportorial to administrative. He started as a newscaster in 1976, became senior editor of *All Things Considered*, went to London to operate NPR's bureau for four years, and was news director in Washington before he took over the hosting assignment on *ATC*. Robert has a deep love for the radio medium, an attraction that began during his childhood in New York City. As one of the old-timers on the NPR staff, Robert was exposed to all the discovery and experimentation of the early years. (He recalls showing his friend Robert Krulwich how to fiddle with a tape recorder to create his famous "mice" voices.) But Robert was also actively involved in the changes during the eighties that moved NPR toward harder news and a more sober approach to reporting. And while Robert believes that sound has an important role to play in radio, he argues strongly that its proper function is to supplement and to enhance the words of reporters and hosts.

"I've always had certain problems with the notion that 'sound' on the radio can be an aesthetic experience in itself," Robert explains. "I know of hardly anyone who returns to listen to a speech production in the way that they go back and listen to the same piece of music they like. There's almost nothing we'll ever do, in any sound production, in any news broadcast or documentary, that will compete for an instant with a Beethoven symphony, for example. Is there something inherently stirring and beautiful, you know, in a recording of the sound of leaves crunching underfoot when you're walking through the forest? No. Not to my ear.

"Sounds make our job as storytellers and reporters easier, and they can enhance our work," Robert continues. "They permit you in the audience to listen to something for a length of time that you wouldn't otherwise. They also give you variety. But a lot of the German, highly sound-oriented stuff strikes me as ultimately pointless. I'd call it a *pseudo-experiential* use of the medium, where, you know, the sound of a wrestling match — perfect and intense, beautifully edited, copy melded to sound — is supposed to convey to you the *experience* of that wrestling match. I think this is bogus. I much prefer an *informational* use of the medium, where sounds are used to abet an ulterior aim, which is to inform and to tell a story.

"I'm reminded of a parallel in television: take the person who sits and watches the smoke rising out of the compound in Waco, Texas, for an hour, mesmerized by the fact that this is actually happening *right now:* 'I'm seeing this, people are burning in this building, and I am watching it.' The television journalism that ultimately only offers you the instantaneous picture of the event — journalism that is satisfied with holding up a camera and presenting 'live' images of an experience — is giving you, in fact, only a one- or two-dimensional approximation of an event. We are ultimately not learning very much at all. There's no information here."

Robert Siegel was NPR's news director from 1983 to 1987 and set as his strategic aim the addition of hourly newscasts throughout the day and the expansion of newsmagazine programs so that they would be broadcast seven days a week, mornings and evenings. As a former editor himself, he embraced the enlarging of the editorial desk system and supported the hiring of many print reporters to beef up the journalistic side of NPR. Furthermore, Robert's on-air presence exuded a kind of reportorial savvy and intellectual rigor, well suited to a more news-oriented broadcast.

Robert was thus an ideal choice to host *All Things Considered* as the program shifted its orientation away from the lighter, more eclectic format of the past. For Robert, public radio is preeminently a medium of ideas — of language and conversation. Robert encouraged the improved coverage of breaking news on *All Things Considered* and the development of something called "the spindown" — a sequence of reports on a major story that begins with a reporter's explanation of the latest news; continues with a two-way (or three-way conversation) with a host that examines an aspect of the story in greater depth; and concludes, characteristically, with a commentary, often from veteran news analyst Daniel Schorr.

The spindown has become a familiar formula on *All Things Considered*, praised by many for providing depth and reflection on breaking news, criticized by a few as having become rigid and predictable (in some quarters, the spindown has become the stuff of parodies about NPR).

Robert Siegel's on-air presence captures perfectly his particular approach to radio news. His voice crackles with a certain formal friendliness and seriousness of purpose. Yet though his questioning of guests can sometimes take on a didactic edge, over the years Robert has allowed more of his natural wit to emerge on the air. If his overall tone remains professorial, the deep enjoyment he takes in his work — and his essential good-naturedness — does communicate itself clearly to listeners and usually prevents him from seeming stuffy. The pitch of his voice, which is a throaty rather than a chesty baritone, further lightens the impression he makes on his audience.

Shortly after Susan Stamberg left *All Things Considered,* Noah Adams moved from NPR to Minnesota Public Radio, where he spent a couple of years hosting the program that replaced *A Prairie Home Companion.* Renée Montagne hosted *ATC* with Robert Siegel until 1989, when the selection of her successor again underscored the newsier approach now in favor at NPR. While the cohost for the weekend version of *All Things Considered,* Lynn Neary, seemed to be a natural choice for the daily position, the job went instead to Linda Wertheimer, longtime Washington reporter.

If the work Susan Stamberg did during the seventies as host of *ATC* had been crucial in making audiences aware of NPR, the superb reporting done by Linda — and her colleagues Cokie Roberts and Nina Totenberg — had been central in establishing NPR's credentials as a news organization. Linda joined NPR at about the same time as Susan, after a varied and somewhat frustrating career at WCBS radio in New York, where she wrote and produced pieces but never appeared on the air. Women had not yet fully broken into commercial broadcast journalism in the early seventies, but at NPR Linda soon found herself on Capitol Hill, a beat she would pursue with consummate skill and success for fifteen years. Nina joined NPR in 1975 as legal affairs correspondent, and Cokie — whose close friendship with Linda went back to college days at Wellesley — came over to public radio in 1979. "The Troika," as the three women reporters were sometimes called, became famous not simply because of their gender, but more because of the wonderful quality of their radio reporting, which turned the simple acts and tracks format into a kind of oral art.

During their years at NPR, the three women had often anchored live broadcasts of congressional hearings and presidential speeches. Linda Wertheimer, in fact, made history in 1979 when she introduced the first-ever live broadcasts of a debate from the Senate chamber during consideration of the Panama Canal Treaty. (Frank Mankiewicz's political clout had managed this particular broadcast coup.) Members of The Troika also filled in, from time to time, as hosts on both *All Things Considered* and *Morning Edition*. While Linda, Nina, and Cokie were impeccable on-air reporters and became increasingly impressive as anchors for live events, they were not quite as naturally effective as Susan Stamberg or Bob Edwards — or Lynn Neary for that matter — when they took on the role of *show host*. A reporter does not need to vary her delivery as much as a host. Where a no-nonsense, straightforward connection to the audience works fine when you have the responsibility of telling a single story, a host's role is to bring an audience along on a journey through a number of different kinds of pieces, and a host's voice must speak with equal effectiveness in a variety of moods and tones. Most intangibly, the kind of aural *authority* required in a host is different from that needed by a reporter. "Why should I be listening to this person?" is a question that a host must continually answer, on a level beyond logic and beyond language.

Hosting is not so arcane an art that it cannot be learned, though the great hosts do seem to have some innate talents or instincts that are difficult to engender. Though some people at NPR questioned how ultimately effective Linda Wertheimer would be as an *ATC* host, no one doubted her ability to adapt effectively to her new role. And NPR managers assumed that the audience's familiarity with Linda as a reporter would enhance her on-air presence and authority — and also help sustain the show's popularity.

Though she had a varied background in radio news, Lynn Neary had not done the extensive hard-news reporting pursued by Linda, Nina, and Cokie. Lynn had worked closely with Alex Chadwick on *Weekend ATC* and shared his orientation toward sound production as well as some of his curiosity for unusual subjects like the origins of striped toothpaste. The choice of *All Things Considered* host in 1989 provoked a good bit of office politics and even hit the pages of some newspapers. Press accounts of the brouhaha (which discussed alleged pressure brought to bear on NPR president Doug Bennet by members of The Troika in favor of one of their own) did not address the deeper implications of the events for the future of public radio. Due to whatever constellation of immediate circumstances, Linda Wertheimer, a stellar news reporter and a solid host with little background in creative sound production, was chosen over Lynn Neary, a sound-oriented producer and reporter with considerable versatility as a host but less obvious credentials as a hard-news journalist. In historical hindsight (a perspective with plenty of inherent biases in itself), the surprising element of the 1989 decision may not be that Linda was chosen as *ATC* host but that Lynn should have been considered seriously for the position in the first place.[1]

In 1989 Garrison Keillor returned to Minnesota Public Radio and Noah Adams showed up back at NPR. He was given his old job as host of *All Things Considered*, and a new format of rotating hosts was created, with Robert, Linda, and Noah playing musical chairs from night to night and week to week. The new approach to hosting fit the new reportorial focus of the program so well that it's hard to believe it evolved solely by accident. The rotation meant that hosts could more often take trips and do reporting from the field — and travel they did: Robert from Israel to Quebec, Noah from Bosnia to Alaska, Linda from Oklahoma to Africa. Interestingly, the producers who accompanied the hosts on these trips tended to be *aural* producers who loved sound and who carried a torch for production styles some at NPR now considered old-fashioned, people like Art Silverman, Michael Sullivan, and Margaret Low Smith. So, while the main trunk of *ATC* grew ever more solidly "hard news," with more acts and tracks reports and more two-ways, the "host feature" side of the program developed an increasing flexibility, allowing for longer, more creatively produced pieces.

The rotating hosts plan also fit in with another long-term strategy, downplaying the extent to which particular hosts would be identified with particular shows. Some public radio managers argue that less personality is a good thing for a news service — listeners should be turning to NPR for its *content*, not for its *style of presentation*. Additionally, many local stations worry that if an audience becomes too dependent upon an individual — such as Susan Stamberg — when that broadcaster leaves the air, ratings may plummet. Yet National Public Radio

---

[1] Lynn Neary came to NPR in the spring of 1982 as a newscaster for *Morning Edition*. Previously she had been a reporter and newscaster on radio stations in North Carolina and Ohio. She covered everything from fires to school board meetings and enjoyed "that sense of being there with a tape recorder, talking to people I might not normally come in contact with." Even before she'd received much radio training, Lynn demonstrated a distinctive ear for sound. She opened her very first newscast on a small commercial station in Rocky Mount, North Carolina, with a tape of sanitation workers chanting at a strike rally.

used to distinguish itself from the rest of the American media partly in the way it embraced radio as a medium of personal quirkiness and creativity. Reducing the "cult of personality" carries a danger of creating blander, more homogenized programs . . . radio that people turn on but do not listen to with the same degree of involvement.

Of all the current hosts on National Public Radio, Noah Adams remains, in a sense, the most enigmatic. Noah possesses one of the most aurally beautiful radio voices of anyone now broadcasting on NPR. His roots go back to NPR's earliest years, and he seems solidly committed to the evocative, even the poetic, side of public radio. He also has the reputation for pursuing the human perspective on a story, whether he is reporting from the hills of West Virginia or from the battle zones of Bosnia. Yet Noah also encapsulates that quirky, eccentric side of radio: an intensely private person who is described by friends as "shy" and by some others as "misanthropic," Noah dislikes being interviewed and usually declines to be observed while broadcasting. Scott Simon quotes Noah as saying that he doesn't like to be watched because he works in a radio studio, not a public zoo (or an aquarium). A short, often rumpled figure with thinning blond hair and rimless glasses, Noah can flash a small yet winning smile at friends and then withdraw into an icy vacancy when approached by people whom he considers outsiders. But the apparent contradiction of an extremely shy person producing wonderful radio is in fact not a contradiction at all: everything about the medium of radio is at once intensely intimate and profoundly isolated. No two people will share exactly the same image of whom or what they hear on the radio, even though everyone listens to the same voices and the same sounds. There is a veiled quality to radio — though at its best, that shroud is like the curtain which in some cultures surrounds oracles who speak wisdom and insight and shared history.

People who like being seen go into television, more a medium for extroverts. Like many other people who have made the most creative use of radio, Noah Adams guards his privacy, and it may well be that a good deal of the power of his work derives from the tensions inherent in the simultaneous impulses to be heard but not seen — listened to yet not "known."

In Noah's voice lies the key to his art. "Noah's voice is unique," says Barry Gordemer. "It's so soft and resonant, very thoughtful. Noah's narrations are almost like small stanzas of poetry. He speaks in small phrases — you know, he types his scripts without punctuation. He told me once that he uses dashes and dots so that he's not forcing an interpretation on himself: he can read the words and understand them almost as he's hearing them. So his delivery becomes . . . a series of phrases . . . with a pause . . . a moment to absorb it and think about it. Another few words . . . Now think again. Noah doesn't *spoon-feed* you, which some announcers do — that feels condescending, and I start getting angry. But he uses what you might call an interactive style: it's almost as though he has eye contact with you and he's waiting to see that glint that you've understood what he said." Barry laughs. "Of course, the downside of this is that sometimes if you tune into Noah and you catch him midsentence or midphrase, you sort of wonder where he is and what he's talking about — it takes you a moment to figure it out."

While Barry Gordemer thinks that many of the changes NPR has undergone over the past ten years have been beneficial, he does miss some specifically *radio* qualities of the earlier period. In particular, one aspect of Noah as host seems to have been lost: "During the Noah and Susan era on *All Things Considered,* the hosts were much more interactive with each other. There was a definite chemistry between Noah and Susan — I'd say a lot of that came from Susan, but it's definitely part of Noah's personality, too. I worked on that show for a year, and I remember that there was an effort on the part of the production staff to write *to* them and have them play off each other. These days, sometimes it seems that the hosts could be in different parts of the world, and you just splice everything together. There's not as much interplay."

Beneath the Dinosaur

In spite of all the changes in style and content of *All Things Considered* over the years, certain aspects of production have remained constant throughout the program's history — and this consistency may explain why *ATC* is surrounded by such a thick layer of tradition, such a palpable aura of pride.

Behind the scenes, the famous *ATC* horseshoe exudes nervous energy. *All Things Considered* compresses the three *Morning Edition* shifts into a single, daylong sprint that starts at about nine-thirty in the morning and races along to the start of the program at five o'clock and beyond. Ever since the show first went on the air in May 1971, *ATC*'s ninety-minute time slot has loomed like a great maw into which generations of producers, editors, hosts, and reporters have poured an extraordinary amount of tape, toil, tears, and sweat. The pressures are enormous and have taken their toll. "*ATC* is famous for chewing up people and spitting them out," more than one NPR staffer has said. Indeed, the turnover rate for all levels of personnel, except hosts, has been extremely high, though there remains a small, dedicated core of people who have been associated with the program in one capacity or another for ten or fifteen years or more. These old-timers change jobs every so often (from editor, to producer, to executive producer, back to producer), and they take sabbaticals — but somehow they all find their way back to *ATC*'s turf.

The breakneck schedule of *All Things Considered* helps inspire a certain bravado — and even machismo — among the production staff, in spite of the presence of a large number of women. (During 1993, women held the three top production posts: executive producer, producer, and editor.) The *ATC* swagger is understandable when you consider the amount of radio production that's accomplished daily in the space of eight hours, or even less. "I mean, let's face it," explains Michael Sullivan, known as "Willie" to everyone at NPR, "when you get right down to it, the show is usually put together in *four-and-a half*-hours. You're supposed to have eight, but somehow it doesn't work out that way."

Most of the staff arrives between nine and nine forty-five. The first people on the scene find the *ATC* horseshoe in semidarkness, abandoned by the overnight foreign editor. Sunlight filters through several glass windows in the doors of offices lining the outer wall of the building. Partitions placed around the horseshoe divide the office space into a rabbit warren of cubicles filled with chairs, telephones, and tape recorders. The horseshoe itself is, in reality, an arrangement of many small and irregularly shaped tables and desks. On the inside of this hollow square, separated by yet another small tabletop, sit the *ATC* producer and editor. They each have a console tape recorder, a computer terminal, and a multiline telephone. When typing on their keyboards or talking on the phone, the producer and editor face the large white storyboard looming on the wall just a couple of feet away. Above the board, a big Favag clock impassively ticks off each discrete second of passing time.

In the light of day, the shapes draping from the ceiling above the horseshoe become clearer than they were in the darkness before dawn. A few pennants are attached to the soundproofed panels. A number of thin wires and cables descend like vines and connect with computer terminals and telephone consoles scattered throughout the *ATC* work area. The pink dinosaur mascot hangs like a three-dimensional fresco above the producer's section of the horseshoe, its arms outstretched in an awkward, childlike greeting. As staff members arrive, no one seems to notice the little animal. He's become as much a part of the natural scenery of the "electronic jungle" as the terminals, the telephones, and the tape recorders.

A range of morning newspapers has already been spread out across the backside of the horseshoe: five copies of *The New York Times*, five of *The Washington Post*, three of *USA Today*, two of *The Baltimore Sun*, one each of *The Chicago Tribune*, *The Wall Street Journal*, *The Boston Globe*, and *The Christian Science Monitor*. Early arrivals among the staff get their pick of the papers.

The *ATC* board, at the front of the horseshoe, is still covered with the previous day's show. The board is somewhat larger than *Morning Edition*'s; it is also more open and freeform, reflecting the unsegmented style of the afternoon program. Three broad columns, with no permanent subdivisions, allow the producer to write in the story lineup for each half-hour with no rigid constrictions as to length. A fourth column lists reports that are ready to be aired and pieces that are pending. Erasing the old road map is one of the first tasks performed by *ATC*'s producer when she or he arrives in the morning. But there's no fixed time when the board is then reinscribed with the tentative outline of the new program. On some days stories will be marked in before lunch, but it's not unusual to come by the *ATC* horseshoe at one o'clock and see the three show columns blank.

This particular morning, Robert Siegel walks in from the elevator at nine thirty-five. A short, slightly stocky man, balding, with a neatly trimmed but full black beard and dark-rimmed glasses, Robert is wearing a dark blue pinstriped suit and is carrying a leather briefcase. He might be a banker or a lawyer, except perhaps for the easy, relaxed way that he smiles as he strides down the corridor. There's a slight twinkle in his eyes as he greets staff members along the way to his office — a large room, neatly arranged, with ample space for guests on a couple of couches. Robert sits down in the leather swivel chair by his desk and methodically prepares for the day's work.

A few moments later, Linda Wertheimer ambles past the horseshoe wearing a straw sun hat that hides most of her face. On her shoulder she is carrying a leather bag and in her hand she holds a large cloth sack stuffed with papers and a book or two. The weight of her baggage makes her rock slightly as she strolls back toward her office, in a corner just across from Robert's. Linda's office looks slightly Pickwickian — relaxed and in pleasing disorder, with stacks of books and papers piled on every available surface. The room is dominated by a thickly upholstered easy chair, with its back to the window, into which Linda sinks when she wants to read or carry on a conversation or make telephone calls. The chair is surrounded by books, stacked up from the floor; one column forms a pedestal on which she often puts her phone.

Linda's clothing and general appearance couldn't contrast more strikingly with Robert's nattiness. Today she is wearing a burgundy-colored oversized shirt, loose-fitting khaki slacks, and a pair of well-worn, comfortable shoes. In contrast to the southern-lady sophistication of Cokie and the urban street smarts of Nina, Linda has always projected a more subdued, down-home aura, befitting her southwestern background. (She's from New Mexico.) Even when she was covering the high-pressure congressional beat, Linda generally maintained a calm naturalness in her dress and demeanor. Now that she is a host and has entered her fifties, she seems even more laid-back than ever. Her pleasant smile, blue-gray eyes, and low-key manner create an aura of easygoing friendliness and relaxed composure.

Of course beneath her southwestern calm lurks a sharp intelligence and a stony will. Linda began reporting on Washington politics at a time when both professions — journalism and government — were totally dominated by men. She could not have risen as high as she did in her field if her character had been simply that of a gentle western "ma'am."

After dropping her bags in her office, Linda returns to the horseshoe carrying a blue porcelain cup into which she pours some coffee. A number of staff members are sitting in the vicinity of the main desk drinking coffee and reading newspapers. Melissa Block, the show producer, sits, straightbacked, in her chair where, a few hours earlier, *Morning Edition*'s foreign editor had been ensconced. Melissa scans the news wires on her terminal and makes notes on a yellow pad. Her hair is dark, cut neatly at medium-length and pulled straight back from her face. She is wearing a trim beige business suit and black shoes with medium-high heels. Intent, composed, Melissa works efficiently and with a keen attentiveness to detail. She has persevered in the demanding job of producer for almost two years — a long stint by *ATC* standards. Like so many others on the program, Melissa jogs whenever she can, not only to keep fit, but to release some of the tensions that build up in the course of a workday.

Production assistants Akili Tyson and Gwen Macsai and director Marika Partridge are standing to the rear of the horseshoe in an area crammed with playback equipment — a CD player, a tape recorder (which you have to stand up to use), an FM tuner, and several sets of headphones, including one that is wireless. There's also a tall metal cabinet filled with shelves of CDs. This area is the functional equivalent of Barry Gordemer's office over at *Morning Edition:* it's the director's station, where Marika (or Bob Boilen, who directs *ATC* for half the week) hangs out, listening to upcoming spots, watching the evolution of the program, and beginning to plan what music to use in the bridges between reports. Marika is a tall woman with long dark hair who wears floppy, unusual hats and attractively unconventional outfits.

Gwen is talking with Marika about the long piece she's been preparing about Emily Dickinson: it looks as though the spot will run tonight. A professor in North Carolina went through Dickinson's letters and "discovered" in the pages of prose five hundred "hidden poems" — lines that if extracted and placed in stanza form sound like much of Dickinson's formal poetry. Linda Wertheimer did a two-way with William Shurr a few days ago, and today Gwen will edit it down into a seven-minute conversation. Gwen is one of NPR's many "floaters," people who make themselves available to fill in as needed. A graduate student who is interested in writing but fascinated with NPR, Gwen has produced a number of humorous commentaries and offbeat pieces as "ornaments" for Bob Ferrante's morning program; she has also done some artful pieces for *ATC*. She wears her dark hair cut short and often grins ironically from behind her glasses.

A Harvard graduate, Akili Tyson is a thin, smiling man of medium height who came to *ATC* from the performance unit of NPR in 1990. Now a permanent member of the *ATC* staff (his formal title is assistant producer), Akili directs the program from time to time. He has started to accompany hosts on field trips and, assuming he advances along traditional lines, he may soon become an associate producer of the show. (At NPR, the distinction between "production assistant" and "assistant producer" is mostly a matter of pay scale. In casual conversation, staff members seem to use the phrase "production assistant" or PA more than "assistant producer." In a further confusion of language, PAs will often be called "producers" when they are in charge of a story or "editors" when they are cutting a particular piece.)

The regular executive producer of the program, Ellen Weiss, has recently gone on maternity leave. Her replacement for the next six months, Michael Sullivan, is sitting in his office, several yards from the horseshoe, along the far wall. Willie is drinking a cup of coffee while looking through *The Washington Post*. A thin, curly haired man, barely into his thirties, he's wearing half-sized reading glasses and a dark blue blazer, which conspire to make him look older than he is — until you notice his dungarees and penny loafers, worn without socks. By the time *All Things Considered* is on the air later this afternoon, Willie will have shed his jacket and loosened his tie. He will also have taken off his loafers and, like some latter-day Huck Finn, he will be walking around the office barefooted.

Willie Sullivan represents one of the last of the *ATC* staff members to experience something of the show's pre-hard-news traditions. In the mid-eighties, a couple of years after graduating from the University of Massachusetts, Amherst, Willie moved from a public radio station in Seattle to NPR's national desk as western editor. Soon he began filling in as a production assistant at *All Things Considered* and, within two and a half years, he had climbed the ladder to become show producer. Willie says that Robert Siegel was one of his mentors, but he credits Neal Conan and Noah Adams with having taught him most of what he knows of radio production: Neal was executive producer during part of Willie's tenure as producer. After his inevitable burnout, Willie did a stint in Robert Siegel's old post in London before joining the list of floating producers at NPR who sometimes fill in on *ATC* and more often go on trips with correspondents, helping them prepare and file their stories. Willie is widely traveled and has worked on both hard-news and feature pieces. He accompanied Robert to Czechoslovakia in 1988; he went to Romania with Noah Adams and commentator Andrei Codrescu in 1989; he produced pieces from the Middle East during the Gulf War in 1991 and from Somalia in 1993. He feels most comfortable as a producer, bringing out the best of the reporters with whom he works.

When he was just a production assistant, Willie hung out with the old guard on the *ATC* production staff, playing poker and basketball and joining the jogging tradition. In addition to the *ATC* social culture, he absorbed a good deal of the older radio culture, and today, even as Willie actively participates in the newer focus on hard news, he worries aloud that careful sound production is too often sacrificed in the rush for breaking news. He wishes *ATC* could maintain a bit more of its original quirkiness and unpredictability, which he had enjoyed, as a listener, during the seventies.

Willie Sullivan encapsulates some of the charm and many of the contradictions within today's NPR. He might be seen, in part, as a logical (or illogical) extension of the carefree, barefoot past of public radio, which has been brought into the mainstream of American media culture and told to grow up and become "civilized." Willie is no hippie — he's a competent administrator and a producer who can be relied on to get results, even under the most trying circumstances. But for Willie, doing the best job you can does not mean you cannot also be playful — and while he does not take his responsibilities lightly, neither does he take himself, nor his job, with dour seriousness. Some of the more traditional editors and reporters who now work at NPR view Willie's antics as unnecessary and perhaps even unprofessional affectations. Yet other people — particularly those with backgrounds in radio — have seen oddballs before and are tolerant of the kooky traditions Willie seems to have imbibed.

The executive producer of *All Things Considered* has ultimate responsibility for the program, handling the budget and various managerial tasks and arranging the schedule of who will host and who will produce and edit. Today the usual show editor — Linda Killian, who used to write for *Forbes* magazine — is over at the White House attending to some business. Willie has decided to save some money, and rather than hire someone else to fill in as editor, he will take on that role himself. This means, of course, that he is placing himself in a subordinate position to Melissa, vis-à-vis today's program, even though he is, technically, also her superior. As the day proceeds, Willie will occasionally direct to Melissa questions that staff members bring him . . . while tomorrow Willie will be replacing Melissa in the producer's chair and Linda Killian will be sitting again on the right-hand side of the horseshoe. Such swapping of roles is so common at *ATC*, however, that it produces little awkwardness.

Between nine-thirty and nine-fifty, a parade of editors swings by the *ATC* horseshoe. Bruce Drake, head of the Washington desk, Elizabeth Becker, head of the foreign desk, and Larry Abramson, head of the national desk, all arrive with story ideas or with information. Both Bruce and Elizabeth came to NPR from print — Bruce worked at *The New York Daily News* for many years; Elizabeth was a writer specializing in Southeast Asia who had once been with *The Washington Post*. Larry is one of the few editorial managers whose background is radio. His group of national editors ride herd on NPR's small cadre of regional correspondents and also coordinate, cajole, and nurture submissions from freelancers and from any public radio member stations who wish to sell pieces to the network. The thinness of NPR's financial resources becomes most clear, perhaps, in the struggles of the national desk to stay on top of stories from around the country.

A short man, bald, with an elegant dark beard and wearing a white shirt and a tie but no coat, Larry Abramson has come back to *All Things Considered* to discuss what is likely to be the lead story for today's program. In New York City, arrests will shortly be announced in a startling terrorist plot, perhaps connected in some way to the bombing of the World Trade Center that took place four months ago. The wire services are reporting that a number of foreign nationals will be charged with a wide-ranging conspiracy that included plans to bomb the United Nations and other facilities such as the Lincoln and Holland tunnels, which connect New York with New Jersey. Certain individuals were also reportedly on a hit list for assassination, including Boutros Boutros-Ghali, the secretary general of the United Nations, and Alfonse D'Amato, Republican senator from New York. The men being arrested have been linked with Abdal Rahman, the blind Muslim cleric from Egypt at whose mosque these plots were reputedly hatched.

There's a great deal of discussion in the offices and corridors of NPR this morning about how to cover this breaking news. Final decisions will be made at the general editorial meeting at ten-thirty, which brings together each morning representatives of all the programs and all the editorial desks, along with management (John Dinges and/or Bill Buzenberg), to review current and future stories. But Larry is making his initial contacts with Melissa concerning this major event over his morning cup of coffee.

Willie emerges from his office and stands beside the editor's chair, still wearing his blue blazer and his half-glasses. He, Larry, and Melissa discuss what reporters are available in New York. Larry says that the main news conference will be covered by Jim Zarroli, a contract reporter who has been following the Trade Center bombing since the day it occurred. Larry does not offer anyone else in New York to do follow-up or pursue other angles on the story. Melissa and Willie make it clear to Larry that they would like more coverage. Larry smiles pleasantly but gives a noncommittal response (NPR has only a very small bureau in New York) before walking off in his characteristically graceful half shuffle.

The big Favag on the wall above the show board reads nine fifty, and the morning meeting for *ATC* should be starting shortly. Many staff members gather around the horseshoe in anticipation of their daily walk to the upstairs meeting room. Linda comes out of her office, still carrying her coffee, and she sits at a back corner of the horseshoe next to Gwen, who is reading *The Baltimore Sun.* Assistant producer David Rector, a tall, handsome man with a gentle smile, stands beside Linda. They all talk about the terrorists' list of assassination targets, which strikes everyone as a little bizarre.

Willie's voice suddenly is heard across the horseshoe and also from a speaker in the ceiling. He is talking into his telephone, but he has plugged himself into the public address system in order to reach anyone who is not in the vicinity. Throughout NPR resonates the traditional morning call: *"ATC.* Let's meet."

Morning Becomes the Meeting

In the third-floor executive conference room, reached by a special set of interior stairs, half a dozen *ATC* staffers gather around a long, imposing, light-wood table. Linda Wertheimer sinks into the middle chair along one side. Melissa sits opposite: she's taken off her shoes and curls her feet under her. The rest of the staff clusters midtable.

Linda leans her face on her hand and puts her reading glasses up above her forehead. Thinking of the story of the bomb plotters in New York, she speaks slowly and with the hint of a funny accent: "So: what are we going to do about the assassination plots. Do we talk to . . . Al-fonse . . . ?" She's referring to Senator D'Amato.

Willie makes a slight bow toward Linda. "After you, my dear."
Linda grins. "No, Gaston."

A general banter begins about the hit list — a sort of cheers and jeers. Someone suggests that it's time for another famous *All Things Considered* contest (which took place more often when Susan Stamberg was hosting the show).

"Yes, 'Terrorist Hits,'" someone exclaims.

Willie's voice rises above everyone else's. "We know there were nine on the list," he says. "They've only named five — you pick the last four!"

"Oh dear," says Linda, laughing.

Meanwhile, Akili has begun passing round Xeroxed copies of today's *ATC* story list — a two-sided sheet that contains a number of headings: *Today's Program, Later This Week, Features Shelf, Host Futures, Requests*. The longest section by far is that entitled *Host Futures*. It includes a range of proposed pieces that involve Robert, Linda, and Noah. Among the stories listed is a trip to Ukraine in December by Robert with producer Art Silverman; a long feature from Linda about teenagers and AIDS; and an interview with a "Ukulele Master" that Marika is proposing but which no host has yet expressed an interest in doing. Melissa starts going over the stories listed under the heading *Today's Program*. Most of these have been added to the list in the half-hour before the meeting, though one or two are holdovers from the previous day's list.

"The budget is supposed to come up for a vote in the Senate today," Melissa says, "and the House will finally vote on the Superconducting Super Collider."

"Who's on the case in the Senate?" Linda asks. As someone who spent almost twenty years covering budget battles, she has a vested interest in the story. Melissa tells her it's Brian Naylor. Linda nods. She knows already that Joe Palca, from the science desk, has been following the Super Collider story.

"It's a court case day," continues Melissa, referring to the Supreme Court.

"All Nina, All The Time," Willie says.

Linda suggests that Nina may be too busy on an upcoming profile of the latest appointment to the court, Ruth Beder Ginsburg, to do a story today. (Linda turns out to be correct.)

Melissa continues down the list. Jim Zarroli will be covering the arrests in New York; Ted Clark will be doing a story from Washington about political developments in Japan; Deidre Berger will report from Germany on a wave of protests throughout Europe by Kurdish militants. "And then there's the story about Fermat's theory," Melissa says.

Some in the room have heard about this curious development in the world of mathematics, others have not. Melissa explains: "Fermat was the guy who scribbled a mathematical theorem in the margin of a page of his notes and said he had a proof that would prove that it was right. But he didn't have enough time or space to write it."

Gwen adds: "This has been one of the big unsolved mathematical problems, and somebody finally solved it yesterday. After three hundred years!"

Jeff Rogers, a blond-haired, ruddy-faced assistant producer who wears a small earring in his left ear, speaks quickly and with enthusiasm. "We should talk to some *geeky egghead* mathematician who thinks this is the *biggest* thing that's ever happened." People laugh, but they know that Jeff is correct. They can all hear in their mind a passionate academic waxing rhapsodic about this arcane theory and being at once informative and entertaining.

Willie says, "Will he bring his yoyo?" A number of people start laughing and begin to make additional wisecracks — but almost without pausing for a beat Willie changes his tone, lowers his voice, and returns to the major story of the day: "Could we back up on the Zarroli?" The *ATC* staff knows that when Willie wants to speak seriously about something, his voice becomes very quiet. The table settles down. "I think we should be sure to get the national desk focusing on this New York story. There *has* to be a second piece."

Robert Siegel leans forward in his chair and speaks slowly and carefully, mixing wry humor with thoughtful discussion. "I'd like to know if they *did* blow up the Holland Tunnel, how long it would take for New York Traffic Control to realize what had happened . . . But I think we should take this all very seriously and be sure we follow up on the FBI angle, and perhaps also the immigration angle. Remember that when the World Trade Center arrests were announced following the shootout . . . that generated good stories about immigration controls. So one thing we might think of is waiting to see who these people are — and how they got here."

Robert makes small gestures with his hands as he launches into a kind of minilecture about events in New York. "The cleric is obviously the most astonishing part of this story. I mean, here we have a guy whose claim of refugee status . . . from America's closest ally in the Arab world

. . . is being heard while people are arrested who are under his influence for bombing New York. This is astonishing. This is a new . . .

"So it seems to me that there's a lot of same-day reporting to be done out of New York in addition to the FBI news conference." Robert's voice imperceptibly moves toward irony. "I know this is an astonishing thought — *two* reporters in New York, you know, getting together on this . . . and working up a package. But that's what I think we ought to be doing — get a couple of reporters in New York who would, in the words of Bruce Gellerman, 'push tush' today and come up with a couple of pieces."

Everyone laughs. "That's a new one," says Gwen.

And then Willie abruptly changes gears again and mentions that Marika Partridge (who is not at the meeting) says she will have her piece ready today on Beau Jocque, a Louisiana zydeco musician. The shift of topic shows no disrespect for Robert. But he has been preaching to the converted: everyone at *ATC* would love to have more in-depth pieces coming out of New York this afternoon, and Willie and Melissa will make a pitch for a second reporter at the general editorial meeting in half an hour. But they both expect that *ATC* will have to generate its own follow-up — a host two-way of some sort. Melissa asks Willie how long Marika's piece will be.

"The usual," Willie replies. "Sevenish."

Linda did the interview with the Cajun musician. She stretches her arms over her head and says, "The guy doesn't have a whole lot to say, but his personal story is interesting. The whole thing is 'very danceable music.' They actually did market research about what got people out of their chairs and composed their music around that. It's a kind of rock 'n' roll zydeco."

David Rector smiles broadly. "Market research zydeco, is that what you're saying?"

"It's the nineties," says Willie, gravely. "Get used to it."

Laughter forms a bridge to discussion of a few other stories. Melissa mentions a small item she's seen in one of the newspapers about a citizenship ceremony that the INS (Immigration and Naturalization Service) will hold today in Tucson: all the proceedings will be conducted in Spanish, except for the oath of allegiance itself. There's a bit of controversy surrounding this ceremony. "I thought it might be worth a little two-way," she concludes, and looks at Linda, the native southwesterner, who nods in agreement.

Then finally, the story comes up that, in many news organizations, would have been primary in everyone's mind. Last night Lorena Bobbitt attacked her husband in a Washington, D.C., suburb, severing his penis and throwing it into a nearby field. Police managed to recover the member, and doctors then reattached it to John Wayne Bobbitt. Arrests are pending. Lorena claims her husband raped her. John Wayne's case against Lorena is, as the legal folks say, prima facie.

Accounts of the Bobbit affair first appeared on the local TV news late last night, but many NPR staffers only heard about the story this morning, when colleagues directed their attention to the Metropolitan pages of *The Washington Post* or *The Baltimore Sun*. By the time of the morning meeting, all the women on *ATC* — but not all the men — know about the case. Melissa describes what happened. When she gets to the part of the police searching for the "severed member," Willie jumps in.

"It's like the leader's nose in *Sleeper*," he says, referring to the Woody Allen movie.

Linda wonders aloud how the doctors can be so confident the reconnecting operation was a "success." She then explains that she heard people on *Morning Edition* joking about the story, but she just kept reading her copy of the *Post* methodically. "I figured I would get to the Metropolitan pages eventually," she says. Linda starts laughing as she remembers the scene around the *Morning Edition* desk. "Absolutely *everyone* over there was talking about it."

Robert has a sudden image. "The Return," he exclaims, thinking of his friend Bob Edwards's humorous thirty-second pieces on the half-hour. Without preamble, Robert launches into an extraordinary imitation of Bob, lowering his voice, assuming a kind of exaggerated drawl, and saying his sentences with the familiar Bob Edwards punchy delivery. "This *woman* cut off his *member* in the *middle* of the *night*," he begins, and then his speech degenerates into a lot of deep-chested *aw-awing* noises that still maintain the familiar Bob Edwards cadence. His voice clears suddenly for the familiar outcue: "This is *Morning Edition*."

The room explodes into hysterics. Linda's high laughter soars over everyone else's, even as she stages a collapse and places her forehead against the table.

After a brief lull, it's back to business — and as though Jerry Lewis had just become John Kenneth Galbraith, Robert speaks calmly and professorially about an extraordinarily dry story that he's been proposing for a few days.

"Remember I talked with Les Cook [economics editor on the national desk] about people who could talk about interest rates? The question is whether lower interest rates over the next five years would be a greater relief to the typical taxpaying household, as Clinton claims, than increased taxes would be a burden to them. This is the thesis of the moment, of course . . ."

Willie interrupts Robert. "Do you think that's possible for today?"

"I have no idea," says Robert. Willie and Melissa exchange words about checking with Les.

Conversation begins to drift through other stories — both for to-day's show and for future programs — ranging from homelessness to reregulation of cable TV. At various points in the discussion, Linda's speech drifts into one regional dialect or another. Sometimes she does it to be amusing, sometimes she seems to be following a habit, an instinctive mannerism such as children fall into when at play. As she talks, her clear blue-gray eyes smile placidly from beneath her tousled hair.

At about ten twenty-five, without any formal word or signal, the meeting breaks up. Melissa puts on her shoes and moves around the table to sit beside Willie. Already the first few editors and producers from other programs have started to arrive for the general editorial meeting. Willie crumples a few sheets of paper and swivels in his chair. He leans back, cocks his right hand, and begins tossing the paper balls toward a wastepaper basket about six feet away. He sinks two, misses one, stands up and retrieves it, tries again, sinks it. Then he settles into his chair and, with Melissa, awaits the start of the meeting.

At *All Things Considered*, basketball is never more than a trash can away.

No Two-Ways About It . . .

For Laura Westley, a small, dark-haired woman with a broad face and a ready smile, the late-morning and early-afternoon hours constitute the busiest part of her workday. Laura's title is editorial assistant, and she is the principal booker for *All Things Considered*. Next to her telephone console sit two gargantuan Rolodexes and around them a number of smaller files of phone cards — the accumulated contacts of many years of *ATC* bookers. Laura's job is to track down people for the *ATC* hosts to interview: to screen them as candidates for two-ways, to arrange mutually agreeable times for a conversation, and to pass on to the hosts relevant information that will be helpful in getting the best material from the interviewee. To be a good booker you need to be able to "work the phones" with consummate skill. You cannot be daunted by protective secretaries, administrative assistants, and spouses. You must have a high tolerance for telephone answering machines. You have to be brazen enough to chase people down to their homes, if necessary, and charming enough to get away with your intrusiveness.

As Laura walks downstairs from the conference room, a little before ten-thirty, she runs into Peggy Girshman, from the science desk, coming up the staircase. She asks Peggy for the name of someone to call about Fermat's Last Theorem, and Peggy mentions a contact in the math department at one of the most prestigious institutions in the country. "If you don't like anyone you find there," Peggy adds, "I can give you more names." Eventually, she might even suggest her own former math professor. Laura thanks Peggy and continues her walk back to *ATC* and her telephone.

Critics of the media often complain about the way that "experts" are chosen to appear on television and radio programs. The familiar diatribes center, again, on simple-minded political considerations: self-appointed watchdog groups will investigate one organization or another and count up the number of times liberals or conservatives, men or women, whites or minorities, religious zealots and atheists, have been guests on particular news programs. This kind of numbers game can result in anecdotally interesting statistics (how many anarchist Laplanders *have* appeared on *Good Morning America?*); but the "studies" seldom reach any genuinely meaningful conclusions and they usually reveal more about the researchers than about the organization being researched.

Rarely spoken about — in large measure because it's a complicated and subtle question — is the extent to which the broadcast medium itself shapes the choice of people who go on the air. For example, if you cannot present your ideas in thirty-second sound bites (in the case of television) or in forty-five- to ninety-second paragraphs (in the case of NPR), you will not succeed as a "media expert." Furthermore, the particular verbal skills that work on TV or radio decisively affect the kinds of thoughts that can be expressed. This argument is sometimes framed in partisan political terms or in the context of cultural and ethnic bias. (The American media favors a particular kind of white, middle-class, middle-of-the-road thinking.) The point here is much broader: a whole range of ideas and opinions — a vast region of experience and understanding — eludes articulation in a two- or three-minute exchange, in the case of television, or a four- or five-minute presentation, in the case of NPR. Typically, discussions that add historical perspective or that argue more than two or three alternatives to a question will not fit into such shortened frameworks.

The question media critics ought to be asking is not how "biased" are particular news organizations, but, rather, is the kind of talk that sounds articulate on *all* television networks — and on most radio programs — sufficiently dense or nuanced or supple enough to speak usefully to the predicaments of our lives, our culture . . . our civilization?

NPR has never had a large enough staff to fill all the hours of its daily magazine programs with its own reporters and commentators. Right from the start, NPR has relied upon the two-way — the conversation with an "outside expert" — as an element of its broadcasts. NPR differs from the other media in that, generally speaking, the organization has been far more sensitive to the limitations of this kind of interview. More important, NPR traditionally has conducted longer conversations (a good two-way can go as long as five minutes, maybe even a little longer) and the segments are almost always *taped* and then edited — which means that an NPR two-way becomes a shaped, or "constructed," piece, more like a report from a correspondent than a live conversation.

The presence of tape means that NPR can open its microphones up to a wider range of voices than can other media. Someone who has interesting ideas, but who tends to ramble off the subject and so could never do live television, can be edited down and become a compelling subject for a radio conversation. On the other hand, even NPR feels the pressures of time constraints. Though theoretically NPR may be able to cast a wider net for its two-ways, in practice, public radio news programs have tended in recent years to choose their guests from lists of familiar Washington insiders and professional talkers. These folks are easier to edit on a tight deadline than less "media-articulate" people, and, it must be said, many people at NPR are pleased that so many VIPs and power brokers are now willing to hold forth on public radio's air. Older staff at NPR remember the days when, because of the network's obscurity and because of its untraditional approach to the news, "movers and shakers" would either never have heard of *All Things Considered* or would choose not to appear on the program. Now that NPR has become more legitimate, more established, the Establishment is heard more often on NPR's air. One consequence is that the glibness which has become so much a part of our national dialogue has begun to enter some of NPR's language as well.

Laura Westley returns to her desk at *All Things Considered* and begins making telephone calls, trying to line up host two-ways for the early afternoon. She must track down someone at the INS in Tucson, so Linda can find out about the Spanish Language Citizenship Ceremony. She needs to find an articulate mathematician for Robert to interview. Shortly, she will be receiving a list of economics gurus who are candidates for a discussion about interest rates. Her list of potential interviewees will wind up being fairly typical for an NPR program: some well-known experts who have been on the air before, but also a couple of people who — if they work out — will bring new voices to the national media.

At eleven o'clock, the hosts of the show, Linda and Robert, are ensconced in their offices, catching up on their mail. Linda is leaning back in her overstuffed easy chair.

"Prep time," someone says, walking by.

"Zat's right," says Linda, in a vaguely European accent. Then she laughs and gestures at the books piled up in her office. "You know, we get so damn much stuff sent to us — letters, articles, books . . . But it's nice to have a job which includes that you sit down in your office from time to time and just read."

Marika Partridge knocks at the outside of Linda's door; she's carrying a rough-cut of the story she's been working on about the Louisiana musician Beau Jocque. She goes to Linda's tape recorder, and the two begin listening to the piece.

A few minutes later, Willie and Melissa return from the general editorial meeting. Melissa goes to the board and adds two lines to the story list. "? Gonyea, Malice Green" and "Jordan, P & G Layoffs." Both pieces have just been offered by the national desk. The Gonyea report concerns a trial in Detroit of two white police officers accused of beating to death a black man, Malice Green. Key testimony is expected from the medical examiner who did the autopsy on Green. Melissa adds the question mark because today's proceedings may end too late for the reporter, Don Gonyea, to file a story. Lorna Jordan is a reporter at an NPR station in Cincinnati who is proposing to cover a round of job cutbacks announced by Procter and Gamble.

Melissa stands with her arms folded across her chest, her weight on her left leg, and begins thinking about a tentative road map for the program. It's a bit early to start outlining out the entire show, but today Melissa has a meeting to attend at eleven-thirty that may run through lunch, so she wants to get a head start.

Meanwhile, Willie tells Robert that it became clear at the general meeting that the national desk was not going to "push tush" and come up with a second reporter in New York for the terrorism story. Nor was the Washington desk keen on following up the story from a national angle — at least not this afternoon. Once again, too many stories, too few reporters. So *ATC* will have to line up its own two-way, following Zarroli's report. "I think what we have to do is watch the FBI news conference at two o'clock and decide what to do based on what we hear," says Willie, speaking quietly. Robert nods.

Willie then shows some names of economic experts to Robert, who says they look promising. Willie hands the list to Laura. He then joins Melissa as she sketches in some mini-outlines of the show in an empty corner of the board. She's writing very small. Willie watches her. "Compare and contrast," he murmurs at one point, stressing the need for variety of tone and style in any sequence of stories.

As Melissa and Willie stand together at the board, Laura is on the phone with Norton S. Bailey, head of the mathematics department of the Chicago Institute of Technology.[2] She talks with the professor for almost half an hour about Fermat's Last Theorem and about Dr. Andrew Wiles, who has discovered its solution. All the while, Laura evaluates Bailey's potential as a two-way for Robert. She has learned so far that Fermat's theorem states that the equation $x^n + y^n = z^n$ is *never* true if n is a whole number larger than two. But she's not yet sure that Bailey can render the equation, its solution, or its significance comprehensible to a radio audience. "Let's back up for just a moment," Laura is saying. "The point of the proof is to show what . . . ?" She listens for a few moments. "Okay. Good," she says, encouragingly. She jots down some notes while Bailey continues to talk.

Marika emerges from her listening session with Linda.

"How are you doin'?" says Melissa, inquiring about the Beau Jocque spot.

---

[2] For reasons that will become apparent, I am using pseudonyms for both the professor and the college or university involved.

"Fine," says Marika, stopping beside Melissa. Marika is several inches taller than Melissa, even though the producer is wearing heels.

"How long were you thinkin'?" says Melissa.

"Eight," says Marika. "It's four and a half of tape [that is, of conversation with Linda], and it's going to have at least half a minute intro, and we *really* need three minutes of music."

Willie, who is nominally the editor today, assumes his executive producer's hat momentarily. "More music, less talk," he says in his quiet but pointed way.

"He's a slow talker," Marika answers. A playful kind of whine enters her voice. "But there's going to be *music* underneath *everything* . . ." Willie smiles. "*O-kay,*" he says, echoing Marika's tone.

Back at her desk, Laura seems to be running into some problems with the mathematics professor. "I'll tell you something," she says in a pleasant but emphatic manner. "I wonder if it's going to be possible to make this understandable in a short period of time." She listens for a while, then continues, "Well, no, I mean I'm interested in explaining for people what the equation is and why it is important. But it's just too difficult for the average listener who's also driving a car, coming home from work . . . Um-hmm. Yeah, it goes by once, and then it's gone . . . Right." She starts listening again. The professor is trying another tack.

It's eleven-twenty when Melissa is ready to abandon her small-scale outline and propose her first full-fledged road map for the show. She moves over to face squarely the three blank columns on the board that represent the three half-hours of the program. Willie has returned to the editor's chair and taken his lunch out of a brown paper bag. He begins chewing on a sandwich while watching Melissa. She fills in the columns beginning at the bottom of the final two thirds. She puts "Beau Jocque" at the conclusion of the second third and makes Gwen's five-minute piece on Emily Dickinson the final piece in the third third. She then groups in the first third the wide range of economic stories: Naylor on the Senate budget debate, Robert's interview about interest rates, Palca's report on the House Super Collider vote, and the new story about Procter and Gamble layoffs.

She then adds Zarroli's piece on New York terrorists as the lead for the second half-hour and puts in Gonyea's report on the Malice Green trial (which may not end till five o'clock) at the top of the third third. Willie stops eating for a moment and suggests that Zarroli would make a better lead for the first third. If the Senate budget vote comes this afternoon, it will almost certainly be later than five o'clock. Melissa agrees, but wonders if Zarroli — a very good but notoriously late reporter — could be counted on to make the top of the first third.

After Melissa completes her program outline, she writes in large letters across the top of the board, "Subject to Change!"

At eleven-thirty, as Melissa is getting ready to leave the horseshoe, Neal Conan wanders by and looks over the board. He's been doing some reporting for the Washington desk for a couple of days. Robert Siegel walks out of his office carrying a can of diet Coke, and the two New York Yankee fans start talking about the current series their team is playing, which they are following mostly on AM radio stations outside Washington.

"This is a *very* big game tonight," says Robert with weight in his voice.

"*Very* big game tonight," Neal agrees.

Neal looks at the board and brings up a breaking story which NPR has not started to cover yet.

"Anyone have any idea why people are sending letter bombs to obscure academics?" He explains that a Yale professor has received such a parcel in the mail today, and earlier in the week, a professor in California had his hands blown off by a similar device. Robert goes to a computer terminal and calls up the latest story from a wire service.

Neal speaks in the general direction of Willie and Melissa. "You could put today's letter bombing on after Fermat's theorem. Different kind of academic story."

"I like Neal better when he's got something to do," Willie says, taking a last bite from his sandwich.

(The Yale bombing will make NPR's newscasts today, but a full piece won't appear on *ATC* until tomorrow afternoon, when a Boston-based reporter, Anthony Brooks, will file a story.)

Laura comes up to Robert and gives him a quick rundown of the mathematician with whom she has been speaking. She has scheduled a two-way at three o'clock: she thinks it will work out, but she suggests that Robert try to avoid getting too technical. Robert says he'll read the story in *The New York Times* about Fermat when he gets back from lunch. Willie and Melissa go off to their eleven-thirty meeting. A few minutes later, Laura leaves. Gwen Macsai is cutting her Emily Dickinson two-way in one of the *ATC* edit booths. Marika is trimming the Beau Jocque piece. But just about everyone else has left the office. For about an hour, from noon to one, the horseshoe is deserted — the calm before the final race to deadline.

Into the Starting Gate

The first interviews of the day for *All Things Considered* are conducted at one o'clock, in Studio Seven, by reporter Ted Clark. Ted is another one of the NPR workhorses who has been around the organization for years as an editor, a producer and executive producer, and a reporter. A gentle, understated man with a soft voice and a soft, young-looking face, Ted may be one of the most undersung professionals at NPR. For the past few years he has mostly reported on foreign affairs, covering the state department and putting together many stories that go into the background of developments overseas. He has long loved radio and appreciates the importance of sound in radio reporting, even though most of the stories he does now do not lend themselves to complicated production. These days, he uses his "radio ears" when selecting the excerpts from interviews that he will use in his acts and tracks pieces.

Many at NPR consider Ted Clark the master at finding and using the "telling actuality" — the piece of tape that evokes more than a mute quotation can in a magazine or newspaper. Ted may use moments in which someone pauses, or hesitates, or stumbles, in a fashion that reveals that he or she is dodging a direct answer. "What people don't say is as revealing as what they do say," Ted says. "And if they're feeling discomfort in their answer to a question, that's often as important as the answer itself. So oftentimes, long pauses should be kept in — they communicate. Silences can be as eloquent as words."

Ted Clark listens to the people with whom he talks in a slightly different way than a print reporter might. His interviewing technique is also radically different from what it would be on television, where cameras, lights, and the presence of a production team can hinder informal or intimate conversation. Like other radio reporters, Ted works alone, his only equipment being a small cassette recorder and a microphone. He often uses this technology to establish a connection with his interviewee. "I always try to sit on a couch with somebody," Ted says, "partly so that my arm doesn't get so tired — you know, holding out the microphone across the space between you and the person you're talking with — but partly because it puts us on equal footing. I mean, with people who consider themselves powerful and important, it's not a bad thing to get them out from behind their desks and sitting next to you. In that sense a microphone can draw you closer together. Also, you talk *over* the microphone and keep eye contact with the other person. Partly this helps them forget there's a microphone present, but, of course, it also draws them out."

Ted is regarded by his peers as one of the best writers of news spots at NPR. He explains, "The first thing I think about is clarity. Your report has to be more clear, more immediately understandable than any other kind of writing. Television writing is augmented by pictures: if people don't understand what a reporter is saying, they still see the pictures. In newspaper writing, you can reread a paragraph that you didn't understand at first. You can't relisten to a radio story. It has to be as simple, as clear, as possible — which means building in some repetitions which would seem like redundancies to a newspaper editor. 'You've already said that,' and he'd pencil it out. Well, in a radio report, sometimes you have to repeat yourself — maybe two or three times — particularly if you're talking about a new concept or if it's a complicated concept.

"Writing for radio also has to be much more conversational than either print or television. Stilted writing sounds even more awkward on radio than it does if you read it on a page or hear it on television. I guess that's because all you have is the voice saying the words. Language comes across a little differently when you simply hear it out loud — with no facial expressions, with no punctuation. The writing has to sound, as much as possible, as though you're *simply talking*. You know, it's funny, but I think sometimes if you write too beautifully on the radio — if you avoid all clichés, even in situations where people normally would use a cliché — your listeners may not understand the point you're trying to make . . . in a sense because the writing is too good. Sometimes you can write most clearly if you speak a bit informally — though you have to be careful."

This afternoon, Ted has arranged two back-to-back phone interviews with a couple of Washington experts on Japanese politics. He sits quietly in the small studio wearing a blue button-down shirt and a red tie, waiting for the tape to start rolling. When the engineer signals everything is okay, Ted starts talking into the microphone in front of him. He then listens to his guest's voice coming back through his headphones, big white ones that cover his ears in such a way that his face, with its even features, seems younger and more childlike than ever. Ted will keep his conversations short and a little after one-thirty will head back to his desk, in a cubicle at the other side of the building, to prepare his four-minute report.

At ten minutes after one, Melissa has returned from the meeting and from lunch. Laura has been back for a few minutes, and she tells Melissa of her progress booking interviews. She's found an INS official in Arizona who sounds very good and has scheduled a two-thirty two-way for Linda. The mathematician will expect a call at three o'clock. Laura is currently looking for economic experts to talk with Robert about the interest rate question. Robert has decided that he would like a *three*-way conversation — more difficult to arrange, more difficult to edit but perhaps allowing for a greater breadth of discussion on this complex issue. She's hoping she can get people lined up for a three-thirty interview. Melissa nods; Laura returns to her telephone.

Linda Wertheimer walks in slowly, wearing her big sun hat and carrying a large paper bag. She deposits her hat in her office and comes back out to the horseshoe carrying a large cobb salad from C. F. Folks, a restaurant just around the corner.

"It's cobb salad day," says Laura from her desk.

"Yes, would you like half?" Linda says.

"No thanks, I've just eaten," says Laura. Then she brings Linda two pages of copy. "Here's your immigration two-way." Laura has printed out information about the man Linda will interview and a series of possible questions for her to ask. Linda takes out her glasses and reads over the copy as she eats.

Melissa fills in the story list at the far right-hand side of the board — and the contours of the afternoon's work crystallizes. In addition to the two-ways, Robert and Linda are scheduled at four o'clock to pre-record a segment devoted to listener mail. Linda wrote up the four-minute script earlier in the morning. David Rector will produce the piece. A number of spots from reporters will be coming into Record Central later in the afternoon, and then various production assistants on *ATC* will have to edit out any flubs and mix in any pieces of actuality that are included in the reports. Jeff Rodgers has already been assigned to Dierdre Berger's report on Kurdish attacks in Europe. Franc Contreras, the newest member of the *ATC* production team and another southwesterner, will be handling Brian Naylor's feed from Capitol Hill about the budget vote. Franc came to work at lunchtime today because he will be doing the "rollovers" this evening — that is, he will hang around and supervise the later feeds of the program to other time zones. The task is often fairly simple, but the possibility of a late vote in the Senate tonight means that Franc might have to make some changes in the program, perhaps during the final feed to the West Coast.

The other reporter pieces will all be coming in late, from four-thirty on. Joe Palca's coverage of the Super Collider must await a Senate vote. Don Gonyea's report from Detroit depends on the course of the trial and whether the medical examiner is cross-examined today. Zarroli's story from New York will draw upon a press conference that hasn't happened yet. Jordan's story about Procter and Gamble is still being arranged by the national desk.

The only spot that causes no one any anxiety whatsoever is Ted Clark's report on Japan. He will get it done on time, he will do all of his own tape editing, including his talk tracks, and the story is bound to be interesting and well crafted.

At ten minutes to two, Melissa and Willie are back in their chairs at the horseshoe. Linda is still working on her salad, Robert is sitting near her reading a newspaper.

"By the way," Linda suddenly says, to no one in particular and everyone in general, "I'm carefully not laying my hands on those portions of this salad that I'm trying to give away. But if I don't give it away soon, I may eat it all."

Meanwhile, Willie begins cleaning up his desk, crumpling the waxed paper that had wrapped his sandwich. He takes aim for a tall wastepaper basket beyond Melissa's chair. He shoots — he scores. Melissa then squeezes some old copy into a smaller ball and sends it sailing into the same basket. Willie and Melissa look at each other. Wordlessly, they rise in their chairs and slap their fingers together in a high-five salute.

Melissa sits down and resumes scanning messages on her computer terminal. Willie takes out a box of cookies from his lunch bag and offers them to people near him. "Animal cracker?" he says, holding up the traditional red, yellow, and white package. For a moment the horseshoe feels more like a family picnic than the center of a broadcast news program.

At seven minutes after two — less than three hours before *ATC* goes on the air — Willie turns up the volume on the old television set that stands to the right of the board. CNN has started to broadcast the FBI briefing from New York City. Robert hands Willie a yellow notepad, and Willie twiddles a pen in his fingers as he prepares to take notes on the news conference. Robert leans back in his chair, arms across his chest. Melissa has dropped off her shoes and put her feet up on the edge of the table in front of her. Several other staff members gather near the TV set.

The news conference begins with a statement that outlines in general terms the morning events. Eight people have been arrested and charged with plotting to plant a number of bombs throughout New York City. The spokesman sounds like a voice from an FBI promotional film of the forties and fifties when he says, with a ponderous tone, that when something like this terrorist plot is being hatched, "the joint task force on terrorist bombing is ready" to meet the challenge. He praises the operation that resulted in today's arrests as an "extraordinary" effort, "carried off with precision timing by an elite group of law enforcement officials."

Willie Sullivan looks up from his notepad: "Translation: they ran into these guys at Dunkin' Donuts."

Jim Fox, of the FBI, then comes to the microphone and tells the story of how the plotters were caught. The suspects had been under surveillance for a while, but only recently did their plans seem to be coming to a head.

"They acquired a safe house, which in the last few days ultimately became a bomb factory," Fox is saying.

Fox goes on to detail that the conspirators bought materials necessary to make bombs and began purchasing plane tickets. The FBI got arrest warrants and moved on the plotters this morning.

"As we entered the bomb factory," Cox says, "five subjects were actually mixing the witches' brew."

Laura Westley repeats the phrase with approval. "The witches' brew!"

"Umm!" Willie grunts, making a note of it. In fact, everyone sitting around the television hears the same thing: by the end of the day, Jim Fox's phrase "the witches' brew" will have appeared in almost every story broadcast and written about the arrests. Catchy, unexpected, short, vivid — and delivered with a voice filled with character and personality — "the witches' brew" becomes an instant quotation attached to this event. Within a couple of days, given the wildly imitative and repetitive quality of the American media, the colorful phrase will be well on its way toward becoming a tiresome cliché, a bit of hyperbole that no one else will ever dare use again.

The birth of the sound-bite happens in an instant — it takes no longer for the metaphoric light bulb to go off in the minds of thousands of reporters around the country and for the moment to be captured, like a fly in amber, on videotape, audiotape, and notepad. But meanwhile events in the real world keep rolling on, without a ripple, as though nothing of significance has just happened. Jim Fox continues his story of the morning's arrests. SWAT teams were used to break into the location. "We entered so fast," Fox is saying, "that some of the subjects said they didn't realize strangers were in the bomb factory until they had the handcuffs being put on 'em."

Robert smiles. "Even *they* were impressed with what a *good* job we did!" Then he adds, in a voice that has echoes of comedian Jackie Mason, "This is the greatest arrest we've ever seen!"

Willie grins but keeps taking notes. Robert, too, is paying attention to Fox, even as he murmurs his own comments.

"They were mixing the concoction in five large fifty-five-gallon drums," the FBI man is saying.

"Jeez!" says Robert, deep in his throat and shaking his head. He stretches his legs out straight and holds his two hands across his belly.

It's two-fifteen, the bulk of the information has been released, and much of the *ATC* staff returns to its other work. Melissa lowers her legs, turns to face her computer terminal, and begins scanning the news wires. Shortly, she will print up the first wire service stories to come out of the news conference and will hand them to Robert. Akili Tyson returns to his editing booth.

But the news conference continues. The first questions from reporters following the official statements unearth some additional information. Some of the people arrested were Sudanese nationals. As Fox puts it, "Of the eight individuals, five are current residents of the United States. And they are from the Sudan. The other three . . . their status remains unknown at this time."

Robert repeats the final words, "their status remains unknown," as though ruminating.

Meanwhile a couple of follow-up questions at the news conference provide ample indication of the degree to which some reporters *listen clearly* to what they hear. A few moments after Fox has talked about the nationality of the accused, two reporters ask him for the same information again.

Willie stares at the television set and says with a touch of irritation, even before Fox has a chance to answer. "Five are Sudanese, three we don't know about!" He speaks slowly, like a schoolteacher, shaking his head.

Another reporter asks about "the witches' brew." How far were they from completing it when they were arrested?

Fox says he cannot comment on this detail. Someone around the *ATC* horseshoe says, "It was just beginning to bubble."

Linda laughs. Laura says, "Well, it still needed the eye of a newt!"

A CNN reporter on the scene launches into a lengthy statement about the devastation that would have occurred if the UN, the tunnels, and the building housing the FBI had been blown up in a single day. After this review of the obvious — perhaps meant to prove that he *had* been listening to the previous twenty minutes — he asks how could the city and the FBI could have handled the situation.

Laura paraphrases the question: "Mr. Fox, how would *you* have felt if you had been blown up?"

Fox senses the inanity of the question and replies dryly: "It certainly would have ruined my day."

The *ATC* crew erupts in laughter again. "You deserved that!" Robert says to the unseen reporter.

"I *like* this guy!" says Willie.

Throughout the news conference, Robert has been thinking about the "Sudanese connection" to these accused terrorists, and as the news conference starts winding down, he mentions to Willie the possibility of pursuing this angle in a follow-up to Zarroli's report. He remembers seeing an article in *The New Yorker* by reporter Mary Anne Weaver about militant Islam and Sudan. Willie nods. Laura looks at Robert. No decision is made immediately, but by two-forty Laura will be working the phone trying to track down Weaver for an interview with Robert — as soon as possible.

Linda Wertheimer leaves the horseshoe before the end of the news conference. It's two-thirty, and she walks slowly toward Studio Five to conduct her first two-way of the day.

Laura's voice is heard over the paging system. "Akili-san, please call 9932. Akili, 9932."

Akili is to edit the INS piece, but no one knows where he is. Laura places the call to Tucson, reaches INS officer Bill Johnston, then asks him to hold while she has the telephone line transferred over to Studio Five. "Has anyone seen Akili?" Laura asks as she prepares to follow Linda into the studio.

Willie picks up his phone and goes on the pager. "Noodles, call 9975 [no longer Laura's desk but the number for Studio Five]. Noodles, call 9975."

During his years working at *All Things Considered,* Willie Sullivan has developed nicknames for many of the staff members. Melissa he will call "Sunspot" or sometimes just "Spot." Akili Tyson became "Noodles" at one point or another because a favorite lunch of his comes from an Oriental noodles restaurant near Dupont Circle.

Laura is standing up at her desk about to go into the studio when her phone rings. One of the economic experts — Robert Reischauer — is returning her call. She explains that she is asking for twenty minutes of his time, starting about an hour from now. Would that be possible? He seems agreeable, and she takes down his phone number for her Rolodex. She then asks if he could talk for a few minutes right now in preparation for the later, taped conversation. He says fine, and she asks him to hold for a moment. It's two thirty-one. Bill Johnston in Tucson is holding on one line, waiting to be plugged into Studio Five. Reischauer is holding on another line. Laura seems momentarily stressed for the first time (but not the last time) today. She calls to Robert, who is just about finished with the CNN news conference, and asks if he would mind talking with Reischauer now and doing the preinterview. Robert understands and is happy to oblige. He goes into his office and picks up on Laura's extension.

Laura walks quickly toward Studio Five, where she finds Akili waiting for her. Willie also comes into the control room in his capacity as show editor. He'll make suggestions to Akili about how to cut the interview. In a few moments, Bill Johnston is patched into the main board and Linda begins recording her two-way. Laura returns to her desk and starts trying to track down the reporter for Robert's proposed conversation about the "Sudanese connection."

It's almost two-fifty when Willie returns to the horseshoe and tells Melissa that the Spanish INS piece went nicely and that Akili will edit it down easily to a four-minute piece. Melissa is revising the board, moving stories around and adding new information. The list of stories has been updated. Laura has been able to confirm guests for the three-way about interest rates: economist Robert Reischauer will be joined by mortgage banker Lyle Gramley. Veteran producer Margaret Low Smith, who will be going on maternity leave tomorrow, has been assigned the sometimes complicated business of cutting a three-way conversation. Reischauer will be coming into the NPR studios at three-thirty; Gramley will talk on the telephone.

Also, the Washington desk has just brought over a late-breaking story: Defense Secretary Les Aspin has delivered a major speech in which he outlined some changes in worldwide military strategy. The new Pentagon correspondent, Martha Raddatz, will prepare the report. (Martha is something of an anomaly at NPR, having previously worked at a local television station in Boston.)

Melissa and Willie thus face the following collection of stories, which they must arrange in some sensible order and then nurse through to completion in time for broadcast:

TALENT	SLUG	Estimated Time (mins.)
Zarroli	NY Terrorists	4
(R)	Sudanese Connection/?	4 1/2
Clark	Japan Political Turmoil	4
Berger	Kurds Get Their Way	3 1/2
Raddatz	Army	3 1/2
Naylor	Budget Vote	4
Palca	Superconducting Super Collider	3 1/2
(R)	Interest Rates & Taxes/Reischauer, Gramley	5
Jordan	P&G Layoffs	3 1/2
Gonyea	Malice Green [Trial]	4
(L)	Spanish INS Ceremony/Johnston	4
(R)	Fermat's Theorem/Bailey	4
(L)	Emily Dickinson Letters/Shurr	5 1/2
(L)	Beau Jocque	8
	Letters	4

Each half-hour of *All Things Considered* in reality consists of twenty-nine minutes, sixty seconds being given back to the local stations (at the end of each third) to do with as they wish. Of that twenty-nine minutes, seven are taken up by news in the first and last third of the program; the middle third has a five-minute newscast. In addition NPR funding announcements consume thirty seconds — music bridges, credits, "zippers," and other odds and ends further eat into the time available for stories. (The zipper is a thirty-second-long musical interlude that *ATC* has added to the first and third half-hour so that local stations can break for "business" if they want. The zipper "opens the show up" at a different time each day, adjusting to the particular flow of pieces.) The net result is that, taken together, the hour and a half of *All Things Considered* includes somewhere between fifty-nine and sixty minutes of reports, two-ways, and produced pieces. Though the timings are all tentative because none of the pieces are in the can yet, at this moment the show appears to be running five or six minutes too long. More than this, the program *feels* long to Melissa, who has been producing long enough to develop an intuitive sense about how much will fit and how much won't.

Melissa has been sketching out tentative road maps with an eye toward seeing what piece or pieces can be dropped. As a general rule of thumb, the more stories you have, the less likely it is that a long feature is going to survive to the final rundown. And sure enough, as Melissa lines up the various half-hours, she finds it increasingly difficult to reserve a section long enough to hold Marika's eight-minute profile of the Cajun musician. While it is always nice to have variety in a newsmagazine, the current climate at NPR would not encourage an *ATC* show producer to drop a breaking news story — such as the speech by Les Aspin, the Malice Green trial in Detroit, or the terrorism by Kurds in Europe — in favor of a long music piece about a Louisiana musician, which could easily be rescheduled to run on another, less busy news day.

Melissa grabs Marika as she walks by the board. "'Rika, I'm just not sure this is going to work," she says calmly. "We've just added a lot of stuff to the program."

Marika is visibly disappointed. But if it is a tradition for those in charge of NPR programs to squeeze and trim and bump and refuse stories, it is also a tradition for NPR reporters and producers to argue and cajole and prod and push in order to get their reports on the air. Nowhere is the jockeying back and forth more intense than on *ATC*, which has always been one of the most highly competitive and highly selective programs. So Marika does not abandon her story on Beau

Jocque without some complaint. She argues from her position as the designer of the piece (and the director of the program) who wants to make sure that her creation is displayed to its best effect. "I'll be away for two weeks, starting tomorrow," she reminds Melissa. "And I was going to mix the piece with the deadroll *on the air* the way I want it to sound."

"Well, why don't you mix the whole thing . . . and then, you know, leave instructions?" says Melissa evenly though not unsympathetically.

Marika knows that some of what she's talking about cannot be done ahead of time nor can it be conveyed in writing to another director. But she does not make a big deal about it: "I just like to be here when my piece is aired," says Marika simply. Melissa nods. In any event, it's still too early to make a final decision.

Melissa returns to working up tentative schedules on the board. Willie stands nearby, watching her and occasionally murmuring some comment and suggestions. The road map has changed significantly since eleven-thirty. Given that the Senate's vote on the budget looks as though it will be happening quite late, Melissa has decided to lead the first third with the New York terrorism story rather than the budget, making the big assumption that Zarroli will get his story in on time. She tries out the following outline for the first half-hour, though it contains about a four-minute hole:

NYC Arrests	4	
		Zarroli
Who Else?	4 1/2	
R/ ?		
Kurdish Terrorists	3 1/2	
		Berger
Emily Dickinson	5	
L/Shurr		

The budget story could lead the second third or the third third. If the latter, the half-hour might start like this:

Budget		
	4	
		Naylor
Interest Rates		
	5	
R/		
Superconducting Super Collider		
	3 1/2	
		Palca
P&G Layoffs		
	3 1/2	
		Jordan

This design also is four minutes short. In addition, the arrangement leaves a hodgepodge of unrelated stories to be thrown into the second half-hour or used to plug up the various holes in the other thirds.

"Where am I going to put Gonyea?" says Melissa, thinking out loud.

"Gonyea?" says Willie, quietly but insistently. "Put him in the first [third]."

"No," Melissa says softly. "Definitely not the first."

"Why not?"

"I don't have enough room for him."

Willie asks why Melissa has Dickinson following the Kurds. Melissa doesn't see how Dickinson can fit in the third third with all the economic stories ahead of it. "I had sort of written Palca out of the show — something has to go, we have too much. But the vote on the Super Collider is going to be about five o'clock and the science desk really wants us to cover it." Melissa sighs. It's hard to argue against a breaking-news story. "Palca, Gonyea, Raddatz . . . We just seem to have too much at the moment."

Willie expresses some coolness about the Raddatz piece. Melissa shakes her head. That, too, is a major story. Willie is somewhat less impressed with its significance and with the need for NPR to report on this particular policy speech, but he also knows that many editors would disagree with him.

With two hours to go before the start of *All Things Considered*, the board remains in a state of flux. Both the rundown of stories and the timings of those pieces remain fluid and indeterminate. Within the next hour, though, the various puzzle parts will start coalescing, and from the confusion will emerge a clear design. The shaping is not accomplished wholly by the conscious acts of the show producer and show editor, however. Many parts of the process are beyond their immediate control.

A little before three, Laura Westley finds herself in another time crunch. She is still trying to find someone with whom Robert can discuss the Sudanese connection to the New York City bombings — *The New Yorker* reporter has not returned her call — but in a few minutes Robert must interview the mathematician about Fermat's theorem. Someone needs to call Professor Bailey so that the two-way can proceed. Laura goes looking for Gwen and finds her in an edit booth, where Professor Shurr is hemming and hawing, hemming and hawing, while discussing Emily Dickinson. Gwen is wielding grease pencil and razor blade, marking and then editing out as much of the academic cadence from Shurr as she can. "Gweny," says Laura from the doorway, "are you still cutting the three o'clock two-way?"

"I don't know," Gwen answers, not looking up as she carefully lays a piece of splicing tape into the editing block. She rubs the tape down with her finger, then quickly replays a sentence that has now lost few diversionary clauses and a number of tedious "ums." Gwen looks over her shoulder at Laura. "I don't know if I am or if Jeff is. We were going to trade."

Laura explains her situation. Gwen puts down her razor blade and goes off to see whether Jeff will indeed take over the mathematician piece, as Gwen needs to spend more time on Dickinson. Laura returns to her desk and resumes her pursuit of an expert on the Sudanese connection. She reaches a candidate for the two-way just as Jeff appears, ready to help out with the mathematics story. Laura puts her phone call on hold, hands Jeff the information about mathematics professor Bailey, then walks quickly over to Melissa and Willie, sitting a few feet away. "I've got Steve Emerson on the phone — Mary Anne Weaver seems unreachable. She may be available, but do you want to see if we can hedge our bets with Emerson . . . to be sure we have someone?"

"Yeah, okay," says Melissa.

"He's sort of a know-everything about that part of the world," Laura says encouragingly. "He's good."

Willie looks over the top of his glasses at Laura. "Weaver's unavailable *completely* for the rest of the day?" He is not doubting Laura exactly, but he is nudging her, in his quiet, slightly ironic way, just to make sure that she has really tried everything possible to reach the elusive writer.

"I don't know," Laura says candidly. "I just get an answering machine. Robert tried *The New Yorker*, too. We're coming up dry."

Willie nods.

Laura asks, "When would we want to talk to him if we're going to talk to Emerson?"

"Anytime," Melissa replies, looking at the board. At the moment the two-way about the Sudanese connection — with unnamed reporter — is scheduled to go on the air at about five-fifteen, a little over two hours from now.

Laura goes back to her desk and resumes her conversation with Steve Emerson.

Meanwhile, unaware of what Laura is currently up to, Robert Siegel walks out of his office on his way to Studio Five and his two-way on Fermat's theorem. He's smiling and seems quite pleased with the prospect of trying to turn a somewhat arcane mathematical formula into a short radio spot.

Formula for a Two-Way Collapse

Robert sits on the edge of his chair in Studio Five, his white-sleeved arms extended in front of him, his face, framed by headphones and slightly cocked to one side. An open can of diet Coke sits on the table beside his script and a blue pen. Robert's balding head, dark-rimmed glasses, and dark beard look a little incongruous surrounded by all the paraphernalia of broadcasting — the headphones, the large Neumann microphone, the various clocks and cables and wires. For a moment, Robert seems a bit too formal, a bit too erudite, a bit too *serious* to be enmeshed in all this electronic equipment. Yet one look into his face as he glances up through the glass window into the control room dispels any sense of incongruity: Robert's eyes are bright, even twinkly; a small smile plays around his lips. Here is someone not merely content and at home, but indeed quietly, yet profoundly, *happy* with where he is and what he is doing.

In the control room of Studio Five, Jeff Rogers has the phone to his ear and is explaining to Professor Bailey that Robert Siegel will be talking with him shortly. Jeff puts down the phone, gestures in Robert's direction, then leans on the directorial console, prepared to take notes.

Willie is sitting in one of the high chairs, his chin against his hand, twirling his pencil.

Robert's voice is heard suddenly over the control room's speakers, sounding deep, resonant, and a bit tentative — as though he were poking his head into a darkened room. "Hello?"

The professor's voice comes back over a somewhat crackly telephone line. "Yes?"

"Howdy!" says Robert. "This is Robert Siegel from NPR in Washington." Robert speaks to Professor Bailey on the telephone in precisely the same cadences and tones that he uses over the radio, which means he sounds slightly formal yet friendly and interested.

"Yes," says the professor again.

"How are you today?" says Robert a bit briskly.

"Fine, thank you." The professor answers slowly and stiffly. He speaks in a European accent that is hard to identify — perhaps it is that of a Central European who has been in America or England for a long time.

Robert exchanges a few pleasantries in his gracious, slightly stylized delivery before moving to the first order of business in any two-way. "Well now, if you could oblige us with a voice level," Robert says. "Could you tell us . . . what you . . . had for lunch today, for example."

"What I had for lunch," says the professor gamely, but sounding a tad confused by the request. He chooses his words carefullly. "Let's see, I had two pieces of toast, and a banana . . . and some tea."

"And some tea," says Robert in his deep, serious voice. Their exchange begins to take on a slightly surreal aura.

"And a game of tennis."

"The lunch was before the tennis," Robert surmises.

"That was before the tennis," the professor concurs.

In the control room, no one likes the quality of the sound they are getting through the telephone.

Willie speaks to Robert over the intercom. "Ask him to hold the phone a little farther away."

"I wonder if you could try holding the phone a little bit farther away from you," says Robert. Then it's back to the chitchat. "Well, let me ask you what you look forward to having for supper."

"Hmm. I'll probably eat some fish. I think it would be salmon."

In the control room, Jeff Rogers exclaims, "He sounds *awfully muddy*." Though one of the younger production assistants, Jeff already has a highly developed aural sensitivity. He cares about sound and works hard to perfect his mixes and edits.

Robert says, "Any idea how it might be prepared, the salmon?" — thus demonstrating that an experienced interviewer can find questions to ask about anything, anytime, anywhere.

"Ah . . . probably broiled."

"Broiled salmon," Robert repeats. He is carrying on this preliminary conversation in such a diligent and interested manner that he almost makes these exchanges sound *significant.*

The engineer, Marty Kurcias, has done all he can with tweaking the EQ of the phone line. It's time to take a more direct approach. Marty speaks into the intercom. "Robert, ask him to rap the phone on a hard surface."

"Ah-ha!" says Robert enthusiastically. This is a bit of old-fashioned radio magic with which he is familiar. He speaks to the professor in a more animated fashion. "Now I am advised to ask you . . . could you take the telephone and try rapping in on a hard surface for a moment?"

"Rapping it?" says the professor in complete surprise.

"Yes, that's right, that's right," says Robert, trying to sound reassuring. "Like kicking the television set."

Of course, Robert has not explained to the professor that the phone line does not sound very good and that sometimes knocking the mouthpiece of a telephone will dislodge bits of carbon and other grunge that may have formed on the electronic contacts. Still, Professor Bailey plays along and does as he is told. Marty lowers the volume on the phone as Bailey bangs the receiver against his desk. He comes back on the line.

"Okay?" he asks.

"Well, let's hear. Can you tell us about the weather today?"

The professor seems to have accommodated himself to the more bizarre aspects of this experience and jumps in with only the slightest hesitation. "Ah . . . well, it's a beautiful day, with a slight wind. Makes the backhand hard to hit." He laughs gently. "I don't think there's a cloud in the sky. And, ah, no humidity."

Through the shared experience of discussing broiled salmon and banging the telephone — which *has* cleared up the muddiness on the line — Professor Bailey and Robert Siegel have established a tentative connection. Robert looks into the control room. "Are we happy now?" Marty switches on the tape recorder and nods.

Robert looks down at the table and then stares into the empty space that separates him from the crackly, disembodied voice he hears through his headphones. He begins his first question: "Now let me explain that

. . . every time we either ask anyone or read anything about this, we eventually come to a point where everyone says that in order to understand the mathematics of this theorem . . . it's impossible, so we shouldn't even try. But I will ask you if you can give us some handle, some schema, of what this novel method is which Andrew Wiles has used to solve Fermat's theorem . . . but first . . . well, how *serious* has the pursuit of a solution to Fermat's theorem been through the past couple of centuries?"

Robert hopes to elicit from the professor a brief sketch of mathematicians either spending a lot of time, or not spending a lot of time, chasing down the solution to Fermat's tantalizing notations. But the language of his question leaves itself open to a number of interpretations, so, in a subtle way, right from the start, Robert unwittingly leads Professor Bailey toward the tar pit of his own erudition. The consequences of this approach only slowly reveal themselves. For the moment, all that's apparent is that the word "serious" does not trigger the same associations for the professor as it does for Robert.

"Serious . . ." says the professor. "Well, there's one part that's been quite *un*serious. Since Fermat's theorem is so easy to state that every high school student can understand it, it's attracted many crackpots, as well as just plain amateurs in mathematics, feeling that — you know, that they might be able to solve it. So that there are literally hundreds and hundreds of solutions that . . . we're looking at several now that have been sent to us, ah . . . you know, by people trying to get some elementary solutions . . ."

Robert hunches slightly in his chair. He listens closely, nodding in response to Professor Bailey's story.

Bailey continues: "I think what's helped also has been this statement that Fermat made in the book. You know, he says in Latin, '*Hanc marginis exiguitas non caparet.*' That is, he has a beautiful theorem but there's not enough room in the margin to write it down."

Willie and Jeff laugh as they jot down some notes. The professor is wandering a little, but he is speaking fluidly, in an interesting voice, and with engaging passion.

Bailey keeps talking: "Everyone who does this as an amateur has heard of this quotation and feels that there must have been some rather short solution."

Robert jumps in with a slight chuckle: "The only hint was that it's bigger than the margin of that page. It was the only information you'd got."

The professor laughs in response. "Well, yes, but we do have more than that. He also gave a proof for the case of n equals four, that is to say, the equation x to the fourth plus y to the fourth equals z to the fourth. He showed that there is no positive integer solution in that case. So he did have a method and it was followed up in the next century. Euler then proved it in the case — these are now serious mathematicians, the great mathematicians — Euler proved it for n equals three, that there's no solution. And then in the nineteenth century, there were all these special cases for a while solved. The n equals five case was done in 1823, I believe, by Legendre . . . in 1832, Dirichlet did another case — fourteen . . . and finally Lamé did a case, n equals seven in 1840. The first really stronger and more general account was made by a great German mathematician called Kummer in 1849 . . ."

In the control room, Jeff suddenly exclaims, in an upset voice, "I don't know how I'm going to edit this! He's all over the place."

Robert takes a swig of diet Coke but does not make a move to cut off the professor from his didacticism.

Bailey keeps talking about Kummer. "And he showed that for certain numbers, regular primes, as exponents . . . that those are cases which again, ah, there was no solution. That is to say, Fermat's theorem is true for those. But even of those, all that were known were a certain finite number . . ."

Robert says "Um-hum!" into the microphone, which is perhaps an attempt to interrupt. But the professor is fully launched, as though speaking to a college classroom. He piles example upon example.

Jeff is seized with vivid images of spooling minute after minute of tape onto the floor of the editing booth. He explodes in frustration: "God Almighty! Shut up!" But the professor is completely innocent of the anguish he is provoking in the control room. He has no frame of reference for his discussion. How often has he tried to teach mathematics into a telephone? And for reasons that perplex the onlookers in the control room, Robert does not seem to be intervening to rescue the professor. Of course, part of the problem is that Bailey's words are now tumbling out like an avalanche.

"Kummer pointed out that Lamé had made an assumption that was wrong. That he was assuming that something called 'algebraic integers' had a property which he thought they shared with the ordinary whole numbers . . ."

"Doesn't he realize that he's speaking a foreign language?" Jeff says.

". . . he had to introduce the new concept, what he called 'ideal complex numbers'. . ."

The monologue continues for five minutes. Laura walks into the control room to see how things are going. She's been concerned that Professor Bailey might be a problem but hoped that Robert would be able to work with him. She listens for a while to the two-way — which has become a one-way — and then says to Willie, "It's too hard, isn't it?"

Willie shrugs his shoulders. "Not yet," he replies, hopefully. He still hears potential in the professor, who occasionally comes up with interesting turns of phrase and is certainly filled with enthusiasm.

Jeff remarks, only half-humorously, that Willie is just saying that because he doesn't have to cut the two-way. At the morning meeting, when he proposed that Robert interview "some geeky egghead," Jeff had a clear picture in mind of some passionate, weird, yet involving conversation that would make for a good three-minute piece about this unusual "mathematical event." Bailey is proving to be not a geeky egghead, but an overscrupulous scholar.

The mathematician talks on, discussing how elliptical curves, number theory, and the Taniyama-Shimura-Weil Conjecture all connect with Andrew Wiles's historic solution of Fermat's theorem. In the control room, Jeff becomes momentarily philosophical. "You know, we could do something really funny with this. There's *got* to be something we can do with this! It's so . . . dense. Maybe we could mix it together . . ." His voice drifts off as he tries to imagine a creative use for the professor. But he cannot.

Laura says encouragingly: "I was just about to give up on this guy on the phone when I asked him to start over — and then he was perfect. But I had to *interrupt* him and tell him that this was for radio and he was being too dense."

The professor starts to wind down. "So one of the things I want to emphasize that perhaps is not seen by the general public is that although every science tends to break up into different specializations — this has happened in biology and physics, and also in mathematics — there's also, every so often, a great *confluence* of different subjects, different areas . . . as in this theorem, where things come together, they're unified, and they give you ways to get *new* results by applying results you have gotten from other fields."

Finally, Robert jumps in. But he does not circle back to the beginning nor does he ask the professor to be more concise. Instead he picks up the theme that the professor has just raised. "It's remarkable that, from a lay perspective, what we're seeing is the narrowest, most utterly academic project solving an age-old problem that breaks through all sorts of walls and brings together — or eventually will bring together — work in many different fields of mathematics."

"Absolutely," says Professor Bailey eagerly. His words stumble over themselves. "I mean we see this, you know, these . . . For instance, let me give you another example . . ." And Bailey spins out a number of esoteric ramifications that result from Wiles's mathematical solution.

Laura says to Willie: "He assumes Robert is understanding what he's saying, and he just keeps talking."

But Bailey's answer is relatively brief. Something more like a give-and-take rhythm has entered the two-way, and the next exchange produces some marginally usable tape. Robert says: "My assumption here is that Professor Wiles in his presentation satisfied the number theorists and therefore has indeed *proven* that x to the nth plus y to the nth will not equal z to the nth, x, y, and z all being non-negative integers." He has summarized Fermat's Theorem quickly and half under his breath in a familiar Robert Siegel way. Then he resumes his question. "I'm assuming he's right. But do we know for *sure* . . . is everyone satisfied?"

"What will happen in the next few months," the professor replies, "is that the proof will be scrutinized, but for a man in the field it's often possible to get a good idea whether this is going to be a correct proof without going through it line by line. What happens is, you get a *feeling* for the concepts involved — it's a highly conceptual subject — and you ask, Are there new ideas? Now, Wiles's approach has new ideas in it . . ."

The professor amplifies his answer slightly, and most of what he says is interesting and personable. Perhaps hoping that Bailey has established a solid foundation upon which to speak, Robert decides to return to some earlier points and give the professor a second chance to make the mathematics comprehensible.

Robert speaks quickly and in a businesslike fashion. "Now, Professor Bailey, if you don't mind, I think that . . . what we've gotten, which we'll edit obviously . . ."

"Yes," says the professor, seeming to anticipate where Robert is going.

". . . the latter questions are fine and clear. I want to go back to the beginning questions."

"All right."

"So that we can perhaps communicate what I didn't ask at the outset, which is what Fermat's last theorem is, and then try to give a hint at the method — one more crack at the method of Wiles. What he used to solve the equation. So first, I guess, in the way of introduction, I think I understand what you're saying: since we all learned the Pythagorean theorem in high school, it's not too hard for us to imagine that same equation being raised to higher exponential powers."

Robert is taking an interesting approach, linking the somewhat obscure formula of Fermat to the familiar geometrical law ($a^2 + b^2 = c^2$). Robert hopes that the concreteness of triangles will both clarify matters for the radio audience and help the professor make his explanations more down-to-earth.

As Robert is speaking, Melissa walks into the control room with the news that the national desk has canceled Jordan's report on Procter and Gamble. The overstocked show is thinning out. She wonders how the math two-way is going. "It's getting right to the point," says Willie. "Still has potential, though it's been rough going." Melissa leaves as Bailey begins his new answer.

"So now . . . The Pythagorean theorem . . . Of course, we're talking, remember, not just about the Pythagorean theorem, but only for whole numbers. You know the Greeks were the first ones to study these questions, not just other solutions as you were now saying in the real numbers or in the complex numbers as they were later done, but in terms of . . ." And Bailey goes off on another abstruse tangent.

It seems that the professor doesn't want to speak about Fermat's theorem in the context of Pythagoras because the analogy doesn't make sense to him — though it might to many radio listeners. Robert holds Professor Bailey on a tighter rein for the next few minutes, interrupting him more frequently, but the professor never finds a way to describe Fermat's theorem in a way that will be clear to listeners whose eyes glaze over when someone says, "x to the n plus y to the n."

In the control room, Laura makes a final plea to Willie: "If we could get him to talk about how excited he was when he heard the news — what it was like being there. When I was talking to him, he sounded like a kid. He said it was the thrill of his lifetime."

Willie stares through the window into the studio. He does not feel he can intervene at this point.

The professor struggles to be more concrete, at one point even saying that what's important about the way Wiles solved Fermat's theorem is that it helps mathematicians keep their feet on the ground. The methods used to solve the classic theorem did not exist fifty years ago, and it's gratifying to have an old problem solved by brand-new theories.

Robert interjects: "Yes, well . . . What can you tell us about the methods that Andrew Wiles used?" Robert speaks in an encouraging, friendly voice, but the informality in his tone does not communicate the message to the professor that he needs to lighten up his discussion.

"The underlying method," Professor Bailey begins, "is one I sort of started to say something about, but let me now *explain in more detail* . . ."

Everyone in the control room — from the engineer to Willie — yells, "No! No! No!"

The professor is off and running. This time he tries to involve Robert more directly in his discussion, soliciting replies as he might in a tutorial setting. But the level of discourse remains too abstract for a lay audience to follow aurally.

". . . Wiles converted the Fermat equation into a series of equations, a class, called equations for elliptic curves." He recites some examples, then asks, "Do you understand what I'm saying? . . . And Frey says that if I have an elliptic curve over rational numbers, then it is modular. Do you see? . . ."

At first Robert grunts and tries to make some responses. But the two-way is collapsing. Marty looks at the amount of tape left on the reel and says, "If he does a couple more minutes, we can fill a whole third."

"We've done the intellectual," says Willie. "Let's go for the emotional."

Melissa returns to the control room and reminds Willie that another two-way is scheduled to begin at three-thirty, in just a few minutes.

". . . on the other hand, that equation that Frey made out of the Fermat solution turned out — and this was proved by another mathematician, Kenneth Ribet . . ."

Laura looks directly at Willie. "Flush?" — by which she means, "Is the two-way down the tubes?"

Willie says: "I don't feel it anymore."

"It's too bad," says Laura. "This is such a good thing. But . . . I was afraid we should have found someone else."

". . . So if you knew that the conjecture of Taniyama was true, then that would contradict this result of Frey, right? Do you see? But this is where Andrew Wiles starts from . . ."

Willie presses the intercom button and speaks very quietly to Robert, so that Robert will be able to hear both him and Bailey in his headphone. "A reminder that your guest is here for three-thirty."

Bailey winds up shortly thereafter, and Robert laughs pleasantly into the microphone. "Well, as general as it is, that's going to have to do it for us . . . It may yet be far too technical for us. I mean there's a limit to our capacity for education on the radio." The professor laughs along with Robert. "So let me just ask you very simply one last question. Having done this, has Professor Wiles achieved a status in the world of number theory?"

"Oh," says the professor, sounding a bit surprised at the simplicity of the question. "He already had a first-class status, I can assure you of that. I mean, he is one of the most eminent number theorists, even before this result."

Then suddenly the professor's tone shifts, and he launches into a curiously touching coda to the entire conversation. "But you know, I'm sorry . . . I tried . . . You know, it's very hard for a mathematician — harder than let's say for a theoretical physicist — to explain anything to laymen about mathematics in this form." Professor Bailey then relates a charming story that Einstein reputedly told a student who wanted him to explain the theory of relativity:

A blind man asks a friend to describe the color white. The friend says, first, that "white" is like a swan; then he explains that a "swan" is a large bird with a crooked neck; finally he describes "crooked" by saying it's like an elbow. "Ah!" the blind man cries. "Now I know what 'white' means!"

Bailey summarizes the point of the story neatly. "To people without mathematical backgrounds, I can only speak in a metaphoric language which is quite limiting." The professor has eloquently expressed the problem with which he has been wrestling for the past half-hour. Interestingly — sadly — the story about the swan would work very well indeed in a radio spot . . . were there anything of equal clarity to go with it.

Then, like a drowning man struggling against the inevitable, Bailey compulsively keeps talking. He goes back over ground he's already covered, sometimes managing to speak more concretely than before (the electrical appliances we use today evolved from abstract mathematical formulas developed in the nineteenth century) — but it's all too late.

The Favag on the wall reads three-thirty-two. People are lining up at the studio door. Professor Bailey keeps talking on and on.

". . . All of a sudden particle physics is transformed . . ."

"Uh-huh, uh-huh. . ." says Robert, trying to interrupt. But the professor doesn't let him.

". . . theories about things called electromagnetic waves . . ."

Laura Westley has left the control room for a few minutes to place a phone call to Lyle Gramley, the second participant in the upcoming discussion about interest rates. When she comes back, she cannot believe that Bailey is still on the line. "Good-bye!" she exclaims. But the professor is talking about James Clerk Maxwell and Faraday.

"I don't understand this," Laura says. "We have a former director of the Congressional Budget Office [Robert Reischauer] sitting outside in the hall, waiting for this phone call to end."

". . . And these all in the end depend upon this insight of mathematical physics."

"On that note," Robert intervenes, at long last, "I'm going to have to cut us off." Gracious to the last, Robert says "us" rather than "you."

"All right!" says the professor, sounding resigned.

"Thank you very much, Professor Bailey."

But the professor is not quite ready to say good-bye. His next words feel like the twisting of a knife in a wound.

"Can you tell me when you're going to . . ." Robert interrupts before he completes the sentence. It's painfully clear that the professor is asking when the spot will air. He wants to tell his family and his colleagues about it.

Robert handles the embarrassing moment with aplomb. "I'm not sure. I don't know that now. The producers will probably know later."

"Okay," says the professor. "But it will be today?" His plaintive voice seems to float up from a dark well — far away from the world of radio.

"I hope . . ." says Robert, quickly sorting out how to be diplomatic yet honest. "Well, it would be today — or else it gets bumped from the program. One or the other, I'm afraid."

"All right. Will you let me know? Or . . ."

"Yes," says Robert, though he knows this may not happen.

"Okay," says the professor calmly.

"Bye-bye," says Robert.

"Thank you. Bye." And Professor Bailey finally vanishes into silence.

. . .

Willie and Jeff have a brief discussion out by the horseshoe, wondering if there's any possibility of saving the two-way. But the decision to drop the interview is inevitable and comes very quickly. No single person appears fully responsible for its failure. The tragedy of the "Bailey affair" lies in the potential that Laura and Willie — and Robert — sensed in the professor but which they were not able to bring out of him. The problem comes down to environment and format. As Willie knows from his work at a university's public radio station, the best way to turn brilliant but loquacious professors into interesting radio conversationalists is to sit with them, eyeball to eyeball, and record much more tape than you are going to use. Often it takes an hour of coaxing and prodding and circling back and rephrasing before you wind up with the necessary raw material for a good radio piece. Then comes the crucial cutting and splicing of the tape, which may take several more hours.

A program like *All Things Considered* rarely can indulge in such intense work, certainly for a piece that must be turned around in an afternoon. Here is one example of why media experts — professional talkers — are more likely to be heard these days on daily NPR programs.

Rounding the Far Turn: Ninety Minutes to Go

At three thirty-five, the *ATC* horseshoe has become the center of a multi-ring circus of activity. The adrenaline rush is starting.

Melissa is creating a new road map. Since the mathematician and the report on Procter and Gamble have both fallen through, the show no longer has too many stories. It may be coming in a bit short. Marika's piece on Beau Jocque is back at the bottom of the second third. The New York City terrorism story now leads the first third, followed by the two-way on the Sudanese connection (the first two thirds of a classic spindown). The show does not yet have either piece in hand — in fact, only within the past few minutes has Laura confirmed absolutely that she will *not* be able to reach Mary Anne Weaver, author of *The New Yorker* story. Writer Steve Emerson has agreed to come to NPR at four-thirty for the two-way. As the piece will air at around five-fifteen, Robert will want to interview Emerson as close to time as possible, thus avoiding a lot of editing. However, Emerson is an expert who appears regularly on many of the television networks. There's a bit of time pressure, here, but it does not generate concern.

The lead story from Jim Zarroli causes some worry. "The Canolli," as Willie calls him, is a fine reporter, but he invariably pushes his deadlines. He is supposed to be filing from the New York Bureau at four (the news conference ended at two-forty). Melissa and Willie will feel considerably more relaxed when the tape of Jim's piece has actually arrived in Washington.

Standing at the board with a black marker in her hand, Melissa is juggling the remaining parts of the show. Suddenly she announces to Willie and whoever else is in the vicinity, "Okay! I'm having an idea here!"

"Let's watch!" exclaims Willie.

"Creation!" says Jeff.

Melissa goes over to the third third and points to Gwen's piece on Dickinson. "These are poems in letters, am I right?" She draws a line above the Dickinson slug with her marker and writes in "Letters" — referring to Linda and Robert's segment of letters from listeners — while proclaiming "Poems . . . in . . . letters!"

Some cheers go up.

Willie stares at Melissa blankly, acting as though he is unimpressed. "That's your idea?" he says with feigned incredulousness.

"Come on! You take what you can get," Melissa answers. Then she starts rearranging the second and third thirds. Originally, there were going to be three or four economic and budgetary stories in the show, and a few minutes ago Melissa decided to group them in the middle half-hour, thus putting the squeeze on the Cajun musician. Now there are only two or three reports on the economy, so Melissa moves them back to the third third, above Letters and Emily Dickinson. The second third remains a bit fuzzy, except that Beau Jocque anchors the half-hour. Linda's two-way about the Spanish-language citizenship ceremony is currently scheduled toward the end of the first third.

In Studio Five, Robert is conducting his three-way about interest rates. Robert Reischauer is sitting with his back to the control room, the typical position for guests. (There's no reason to have them distracted by all the faces and the activity on the other side of the glass window.) Lyle Gramley listens and responds over the telephone: the two men in the studio hear him through headphones. Robert Siegel sits on the edge of his chair, as before. He has rolled up his white shirt to his elbows. He leans his chin on his left hand as he listens, then makes small gestures with both hands in front of him when he asks questions. He takes a sip of diet Coke from time to time. He smiles and nods.

"I just want to ask both of you about the prospects of interest rates remaining low," he is saying. "Let's turn that around. If the deficit program *doesn't* succeed, do interest rates go sky-high as a result? Lyle Gramley?"

Robert is in his element. He gracefully moves his questions from guest to guest, while elegantly — if sometimes grandiloquently — summarizing points and perspectives. Gramley and Reischauer are old hands at this kind of conversation and make reasonably concise presentations. The three-way will continue for about twenty minutes, and while its subject matter is pretty dry, the resulting tape accomplishes exactly what Robert had hoped. It affords a cogent (if somewhat characterless) discussion and critique of a central plank of the Clinton administration's economic policy.

In Studio Seven, at three thirty-eight, Linda is catching up on a bit of business that the extended mathematics two-way bumped from Studio Five. Several years ago, NPR started distributing *Fresh Air,* an interview program produced at WHYY, Philadelphia. Many stations carry *Fresh Air* in the hour before *All Things Considered,* and so *Fresh Air* host Terry Gross regularly records a promotional spot with one of the *ATC* hosts, usually around three o'clock.

Linda has put on her headphones and is leaning her right cheek heavily against her hand. The direct line to WHYY in Philadelphia has been patched properly, and Terry Gross's substitute host, Marty Moss-Coane, is about to introduce the *ATC* promo. The engineer at WHYY punches up a special music cartridge, and Marty begins, "Linda Wertheimer has joined us to talk about *All Things Considered* today. Linda, what stories will you be covering?"

"Well," says Linda, looking down through her glasses at a list she has written but speaking in a voice that sounds halting and extemporaneous, "Well, we're leading, Marty, with the arrests in New York City of . . . ah . . . terrorists planning to bomb the United Nations and to assassinate . . . certain officials. We'll also be talking about the Sudanese connection to those people. The budget debate goes on in the Senate: we expect a vote, and we'll have a report. We'll also be discussing interest rates and how keeping them low will make some of the things that President Clinton wants to do possible. We have letters, we have new Emily Dickinson poems, we have zydeco. . . . We have it all."

"Thanks, Linda," Marty says. "Those stories and more later today on *All Things Considered* from National Public Radio." The promo music fades up and then out.

After a pause, Marty's voice is heard from Philadelphia: "I think that was just fine."

"Okay, good," Linda replies. "I'm sorry we were late," she says graciously. She removes her headphones, takes off her glasses, and holds them in her hand as she leaves the studio. She emerges into a flurry of conversation and activity around the horseshoe.

Having just given *Fresh Air* a preview of tonight's program, Linda now stops to look at the new road map. Fortunately, Linda did not say anything in the promo about the *order* in which stories would appear. Each third is short by about a story, but two pieces are not yet included in the schedule: Gonyea's report on the Malice Green trial (still iffy) and Palca's report on the Super Collider vote (assuming it takes place). Furthermore, Margaret Low Smith has a shelf filled with commentaries, three- to three-and-a-half-minute essays from about a dozen regular contributors around the country. The idea of having an occasional short "talk" piece, like an editorial column in a newspaper, started a long time ago on *All Things Considered*.

ATC commentators include interesting characters, such as Bailey White, with her distinctive southern drawl, and Daniel Pinkwater, the oversized-yet-cuddly writer of children's stories from upper New York State. But in recent years the commentators have not been used quite as much to enhance the flow of a program as to plug up holes that appear at the last minute. Margaret tries to keep a wide enough variety of commentaries on file so that there's at least a chance of having them follow logically from the previous story in the show, but format often overshadows function in this particular area of *ATC* programming.

It's not yet time to "reach for the commentaries," however. Willie is checking out the status of stories. "We got the Berger?" he asks.

"Berger will be here," says David Rector. "It will need fixing." Meaning that the foreign desk has already apprised *ATC* of some technical problems with the tape that will have to be repaired before broadcast.

"Do we know if the medical examiner has been cross-examined yet?" asks Willie, thinking about the Gonyea story. Melissa says she'll put a call into the national desk and find out what's going on.

Willie looks at the current lineup of stories in the first third. "Zarroli, Sudan . . . Spanish INS ceremony is kind of pretty. That's good." He likes the idea of having a slightly softer piece toward the end of the first third — a section of the show that, in Willie's opinion, can often become too dominated by hard news.

Linda is wondering when she and Robert will record the Letters segment. "Rob is still in his three-way, right?" she says to David Rector, who will be producing Letters.

"Yeah, that's why I said we'd record at four."

Linda nods and walks to her office.

At a little past three-fifty, Robert concludes his three-way. Out of the control room, Margaret walks — or, rather, rocks, as she's extremely pregnant. She glances over her notepad. Cutting a three-way is a little trickier than cutting a two-way because you want to be sure that no one guest dominates the time.

Margaret stops by the board and asks Melissa if she really wants the three-way cut to five minutes.

"Do you need more?" asks Melissa. "I can give you a little more."

"Well, because it's three people, it's always a little hard to get it down."

Melissa looks at the road map, then picks up her felt marker. "Well, call it five and a half."

"Okay," says Margaret. Thirty seconds does not sound like a lot, but it adds a few extra beats to the pacing of a radio piece and will make Margaret's job of editing that much easier.

Marika now brings the word to Melissa and Willie that Zarroli's piece will not be coming in at four o'clock. The New York bureau reports that it will be fed at four-thirty.

"Aie!" Melissa exclaims.

"Ouuugh," Willie groans.

"Scary," says Marika.

"*He* pushed it back to four-thirty?" Willie asks Marika, double-checking that the delay has not been caused by any technical problems. Marika confirms her understanding that it was Jim's decision.

"That means he won't be done till a quarter to five," says Willie. Like watchful parents, the producer and editor of *ATC* must know the quirks and foibles, as well as the skills and the strengths, of their staff. A good producer will always hope for the best and plan for the worst.

"Well, we could always do it live — and schedule to do that, just in case," says Willie. Melissa is sitting in her chair, straightbacked as usual. She looks steadily at Willie, doesn't say anything, but agrees with his general assessment. Five minutes to four, and questions now loom over the lead story of the program. No one doubts that Zarroli will get his report done and that he will do a good job. But his piece may be a cause for some excitement in an hour or so.

Robert has gone to retrieve another diet Coke from the distant vending machine, and now he appears at the back of the horseshoe. "Was the three-way okay?" someone asks.

Robert shrugs noncommittally. "It doesn't *sing*, but we can spend five minutes on it."

Margaret says, "Yeah, let's talk a little bit about it."

Robert smiles and speaks slowly. "Okay. I think it should begin at the beginning . . ."

"Yes — and end at the end," Margaret continues, speaking rapidly and laughing.

Robert doesn't laugh. He continues in his measured pace. "I'm not sure if it has to end at the end." He explains that in his view, the whole last set of exchanges can be dropped. "We don't have to get that specific about the debt," he says. "But I *do* want . . . that is, if you keep in my question (which I think you have to keep in) where I say, 'What kind of a watershed *is* this? — not much in the way of new taxes, not much more to deficit reduction, and low interest rates haven't made that much difference' . . . if you leave in *that*, then we owe Reischauer his disclaimer. I was taking some liberties with his remarks, and we want to be sure we keep his reply to me."

Margaret understands fully and agrees. Careful tape cutting means you worry about fairness and accuracy as well as comprehensibility. After a few more comments, Margaret walks slowly off to the edit booth, her hand on her hip, to begin her cut.

Robert notices that the rundown of stories on the right of the board now lists the Sudanese Connection two-way for four-thirty, though no name has been filled in.

"Oh, good," he says to Melissa. "What's her name again?"

Melissa replies, "We're using Steve Emerson. Mary Anne Weaver's AWOL. We can't find her."

"Oh! We're doing Steve Emerson," Robert says thoughtfully. He sounds pleased.

"Do you want to see *The New Yorker* piece anyway?" asks Melissa. "It's not absolutely necessary now."

"Yes," says Robert, looking at the clock. "I'll see it in about fifteen minutes." First he has to do Letters with Linda.

Melissa turns to David Rector and asks him to be sure that he "runs a clock" when he produces the segment. Letters must last exactly four minutes and Melissa is double-checking that Linda and Robert will be able to see a timer counting down in the studio so they can record to time.

David goes off to Studio Seven, where Linda and Robert soon join him. At four o'clock, Marika is using Studio Five to mix her Cajun music piece. She will have to be finished shortly because Robert has the Sudan two-way scheduled at four-thirty, and sometime before that, Robert and Linda will need to record the opening billboards for each half-hour. Everyone prefers to pretape *ATC* billboards because they involve a number of elements combined into a fifty-nine-second production: in addition to the theme music, two hosts alternate their brief descriptions of upcoming stories, and at some point a teaser is dropped in — a snippet of tape from one of the half-hour's pieces. Given the hectic schedule of *All Things Considered*, these openings must sometimes be done live, and flubs are all too common during live billboards. These goofs are some of the most glaring and exposed ever broadcast on NPR. (The other familiar kind of glitch is the "double take," when an editor has neglected to cut out a false start from the talk tracks of a piece. When this happens, listeners hear a reporter or host say exactly the same sentence or phrase twice at the beginning or in the middle of a story, much to the embarrassment of everyone concerned.)

The billboards cannot be recorded until the road map for the program is locked up. So while Robert and Linda record Letters, Melissa and Willie are checking in with editors from the national and foreign desks trying to pin down the status of all outstanding stories. They are also engaged in a continuing discussion about the program's flow, though now, after four o'clock, "flow" tends to give way to "fit": that is, the board becomes a puzzle into which pieces of various lengths must be put so that each third lasts exactly twenty-nine minutes — no more, no less. It's nice if there is *some* logic — some sense of connection — from story to story, but at this hour, "aesthetics" will yield to pragmatism. In live radio for a *network*, the clock defines the bottom line.

Robert and Linda crowd into Studio Seven, a space about a third the size of the broadcast studio. It holds two people snugly, three with some sense of crowding. Linda sits to the left, Robert to the right, reversing the seating position they take when broadcasting in Studio Five. Since *ATC* is a monaural program, no one will know the difference.

Linda puts on her glasses and looks over the script. "Now . . . let's see. You start."

"Right," says Robert, leaning his copy against a little stand on the console between them. The two seem very comfortable with each other, though businesslike, since, with less than an hour to go before broadcast, much work needs to get done. "Let me see . . . who does the *Wonderful Life* material?"

Robert is referring to a letter that discusses the expression "Adam's Off Ox," which was mentioned in a story about President Clinton last week on *ATC*. The letter writer alludes to a scene from Frank Capra's movie *It's a Wonderful Life*, and Linda has come up with the idea of playing an audio clip from the movie to spice up the segment. David Rector rented a video of the movie and then got Record Central to dub a few seconds of the sound track onto a reel of audiotape.

Since Linda has written this week's Letters segment, Robert is scanning the copy quickly to become familiar with its ebb and flow. The two hosts alternate reading the various excerpts. Robert also wants to be sure he pronounces all the names correctly.

"*Ban*dlestam?" he asks.

"*Man*delstamm. I'm sorry. M-a-n . . ." She spells it out for him.

Robert reads more snatches of the script out loud. Linda picks up some of her cues, as necessary. They come to the section about "Adam's Off Ox." Robert begins reading, "Peter Lopilato, of Bloomington, Indiana, writes . . ."

Linda interrupts to correct his pronunciation of Lopilato.

Robert says it her way a couple of times. Then he reads, "Adam's Off Ox," enunciating slowly. Without looking up, he asks Linda, "Is that how you say it?"

Linda keeps staring at her script. "Adam's Off Ox," she repeats. The two hosts return to their silent reading, a bit like a bespectacled couple sitting around an afternoon tea, sharing different sections of the same newspaper.

Robert comes across another name. "Richard Boehm." He pronounces it several ways, questioning.

Linda shakes her head. "I don't know."

She looks into the control room. "David," she says, peering over the top of her eyeglasses, "we've got two 'pronouncers' that we don't have and we need to get."

"Should I ask Laura to call?" David asks. Linda answers by taking off her glasses and getting up from her seat. Robert stays behind to read through the rest of the script.

Outside, at the horseshoe, it's decided that Laura will phone one letter writer, Linda on the other: it's already five minutes past four and time is precious. Laura is able to confirm the pronunciation of Lopilato fairly quickly. David relays the information to Robert: "Low-pea-lotto." But they must wait a few minutes more for Linda to get back from her office. Mr. Boehm is proving harder to track down.

Shortly after four o'clock, Peggy Girshman from the science desk drops by *ATC* and talks with Willie and Melissa about the vote on the Superconducting Super Collider. It will definitely be occurring soon, and reporter Joe Palca is covering it. Melissa tells Peggy that Joe may have to go live if he wants to do a report simply because *ATC* may not have a production assistant free to handle a tape. "Akili has got a lot of other stuff backed up. If he gets freed up, we can take in a piece early."

Melissa looks at the clock. "Robert should start Letters."

Someone mentions that Linda is checking the pronunciation of a name.

Gwen appears and holds out to Melissa a reel with a small amount of tape on it. "Here's Emily," she says. Melissa takes the five-minute-thirty-second report that represents half a day of editing. Gwen has more work to do for the program. She will cut the interview with Steve Emerson, now scheduled to take place at four-thirty; she will supervise any mixing that's necessary in Ted Clark's acts and tracks report on Japanese politics; she will help out as needed with other stories that are coming in late — such as Jim Zarroli's from New York and Don Gonyea's from Detroit.

Gwen considers her immediate responsibilities. "Is the 'Sudanese Connection' going to be a countdown kind of two-way?" she asks Melissa — meaning, again, is Robert going to try to conduct the conversation exactly to time?

"Well," Melissa says, "you can try."

"And Zarroli is supposed to be here at four-thirty?"

"Yeah," Willie says tonelessly.

· · ·

Linda returns to Studio Seven. She wasn't able to reach the letter writer himself. "But there are two other people in Great Neck [New York] with the same name, and they both pronounced it 'Bame.' So we'll pronounce it 'Bame' and hope for the best."

Robert repeats "bame" to rhyme with "fame" and then says the name again with a southern twang. Linda picks up the challenge and says the name with a *deeply* southern drawl.

"Okay," says David from the control room. "Stand by."

The engineer hits the cartridge holding the music-and-typewriter theme that announces the Letters segment. At the appropriate moment, Robert starts reading the first letter: "Mary Turner of Ashland, Oregon, writes us to object to our coverage of the occasion in which the president announced the nomination of Judge Ruth Bader Ginsburg to the court . . ."

Robert and Linda read the copy easily, smoothly, with no glitches or stumbles. Robert sits, as always, on the front of his chair. Linda assumes a more relaxed posture, holding her script in her right hand. Sometimes she leans her chin against her left fist, sometimes she gestures gently with her left fingers, as though directing herself up and around the cadences of language that she's speaking. Though Linda and Robert alternate their reading several times in the course of the four minutes, and though their voices evoke a clear sense of interweaving and intertwining, and though they frequently smile at what the other one is reading . . . not once do they actually *look* at each other. Their eyes remain focused on their scripts.

Linda begins the final part of the segment that will lead to the clip from *It's a Wonderful Life*. "And on our explanation of an expression used by President Clinton in asking a reporter's question, we had several letters . . ."

Four people were listening to Linda read, including Marika Partridge, who came into the control room a few moments before Linda began the letter. Robert was following with the script, as was the director/producer, David. No one heard the slip of the tongue — so obvious in print — when Linda said "asking" instead of "answering." Very often such mistakes are picked up by the engineers, who are constantly aware of the sounds being taped or broadcast. But the intense pressures of *ATC* inevitably mean that for all the diligence and concentrated effort, flubs often happen. On the other hand, there are two schools of thought about small bloopers like this. While some producers and hosts want their shows to be "perfect," in the way that musicians want their recorded performances to have no blemishes, others say that the occasional mistake, if not egregious, adds a quality of spontaneity to the show — the illusion (which is not *always* an illusion) of a *live* broadcast.

In any case, Linda continues reading her script: "Peter Lopilato of Bloomington, Indiana, writes: 'In *It's a Wonderful Life*, George Bailey, played by Jimmy Stewart, wanders through Pottersville searching for someone who knows him. In one memorable scene he turns to the bartender, Nick, whom he's known for many years, and says, "Your name is Nick. Isn't it?" I've watched *It's a Wonderful Life* many times, but never have been able to quite make out Nick's reply. That is, until today, thanks to Bill Clinton and *All Things Considered*. Nick replies, "I don't know you from Adam's Off Ox." Thank you for filling in a gap in one of my favorite movies.'"

Robert now reads the second letter. "And Richard Boehm, of Sea Cliff, New York, points out . . ."

"Ready, Four," says David to the engineer in the control room, alerting him to the tape clip coming up.

Robert continues reading: ". . . 'This evening's broadcast implies that the idiom is of southern origin. In the movie, Nick, played by Sheldon Leonard, delivers the line with a downtown Brooklyn accent, which is about as far from a down-home country accent as you can get.'"

"Hit it," says David, and the short tape excerpt starts playing. "You can take them out," David continues. Linda laughs as she listens. Though using the movie sound track was her idea, she hadn't actually heard the excerpt before now.

Robert sits with his arms folded across his chest while Linda reads the wrap-up to the segment. She is smiling broadly, and you can hear it in her voice as she says, "All cross-cultural references appreciated. Send them to *All Things Considered*, National Public Radio, Washington, DC 20036."

Robert and Linda take off their headphones, exchange some laughs about the final letters, and then head out of the studio.

As Letters is winding down, some final rethinking and rearranging is going on around the show board. At seven minutes after four, Willie calls the national desk and asks if it is possible for Gonyea's piece on the Malice Green trial to lead the second third, that is, to be in hand and ready to go at five thirty-five. Apparently the court *has* adjourned a bit earlier than expected, so Gonyea will be able to meet that deadline.

The board at four-fifteen does show what each third of the final program will contain, though the actual *sequence* of stories, especially in the first third, will remain in doubt until the last moment.

[5:00 — 5:29]	[5:30 — 5:59]	[6:00 — 6:29]
NYC Arrests 4 JR/GM Zarroli	Malice Green 3 AT Gonyea	Budget Vote 4 FC Naylor
Sudanese Connection 4 1/2 GM R/Emerson	Kurds Attack 3 1/4 JR Berger	Interest Rates 5 1/2 MLS R/
Aspin Speech 3 1/2 DR Raddatz	Japan Politics 4 GM Clark	Super Collider Live? 3 1/2 JR
Spanish INS 4 AT L/Johnston	Letters 4 DR	Emily Dickinson 5 1/2 GM L/Shurr
A Cat Named Hamish 3 1/2 McIlwraith	Beau Jocque 7 1/2 MP	

In addition to the time and the reporter, each story includes the initials of the production assistant or producer responsible for the piece. One of Margaret's commentaries by writer John McIlwraith has indeed been inserted into the final four minutes of the first third.

With the road map in place, the billboard that opens each third can be written and recorded by Robert and Linda. Usually the producer or the editor writes the copy. But the hosts sometimes compose the billboards, and as Robert is prepping himself for the two-way about the "Sudanese Connection," Linda goes into her office to work on the opening for the first half-hour. She sits with one foot flat on the floor, the other lifted out of her shoe. Like a number of writers for radio, Linda sometimes murmurs quietly to herself as she types, hearing the words in her ears as she composes on the page. For his part, Robert sits in his leather swivel chair, puts his feet up on the arms of the couch in his office, and starts looking through the *New Yorker* article on Muslim fundamentalism.

Meanwhile, Melissa is listening to the Spanish INS report, checking out a teaser for the first third. She has already asked Marika to pull ten or fifteen seconds from the Beau Jocque feature to tease the second third, and Gwen has suggested a cut from the interview with the Dickinson scholar to go inside the third billboard. Akili will direct all these openings and he is already in Studio Five, dubbing the teasers off the original tapes. He'll then splice on the appropriate pieces of white paper leader tape so the recording of the billboards can go smoothly.

Jude Doherty from the national desk, who's been working with Jim Zarroli over the telephone, comes by to discuss the latest news from New York City. Willie joins the conversation, standing in the doorway of Robert's office. Jude outlines for Robert what will be in Jim's report, which will include more information than what was in the news conference this afternoon. Reports on the wire services, though, are already confusing some of the facts in the case, specifically the nationalities of the eight men arrested. Robert has seen that Agence France Presse (AFP) is listing all eight of the terrorists as Sudanese. Jude's understanding, through Jim and other wire services, is that five or six are Sudanese, but of those one is American-born, though of Sudanese extraction. The other two or three are identified by the FBI as Muslim fundamentalists. "Or what we call 'Islamic militants,'" says Jude.

Robert and Jude get into a moderately pedantic discussion about what to call this political group. But it is the *numbers* game that principally concerns Willie, Robert, and Jude, and as the broadcast nears, getting the numbers right will continue to loom as a major issue.

Four-twenty: Robert is alone in his office. Melissa and Willie are scanning the news wires. Marika is standing by her CD player, behind the horseshoe, listening to possible music bridges for the show through her headphones. People hear her murmur something about the Grateful Dead.

Jonathan "Smokey" Baer — one of the oldest of the old hands at *ATC*, who has developed something of a legendary status among tape cutters as the "Fastest Blade" at NPR — has turned up late in the afternoon to help out if needed. At the moment, he is standing behind Melissa, giving her a neck rub. "'What a long strange trip it's been,'"

Smokey says, picking up on Marika's mention of the Dead by quoting some well-known lyrics.

Melissa answers Smokey's words with another Grateful Dead quotation: "Trouble ahead, trouble behind."

Willie starts singing quietly: "And you know that notion just crossed my mind." Others join in: "Trouble ahead, trouble behind . . ."

Melissa turns from her keyboard and slaps the Letters reel onto her tape machine. She starts rewinding the tape, and the noise of her Scully tape recorder partly drowns out the quiet singing. The *ATC* producer has an old, particularly clunky machine that whirs noisily when winding and rewinding, a bit like an old airplane propeller. The roar continues long after the rewinding has stopped — something about the inertial flywheel continuing to spin.

Smokey, a tall man with a droopy mustache and a perpetual grin on his face, goes prowling about the office looking for leftover food (another habit for which he is legendary).

Melissa smiles as she listens to Letters at high speed. She exclaims, "We got movies, we got clips, we got music . . . oh, my God, what a production!"

When she arrives at the "Off Ox" letter, she slows down the tape to normal speed so she can hear clearly how *It's a Wonderful Life* was mixed into the segment. Others at the horseshoe listen in. At Linda's sign-off, people start applauding.

It's approaching four-thirty. Akili comes out of Studio Five. The teasers for the billboards are ready. The hosts are not. Meanwhile, there's been no word on Zarroli. And where is Steve Emerson?

Melissa is now listening to Gwen's cut of the Dickinson piece, sometimes at high speed, sometimes at normal speed. She starts checking an edit. Professor Schurr is speaking: "You say something about this one. It starts out, 'The pansy is transitive.'" Melissa stops the tape, rewinds briefly, listens again. "'The pansy is transitive.'"

Laura gets on the phone. Steve Emerson has told her that he's arranged a five-o'clock television interview somewhere. Had he gotten to NPR at four-thirty, his schedule would work out. But something has happened.

"I think we should start to think about covering our ass," Willie says in a low voice to Melissa. He speaks in an almost teacherly tone, as much as to say, "In a situation like this, we ought to start thinking of fallbacks."

Robert emerges from his office at four thirty-one. "Is Steve coming here or are we doing a phoner?" He's told that Emerson is supposed to be here.

Laura rises from her desk and comes toward Willie and Robert. "Okay. Emerson is in his car. He's at the Washington Hilton. He's driving down. He's on his way."

People look at the clock and start murmuring. With no traffic, the Hilton is perhaps five minutes from NPR. But this is the start of Washington's rush hour.

Willie raises his voice above the din, a note of tension finally entering his voice. "First question to ask him: can he stick around and go live at twelve minutes past?" Willie is trying to avoid having things get so backed up in Studio Five in the next half-hour that nothing is done right. He'd also like to avoid Gwen having to do a "crash edit" on Emerson. (A crash edit occurs when a tape-cutter has hardly any time to prepare a piece of tape for air.)

Laura replies definitely, forcefully. "No. He can't. I told you. He can't."

Willie assumes his singsong, nudgey, "C'mon, you can do it" tone, though he speaks calmly and quietly: "Ask him again."

Laura goes back to the phone.

"Sunspot?" Willie calls, raising his voice slightly. "Is the Open for One done?" Meaning, Is the billboard for the first third written? It's clear that Robert and Linda have got to record the openings now, before Emerson arrives.

Meanwhile, Jeff Rogers is standing near Record Central (which everyone calls the RC) some distance down the hall waiting for the Zarroli feed to start. The last word from New York was that the feed would start at four-forty instead of four-thirty. Gwen is sitting at the horseshoe, available to help out.

In a typical feed of a story from a reporter, acts and tracks will be sent separately to NPR, and then the elements will be edited, as necessary, by NPR tape cutters and mixed by an NPR producer and engineer. Jim Zarroli is preparing his report in the New York bureau, however, and since he is running late he will do the mixing in New York and feed the completed report. Jeff and Gwen are available, however, if there are any screwups in New York or if the piece has to be fixed or redone here in Washington.

Two other late-arriving stories will definitely have to be mixed by the *ATC* staff: Don Gonyea's piece on the Malice Green trial — now scheduled to go on the air at five thirty-five — and Brian Naylor's report on the budget debate in the Senate. Franc Contreras is currently working with Brian's Washington desk editor, Ken Rudin, in an edit booth removed from the activity around the horseshoe. Brian's piece won't be on the air until six o'clock, so Franc has a bit of time to edit the talk tracks, prepare the actualities, and mix the two elements together. (Brian will feed his narration to the RC from a small studio that NPR maintains on Capitol Hill.)

Down the Backstretch:
Billboards and Late Reporters

Four thirty-five. Linda and Robert at last take their seats in Studio Five, Willie, as show editor, having passed on the billboard that Linda wrote. Akili and two engineers, Marty Kurcias and Terry Knight, are in the control room.

Linda and Robert sit at opposite ends of the table in the studio wearing their headphones. They begin to read out loud the opening to the first third, partly to get the feel of it, partly to let Marty make sure all the levels are set properly.

"Suspected terrorists arrested in New York," says Linda, characteristically ending the "York" on an up inflection.

Then Robert says: "It's *All Things Considered* from National Public Radio."

Linda continues: "Eight men were arrested . . . hmm?" She stops as Robert begins discussing the "problem of the numbers." Robert will be following Linda with a brief line: "Of the eight, five are from Sudan. What is the Sudanese connection?"

When Linda and Robert look into the control room, Akili asks, "Are we ready?" and sees small nods of acknowledgment from the hosts. Robert is leaning on his elbows again with his hands straight in front of him. Linda is resting her chin in her left hand. Akili says, "Hit it" to Marty, and the theme starts, playing from a DAT tape. "Ready on both. Coming up." Akili raises his hand high, palm toward the studio, signaling "Prepare yourself" and then, at the appropriate music cue, points sharply toward the hosts.

"Suspected terrorists arrested in New York," says Linda, her rising inflection even more pronounced for the actual recording.

"It's *All Things Considered* from National Public Radio," says Robert.

The music swells, and the recording of the first billboard continues — flawlessly, as it turns out. Linda and Robert alternate their copy, the teaser comes in properly, and everything ends in fifty-nine seconds.

At the conclusion of the billboard, Linda has her hands cupped together on the desk in front of her. She and Robert smile at each other. It is four thirty-eight.

Willie strides into the control room. He's rolled the sleeves of his pink shirt up over his forearms, he's loosened his tie — and he is barefoot. He hands Akili copy for the second billboard, which he has just completed. Gwen comes in while Willie is standing next to Akili. "I have to pull Robert out for a two-way," she announces.

"Is the person here now?" says Akili.

"Yeah," says Gwen. Apparently Steve Emerson has just arrived, having made the drive from the Hilton in about fifteen minutes. "Well, actually," Gwen corrects herself, "he's on the third floor, coming down." (Guests to 2025 M Street always enter NPR through the executive offices above the news floor. An administrative assistant or a production assistant then goes upstairs and walks the person down to the appropriate studio.)

Akili gets on the intercom: "Robert, your person is on his way down. You want to try this second billboard or . . .?"

"Do we have copy?" Robert asks.

"I'll bring it in right now," Willie says in his quietly intense voice.

"Then I'll stay here," says Robert. Willie walks quickly out of the control room and heads into the studio. Gwen takes a seat beside Akili. The Favag on the wall reads four forty-four and forty seconds.

Akili says to the hosts: "Ready? Here we go." Marty punches the DAT player. The theme starts again.

Akili says, "Ready on both. Bring them in." He gestures to the studio.

"Testimony in the Malice Green beating trial," says Linda.

"In this half-hour of *All Things Considered*," says Robert.

"Close their mikes. Music up," says Akili quickly. Then he gives the cue to Marty for the teaser, which will be coming up in about thirty seconds. "'His dad tricked him into it' . . . What a mean dad," Akili adds in an aside, and Marty smiles. "Ready on both." Akili speaks quickly.

Linda holds her forefinger under her chin as she starts to speak, though she moves it away and to the side as she reads.

"In the trial of three white police officers charged with beating

Malice Green to death, a medical examiner testifies that the victim died of blows to his head." Once again Linda is referring to a piece that does not yet exist, though Willie has talked to the national desk about what Gonyea will report.

"Also, Kurdish militants attack Turkish embassies and consulates all over Europe today," Robert says, and then he continues, with no break in his intonation, ". . . wait a minute. They're not *militants*, they're *terrorists*." He sounds a trifle impatient with the language of the copy. Willie has remained in the studio, sitting between Linda and Robert. He goes over and stands beside Robert, and they look at the copy together.

Marty immediately stops tape and rewinds to the beginning of that take.

"Yeah," says Akili with a slight laugh. "I'm not going to argue with that."

The staff in the control room waits as Robert and Willie edit the copy.

"Do it again," says Akili. The music starts. "Ready on both. Bring them up."

"More testimony in the Malice Green beating trial."

"In this half-hour of *All Things Considered*."

The Open begins as before, then Robert reads his revised script: "Also, Kurdish terrorists attack Turkish embassies and consulates all over Europe today, taking hostages and making demands."

"Stand by on Two," says Akili, meaning Tape Recorder Two, which has the teasers cued up on it.

"And Beau Jocque," says Linda, "the leader of a Louisiana zydeco band — that's an irresistible invitation to dance around . . ."

"Ready . . ." Akili warns Marty.

"He says his dad tricked him into it," Linda concludes.

Marty is ready to hit the play button, but Akili does not give the cue. "No, we can't do it," he announces to the control room. "No, we ran out of time."

At the start of each billboard, Akili begins one of the electronic timers in front of the director's station. He sets the timer to count backward from fifty-nine seconds. He knows the teaser is fifteen seconds and when Linda gave her cue-to-tape, Akili saw that only fourteen seconds were left on the timer. Akili talks to the hosts and to Willie through the intercom. "We're out of time. We have to take it again."

In the studio, Robert, Linda, and Willie are conferring on how to cut a few seconds from the billboard. Marty recues teaser and tape.

The clock reads four forty-six and thirty-nine seconds.

Linda and Robert are editing their copy separately. Robert eliminates the reference to Kurds "making demands" while Linda simplifies her introduction to Beau Jocque.

"What are you taking out?" asks Robert, so his script will look the same as Linda's. She tells him.

"Okay," says Akili. "Here we go."

Marty starts recording and hits the music.

Robert says quickly to Linda, "You're up to date on the end of the Kurds?" He gives her the new cue. Linda nods.

"Ready on both," Akili says. "Bring them up."

The opening of the billboard runs as before, but then Robert reads: "Also, Kurdish terrorists attack Turkish embassies and consulates all over Europe today."

Linda comes in: "And Beau Jocque: he's the leader of a Louisiana zydeco band — he says his dad tricked him into it."

"Hit it, mike out," says Akili to Marty. The billboard now has plenty of time. Not only did Robert and Linda cut several phrases, they also punched up their reading ever so slightly.

"My dad had an accordion, a Cajun accordion . . ." Beau Jocque begins.

"You have four seconds," Akili tells the hosts, informing them how much time will be left after the teaser.

"I'll take that," Robert says, meaning he will do the tag line leading to the news.

"Okay," Akili says to Marty. "Robert only."

Marty repeats, just to be sure. "Robert only."

The Beau Jocque tease is rapidly coming to a close.

"Uh-huh," says Akili, then, "Open his mike."

Robert makes sure his words fill the remaining four seconds: "Those stories, and your letters, after this news update."

The billboard ends on time. "Great!" Gwen exclaims. She looks at Akili sitting beside her. "Does Robert know he's going live with Emerson?"

"Going live?" says Akili, surprised. Last he heard around the horseshoe, Emerson needed to dash off to a television appearance. "Well, Willie's in the studio with him — he must have said something."

Marty asks if they are going to do the third billboard. It is four forty-nine. "I don't have a third one," says Akili. And indeed, in the studio Robert is taking off his headphones and standing up.

Gwen and Robert meet Steve Emerson together on the sofa that sits just outside the door to the Studio Five complex. Gwen says, "We're going to go live, you know, Robert."

Robert shakes Steve's hand while saying, "So I gather, fine. Always good to see you, Steve."

"Nice to see you again," replies Emerson, a compact, soft-spoken man, as well dressed as Robert and also sporting a beard.

"So what do you think?" says Robert. Emerson begins to reply, but Robert smiles and says, "Let's take a walk to the vending machine while I ask you what you think." They laugh.

"Well," says Emerson, "I think two things are interesting — three things. One is that the Sudanese government . . ." The two men walk off, deep in conversation.

It's four-fifty. Linda and Akili walk back toward the horseshoe. As Linda crosses the board on the way to her office, she yawns. Melissa calls to Akili.

"Yeah?" he says, coming over.

"Do you see that I have you down for Gonyea."

Akili looks up at the board and nods. The report is scheduled to come in at around five-fifteen, which will give Akili twenty minutes to prepare the elements and then mix the three-minute report.

Melissa is listening again to the Spanish INS piece and draws Akili into the discussion. They need to cut fifteen seconds from the spot, scheduled to air toward the latter part of the first third, in order to give the live two-way between Robert and Steve Emerson a little more elbow room. Melissa has an idea for an edit and plays a section of tape for Akili.

Four fifty-three. Melissa hands Akili the INS tape so he can make the cut. Robert returns to the horseshoe with Steve Emerson; their conversation has drifted into a more general discussion about the Middle East. Robert now fills in Emerson on procedures. Their two-way is scheduled to begin at twelve minutes past five. They will listen to Zarroli's report from New York together before they talk. "It's quite important that we should hear the story that precedes us. You'll recognize some of the tape he uses, I'm sure, which will be from the news conference." Then Robert remembers something. "Oh, Meliss," he calls. "We have to decide how to describe Steve. 'A freelance journalist who writes about terrorism?'"

Melissa starts typing a script for the two-way, while Robert dictates some more ideas: "He's written a great deal about fundamentalism . . ."

"And my address is . . ." says Steve Emerson. Robert laughs.

Four fifty-five. Willie is conferring again with Jude Doherty as he writes up the introduction to Jim's report. "Six were born in Sudan?" Willie is asking.

Jude speaks with a singsong, didactic voice, trying to make everything clear. "Five were U.S. residents with Sudanese passports. The sixth was American-born, of Sudanese descent."

"We're still short two," says Willie. "There were eight arrested altogether."

"Right," says Jude, "The other nationalities are unknown."

"This intro works the way it is, then, yes?" says Willie, and he moves out of the way so Jude can read what's on his screen. She nods in approval.

But where *is* the Zarroli piece? — which now has been included in the opening billboard, which now has an introduction written for it, which now has a follow-up two-way ready to go. The report has not yet been sent up from New York. The four o'clock target has slipped to a four-thirty deadline, which has slid to a four forty-five probable feed. It is scheduled to go on the air following the five o'clock newscast and a thirty-second introduction from Linda — that is to say, it will be broadcast at eight and a half minutes past five. Less than fifteen minutes from now.

Jeff Rogers still waits in RC. Gwen Macsai remains free to help. The rest is up to the production crew in New York and to the reporter himself.

Back at the horseshoe, Linda has joined Jude, who is standing behind Willie as he types up the script introducing Zarroli's report. Akili walks over to Willie holding the newly cut INS tape. Willie looks up while he types a few words and says in a loud voice, "Vat do *you* vant?"

"Two fifty-three on the Spanish language INS," Akili says.

Linda speaks up: "And you have the intro? I feel like I'm working only slightly. Is the intro okay, Akili?" She remembers Melissa saying that the latest cut would require a slight rewriting of the introduction.

Willie looks over his shoulder at Linda while he types. "We don't really *want* you working, Linda."

Akili hasn't checked the intro yet. "Did you dupe it over to me?" he says, meaning did Linda send the copy to his computer mailbox.

"It should be in group," says Linda. "Group" is the common computer location that all members of the *ATC* staff can access and the place where all portions of the show script are sent.

"Okay," says Akili.

Willie takes a pause from writing the Zarroli intro, looks directly at Akili, and speaks in his quiet, yet firm voice. "Tell Melissa the times. Let's keep the divisions straight here." Willie is *editor* tonight, not producer — it's Melissa who must know the precise lengths of all the pieces. As work on the show nears its climax, Willie understands that it's particularly important now to maintain the proper lines of responsibility and authority — otherwise foul-ups are sure to happen. "I know it's hard," he adds with genuine understanding. Akili nods and takes a few steps over to Melissa's side of the horseshoe.

Willie goes back to the Zarroli introduction. He addresses Jude. "Now here's where I'm confused." He speaks patiently but with a bit of tension in his voice. He's brought up the script of Zarroli's report, which is in the computer, even though the tape of his spot has not yet been fed from New York. "He's saying that 'six of the men were born in the Sudan, while the seventh, reportedly, is American-born.'"

"All right," says Jude.

"'The nationality of the last man is unknown,'" Willie continues reading.

Linda says, "The wires have been saying that there were five Sudanese."

"Right," says Jude. "Except for AFP, which said eight." What Jude doesn't say, but everyone knows, is that Agence France Presse is notoriously inaccurate in its details. "Well, stick with what Jim has because he was at the news conferences and the wires have really been confusing."

"I thought I wrote it down as five," says Willie, remembering what he heard on television earlier in the day.

Melissa has switched on small monitor speakers near her tape recorder that carry what NPR is feeding to the network — and suddenly the *ATC* theme starts. It's five o'clock. And where is Zarroli's tape?

Robert comes over to the group standing around Willie. "I understood that five of the arrested men were permanent U.S. residents," he says. "They had green cards."

Willie explains that Zarroli is reporting *six* native Sudanese.

Jude picks up the telephone. "I hope Jim is out of the studio now so I can verify this with him." She reaches the New York bureau. "Hi, this is Jude," she says carefully, trying to mask her tension. "I'd like to talk to Jim. Thank you." She looks at Willie. "I hope the receptionist knows who I'm talking about."

Willie sums up the situation facing them as he understands it. "Look, if he's wrong, he can read his first track again."

Jude is supporting her reporter. "Right. But I don't think he's wrong."

"Whereas if we're wrong, we'll redo the billboard," Willie adds, still sounding remarkably calm.

His mind is racing at high speed, however. While Jude is waiting to talk to Zarroli, Willie picks up his phone and pages Martha Raddatz. Willie wants to know immediately the status of Martha's piece (which he *thinks* she has already recorded) because if the Zarroli story is late, Willie will suggest using the report on defense secretary Aspin's speech directly after the newscast. The Favag ticks off the seconds and Martha does not answer the page.

Meanwhile, the taped billboard identifying five of the suspects as Sudanese has now been aired and Corey Flintoff has begun the first *ATC* newscast. His lead story concerns Haiti — President Aristide announced late today that he will meet with the military rulers of the country next week. The second story is a report from Anthony Brooks about the letter bomb that severely injured a Yale computer science professor.

"Where am I," says Willie, turning around and temporarily losing track of what he was planning to do next.

"You have Zarroli's copy on your chair," says Melissa.

Willie suddenly reaches up over Melissa's tape recorder and rubs the pink belly of the stuffed dinosaur. "Save us *Dee*-no," Willie says, in a high but quiet voice. "*Please . . .*"

Then he sits down and returns to the Zarroli intro on his computer screen.

At the same time, Linda is talking with Jude as she talks on the phone with Zarroli. Jim confirms the number of Sudanese as six. Robert is discussing with Steve Emerson whether Muslims themselves use the word "fundamentalist," or is this a strictly Western usage? Melissa is talking to Akili, David is talking to Gwen . . . the noise level around the horseshoe gets louder and louder, all while Willie is trying to finish writing his script. He suddenly raises his voice above the cacophony. "Can we have a little *more* noise, *right* here, please!!??"

Linda ends her conversation with Jude and walks off to the studio.

Robert follows with Steve. As the noise subsides, Willie completes the intro. While it is being printed out on a whiny Okidata dot matrix some distance away, Willie says to Melissa, "Spot? I want to bring this script to Linda because I want to ask her a question." Typically, during a broadcast, the producer carries copy to the hosts and to the control room. Melissa nods. Then Willie focuses his mind on backup options. He remembers his unanswered page to Martha Raddatz.

"Where's Martha's tape?" he asks. "Just in case the Zarroli is totally fucked. Do we have her tape?"

Melissa says she will get Martha's tape into the studio as soon as possible. Willie reviews yet another fallback — a direct feed from New York into Studio Five and then out over the air. "Are we patched?" asks Willie, meaning, is the New York control room connected to the Washington control room, just in case? This kind of link has to be coordinated through NPR's Master Control, downstairs.

"Yeah, we're patched," says Melissa.

Jude is on the phone to the New York control room. "Are you going to do it live?" she asks. Willie and Melissa watch her expectantly. "Gotcha, gotcha," she says. Meanwhile, in the background, Corey has just started the second section of his newscast — it's four minutes after five:

"The FBI said today that it has arrested eight alleged Islamic militants on charges of plotting to blow up the United Nations and two highway tunnels under the Hudson River. The FBI complaint said that five of the suspects were arrested as they were mixing a so-called witches' brew of explosive ingredients at an alleged bomb factory. The mixture was said to be similar to the one used to bomb the World Trade Center in February. The FBI said that *at least five* of the suspects were from Sudan."

Corey has cleverly gotten around the problem of inconsistency between what the wire services say and what Jim Zarroli will shortly be reporting. That is, if his report arrives in time. Before Corey has finished reading his story, Jude has hung up the phone. "Okay," she says. "The New York engineer says that there are sixty seconds left in the feed they're now sending into the RC."

Willie double-checks. "It's being fed *right now?*"

Jeff Rodgers has come back to the horseshoe and is listening to the proceedings. "It's being fed *mixed* and everything?"

"Yes," says Jude to both questions and continues with a calm intensity. "Now after the feed he will rerack all the tape and be ready for a live roll if necessary, if Melissa calls."

One of the engineers from the RC has also come down the hallway to bring news of the feed. "I talked to New York right before Jude did," the engineer explains, "and there are no pickups." That is, Jim's talk tracks contain no stumbles and all the transitions from talk track to actuality run smoothly, so no one in Washington will have to edit any of the tape. Apparently one reason that the Zarroli piece is coming in so late is that New York decided to prerecord Jim's narrations, leader them up, and then feed a "live mix" to Washington — that is, run two tape machines, one with Jim's tracks, the other with his actualities. If there had been more time, New York would have prerecorded the entire mix and then fed the completed piece. The most anxiety-provoking scenario was avoided, though — something that happens often enough on a breaking story — when a reporter reads "live to tape." In this form of production, the reporter speaks his or her talk tracks from the remote location and the remote engineer rolls the actualities on cue. The RC in Washington records the results, which often include a few false starts and flubs — either the reporter stumbles or the engineer misses a cue — that have to be edited out before broadcast. Given enough time, none of these mistakes will cause a disaster. Simple tape editing in Washington can clean up all the pickups. But at the moment there's no time left for any edits at NPR.

Though the mix appears to be arriving in good shape, the New York bureau is not taking any chances, and at the end of the feed the engineer will rewind the tapes and be ready to repeat the mix live, directly onto *ATC*'s air, should anything untoward happen to the recording RC is currently making. (It's always possible a freakish accident might occur, such as someone spilling coffee onto the tape or accidentally erasing it.) With this little time to spare, you cannot be too careful, nor have too many backups in place.

"All right, good," says Jude, beginning to feel that everything is going to work out after all.

Melissa tells Jeff that all he will do is "white-line" the tape, when he collects it from the RC — that is, he will put a long white mark with a grease pencil over the last several seconds of the tape so that the engineer in the control room will *see* when the end of the report is coming up. Usually, white leader tape is spliced onto the beginning and end of a piece, again as a visual aid for the people in the control room. Of course, everyone is watching timers and clocks as well, but the physical marks on the tape add one more measure of security, provide one more stay against the chaos that always seems to be lurking in the shadows whenever men and women try to operate, with split-second accuracy, a medium based on complex electronic machines.

Jeff runs back down to the RC to be ready when the feed from New York ends. Akili asks if he should hold open the door of Studio Five for Jeff. When only seconds remain to get a piece of tape from editing booth to control room, it's one of the traditions at NPR for people to hold open the door of the studio and the inner door of the control room so that the editor with the tape has a clear path all the way to the on-the-air tape machines. Someone says to Akili that Jeff will have "plenty of time" to white-line the tape and get it into the control room. Akili and Gwen decide to take up positions beside the doors anyway.

Here's what's meant by the expression "plenty of time" in this context: when Akili asked if he should hold open a door, about thirty seconds were remaining in the feed from New York to the RC. The Zarroli report was scheduled to be broadcast in a little over three minutes — giving Jeff two and a half minutes to get Zarroli's report from the RC into the control room. Two and a half minutes is a long time in broadcasting. During that period, Corey Flintoff will begin and end the business section of his seven-minute newscast. (It actually lasts six minutes and fifty seconds and includes a ten-second funding credit at the end.) A five-second *ATC* stinger — a short piece of music — leads from the newscast back to the hosts. Robert and Linda's greeting ("This is *All Things Considered*, I'm Robert Siegel," "And I'm Linda Wertheimer") will consume another five seconds. Linda will then read a thirty-five second introduction to the report from New York. While all this is happening on the air, Jeff has more than enough time to stop by an editing booth and white-line the Zarroli tape. One might argue that he could even add leader to the front and back of the tape — but limiting his activities to white-lining saves about a minute and also guards against sliced fingers and other mishaps.

Shortly after six minutes past five, while Corey is introducing a brief report from Lorna Jordan, Jeff runs down the corridor from the RC carrying the precious tape. He slaps it onto the machine in his edit booth and spools the tail of the tape onto a take-up reel. Then he directs the tape around the mechanical timer installed between the two reels. He rewinds till he comes to the telltale squawk of Zarroli's voice playing backward at high speed. He joggles the tape forward till he hears (at fifteen inches per second): "In New York, this is Jim Zarroli reporting." He puts his grease pencil down on the outer side of the tape and spools back several seconds from the end, drawing a white line as he goes. Then he rewinds the entire report, letting the tape run across the playback head so he can hear where the piece begins. He cues up the tape at that point, draws another short white line, zeros the tape timer, then fast-forwards through to the end, slowing down the machine (by joggling the fast forward and rewind buttons back and forth) till he stops exactly at the conclusion of Zarroli's sign-off. The story indeed lasts three minutes and thirty-five seconds according to the timer, as New York had promised. Corey is discussing the latest unemployment statistics in his newscast when Jeff finishes checking the length of the tape, so rather than carry the report into the control room "tails-out," he rewinds Zarroli back onto the left-hand reel so that the tape will be "heads-out" and ready to play. He quickly sticks a blank label on the reel, writes down a slug and the timing, then runs out of his edit booth.

Akili and Gwen are holding open the doors as Jeff rushes by. He reaches the control room with about fifty seconds to spare.

"There's something *good* about the door-holding," says Akili, grinning broadly. "Though actually, it doesn't happen all that often."

"I love this part," says Gwen with a quiet smile. "It's my *favorite* part."

Epilogue: The Race Goes On

While the broadcast of Jim Zarroli's story — on time — marks the end of the first part of the *ATC* sprint, other dramas continue to play themselves out through the rest of the program. The live Emerson two-way goes well, and after it Steve heads off to his television appointment. The Gonyea acts and tracks report about the Malice Green trial arrives from Detroit, in pieces, just a few minutes behind schedule. Akili does a crash edit on the talk tracks, while Gwen prepares the three actualities for mixing, placing leader tape between each cut. Akili runs into Studio Seven and has eight minutes to assemble a three-minute piece. The engineer does a cool, quick job — switching deftly from track to act to track — and she leaves Akili with a full four minutes to leader and time the final spot. He runs the piece into the control room at five thirty-five, a couple of minutes before it goes on the air.

Later on during the second segment, Linda is pulled from the broadcast studio to do a quick two-way — on tape, but to time — with Joe Palca about the surprising vote in the House that defeated the

Superconducting Super Collider. The piece runs, as scheduled, in the third third, following Brian Naylor's report on the Senate budget debate, which production assistant Franc Contreras manages to finish editing with a little under five minutes to spare.

And then there are the fixes for the rollovers — lots of them today. Jim Zarroli's piece lived up to his usual high standards. His was one of the only reports in any news media to include enough of the context around Jim Fox's phrase "witches' brew" to give the words richness and character: they were part of a *narrative*, not just a clever sound bite. But Jim Zarroli made one mistake: he was simply wrong about the number of Sudanese arrested. So, before the second feed of the program, Jim rerecords the faulty sentence and that piece of tape is spliced into the master reel of the program. After six-thirty eastern time, newscast, billboard, and reporter are all in agreement about how many of the plotters were Sudanese nationals.

Then, toward the end of the show, in spite of warnings from Willie, Linda pronounces the "h" in the town of Amherst, Massachusetts, during her introduction to the Emily Dickinson piece. The lead-in has to be redone. Also, before going home at ten minutes to seven, Linda records three alternate introductions to updates that Brian Naylor might have to file from the Senate. She covers all contingencies in the ongoing saga: the budget has been *approved*, the budget has been *defeated*, or the vote has *just begun* . . . here's a report from Brian Naylor. Franc Contreras hangs around the office until nine-ten, at which point Willie also returns to NPR following a long jog; but at that hour, the Senate is still debating, so no updates are needed to Naylor's original report. Franc and Willie, the last of the *ATC* production crew still on duty, can now go home.

At nine twenty-nine, when Robert Siegel's taped voice signs off for the last time at the end of the third rollover, there is no one around the horseshoe to hear it. The overhead lights are out, the *ATC* race is finally over. At nine forty-five a departing engineer locks the door to Studios Six and Seven after shutting down the facilities for the night. The *All Things Considered* board remains filled with the scrawled words, numbers, and phrases of the past twelve hours — but these marks of activity, noise, and tension now seem only silent echoes in the gathering darkness.

Crashes and Dreams

How Fast Is Your Blade?

The art of radio as practiced at NPR mixes collective and individual creativities in a fashion that is unique among the mass media. For *All Things Considered* to come up with a ninety-minute program each day, three or four dozen people, spread through the organization and around the world, have to work together as quickly and as efficiently as possible; yet this is a far smaller team than would be involved in television, movies, or even music videos. While radio technology is becoming increasingly complex (what with the advent of digital recording and satellite broadcasting), the medium of the sound and the story retains a small-scale, intimate dimension to its production, analogous to the demands the radio program itself makes upon its ultimate destination — the private imagination of an individual listener.

Many old-timers at NPR bemoan the increasing bureaucracy in public radio, in large measure because these reporters and producers have experienced the genius of the medium in its comparative simplicity and directness: one reporter going out into the field with a microphone and cassette recorder, then assembling, with tape deck, editing block, and typewriter (or computer), the raw elements that a producer and engineer will help assemble into a powerfully moving aural presentation. Yet in spite of the fact that the guidance of managers, the control of editorial desks — and even a certain measure of approval from local stations — have cut into the former independence of reporters and producers, the essential acts of radio at NPR remain surprisingly private, individual, and even solitary. The fundamental image for the creative process has not changed a great deal over the years: a woman or a man sitting alone in a windowless soundproofed cubicle holding a grease pencil and a razor blade, listening intently while hundreds of feet of orange-brown plastic tape, loaded onto large metal reels, wind back and forth across a thick gray and silver playback head that reads the magnetism on the tape oxide as though it were electronic Braille and gives it sound. All forms of radio production at NPR — from the simplest "voicers" and the familiar acts and tracks pieces to the most complex mixes — pass through the crucible of the edit booth. And the diminutive editing block, that piece of machined aluminum screwed to the metal plate above the tape heads, may be considered the touchstone for everything that makes its way onto NPR's air.

A curious mystique has grown up around the craft of tape cutting at NPR. There's a kind of visceral magic to the process by which razor blade and splicing tape can reshape voices and sounds, and few people who work at NPR are immune from its attraction. Like sewing cloth or whittling wood, the tricks by which audiotape is manipulated and transformed are at once simple and profound, a mixture of craft and art — easy to learn, difficult to perfect.

The creativity of tape editing is intensely democratic. Production assistants, reporters, and producers, of course, will spend a good deal of time cutting tape, but hosts will also pick up a razor blade from time to time, as will NPR personnel such as secretaries and administrative assistants, who have no immediate connection with on-the-air work. The lure of the tape even reaches out to many former print people who staff the editorial desks. Though some old radio hands grumble when their work must be approved by people "who have never had to cut a piece of tape," in fact, a number of former newspaper and magazine people feel their fingers itching to pick up a razor blade. Linda Killian, show editor for *All Things Considered*, came over from *Forbes* magazine to NPR, and after her first few months of editing scripts, she began talking about how much she wanted to try her hand at tape editing. She learned from other show producers, like Cindy Carpien at *Weekend Edition Saturday*, that it was rare these days for a show editor to also be a skillful tape editor. "I think I could learn *how* to do it," Linda said one day to Willie Sullivan and Melissa around the horseshoe, "though maybe not good enough to do a two-way. I mean there seems to be a big leap between editing an actuality and cutting a two-way. But the physical mechanics of tape editing don't look that hard, and I'd really like to try it."

The advent of digital technology may change radically the relationship between tape cutter and tape, for it turns out that DAT (Digital Audio Tape) cassettes are not edited, molded, or shaped in the same way as anologue, reel-to-reel tape. Most important, digital tape is not physically cut and spliced. Edits are made electronically at a computer terminal using specially designed editing programs. Digital tape editors look at a screen rather than at tape spooling across the tape head. They use a mouse or a keyboard rather than a splicing block. The *physical craft* of tape cutting will change into . . . something else. There's considerable discussion at NPR about what differences digital editing will bring. Few people at NPR have had extended experience using an "editing workstation," even though many commercial radio news operations and some programs on International Public Radio (formerly American Public Radio) have already "gone digital."[1] Digital editing promises to be very quick. It might take a couple of seconds to make some exceptionally difficult cuts that would require several minutes and a lot of trial and error with a grease pencil, razor blade, and splicing tape. Digital recordings can also be manipulated in sophisticated ways that can clean up a bad recording or subtly change the sound on tape — though some of these capabilities will raise questions of standards and ethics. For example, digital editing software will soon make it possible to alter basic sound waves so that if a speaker's voice goes up in the middle of a sentence just where an editor would like to make a cut, the editing station will be able to change the voice inflection

---

[1] American Public Radio grew up in the late 1970s and early 1980s as an outgrowth of the Minnesota Public Radio network. Originally APR took up the slack in distributing arts and performance programs (concert series and the like) when NPR cut its budget in these areas, but APR soon expanded its operations into news as well. The network established a relationship with the *Christian Science Monitor*'s broadcast service in the early eighties. The resulting *Monitor* radio program has gone through a number of formats and incarnations since then. APR (and now PRI) news shows operate with even smaller budgets than NPR — and their audiences also remain quite small — but the network is determined to build itself up as an alternative source of news programs for public radio stations.

so that it goes down, as though ending a sentence. How much of this kind of manipulation will be considered "proper?"

Some people at NPR worry about the inherent abstraction of editing digitally.[2] Will reporters and producers feel as "close" to their sound when they are looking at it on a computer screen instead of touching it with their fingers? Neal Conan expresses concern that the *linearity* that is so much a part of working with analogue tape (A follows

---

[2] It can be argued that, in its very conception, digital recording adds an extra layer of abstraction to the process of sound production. All sound recording begins with sound waves striking the diaphragm of a microphone and producing an oscillating electrical current that mimics the pattern of the original sound wave. In an analogue recording, the electrical impulses from the microphone are then sent to the tape recorder, where the oscillating current creates similar oscillations in a magnetic field generated by the recording head when audiotape passes across it. The recording head is little more than a complex magnet whose magnetic force can be altered electrically. The changing pattern of magnetism generated by the recording head changes the pattern of magnetic charge on the audiotape as it flows by. While the electrical oscillations that come into the tape recorder are in constant motion (as the microphone keeps hearing different sounds), the magnetic oscillations on the recording tape itself take permanent shape as the tape winds in and out of the magnetic field. You can think of the recording tape as sand on a beach after a wave has washed over it: a rippled pattern, a memory of the wave, is left behind.

Digital recording presents an entirely different picture. Before the electrical current produced by a microphone gets sent to the tape recorder, it first gets passed through a "digitizer," which converts the continuous oscillations of the electrical current into a set of numbers — ones and zeroes — that mean "on" and "off," electrically speaking. The sound is thereby translated into a code that no longer looks anything like the original phenomenon: it's not even continuous, as are all sound waves, but instead it contains a huge series of separate data points — collections of ones and zeroes. These numbers are then recorded on magnetic tape in much the way that data is stored on the floppy disk of a computer. The quality of the sound being captured on tape no longer is a function of the recorder's own electronics — how accurately oscillations in the magnetic field mimic the original pattern of sound. The digital code — millions and millions of numbers — is responsible for getting the sound right.

Thus it can be said that analogue recordings store sound as a magnetic "echo" of the original wave, while digital recordings store "an idea" of the original sound. The significance of these different approaches is hotly debated by audiophiles and sound engineers. Many feel that the digital idea represents the original sound far more accurately, with less distortion and greater fidelity, than the analogue echo. Others hear greater abstraction — more "homogenization" — in digital sound: analogue recordings are called "warmer" and digital recordings "more analytical." Philosophy and psychology hide within many arguments over digital versus analogue sound.

B follows C) — and so much a part of good radio storytelling — might be replaced by something more associative or disjointed. Bob Malesky worries more about *how* digital technology is introduced at NPR. While at PRI's *Monitor Radio* digital editing stations are set up for individual reporters and producers to use, NPR's first discussions of workstations have involved using engineers to run the complex software. "Apparently, at the moment," Bob explains, "a digital workstation can be operated by a reporter or producer alone so long as you are dealing pretty much with just one voice or one interview. The moment your tape gets more complex, even for basic editing an engineer is required. Now for me personally, I will find it very difficult to *edit through* another person. It's hard enough during an actual mix — when you want to get the engineer involved in what you're doing — to explain exactly what kind of *feeling* you're trying to get, how you want the piece to flow and be shaped . . . But to deal with all that in the editing process as well, I would find distracting and time-consuming. But we'll have to see how the technology and our use of it evolves as time goes by."

Few people doubt that NPR News will eventually move to digital recording and editing, though the costs and uncertainties involved will delay the changeover for some time. However, even when razor blades become as obsolete as quill pens and manual typewriters, analogue tape editing will continue to exercise a powerful influence on the creative imagination of radio producers. Over the past twenty years, a great deal of lore has grown up around "the touch of the tape," and these stories and experiences will not easily be forgotten.

Dale Willman started work at NPR in 1986, but his career in radio has taken him through a number of different organizations, including several commercial stations. Dale has tended to keep at least one finger in the NPR waters due to a lingering affection for the organization and the people who work there. In recent years, he's filled in as a newscaster and as an occasional host for live events. Dale has a pleasing on-air voice — he hosted American Public Radio's *Monitor Radio* for a while — though he is viewed at NPR as one of those newscasters who has a slightly commercial feel to his delivery.

Before becoming a newscaster, Dale worked on a number of NPR programs as a production assistant. A tall, long-limbed, gentle-spoken man who wears an earing and a soft brown beard, Dale discusses tape cutting from the perspective of someone who learned his craft during crash edits on *All Things Considered*. "People have different skills as tape-cutters," he explains. "Some people are good feature producers. Ira [Glass] is someone who can take a piece of tape that seems really bizarre and shape it into something quite wonderful. He may spend a little time doing it, but he can *hear* the potential within the tape which someone else might not. That's one kind of skill, or set of skills: to get an idea from raw tape and then be able to cut to it.

"Then there are the 'fast blades.' These are people who are good tape cutters in a technical sense — they won't make 'noisy edits,' they won't leave 'double breaths,' they won't often 'upcut,' and so on — but they also are fast.[3] They are able to make quick choices about what tape to use and what to exclude. Their hands move fast and efficiently . . . razor blade, splicing tape, leader tape. Someone like Ira is an okay editor on a deadline because he's had a lot of experience cutting for *ATC;* but some feature producers might find it difficult to make hard-news decisions quickly — what's the 'good tape' and what you can eliminate.

"Although most people in radio don't like to think this, my theory has always been that surgery of any kind is a mechanical skill, and therefore anybody can learn to do a *certain* amount of surgery. Similarly,

---

[3] A "noisy edit" is a splice the audience can hear. A number of mistakes can cause the problem: you splice together two pieces of tape that have different background ambiance; or the voice levels don't match up, either in volume or inflection, so the flow of speech jumps or breaks in an unnatural way; or you leave a small gap between the two spliced pieces of tape, which will cause an electronic noise. Occasionally a tape editor will do everything right and a particular edit will still make a "bump" as it goes over the playback head. The most common cause for this kind of gremlin is that a glitch of magnetism has attached itself to the tape — perhaps carried by the razor blade itself. Sometimes the glitch will go away by itself; sometimes it will force the editor to redo the splice or reedit the tape.

"Double breaths" occur if you accidentally cut your tape *after* one breath and *before* another. The speaker will then take *two* breaths between words or sentences instead of one.

An "upcut" is one of the most common mistakes. It happens if an editor has tried to make too tight a cut and has lopped off the initial portion of a word. "Hers" will sound like "ers." "White House" will come out "ite House." The danger of upcuts has inspired the number one rule of tape cutting: save your outtakes. That is, throw *nothing* away until the piece you're working on has been aired. The most effective way to repair an upcut is to find the original edit, reattach the piece of tape you spliced off, and make the cut again, more carefully. Alternately, you can try to lift the proper consonant (or vowel, which is much more difficult) from some other outtake — but then you'll be piecing together bits of tape which may be half an inch long, and you'll encounter incredible problems isolating the sound you want and then trying to match background ambiance and intonation.

I think anybody can learn the basics of cutting tape. You might even be able to teach monkeys . . . well, maybe not. They'd probably hurt themselves. But there are many purely mechanical skills in tape editing: rocking the tape back and forth to find the editing point, marking the spot with a grease pencil, cutting with a razor blade, using just the right amount of splicing tape, adding leader tape when needed. You can get just about anybody to a base level of knowledge and ability. But what makes some surgeons stand out above other surgeons is the *art* they bring to it . . . the ability to make those surgeries a little tighter, to make those cuts a little more precise, and to be a little more creative with what they're doing. And it's the same thing here. While anybody can learn to simply 'cut tape,' it's a very difficult skill to be able to take a thirty-minute interview and hear a five-minute piece in your head. The hardest skill is to be able to mash tape together, to take that thirty minutes and mold it into something that is short and succinct but does *not* reduce what the person said — does not change the meaning. *That's* where you separate the great people from the good people. And finally, if you can accomplish this reduction at high speed — cut down thirty minutes of tape in less than half an hour — then you've got a fast blade."

Early on, Smokey Baer earned the reputation as one of the fastest of the NPR tape-cutters. He also developed and popularized some of the tricks that later generations of editors now learn as standard procedure.

In an NPR handbook entitled *Sound Reporting*, Smokey makes some interesting distinctions and comparisons. He writes:

> While *editing tape* is a physical task (cut the tape, join it together again), *tape editing* is a creative process that is as demanding and rewarding as fine writing. Like a writer attending to grammar, a tape editor must be careful to make clean splices that leave the listener unable to distinguish edited material from unedited material . . . Tape is not as easy to edit as the printed word. That's because tape editors must preserve the qualities of speech that linguists call *suprasegmentals*, the cadence and inflection of the voice. This is audible information that you can't see in a transcript but that is picked up and processed by the ear and the brain. Just listen to a bad edit. The text makes perfect sense, but your ear knows something is amiss. There may be no breath where the speaker should

have taken one, or there may be changes in background sounds, or the speaker may have abruptly moved far away from the microphone.[4]

Smokey discusses some of the ways that tape cutters can turn a choppy, unnatural-sounding edit into a smoothly flowing actuality: short pieces of tape can be taken from the "outtakes reel" — where discarded tape is stored — and used as corrective splints or Band-Aids to mask discontinuities on the tape:

> Sometimes you need a pause, breath, or even a sound (like an off-mike telephone ringing) to throw into your tape to make an edit sound right. Consider your outtakes a reservoir of room ambiance and speech effects (coughs, *uhms*, *ahhs*, etc.) that you can use to maintain the natural cadence of a person's voice. You can't necessarily mix outtakes, though. The ambient sound of a certain place is closely related to microphone placement. A person's voice recorded, say, during a tour of a very large room, might change timbre as he or she moves through the room. Taking a breath or a phrase recorded in one part of the room and editing it into a portion of tape recorded in a different location may or may not work. Let your ears be the final judge. If it sounds natural, leave it in. If it doesn't work, take it out and look for another section of tape to help you solve your problem.[5]

"Smokey's a real good tape cutter," says Dale Willman when asked about the legendary Baer. "He's done some wonderful work. Of course," — and here Dale smiles impishly — "I *will* say that when *I* was in my 'cutting prime,' Smokey never accepted my challenges for a cutoff to see who *really* was faster." He pauses and grins enigmatically. "I think I would have won."

For his part, in *Sound Reporting*, Smokey talks about his own prowess by adapting a line from A. J. Liebling, "I edit tape better than anyone who can edit tape faster, and edit faster than anyone who can

---

[4] Jonathan Baer, "Tape Editing," in Marcus D. Rosenbaum and John Dinges, eds., *Sound Reporting, The National Public Radio Guide to Radio Journalism and Production* (Kendall/Hunt Publishing, Dubuque, Ia., 1992), p. 164.
[5] Ibid., pp. 176–77.

edit better."[6] The fraternity of fast blades at NPR contains distinct macho overtones — even though membership in the club is not by any means restricted to men, and even though many of the fastest male cutters are also quite sensitive and unchauvinistic individuals . . . away from their editing booths.

"But you know," Dale continues, "everybody has their own strange style when it comes to editing on a deadline. If I knew I had an acts and tracks crash coming in — where I would be putting the talk tracks and actualities on separate reels and leader them for mixing — I would make preparations ahead of time. I'd cut up leader tape into two-second pieces [two seconds in time means fifteen inches in length] and have a stack of these ready to splice in. I'd wrap longer pieces of leader around the hubs of several blank take-up reels so I wouldn't have to waste any time starting my outtakes, my acts, and my tracks reels. Because those are the things that take time. There's not much you can do to speed up the actual tape-cutting process, but you can make up some time with the ancillary stuff.

"In addition I'd usually *hide* all these things in various places in the edit booth — that's a technique which Michael Lawrence and I still joke about. Michael is now a producer on the *Newscast* desk, but we used to share an edit booth at *All Things Considered*. And it's simply a fact of life at NPR that if other tape cutters run out of supplies in the middle of an edit, they'll come scrounging around other booths, 'borrowing' leader tape, empty reels, grease pencils . . . whatever. So Michael and I devised these hiding places for our blank reels, our leader, our extra razor blades, and our splicing tape. Worst thing to happen is to run out of anything when you're crashing.

"Now many people when they're editing, say, a half-hour two-way, will pull the *good* tape off a reel and thus slowly build up the best ten or twelve minutes from the interview on a rough-cut reel. I always found it faster to work the other way. During the two-way, of course, I would always keep a log, and as things were said that I *knew* I wasn't going to use, I'd put a big X in my notes. Then, in the edit booth, on my first pass through the tape, I would *remove* all the marked sections. That might be anywhere from half to two thirds of the interview. Suddenly, the thirty-minute tape is now a ten-minute tape — much

---

[6] Ibid., p. 181.

easier to listen to and to figure out exactly what you've got, and how best to arrange it. Most tape cutters probably work the other way round: they pull off the good stuff rather than the bad stuff. But then, it seems to me, you keep looking at this mass of bad tape that gets smaller only very slowly. When I was on a crash, I found it overwhelming to stare at thirty minutes of tape for any length of time. Whereas using my system, boom!, in two minutes I could be working with ten minutes of tape — and then the piece would almost shape itself many times. It made the crashes a lot quicker for me."

While it can be a fairly simple matter to reduce a half-hour conversation to the most interesting fifteen minutes, trimming that rough-cut down to four or five minutes can take considerable skill and experience. To make those edits on a sharp deadline takes a mixture of technical prowess, extraordinary confidence, and an enormous rush of adrenaline. Peter Breslow is another one of the old hands from *All Things Considered* with a legendary fast blade. Not only is Peter fast as a tape cutter, he's quick as a field producer, as a reporter — in fact, in anything he does. Yet, like so many of the most experienced people at NPR, Peter's personality, away from deadline pressure, is extremely laid back and easygoing. Peter wears blue jeans and wire-rimmed glasses, and his bristly gray hair is cut long on the sides. His quiet smile and slightly distracted stare sometimes make him look like some refugee from Woodstock or Haight-Ashbury, vintage 1969. The persona is both genuine and a bit of a put-on, a stylized mask behind which Peter coils his enormous energy and talent.

Peter Breslow has spent almost all of his fifteen years at NPR working in one capacity or another at *ATC*. He enjoys traveling, and, like Willie Sullivan and Art Silverman, he gets a big kick out of producing other reporters, though unlike Art and Willie he also enjoys doing his own kind of special-feature reporting whenever possible. Peter's most famous exploit is probably his 1988 climb up Mount Everest, when he joined a team of American mountaineers and sent back a number of award-winning reports for *All Things Considered*. His travels have also taken him to Somalia, to Eastern Europe, and all over the U.S. In 1993 Peter finally was lured away from *All Things Considered* and became associate producer at *Weekend Saturday*. While he enjoys the relaxed pace of a weekly show — with the additional opportunities it affords to produce in the field — Peter speaks with a perverse kind of affection for the extraordinary deadline pressures of his many years at *ATC*.

"The daily deadline thing really trains you, you know," Peter explains. "I mean, I'm sure it's extremely unhealthy, but it's a kick, too, to be under incredible time pressure and know that you cannot waste a moment or you'll miss your deadline. You have to be so *focused*. It's really kind of a yoga-type thing — but the complete antithesis. Yoga is using concentration to slow yourself down and make yourself calm. This time you're using concentration in order to go nine thousand miles an hour." He laughs. "But it does have that kind of Zen quality of complete focus of attention, except, of course, as I say, it's probably really bad for you as opposed to helping you. Sometimes you're so pumped that you can't hold your hand steady to cut tape. I mean, I remember late one afternoon when I was working on *ATC*, I happened to find out that Edward Abbey, the environmental writer, had just died — quite literally just a few minutes earlier. I was calling up someone who was at this place where Abbey was, and she told me that he had just died. I also learned that the guy who was the model for a character in Abbey's novel *The Monkey Wrench Gang* — Seldom Seen Smith — also just happened to be around when Abbey died. So I asked the woman I was talking with whether this guy would be willing to talk with us. And she said, 'Well, I'll ask him, but he's very upset,' then she hung up the phone. This was all happening at about four-thirty, half an hour before we went on the air.

"Well, at about five minutes to *six*, this guy calls back and says, 'Okay, I'll talk to you.'" Peter laughs. "So we have half an hour left to the show, right? Now at the six o'clock news break, there are eight minutes when we can pull a host out of the broadcast studio to conduct a two-way. So Noah comes out and starts the interview in one of the production studios. The guy starts talking — he's good, but he's sort of in shock, you know, and talks a lot. Pretty soon it gets to be seven minutes after six. Noah has to go back to the show, but he doesn't want to interrupt the guy. Noah leaves, *I* go into the studio, take his place, and finish up the interview — the guy never even realizes the switch. Then I come running out of the production studio with, probably, you know, twelve minutes of tape or something. I have to cut it down to a three-and-a-half-minute thing for the last four minutes of the show. Now, Neal Conan was executive producer at the time, and he was also editing the show that day . . . which was a good thing because I didn't have time to write an introduction, but Neal is a very fast writer. So I come screaming out of the studio, and I'm yelling information to Neal about Edward Abbey — Neal didn't even know who he was." Peter raises his voice as he tells the story. "'Edward Abbey is a writer, wrote *Monkey Wrench Gang . . . duh-duh-duh.*' I'm yelling all this stuff to him, and I'm slashing away at this tape." Peter makes a sound of hacking at tape. "Well, Neal writes this beautiful, flowing intro. I get the tape done, you know, with like five seconds to spare, and it got on the air. And it was fine. No one knew the chaos that was behind it."

Of course, in order to edit that fast, Peter had to do a certain amount of work on the tape at double speed, fifteen inches per second — particularly since, unlike some cutters on a crash who will go into the edit booth with a clear idea in mind how they will cut the piece, Peter usually has to hear the tape again as he's making his decisions about what to keep and what to drop. "Even if I'm sitting there during a two-way taking notes," he explains, "I need to listen to the tape again. I mean, I'll remember what I heard, and I'll probably have a few things in mind, but — well, it's hard to explain exactly, but I'll listen and cut simultaneously. I'm always, finally, responding to what the tape sounds like. That's where I make the final decisions about what goes and what stays." As a producer, Peter is particularly oriented toward sound, and so as an editor as well he finds there is no substitute for *hearing* the tape and giving his ears the final say.

NPR reporters and producers are always talking about "good tape" and "bad tape." The point of editing is always to bring out the good tape, and the point of a crash edit is to find the good tape quickly. But people have a hard time defining what makes good tape, other than the fact that it's interesting, involving, and engaging. And while experience obviously helps an editor hone his or her judgment about tape, it seems that some kind of "aural instinct" is also involved. "I think there are probably a lot of people who do fine work here," says Peter, "who nonetheless have to take a little bit of time to find the good tape. It doesn't just leap out at them as easily as for some other people. On the other hand, it's also an acquired skill, up to a point. I mean, during my first years here, I would hem and haw a lot when deciding on my edits. But then you learn to have confidence in your instincts and abilities."

One cardinal rule at NPR — often broken in the hectic pace of *All Things Considered* — is for tape editors to *save their outtakes.* Since good tape is such a subjective idea — and since there are almost always a number of perfectly reasonable ways to cut a piece of tape — saving outtakes allows producers or editors down the line to second-guess and revise. Fast blades often do not save their outtakes. Even though Peter now works on a weekly show with a producer, Cindy Carpien, who frequently asks her staff to recut their stories, he cannot get into the habit of saving his outtakes. "Occasionally, I screw up," Peter explains with a grin, "but on the whole I'm not going to change my mind about how to cut tape after I've done it. And Cindy always gets mad at me for not saving my outs . . . but still I don't." Peter smiles mischievously and shrugs his shoulders.

Dale Willman sympathizes with Peter's point of view. "Particularly during a crash, a lot of your outtakes wind up on the floor," Dale recalls. "Which is where they belong. I mean, there's the other extreme, which used to drive me nuts. People would take the outs that they weren't sure about and *tape* them to the wall. So you come into an edit booth that someone else has been using and there will be fifteen strings of tape, one end attached to the wall, the other end in a pile on the floor. You have no idea what all this spaghetti is. And you don't know if you're supposed to save all this . . . if this is a new art form . . . if it's a shrine of some sort that you shouldn't disturb." Dale laughs, but it is true that NPR edit booths are frequently littered with outtakes of various lengths, hanging off the edge of the tape recorder, or draped from the shelves and the walls, or gathered in clumps on the floor.

Sometimes such forms of temporary storage can be essential as an editor moves around sections of tape from one part of a reel to another. Shorter lengths may be draped over the neck (the way a tailor holds a measuring tape) or stretched across the lap until the reel of tape on the machine is wound forward or backwards to the place where the insert is to be made. Of course, since all pieces of tape look exactly the same and editors do not always have the time or the inclination to mark or label the various outs, it takes considerable concentration to keep track of *what* you intend to go *where*. "The search after the lost cut" is a frequent, time-consuming game played by experienced and inexperienced tape cutters alike.

Franc Contreras, the newest member of the *ATC* production team, is just beginning to learn some of the techniques and some of the lore that Peter Breslow, Smokey Baer, and Dale Willman talk about. Franc has been in and out of NPR on temporary assignments from his native New Mexico for about nine months. After a couple of weeks last summer on the daily and weekend versions of *All Things Considered*, Franc returned to Albuquerque only to receive a call in the late fall from Cindy Carpien offering him a temporary slot at *Weekend Saturday*. But Cindy also suggested that he come to Washington expecting to stay a while. "Will I have work?" Franc asked. "Yeah, we'll find you some work," said Cindy encouragingly. Franc was faced with a career move that he hoped would change his life.

"The first day that I started this current stint at NPR was my thirtieth birthday," Frank explains with an earnest, serious look. "So for me it was a new address, a new life, a new decade. And a new country for me, coming from New Mexico. Washington, the East Coast, is like a different country. We think of space and time so differently back home — we *do*, you know." He laughs, his brown eyes brightening. "I was reluctant to get on the subway. It was very strange for me to think about getting on a train that went underground — and so fast. I wouldn't go to movies at first 'cause *everything* for me kind of was a movie. Life here was already surreal enough. I didn't have to go to another level.

"And I'll tell you one thing: after a month and a half of being here, I was calling my old station and saying, 'Hey, let me know when you post my old position again,' I said, 'because I'm interested.' I was really worried that I wasn't going to make it here. Six months: I couldn't even *imagine* staying here six months!"

Franc scratches his short black beard as he talks. "I knew how to do radio journalism before I got here, but I didn't know how to do it on a deadline *with the kind of quality* that they require. They require two things of you on *ATC*. First of all, extreme quality: you've got to be able to write, and you've got to know good tape from bad tape. You've got to understand how radio works. On top of that, though, you've got to be *fast*. There's no time to think about it . . . you've got to be able to crank. And if you don't understand the tools and the pieces and the way the organization functions and some of the personality types and all of this stuff — you can get lost in the confusion.

"And those crash edits . . . man!" Frank grins and shakes his head. "That's just the right word for *that* experience. It's like you're driving your car through an intersection . . . and you see a van coming . . . and it's going to broadside you — you just *know* it is — so what happens to your adrenaline? It gets spiked off the wall, out the top of your head! You are now in a different time zone. That's the feeling you have when you're crashing. Crashing means that you have some tape that needs to get on, and your deadline is maybe a minute away, and you are scared out of your mind 'cause you know that at any moment you could slip up, your piece won't get on the air, it won't make it, and you'll miss your deadline. And that's about the worst thing that could happen.

"The first crash I did here was when I was cutting a music piece that Bob Boilen handed off to me. Noah had interviewed a writer from *Musician* magazine who talked about his twenty-five favorite guitar solos. My job was to cut the two-way down, make it tight, and then weave in and out these various solos. Well, I produced the thing on a deadline, and it came in too long, and it was just scary as hell 'cause really, at that point, I didn't have the tools to be speedy. I remember that Smokey was standing over me on one side, and he was kind of nervous — it's really hard for another producer who's fast to sit and watch a producer who's slow on a crash. They want to just jump in there and do it. But the problem is they don't know the specifics of the tape, so they could end up goofing it up, so I had to sort of like take control. But Smokey was standing over me, only every so often he would bump me aside and make a cut, and then I'd bump him aside and make the next cut. Now, I'm like — what? — five-foot-six, pretty small guy, about a hundred and forty or something. Smokey's this big guy, well over six-foot, a hundred and ninety, maybe two hundred pounds. I guess in retrospect it must have been a pretty funny sight."

Franc ended up running the finished piece into the control room less than a minute before it was supposed to go on the air. "Everyone was freaking out, partly, I guess, 'cause I was new and even with Smokey helping out, they weren't sure that I was going to make it.

"But I've learned a lot since those first days," Franc continues. "First off, don't crash on a music piece! Crash when Deborah Amos is filing from Sarajevo, and the news has just come in, and there's nothing you can do about it. But don't create crash situations for yourself by working inefficiently! But I also know that, in general, I'm still seen as being a little slow. I've got to learn to speed up a bit. I tend to hang on to the tape a little bit too long. I'm still trying to make it perfect, and sometimes that makes me crash on pieces which should be done more quickly.

"But I'm much faster than I was when I first came here. I mean, for example, I've learned to listen to tape moving twice as fast as normal — fifteen ips. On the other shows I've worked on here — *Weekend Saturday* and *Weekend All Things Considered* — I would plod methodically along, sometimes even transcribing the tape. Now it's hard for me to listen at normal speed. If I could play back at thirty ips and understand it, I'd bump the machines up that fast!"

And the News Came Crashing . . .

"Crashes" on *All Things Considered* and other programs are not always triggered by the need to cut tape at the last minute or by the inexperience of young editors. The biggest excitement — the greatest adrenaline rush — occurs when staff members must mobilize to cover breaking news. Any journalist who has ever worked on a daily newspaper knows the thrill of reporting an event as it is happening. Broadcast news adds even more intensity to the experience, because while a deadline for a print reporter may be measured in hours, a radio reporter's deadline can become a matter of minutes and seconds.

NPR's meager budget and its newsmagazine format — which puts so much of its programs on tape — combine to make it difficult for NPR shows to cover a large number of breaking news events; so whenever a chance opens up for rapid-fire reporting, producers will go to extraordinary lengths to accomplish the feat. It so happened that during the very first week that Franc Contreras was doing rollovers for *All Things Considered*, in May 1993, a major story broke in the middle of the western feed that wound up precipitating a massive adrenaline rush for a handful of *ATC* staff members scattered all over Washington.

During the initial broadcast of *ATC*, that Friday afternoon, NPR's White House correspondent, Mara Liasson, discussed the latest news about the Travelgate scandal with host Robert Siegel. That miniscandal had been playing itself out in the press for a couple of days as reporters tracked down information about people from Arkansas who took over the White House travel bureau after President Clinton's inauguration. In her two-way, Mara detailed some of the charges of impropriety and outlined the defense articulated by the administration in an afternoon press conference. The piece led off the final half-hour of the show.

Six-thirty on a Friday evening is not a time that the *ATC* staff dawdles in the office. (The giddiness of the impending weekend affects everyone at NPR — there's always considerable laughter and noise throughout the second floor, and the celebratory mood subsides only as waves of people start heading to the elevators.) As the first rollover of *ATC* began being fed, the two hosts for the day, Robert and Linda, took off quickly. Robert mentioned that he was going to a movie with his family. Art Silverman had been producing the show. After a few encouraging words to Franc Contreras, Art hurried home to spend some time with his children and with his mother, who was visiting from New Jersey. Art was also about to leave for a few days on a field trip to Montreal with Robert Siegel. Within a few minutes, Franc was left by himself to supervise the refeeding of the program to the Midwest and then to the Far West.

Suddenly, at about eight-thirty, a bulletin moved across the news wires that the White House was firing the Arkansas travel agents who had been the source of the Travelgate controversy. Franc saw the story and knew he had a problem on his hands.

"The breaking story rendered our two-way useless," he explains. "So I had to find a way of reconstructing it. What does that require? Two essential things: a reporter and a host. Mara was nowhere to be found — she wasn't on a beeper. Neither was Robert Siegel. I'd heard him say he was going to a movie, but I didn't know which one. I actually made some calls to theaters to see if I could locate him. No luck. Well, at some point as I was trying to track down a host and a reporter, I left a message for Art Silverman on his voice mail here in the office. I didn't have his home phone number so I couldn't try him there. It was a gentle message in which I simply explained that it looked like I might not be able to update the story, but I was going to try. I just felt the need to leave a record of what was going on. Anyway, while I'm trying to figure out what to do next, Art surprises me and calls me back almost immediately."

Senior producer Art Silverman is one of the last of the strongly sound-oriented radio people to maintain a full-time, official relationship with *All Things Considered*. Art came to Washington in the late 1970s after working at Vermont Public Radio and soon established himself as one of the more creative producers at NPR. He climbed the hierarchy of *ATC*, eventually spending a period of time as executive producer. These days, he focuses his attention on developing longer host reports, but he will often fill in as show producer or show editor when needed. He carries off all his roles with considerable grace and style. A thoughtful, hard-working, intense man in his early forties, with close-cropped dark hair and dark-rimmed glasses, Art has made numerous adjustments to the changing formats and priorities at NPR over the past decade, without ultimately compromising his basic belief that radio ought to be, as much as possible, a medium of creative aural expression. He often worries out loud that in the pursuit of the grail of hard-news coverage, NPR may be producing radio programs that are less interesting than they used to be; yet, when called upon, Art will put on his "hard-news" mantle without complaint, and will work with great skill, tact, and enthusiasm.

Art begins telling his side of the Travelgate story by explaining why it was that young, inexperienced Franc Contreras found himself *so* alone on that Friday evening in May. Art speaks in his typically rapid, businesslike manner, his dark eyes glimmering slightly behind his glasses:

"We used to have beepers, all of us. But over the years everyone's batteries went dead, and now nobody knows where the beepers are. Robert would have been the person to call, but Robert was at the movies. So Franc was left, you know, a young guy, all by himself. He faced a big decision. He had to either leave the piece as it was . . . and it's embarrassing . . . which probably would have been the default position, or he had to take it out. But there was nothing to replace it with except for a big piece of music.

"Now it was just luck that I happened to call into my office phone mail from home. That's *very* unusual, particularly on a Friday night. But it turned out that we'd just finished dinner at home, I'd cleaned up the table, my mother was there with the kids . . . my wife was out at a play. It turned out that I'd been waiting to get a message from one of our contacts in Montreal. I was all packed and ready to go to Montreal, you see. So I called in to the office to check up on this call from Canada and I hear Franc's voice telling me that, yes, this guy from Montreal did call me, and, then, 'Oh, by the way, I'm trying to find either Linda or Robert because the Travelgate story has broken, but I can't seem to find them.'" Art smiles and laughs. He begins speaking even more rapidly. "I mean, Franc told me the news in this very casual offhand way. When, actually, his very first call should have been to me, to let me know what was going on, and then the responsibility would have been mine. If I'd heard early enough, I would have raced down to the office myself and taken charge."

By the time Art heard about the story, it was about eight forty-five. The outdated two-way between Robert and Mara was scheduled to go on the air at nine-ten. There was no time for Art to get back to NPR — there was barely time for anything. Franc himself had already been thinking about possible options, and Art confirmed a number of decisions. First, Franc should definitely not run the original two-way unless all else failed. Second, to buy more time, Franc should rearrange the sequence of pieces in the last half-hour, allowing an update of the Travelgate story to go on the air at around nine-twenty instead of nine-ten. Art would try to locate a host to conduct the two-way. Since Franc had had no luck with Robert, Art would call Linda. But he also raised the possibility of dropping in a commentary from Andrei Codrescu if they were unable to find a host and a reporter for the update. Franc should find that commentary and get it ready, just in case.

"I called Linda's home — not there," Art explains. "And then I suddenly remembered something Linda had said during the day about having to take care of 'the twins.' Now, 'the twins' are related to Cokie — I believe there's one niece and one nephew. So I called Cokie's home, not that I thought Linda would be there but because I figured Cokie would know where the twins were. A phone machine answers. I start talking into Cokie's machine. And suddenly Linda bursts in. 'What is it?' We start talking. Now, I hadn't prepared in my mind for this contingency, that I'd find Linda at Cokie's, so at first I'm just telling her what's going on. Then suddenly I remember that Cokie's house has a microphone in it, directly linked to NPR."

A few of the major reporters — Cokie, Nina, and Dan Schorr — have permanently installed in their homes air-quality broadcast lines that connect them with NPR. Linda has never had one put in her house because she lives close enough to downtown Washington that it is easy for her to come into the office whenever she's needed. Cokie uses her direct connection for her weekly two-ways on *Morning Edition* with Bob Edwards, which usually occur at ten minutes after seven. (This home microphone was a secret as far as listeners were concerned until the morning when Cokie's dog started barking in the middle of the live two-way. Subsequently, attentive listeners may sometimes hear the deep breathing of the dog, who is sleeping on the floor near Cokie as she broadcasts.)

Art continues the story. "Well, when I remembered the microphone my first thought was about the Codrescu commentary. We would now be able to use it because Linda could record an intro for us. 'We're going to give you some copy,' I said to Linda. 'Could you say it into the microphone there and we'll record it here?' Linda said that would be no problem.

"But then it occurred to me that if Linda could record an intro, why couldn't she conduct an entire two-way? Being at Cokie's was a stroke of luck — it was almost as if she were in the studio. So that was the breakthrough. Of all the places in the world where Linda could have been on that night, she was in a private home in Washington that had a microphone directly connected to NPR."

It was five minutes to nine when Art's goal suddenly crystallized. He had found a host — if he could find a reporter, the final feed of *ATC* could carry an updated two-way about Travelgate.

Meanwhile, Franc was doing some fast editing. "I began cutting the show reel about ten minutes before the start of the third third," he explains. "Essentially, I'm moving all the pieces up and I'm opening a window of about five minutes, starting at about nine-twenty. If Art can line up a reporter for Linda, we'll do a live insert at that time, and, afterwards, return to the show tape for the final piece. If Art can't find a reporter, then I've found the Codrescu piece, and Linda will have to record an intro for it. But also, just in case, I also have the original Mara-Robert two-way all cued up and ready to go — that's the ultimate fallback."

Back at his home, Art is working the phone, starting a couple of minutes before nine, trying to find a reporter who will talk with Linda. (For her part, Linda walks upstairs to Cokie's office and spends a bit of time creating "a small barricade," as she puts it, to prevent the twins from coming upstairs and getting underfoot during the live broadcast. When she's all set up in Cokie's study, Linda puts in a call to NPR and waits for events to unfold.)

"First I spoke to the reporter for *The Boston Globe*," Art says, "who happened to be in the White House press room when I called. He was very new to the job and said he was in the midst of filing and couldn't talk to Linda right now — maybe later. I made some other calls and finally raised Michele DuBach, who was our on-duty Washington editor. She suggested David Lauter from the *Los Angeles Times*. I called the *LA Times* office here, and they said, 'He's home, but we can connect you.' They wouldn't give me the number. But they put me through, and suddenly I'm talking to his wife and I'm saying, could he please come to the phone. By this point it's past nine-fifteen. We have less than five minutes to air.

"He comes to the phone and I summed up the situation briefly and I said, 'Have you ever talked on the air?' He said, 'No.' But we talked a little, and his voice sounded good, and he was very familiar with the story. I made the decision to go with him. I said, 'Fine. You'll be talking with Linda Wertheimer. It's going to be live . . .' — I looked at my watch — '. . . in *two* minutes.' Now, normally I would have said to him, 'Stay on the line while we patch you through to the studio.' But I was standing in my dining room with only a single phone line. So I told him to hang up and call NPR directly — I gave him the phone number.

Then I called Franc and told him to make sure Linda's mike was patched through okay and to make sure the *LA Times* guy's phone would be hooked up properly so that Linda could hear him. Then finally I talked to Linda and told her that she was going to be talking to David Lauder in a minute. Franc had already given her an intro — which I guess she had jotted down and edited herself on a piece of paper, I don't think she was tied into NPR's computer — and she was just waiting for the cue.

"And then all I could do was hang up and wait. I was at home, I didn't have the NPR clocks around me . . . all I could do was get the thing set up and hope it turned out. When I finally hung up, I couldn't believe it. I was still at my table, I still had to clean up the dishes . . . and I was amazed at the idea that on my home telephone I had concocted this thing which was about to be broadcast out to all the West Coast stations."

Franc, meanwhile, was sitting nervously in the director's chair at Studio Seven waiting for the various elements to fall into place. At one point, he had Linda on one telephone line and Art on another. Franc recalls his feelings: "The best analogy I can draw is that there's this plane in the sky, the pilot has died, and I'm sitting in the cockpit while the control tower tries to talk me in. I'm talking about the intro with Linda, and then Art is telling me about the reporter who's going to be phoning in shortly. At one point, I put Art and Linda on speakerphones so they could talk to each other, while I go over to the tape recorder and do some final leadering of the final segment of the program — what we'll be going to after the two-way, assuming it comes off."

The engineer — Loren Kelly — did a rapid job of patching Linda in to the studio, and soon she was all set to broadcast. "The second piece of the half-hour is playing through," Franc explains, "but the L.A. reporter hasn't called in yet. We're supposed to go on at eighteen minutes past, as I recall. And at something like seventeen minutes and fifteen seconds, the guy finally calls. Loren patches him in — even does a quick EQ. I repeat the guy's name for Linda to be sure she's got the pronunciation okay. I tell Linda her down clock, that is, exactly how much time she's got for this segment, and I guess she's using her own stopwatch.

"I tell the reporter to stand by, I tell Linda to stand by. The previous piece starts winding down, and at nine-eighteen the leader tape shows up on the master reel, which means we're going live. We don't waste time with a music button, I give Linda her cue, and she starts reading the intro that we rewrote from the original which Robert had used with Mara. And Linda's on live — from Cokie's house! She's sitting in . . . I don't know, Cokie's kitchen or wherever the hell it is!" Franc laughs, his smile widening. "And, you know, I'm so amazed by it all that I don't have the presence of mind to start my *own* down clock until maybe ten seconds into the interview. Well, that just means I have to keep a close eye on the wall clock because my own segment timer is off.

"After Linda's intro, she asks her first question, the guy starts talking . . . and he's great! He's really articulate. Maybe that was just luck, I don't know. But he updated the piece very well. And then, right on time, after four and a half or five minutes, Linda says, 'Thank you very much,' she signs off, and we resume the next piece. And a few minutes later the show ends right on schedule."

"It was quite something," Art Silverman sums up with considerable understatement. "We didn't have a studio, we didn't have a host, we didn't have a reporter . . . we had an inexperienced person here in the control room. But Franc did everything he was supposed to, Linda did everything she was supposed to — and it all just worked. Not only did we get the update on the air, it turns out we were talking to a guy from the *LA Times* at the moment we were feeding the show to California." Art smiles and shakes his head. "Of course, throughout those final minutes, I kept thinking defeat was coming very, very close. We were right on the cusp of failure or success."

Young Blades and Old-timers:
Perspectives on the Future

Three generations of staff members on *All Things Considered*, looking through the rushes and the crashes, muse upon the future directions of their work:

While Franc Contreras has often felt overwhelmed by the pressures at *ATC*, he has also encountered gestures of help and support from many senior staff members. He has come to dream of a future for himself at NPR. He leans forward in his chair and speaks slowly. "This has only come to me recently, as I've started to feel more grounded here . . . but I hope that I can give my life to this place. I do. I'll tell anyone that right now. I would. I'll grow old here if they'll let me — I'll do it.

"'Cause I believe in this place. I don't want to do television, I worked in television. I find it limiting — the technology, the kinds of stories you can do. Here, there's no limit on what I'm allowed to think about. I can conceive of any story, and as long as I'm savvy enough to know how to pitch it, and as long as I'm thinking with enough layers, and really pushing the listeners to think, and coming up with something entirely different — then I can get stuff on. And I love radio, I love working with sound. It's really satisfying. I like to do feature stuff, but I'd also like to cover harder news.

"I have dreams. Yeah, I have dreams. Sometimes I think that I would like to be another Peter Breslow, you know. I love the kind of stuff he does. I want to be able to go rock climbing and take a recorder with me. I think I'd love to roam around the Andes with a tape recorder for NPR and pull out some stories that would really surprise a lot of people. And I think as I learn the craft, then maybe one day that can happen. You know, I'm only thirty. In ten years I could be forty years old and toting a digital audio deck through Colombia or something." Franc grins broadly, his thin beard rimming his face. He gestures with his hands in a way that makes him look more like twenty than thirty.

"And I think of this place as having enough room for someone like me to come in and bring my own perspective. Some people may think of it as a Latino perspective, or a southwesterner's perspective, or a rural person's perspective. 'Cause I've lived in places like Iowa and Tucson and Albuquerque — not big cities, you know. But I think there's something else, you know, that I offer, and I'm learning what that is."

Franc pauses for a moment and looks out the door of the editing booth at the empty corridor beyond. "I'm sure I'm not the only one in this place with dreams like this. Lots of people must have them."

Art Silverman has been interested in sound as long as he can remember. Born in 1949, he grew up in Livingston, New Jersey, in a home that always had a tape recorder in it. "My father had a friend named Chet Smiley who was a tinkerer who played around with modifying tape recorders," Art explains. "He founded a company called Livingston Tapes in the early fifties and traveled around, making experiments in stereo recording on tape. And I was always in his workshop and got interested in all that stuff. When I was a kid I fooled around a lot with microphones and a tape recorder. And I always had a radio in my room, I always listened, as early as I can remember. I also remember visiting the local transmitter for WVNJ, Newark — it happened to be in our town. I used to go up there and dust off the transcriptions of commercials they threw away. I was always bringing those home and playing them.

"I guess my earliest memories of radio programs include NBC's old weekend show *Monitor.* I can still hear their program ID in my head: 'You're on the Monitor beacon,' with a drum roll and the beep-beep sound of a transmitting beacon. Frank McGee used to host the show Sunday evenings, and also Frank Blair. The format of that program was as much like *All Things Considered* as anything that I can imagine — long feature pieces broken up by music. Only it was a network service that went all weekend, Friday night until Sunday evening."

In addition to his love of radio and sound, Art also wrote a lot. He brought a little mimeograph machine back from his father's stationery store and for three years turned out a neighborhood newspaper. While attending Emerson College, Art worked briefly on the undergraduate radio station, writing copy for newscasts. A couple of years later, he had a job as a reporter for a newspaper in New Hampshire, but he found himself spending a lot of time as a volunteer at Vermont Public Radio, just across the river. That was in 1977. A year later, Art moved to Washington and joined *All Things Considered* as a production assistant; he has been with the program ever since.

Art Silverman has lived through all the changes at NPR from the heady Mankiewicz years of expansion and experimentation, through the financial collapse, to the hard-news-oriented present. He has seen *ATC*'s audience grow and felt the style and pacing of the program shift. He has wrestled with the problem of how to maintain a niche for creatively driven, sound-oriented pieces in an environment increasingly focused on more traditional definitions of "news."

"I must say that I feel like a complete dinosaur talking about 'the creative potential of the radio medium,'" Art says, looking out the window of his little office cubicle as he talks. "I mean, not very many people are still producing the kinds of pieces we used to do all the time here. I think we still do it in little brush strokes from time to time, and we still put on extended features from time to time. But it's rare nowadays that we get somebody who bursts in and says, 'Hey, listen to what I've done with sound in this piece!' This program was born in the sort of post-Beatles sixties age, where the recording studio was a novelty — overdubbing was a brand-new device. And suddenly everyone had great sound systems and there was a lot of experimentation in the pop culture of the times. I mean, *The Firesign Theater* came out of the same milieu, people experimenting with sound.

"Now you tend to get that level of experimentation in visual presentations — MTV videos and the like. And maybe people are going out with their video recorders in the way that we went out with our audio recorders . . . I'm not sure. I mean that could be part of what's happening here.

"But NPR has also made many conscious choices to evolve in a certain direction. And the pressures to turn *All Things Considered* into a news service instead of a radio news program also mean that you won't get the same kind of people working here who used to work here, and you won't get the same kind of creative response to the news or the culture. People who can achieve satisfaction from simply reporting the news will tend to gravitate here.

"Now I'm a big advocate of the news — I think that's properly the central part of our program. And there are days when the news is everything. And that's fine. But there are also days you have to pump up half-baked things to be the news. And here is where I'm really in favor of having the show be more plastic, rather than deciding that we *always* have to have a certain amount of news. There are days when it's just plainly not a news day. And I think we need to have a lot more material on hand to figure out how we can kick back a little more and relax. That sounds like a real non-news thing to say. But I think what I'm getting at is that when the news is not exciting, we still put it on. We put ersatz news on. We put on second-tier, third-tier, fourth-tier stories . . . endless stories about Chad. Not to denigrate Chad, and I'm overstating the case a bit. But I do know that a lot of people within the creative radio community turn up their noses at what we're doing now. And although I take a lot of this criticism with a grain of salt, it does hurt me personally when I hear people whose work — and whose *humor* — I respect . . . the Jay Allisons, the Lars Hoels[7] . . . saying, 'I can't listen to *ATC* anymore. It's too boring. It's dull.' Now, to some

---

[7] Jay Allison is an independent radio producer living in Woods Hole, Massachusetts, who has done many longer-form pieces for NPR over the years. Lars Hoel is a former NPR producer, now an independent in New York who writes a sometimes critical and always witty column about NPR in *Airspace*, the newsletter of AIR, the Association of Independents in Radio. Lars is married to the multi-talented and longtime chief engineer of NPR's New York bureau, Manoli Wetherell.

extent, there's some sour grapes going on here. I mean NPR, generally, broadcasts far fewer non-news-oriented pieces these days, and many people who used to produce those pieces no longer find work here. There's some bitterness about this. Just read through a publication like *Airspace*, and you'll see there's a lot of NPR-bashing going on.

"But I do worry that a portion of this criticism may be valid. If a young, new Ira Glass showed up on our doorstep — somebody full of creative energy — I don't think we'd recognize it if he or she didn't have sharp enough journalistic credentials. Yet this is the kind of person that the remade *New Yorker* wants on its staff — and I mean that as a compliment to *The New Yorker*. I worry that fewer young people these days, listening to the show, think to themselves, 'My God, *All Things Considered* — that's exactly my kind of show. They're running all those wild M'Lou Zahner-Ollswang pieces.[8] That's my home . . . my crazy ideas will fit there.' Again, I'm oversimplifying a bit because once in a while we do slip in something funny or something satirical into the program, but the underlying smart, sassy side isn't always apparent. And it needn't be like it used to be — we did go over the top a lot in the early years — but for me the show would be more attractive if we had more of those pieces on.

"Many people are very pleased with *All Things Considered* as it is now, but I think it still needs to be primed to become a truly great news program. And what it needs to be great is to become more relaxed, to leave enough room for other stuff. Doesn't necessarily have to be long pieces. Length itself is really not the whole issue. I'm moving towards thinking that short's not necessarily bad these days, but the question for me is the use of sound and the choice of topic. It's the ability, or the *will*, really, to spend five minutes on . . . well, let's say rhubarb — that was one of M'Lou's more famous reports. I mean it's the playfulness that we used to allow on the air more. Not all the time — just occasionally. Just because people are using us as a prime news source and take us pretty damn seriously, *we* don't have to take ourselves *that* seriously. We shouldn't be beholden to that seriousness to such a degree that we can't let our hair down. Just because we're getting older is no reason we need to hold on to NPR as some institution that can't be shaken up by someone younger with a smart idea."

Playfulness is just one element of what Art means by "creativity"

---

[8] M'Lou was a reporter from the Midwest in the early days of *ATC* who produced unusual features.

in radio. He also includes "inventiveness" as a major component in realizing the full potential of the sound medium. His own work on *ATC* over the past years has included a considerable amount of innovation and experimentation, even within the context of hard-news coverage. As a field producer, he traveled out to San Francisco following the 1989 earthquake and supervised Linda's live cohosting of the show from the West Coast. Having Linda on the scene allowed Art to produce some vivid features describing the devastation and cleanup. Then, in the summer of 1991, he and Linda did a long report on teenagers and their sexual habits. They spent two days down at a beach, interviewing and hanging out.

"We practically lived with these kids," Art remembers, "and brought back lots of tape. And because we were given so much time, I was able to think about musical transitions and sound — delicate nuances. And I did something I never get to do much these days, though we used to do it a lot in the past: I took people into rooms and played them the piece, and watched their reaction. And then we'd talk about it. I wound up changing context, changing direction. I shaped the piece slowly — sculpted it really — with the help of other people. Linda wrote some really nice copy for it, and when the piece aired it didn't sound like an ordinary story. There was an unusual quality to it — people found it quite moving. I'm probably more happy with that story than any other I've done over the last few years. And one of the keys was not being on an immediate deadline. I had the piece in the can a couple of weeks before it was broadcast."

Art finds possibilities for innovation even when he's on a tight schedule. His most recent field trip, again with Linda, took him on a weeklong car ride along U.S. Route 50 through the Midwest. The purpose of the journey was to visit a range of different towns and discover what people had to say about the new administration in Washington, not yet six months old. Using the latest technology (including DAT recorders, cellular phones, and satellite uplinks) Art and Linda were able to air long stories chronicling their visits to an antique store, a granite carver, several restaurants, people's homes . . . all the time chatting about politics. The pieces were produced and aired the same day or the following day, depending upon the availability of a satellite uplink to send their tape back to Washington. The reports glowed with a certain freshness and raw originality. Art and Linda engaged in a spontaneous scene-painting, both through the use of natural sound and oral description. The high-quality audio and the rapid turnaround in production further enhanced the vividness of the stories.

Art is still on a kind of creative high from the trip. "I think I've learned something new about radio, or really it's something old about radio, that I can use," he explains, speaking rapidly and barely finishing his sentences. "I feel renewed and invigorated all over again about possibilities. Interestingly, the logistics of the trip dictated the style of the reports, but the style, as it turned out, had many things in its favor. Radio is full of conceits that are really studio tricks by which you create the illusion that, for instance, a reporter is standing beside the road as she speaks. Well, during our trip along Route 50, Linda recorded her tracks in the environment in which she was. When Linda said, 'I'm in a doughnut shop,' she was sitting in a doughnut shop, and you could hear it. If she was about to climb out of a car and go into the beauty salon, she opened the car door and said into the microphone where she was and what was about to happen. If we didn't like the way her narration sounded, we did another take on it, as opposed to fixing it later on in the studio. This all created a great feeling of immediacy."

Linda does some of her best work when she is out in the field talking with people, and the most memorable scenes from the Route 50 trip included brief sound portraits in the shop of a granite cutter who carved tombstones and in a beauty salon with a beautician who kept insisting that she work on Linda's hair. The reports thus included not only political conversations about the Clinton presidency but also some aural texture from the particular part of the country in which the interviewees lived.

Linda gives much credit to Art for the success of the Route 50 series: "Art is working on all kinds of ways of doing radio, and I am his willing handmaiden," she explains. "It was his notion that we try to do radio in 'real time,' and I think it gave the series a special quality. Journeys are always interesting, of course, in and of themselves. They're a kind of progression — almost like Chaucer. I suppose it's kind of a witnessing thing. You take the audience along with you: you have an experience, they share the experience. I mean, I brought with me a file of political polls as thick as your thumb, and so in a sense I knew ahead of time what people thought. What our trip did was to go out and find those people — where they lived and worked — and I could say to them, 'Tell me why you feel this way. How strongly do you feel about it?' And that evening, or the next, they'd be broadcast on NPR."

· · ·

Art has done many wonderful pieces with *ATC* hosts over the years, and he continues to enjoy his association with the program, even though his perspective on the show is complex. "I hope I'm making myself clear," he says. "I think *All Things Considered* does a lot of fine things. You get more international news than any other broadcast source in this country. You will get literate and insightful reports and discussions of current events. It's very complete, its fairly accurate, surely as accurate as any newspaper, including *The New York Times.*

"I would like to be able to say also that the show is really witty, and it's going to be full of surprises and it will take you places in sound that are really amazing. But I can't say that, at least not on a regular basis. I regret that we don't have more of the completely creative, even oddball sound pieces. But there's no appetite for it with people who produce the daily programs here. I mean, if they hear something great, they will put it on. But there's not such a hunger for this kind of radio that it's a priority, in contrast with everything else. And furthermore, it would sometimes be hard to "get into" these stories. Where would they fit in the program? The way *ATC*'s produced these days, there's so much news that on many days, any kind of arty sound piece would just be at war with the rest of the program. How would you even introduce it? I mean, I remember a famous essay that someone did once. How did it start? . . . 'Did you ever wonder where *dust* comes from?' And this led into a contemplation of *dust.*

"Now, I love those pieces. But they are very hard to do well — that kind of radio is much more difficult, in a sense, than reporting. Reporting, you go there, get the story absolutely right, and write it up beautifully. But this other kind of piece requires you to conceptualize on a very deep level. And you have to take leaps of faith, hoping that the audience stays with you. And you have to be willing to occasionally fall on your face."

Art has survived at *ATC* as long as he has by adjusting his talents and skills to the changing requirements of NPR and also by holding on to his faith that the creative power of radio can percolate up through even the most news-driven program and give listeners a unique experience — if only for a moment.

"You just don't give up," he says, speaking a little more slowly than usual. "You keep trying. We've done a lot of interesting radio here over the years, and because of that past, that history, and the talent that we still have here, we just all have to work harder and not be lazy about how difficult it is to get the good creative stuff on the air. I mean, for about a year, a while back, I was very happy just coming in here every morning — blank slate, no long projects on my calendar. And I asked myself each day, What can I do — for three minutes, two minutes, five minutes — that will make this program distinguishable . . . a little different from everything else that NPR puts out? Even if it's just a brush stroke: what can I do that's funny, what can I do to combine two pieces of tape in an odd, unusual fashion? And the hosts are great about ideas like that. If it makes sense, and even if it's crazy, Linda, Robert, Noah enjoy cooking up stuff. There's lots of sources for playfulness. You hear something in the news, it reminds you of something in an old movie, you could dub the sound, and put it together. We have wonderful opportunities.

"But there's no getting around the fact that the dynamics on the program have changed. It's like the old question of turning *ATC* away from being a beginning-middle-end program. That was another battle that Susan [Stamberg] and others fought and in the end lost. The argument goes that nobody in the audience listens to *All Things Considered* all the way through anymore. Surveys will tell you this. But I think the issues are so intangible that no one could measure it at all. Even if you didn't always listen from beginning to end, you would at least get the *sense* that some people were — and certainly, equally importantly, you would feel that the people who were putting the show together were involved in some enterprise that had *direction*. And even if you caught it in the middle, you knew which way the car or train was moving . . . you knew there was a parade going by. And if you had the feeling that you missed part of the procession, you might sometimes wish that you could hear it all. And so some days, when you had the time, you would listen to the whole program and then you'd *really hear* something. You'd get an extra kick because you'd enjoy the way elements coalesced in a certain way because the program was taking a certain path.

"Well, this is all beating a dead horse. The weekend programs are still produced with a sense of the whole, I think, for the most part. And a few of us who remember the old way of doing things are still around on daily *ATC* . . . maybe because the changes have happened gradually, maybe because we still hope that on any given day we can add a bit of overall shape to what we're doing. But perhaps it's just that some of us are still living a couple years in the past at any given point. You know: dinosaurs."

• • •

Willie Sullivan lies on his side on the roof of the NPR building puffing on a cigarette. He's stretched his legs out and is propped up on an elbow. His feet are bare, his blue shirt is open at the collar, he's removed his tie. Willie is on a smoking break from his job as temporary executive producer of *All Things Considered*. He's wearing only one hat today, as Melissa is producing and Linda Killian is editing. Willie is younger than Art Silverman, though older and certainly more experienced than Franc Contreras. But though his career at NPR started several years after Art's, he speaks even more strongly and more critically about changes at *All Things Considered* and NPR generally over the past few years.

"I mean, look, it's no secret that NPR is becoming less and less of a radio medium," Willie says in his typically quiet, yet focused voice. "There's a lot less sound in our product now. I think it's a shame. I think there's a shortage of good radio producers at NPR now. There's a shortage of good radio editors at NPR right now. I *don't* think there's a shortage of good *reporters*. There are a fair number of good radio reporters. But something's getting lost.

"It may be a function of us getting bigger. The more mainstream we become, the more a source of primary news we become, the less opportunity there is — the less *room* there is — to do radio. You know: sound.

"Danny [Zwerdling] is my best example of someone who works with sound the way one ought to. And it takes time for him to produce his pieces. And, you know, there are those who are impatient with that style. From what I gather, there may be quotas introduced on some news desks now. Reporters have to produce x number of minutes per month. Now, I understand the wisdom of trying to make people productive. But there also has to be a balance. And I think we lose sight of that sometimes.

"On the other hand, putting on my hat as executive producer for a moment: longer pieces cost money. If you want to do the longer pieces, if you want to give a reporter three weeks or more to work on the piece, you have to replace that reporter. You can't steal that reporter from a beat — that will leave the beat uncovered, and the shows will scream, and the news director will scream, and the desk editor whose person you stole will scream. You want to do a long piece? Fine — show me the money. It'll be expensive. And to my mind, we're stretched incredibly thin already. So the question arises again: are we going to be a primary news source? If we are, then we've got to hire a shitload of reporters and editors.

"I mean, look: I think all the debates and questions about the kind of reports NPR is airing, the kind of show that *ATC* is today . . . it all comes down to what our definition is of what we want to be. Do we want to be a primary news source? Some people say we are already *the* primary news source for many people. If this is what we want, then *I* think we're going to give up a lot of our creativity — what all the older people at NPR (they must be all of forty-five years old) remember as the 'good old days.' There was a lot of good stuff out there then. There was a lot of incredibly self-indulgent stuff out there, too. I think that the product is probably sharper now than it was then. But it's probably also lost some of that creativity. Some of that spark. It's a trade-off. Will we lose it permanently? I hope not. I hope not. But sometimes I don't see how else we can do it, given our limited resources.

"Still, we keep trying, and we still have reporters like Danny, and Deb Amos, and Gjelten out there.[9] And on *ATC*, we're still able to send our hosts out on the road from time to time. And they come up with good radio."

It was Willie's decision that put Art Silverman and Linda Werthei-mer onto Route 50. Willie was pleased with the results, but he's already gotten mixed reviews from others at NPR. "Look, I've heard from some people that they thought those pieces were flatulent . . . self-in-dulgent . . . condescending — very little meat. Very little structure." Willie relights a cigarette and speaks slowly, with emphasis. "I heard all of those pieces. In terms of news, they were very soft, yes. Didn't hear anything particularly unusual that the polls hadn't already told you. But: did a lot of normal people's voices get on the air? Yeah. A lot. Did some of them sound stupid? A few. Who cares? Put those people on the air. Don't shape it in any great way. Let those people talk. Ask them what they think and then record what they think and put that on the air. I thought it was *tremendously* refreshing.

"I think Linda's very good with people. And sometimes that doesn't come across when she's hosting in that studio vacuum. I also think she gets excited by talking to people. She's naturally curious that way. She likes to hear what they say. Everyone points to Noah as being the best interviewer to draw stuff from people in that way. But I would argue that Linda is every bit as good at it when she gets out in the field. And

---

[9] In 1994, Deborah Amos joined ABC News. She'd been a stalwart at NPR for some twenty years.

it's our job to get her out there more. A lot more. Get her away from this building!

"There were rough edges to the Route 50 pieces. But to my ear, that meant it didn't sound packaged. I liked that. Plus Linda and Art and everyone involved worked their asses off to get those things on the air. And I thought they did a very good job."

Willie sits up and crosses his legs in front of him. He looks down at the graveled roof surface before continuing. "I had some rather heated discussions with some senior news executives about that product. But I'd do it again in a minute. You've got to let pieces *breathe* every now and then. In fact, a hell of a lot more often than we do. *ATC* can develop a certain relentless pace. Bang, bang, bang. Hard-news piece after hard-news piece. It can sound smart to do the show that way, and it can be very informative. But you also miss something there.

"I mean, that's why I sent Noah and Melissa to Bosnia with the SAT phone and the Switched Fifty-six.[10] Because one thing that I thought we were missing in this whole Bosnian thing were the voices of normal Serbs explaining why they thought this was a just war. Or wasn't a just war. And having the high-quality connections allowed us to get some clear and engaging tape.

"Now you could argue the same thing about those pieces that you argued about the Route 50 pieces — that part of it wasn't polished. Well, maybe some of the people were left to talk a little longer than they should have been. But I don't think we have to think in terms of actualities only being twenty-two seconds long. Noah's good at the back and forth. And we need to have a more flexible pacing in *All Things Considered.*

"I mean, look: that's the direction I guess I'd like *ATC* to take. Change the pace *within* the show. You don't have to change the pace of the entire show. It can be a blend of both elements — the hard news, and the softer piece. And you don't need incredibly long segments to

---

[10] The satellite phone was first used by NPR in its coverage of the war in Somalia. A very expensive technology, it nonetheless allows virtual studio-quality transmissions to be sent back to Washington from anywhere in the world. Switched Fifty-six is an older bit of wizardry that dramatically improves the quality of a normal telephone line. Working with digital technology, the Switched Fifty-six turns a voice into a coded signal, which then gets transmitted along the phone line. When the signal is decoded back in Washington, the voice quality sounds roughly like an AM radio transmission, considerably better than a normal telephone line.

get a different pace going. I think we can have features that tell you a very interesting story, that use the sound the way radio should use it — and be *twelve* minutes long, not twenty minutes long. It's a compromise, but this gets back to what I was saying before, which is the demands that are placed on us now. We're starting to be more of a primary news source, we want to cover more news. If we do that, there's going to be less of a hole for the produced pieces. That means the produced pieces have to be that much better. They'll also have to be shorter. I think we can get that."

Willie goes on to speak admiringly about the kind of reports that are broadcast on the weekend shows, especially *Weekend Edition Saturday*. He calls its producer, Cindy Carpien, "relentless in her pursuit of perfection" and "the finest show producer in the building." But for all his critique, Willie remains clearly attracted to the pace and excitement of daily *All Things Considered*: "The work is so hard — so impossible really — and at the same time very satisfying when you finish it. You have the sense that you're doing something with very little time to do it in. That's gratifying and unnerving at the same time. You're ultimately never quite finished. An extra hour, an extra two hours . . . you know you could smooth out so many rough edges. And yet you do the best you can, and sometimes that's quite good in itself.

"There's also something to be said for starting a project in the morning and knowing that at six-thirty the project is going to be over. And then you can move on to another. There's this feeling of closure, as the politicians would say. And that's appealing. At the end of the day, you have done something. And it's over, finished. There's no going back. And tomorrow you'll be doing something completely different."

Willie looks down at the gravel roof again, momentarily thoughtful. Then he stands up, shakes and stretches himself in an almost catlike way, and walks, barefoot, back inside the building . . . to the elevators and then down to the *ATC* horseshoe, where today's program continues to move forward, at a quickening pace, toward the inevitable deadline.

Epilogue: The Unkindest Cuts

In the winter of 1994, Franc Contreras left Washington to join the production team of *Latino USA*, a weekly newsmagazine produced at a public radio station in Austin, Texas, and distributed nationally. The job opportunity arose right after Franc's temporary appointment at *All*

Things Considered had ended. He planned to remain at NPR and had already accepted another temporary assignment, this time at the science desk. But the position in Texas was permanent, full-time, and presented an exciting range of challenges and possibilities. It also allowed Franc to return to that part of the country in which he's most at home.

"I still feel connected with NPR," Franc explains in a telephone call from his new post. "I feel very close to those people." But he is also extremely happy at *Latino USA*, which he feels is on the cutting edge of an important kind of journalism.

Franc has not entirely abandoned his thoughts of returning to NPR in Washington. But these days he's more apt to dream about NPR moving to the *southwest*. "I wish they'd open a bureau out here," he says, smiling audibly into the phone. "It'd be great if they put one of their hosts in the west, for example. Really nationalize their sound." And he laughs.

A few months after Franc Contreras left NPR, Melissa Block gave up her position as producer of *ATC*. She moved to New York for a year to try her hand at freelance reporting. The inevitable *ATC* burnout, predicted for "Sunspot" by Willie Sullivan a few months earlier, had struck again.

Melissa's replacement — Sean Collins, a young but experienced producer, famous within NPR for his dynamic creativity — was at his new post for a week when he suffered a serious back injury, in part brought on by stress. Upon his return, Sean's special flair made itself apparent. From time to time, a few light, witty, even slightly experimental pieces began appearing on *All Things Considered*. A couple of older NPR staffers spoke wistfully of subtle changes in the wind at *ATC*; yet, in the same breath, they wondered how *much* difference a single producer could make . . .

And so the crashes — and the dreams — continue at *All Things Considered*.

Weekends: Mornings and Afternoons

Old-time NPR

Good evening. From National Public Radio in Washington, I'm Katie Davis, with *All Things Considered.*
— *Weekend All Things Considered,* 1993

Before there was *Morning Edition,* before NPR started thinking of itself as a primary news source . . . in the days when Susan Stamberg and Bob Edwards cohosted *ATC* and the theme music for the program was played on a sassy synthesizer instead of a richly textured brass band . . . at a time when an extremely young Jay Kernis worked in the promotions department and then became production assistant at *Voices in the Wind* under Bob Malesky, who had just inherited the weekly, hour-long arts magazine from Robert Montiegel . . . at a time when there were no news desks, very few news editors, and when the weekly education magazine *Options in Education* was the second most recognized show on public radio — at such a very early moment in NPR's history, the news division (then only one small part of the entire public radio organization) took its first tentative steps toward enlarging its program schedule by launching, with some fanfare, a sixty-minute Saturday and Sunday version of *All Things Considered.* A number of younger staffers from the daily show were moved over to handle the new enterprise,

which Susan Stamberg often promoted with an almost motherly enthusiasm at the conclusion of the Friday edition of *ATC*. Noah Adams
was one of the first hosts of *Weekend All Things Considered*; Deborah
Amos and Neal Conan were two of the early producers.

The initial audience was quite small for *Weekend ATC* — which eventually developed a second nickname, *WATC* — pronounced "WATT-
cee." During the late seventies, weekends on public radio stations were
about as popular as "garbage time" is to basketball fans. Until Garrison
Keillor began his rapid rise to fame on American Public Radio's Saturday evening show *A Prairie Home Companion* in the early 1980s, public
radio weekend fare was consistently aimed at extremely small slices of
the listening audience. Even today, with a few notable exceptions,
weekends continue to be a time when stations air programs that they
know will not draw large audiences. Saturday and Sunday have always
represented the musty back rooms of the public radio programming
museum. But *Weekend ATC* persevered with small staff, limited resources, and marginal listenership. NPR brass liked the idea that the
news division was now producing programs seven days a week. *Weekend
ATC* provided a training ground for tape cutters, producers, newscasters, and hosts who might move on to the daily show. And the fact that
WATC had a week to prepare two one-hour shows gave the program
the chance for more leisurely experimentation with the radio form. The
talents and creativities of many staffers flourished in the program's
relative obscurity.

When *Morning Edition* was launched in 1979 as the first major
expansion of NPR News under Frank Mankiewicz, *Weekend ATC* for a
time became even more overshadowed by the daily programs. As the
editorial desks were established and expanded their operations, the
weekend program often found itself having to remind the rest of NPR
of its existence. The daily shows worked reporters so hard during the
week that a tradition developed of giving staffers the weekends off.
WATC would often have to use freelance reporters — or do two-ways
— to cover news stories that full-time NPR correspondents routinely
handled for *Morning Edition* and daily *ATC*. A bit of show-business
sensibility entered the mix as well. Audiences for *Weekend ATC* were
minuscule compared with the daily shows, at times maybe a quarter
the size. Some NPR correspondents didn't like the idea that their work
might be heard by so few people.

But, as Lynn Neary, a longtime host of *WATC* recalls, the lack of
attention paid to the weekend program by NPR's own staffers was

always "one of those proverbial doubled-edged swords." "It could be annoying that you didn't have everybody gearing toward you and what you created," Lynn admits. "On the other hand, sometimes being left alone was great because you were able to 'do your own show' without anybody bugging you. The program was on the air before anyone had time to say anything to you about it!" Lynn laughs one of her deep, hearty laughs. "So we could push the edge of radio a little further, maybe, because we were on the weekend."

Over the years, through a number of different hosts and producers, *Weekend ATC* maintained a spacious, flexible format. The first half-hour began with a five-minute newscast, and this was followed by a twenty-three-minute segment that could be apportioned however the producer wished. The second half-hour stretched out for some twenty-eight or twenty-nine unencumbered minutes. (The push toward hard news in recent years has meant that *WATC* has added a break for headlines at the beginning of the second half of the show, but this uses up little more than a minute.) Not surprisingly, *Weekend ATC* developed a tradition that embraced long-form radio. "Even though the program has gone through many changes," says Lynn, "I think the show has always placed a tremendous value on the long piece that makes creative use of sound. Even today there's still a sort of experimental feel over there. It was the *original* weekend show, and so it always had a more laid-back quality to it, which gave it more time to breathe and to think creatively. The show has held on to that approach, I think."

Throughout the seventies and into the early eighties, *WATC* remained NPR's only weekend news presence. The financial crisis of 1983 scotched ideas that Frank Mankiewicz and his staff had to expand NPR programming into weekend mornings. Oddly enough, the period of retrenchment that followed the implosion of '83 provided encouragement for the new NPR president, Doug Bennet, to add a Saturday-morning program as soon as he could. After Bennet presided over the initial downsizing of the network, he reportedly felt that it was extremely important for NPR to make some move — any move — connoting expansion and growth. "It was enormously important symbolically to start something again," Bennet has told writer Mary Collins. "Once you could, then it became possible to talk seriously about an agenda."[1]

---

[1] Collins, p. 92.

By 1985 Bennet felt that NPR was strong enough financially to add another news program to its schedule. Jay Kernis, one of the original wizards of *Morning Edition*, was asked by then-news director Robert Siegel to create a two-hour Saturday-morning vehicle for one of the star reporters in NPR's lineup, Chicago-based Scott Simon.

Almost since his first arrival on NPR's air in 1976, initially as a freelance reporter (his contact in Washington was Robert Krulwich, then a national editor for *ATC*), Scott's work had been gaining enormous recognition among listeners and colleagues alike. Everything about his reporting was laced with both aural artistry and oral originality. His voice was one of the most distinctive on public radio. Sounding quirky, even old-fashioned, Scott's slightly unusual accent and throaty timbre suggested a friendly kind of jowliness — a curious mixture of eccentricity and trustworthiness. Part of Scott's radio charisma may have grown out of a fundamental anomaly about his on-air presence: his voice sounded old and mature, like someone who had been doing radio for years, yet his *words* were clearly those of a young man of the 1970s — vivid, metaphoric, colorful, and filled with compassion and commitment.

When Scott Simon started working for NPR, he was among the youngest reporters on the staff — barely into his twenties. The son of a well-known Chicago comedian who had run into political problems during the McCarthy era, Scott had grown up in a family with a tradition of both performance and social commitment.[2] He'd studied anthropology at the University of Chicago and then moved into community organizing. "I was always writing pamphlets and the like and I always put out underground newspapers wherever I was," Scott recalls, "so I had done some 'writing.' But I'd never worked on *The Maroon* [the University of Chicago student newspaper] or anything like that. I was not interested in writing or in journalism, as such, at that point in my life. I think it'd be fair to say I was more interested in overthrowing the government." And Scott gives one of his characteristic smiles — a mixture of disarming innocence and puckish self-deprecation.

In 1975 Scott began doing a little work for public television in Chicago on a show called *The Public News Center.* "I was producing essays three times a week," he remembers. "This being local public

---

[2] Scott's father worked in vaudeville as a teenager and was also a successful morning radio personality for a time. ("He was inevitably called things like 'zany' and 'madcap,'" Scott says.) Studs Terkel was a close family friend.

television, WTTW, they had only two video units, so often my pieces would be covered by still pictures. And occasionally we would use 'wild sound' [sounds occurring naturally in a particular place] collected by audio recorders. Well, our show went on the air at seven o'clock every night, and we would often be working late at five o'clock, selecting the pictures to go with the essay. And often we'd put on *All Things Considered* while we worked. This was the first time I'd listened to NPR, and, my God, I just thought it was the most wonderful thing I'd ever heard. I mean, this was a narrative form of journalism that I'd always admired. It was like Murrow, it was like some of the great reporting I had read in the *Chicago Daily News* or the *New York Herald Tribune* — which were both *writers'* newspapers. I was so taken with what I heard that I contacted WBEZ, the local public radio station in Chicago. I mean, I didn't know from NPR . . . I'd never really done any radio. And for their part, WBEZ's contribution to NPR was minimal at that point, but a very nice woman named Carole Nolan invited me over to see the facilities, and while I was there, an engineer named Claude Cunningham put a tape recorder over my shoulder and showed me how to operate it, and told me vaguely what editing was, and all that sort of thing. And I think it was during the 1976 election year that I began to file for NPR."

Once Scott started sending material to NPR as a freelancer, editors and producers in Washington rapidly came to know him as an extraordinarily gifted reporter with a unique on-air style. It was hard to say what was most distinctive about Scott Simon — his writing (vivid and clear but with a longer cadence, a more stately rhythm than what was usual on contemporary radio) or his use of sound. He seemed to know instinctively how tape could enhance his radio reporting. The eloquence of his language was regularly matched by a richness of aural scene painting, as Scott combined evocative sound with revealing excerpts from interviews. His reports often became narrative tapestries of interwoven voice and sound.

In 1977, NPR hired Scott to head its newly created Chicago bureau, and over the next several years, a small team of talented production people coalesced around Scott and began regularly turning out some of the most striking radio pieces ever aired on NPR. Scott's award-winning coverage of an American Nazi Party rally in Chicago is still listened to as a model of how to mix sound-portrait techniques with hard-news reporting. Scott also traveled around the country and abroad

— particularly to Central America — on various reporting assignments for the network.

By 1985 Scott Simon seemed like a natural choice to host a weekend morning program that would have a more leisurely pace than daily *Morning Edition* and yet would emulate some elements of the weekday format. Jay Kernis and Scott began exchanging memos and conceptualizing the new program.

Weekend Edition — as the program was called before the creation of its sibling show on Sunday — became Jay's swan song at NPR. He remembers his two years on the program as the time of his best work in radio. "You know, Scott and I were like one human being sometimes," Jay explains. "I mean, we inhabited separate worlds, but we were so close — our understanding of radio, our sense of what we wanted to do with the medium. For instance, we were able to devise the show in just a few weeks. And then, where Bob Edwards and I, in the early days, had to do much testing and have a lot of discussions about his work on *Morning Edition*, right from the start on *Weekend Edition* Scott and I were talking in shorthand with each other. 'How about *this?*' 'Yes, of course. And *that.*' 'Sure. But *then* we'll do *this.*' 'Naturally . . . ' I mean sometimes I used to think that we really should talk things out more *completely*, but it was just so right that much of the show just sort of happened."

The format that Jay, Scott, and others came up with for the new Saturday program consisted of an expanded *Morning Edition* pie. The show remained segmented, but instead of the daily diet of five sections, *Weekend Edition* followed a more leisurely rhythm and was divided into three segments, each lasting essentially eighteen minutes. Subdivisions within each portion of the program broke up the regularity, however. The initial pie slice began with the traditional minute-long Open and continued with a five-minute newscast; *Weekend Edition* producers thus had twelve minutes to fill in the A. The B consisted of a fifteen-minute block, followed by a three-minute cut-away — a period during which local stations could insert their own features if they wished. *Weekend Edition* sent out its own piece during this time slot for those stations who stuck with the network. The C segment ran, uninterrupted, for a full eighteen minutes.

Between each segment (A to B and B to C), two-minute breaks allowed stations to identify themselves or air business messages. What NPR itself broadcast during these breaks varied as *Weekend Edition* evolved. The second minute of the break tended to contain forty seconds of headlines, rounded out with music. The first minute carried promos for other shows or short items that came to be called the "Fo Break" ("Information Break"). These were often similar in tone to Bob Edwards's humorous Returns and were about the same duration. Fo Breaks might also promote upcoming parts of the current program.

The length of breaks and cut-aways meant that local stations could retain as much as seven minutes of presence during each fifty-nine minutes of NPR's *Weekend Edition*. Though they would not be able to interrupt the program's flow as frequently as they did during daily *Morning Edition*, stations still were given a considerable amount of air time for their own use.

Weekend Edition went on the air in November 1985. Scott brought with him from Chicago a number of people who had been working in the bureau there, including Smokey Baer (who had left *ATC* in 1977 to become associate producer in Chicago) and a multitalented young engineer, Rich Rarey, who had joined NPR in 1980, shortly after graduating from Ohio University. Rich represented something of a second generation of NPR staffers, young men and women who had listened to the creative new sound emanating from the network and sought to work there when they were old enough. While a freshman in college, Rich had heard one of Scott Simon's early reports. "I was doing maintenance in one of the academic radio facilities at the time," Rich recalls, "and had NPR on in the background. And I distinctly remember a piece Scott did while covering demonstrations in one of the Chicago neighborhoods. I'm not sure it registered at the time that this was *Scott Simon* — and I sure didn't think that I'd be working with him in a few years. But I clearly remember being shocked — *shocked* — because NPR broadcast the word 'fuck,' which one of the demonstrators had used. Overall, I was very struck by the intensity of the entire piece — Scott's narration, his use of sound. It made a big impression on me."

Rich grew up on a farm in Ohio and has vivid memories of listening to an old tube radio (a 1934 Zenith console) that his father had bought years before. "I always loved radio," Rich says. "I'm not quite sure why. But I found something tremendously appealing about the red beacons on the faraway tower lights of radio stations. I found that to be an exotic kind of image that symbolized . . . I don't know what — the romantic, faraway sounds that I heard on the radio at night. I used to put an old eight-ohm speaker under my pillow and listen to the distant stations beating against each other. I found it relaxing to hear the kind of *moosh* of stations fading in and out of each other."

Rich Rarey quickly became the technical director of *Weekend Edition*, the person in charge of the overall sound of the program. A highly skilled "sound designer" as well as an engineer, Rich was far more than a "spinner of dials" and a "puncher of buttons." He brought a unique aural sensitivity to his field recording and studio mixing and was an important part of the original team that created *Weekend Edition*.

In addition to the gang from Chicago, Jay Kernis collected a number of staff members with whom he had worked on *Morning Edition* — including Neva Grant, a talented editor and producer, and Cindy Carpien, a young woman who had joined *Morning Edition* as a production assistant a couple of months after the show went on the air. Cindy was still in college when she started working at NPR, but she quickly demonstrated a natural aptitude for radio. After just two years with *Morning Edition*, and barely into her twenties, Cindy became the show's director. Now Jay asked her to assume the same role on the new weekend program.

Weekend Edition took a while to find its voice. Scott Simon had to direct his unique talents as a writer and a speaker to new purposes. He was now responsible for anchoring the attention of an audience throughout a two-hour program instead of just a five- or eight-minute report. Sitting in the host's chair permitted a reporter to become more personable, but the role also imposed certain restrictions on that "personality." Of course, in Jay Kernis, Scott had a producer whose oft-stated goal was to make the host sound great. Jay was invaluable in helping mold Scott to the show and vice versa.

With an entire week to prepare one program, Jay could now give full vent to his perfectionism — sharpening the show's overall shape by choosing stories carefully and making sure they flowed smoothly and intelligently into one another. In a sense, Jay was returning to his earliest experiences as a producer at NPR, when he had worked on the weekly arts magazine *Voice in the Wind*. Gone were the hard-news, daily-deadline pressures of *Morning Edition:* while *Weekend Edition* was expected to cover the news, it was equally expected to be a showcase for the best of creative radio.

Weekend Edition did not have the open-ended format of *Weekend All Things Considered*. Though the show's eighteen-minute segments were longer than *Morning Edition*'s, the structure of the program remained more rigidly defined than *WATC*'s: it contained echoes of the daily show's heritage as a *radio service*. Time checks occurred at prescribed intervals, along with periodic program and host identifications. Many segments began with a certain predictable formula — teasing the second story before launching into the first. ("This is *Weekend Edition*. Swallows do indeed come home to Capistrano. *But first . . .*") Of course, as producer, Jay Kernis tried to work creatively with the constraints imposed by the program's structure and he attempted to transcend any repetitive routines. Certainly within each segment, *Weekend Edition* stories were allowed to breathe and to flow more than in any other NPR program, save, perhaps, *Weekend ATC*.

Weekend Edition with Scott Simon began developing a strong and loyal following. Saturday morning turned out to be a good time for local stations to broadcast a nationally produced radio magazine. Many listeners were in their cars doing weekly errands, while others worked on odd jobs around their homes. Even the show's segmentation seemed to fit the rhythm of the weekend morning. As with daily *Morning Edition*, many listeners would dip in and out of *Weekend Edition*, though those who could listen to the entire two hours would experience far more of a "complete program" than those who listened to an entire *Morning Edition* broadcast.

When Scott Simon started his career as a host, he was thirty-three years old. Notwithstanding his relative youth, he quickly developed an even stronger presence as a host than he had projected as a reporter. His writing style blossomed, becoming a tad more florid, occasionally even Dickensian — yet perfectly consistent with the breadth of personality, conviction, quirkiness, intelligence, and humor that soon was pouring out of the pieces he did for *Weekend Edition*. The show broadcast reports and features from other NPR correspondents as well and also developed a cast of commentators with whom Scott conversed regularly, ranging from NPR's distinguished elder statesman (a man with his own touch of quirky genius), Daniel Schorr, to West Coast movie critic and NPR freelancer Elvis Mitchell (whose often witty approach to film meshed perfectly with Scott's sometimes giggly high spirits). But the bulk of *Weekend Edition* consisted of interviews, essays, humorous "bits," and produced feature reports done by Scott Simon. The show was unabashedly personality-driven and was also, undeniably, an object lesson in how to use the medium of sound creatively.

Like any radio personality — Susan Stamberg is another example at NPR — Scott provoked extremely positive and extremely negative feelings among listeners. Some in NPR's audience considered Scott verbose, overdrawn, too precious, too filled with himself. Other listeners felt, with equal conviction, that Scott was one of the most original, interesting, trustworthy, and *decent* voices in all of American broadcasting. It's the nature of a program that caters to a distinctive voice and does not try to eviscerate personality that different ears respond with different emotions. While it may be to the credit of NPR and its local stations that they have, on the whole, given substantial support to *Weekend Edition* almost since its inception, it must also be noted that, so far, Scott has not often been asked to host any of the *daily* programs. The hosts who do rotate through the other programs as fill-ins tend to be less individually distinctive, less "hot," personalities than Scott. (The one exception to this rule is Susan Stamberg, who has occasionally filled in for Bob Edwards on *Morning Edition*. But Susan remains the most experienced host at NPR and one of the most versatile. Furthermore, her strong radio presence may be considered somewhat less quirky than Scott's, the difference, perhaps, between a nudgey Jewish mama and a lovable but slightly eccentric bachelor uncle.)

Weekend Edition was growing in popularity, and thought was already being given to adding a companion Sunday-morning magazine, when developments on daily *All Things Considered* precipitated the decision to drop the other shoe in weekend programming. After fifteen years as cohost of *ATC*, Susan Stamberg indicated that she wanted to leave the grind of daily broadcasting. A Sunday-morning arts magazine seemed the perfect place for her talents, and so in the fall of 1986 Susan hosted her last show for *All Things Considered*, and in January 1987 NPR debuted *Weekend Edition, Sunday*. *Weekend Edition* with Scott Simon became *Weekend Edition, Saturday*, or *Weekend Saturday*, and then, in the inevitable acronymic jargon of any organization, *WESAT* ("WEE-sat"). The Sunday show with Susan was usually referred to as *Weekend Sunday*, or *WESUN* ("WEE-sun").

Though *WESUN* borrowed the structure of *WESAT*, right from the start it was geared to be a vehicle for Susan and her particular interests. Jay Kernis was executive producer of the two programs and worked closely with Susan in the original conception of the show. But he deferred many day-to-day questions to the staff he put in place, including longtime NPR producer Katherine (Kitty) Ferguson, whose work went back to the early days of *All Things Considered* and *Options in Education*, where she had served as associate producer. Partly due to Jay's primary focus on *WESAT* and to Susan's own strong sense of what she wanted *WESUN* to be, a tradition grew up, which has continued to this day, of a quite separate identity between the two weekend morning programs.

Susan's decision to leave *All Things Considered* was traumatic for everyone concerned, particularly the vast audience for whom NPR, *ATC*, and Susan Stamberg were synonymous. Susan's desire to leave was partly a product of fatigue, partly a feeling that it was time for her to do something different. In her book, *Talk*, Susan discusses publicly for the first time certain private, health-related reasons that also precipitated her decision. (She was diagnosed with breast cancer, a condition that was promptly and successfully treated.) Yet looking beyond the individual stories and particular choices made by individuals, wider, institutional forces were also at work "encouraging" — implicitly if not explicitly — Susan's departure from *ATC*. NPR was changing the kind of radio it wanted to broadcast in its daily programs, and Susan was resisting many of these changes.

Weekend Sunday would present Susan with an easier schedule, and also allow her to pursue her deep interest in arts and cultural reporting. Among the many innovations on which she insisted was that, aside from the hourly newscasts and breaks for headlines, the show would *not* be done live. All of Susan's work — interviews, features, introductions for reporters' pieces — would be recorded on tape, thus allowing Susan not to work on weekends.

Sunday morning is a leisurely time for radio listeners. Longer, slower-paced features profiling musicians, performers, writers, and the like seemed appropriate subject matter for the time slot. But in spite of Susan's "star" status at NPR, *Weekend Sunday* did not enjoy the immediate success of *Weekend Saturday*. Part of the problem had to do with long-established programming traditions at many NPR stations. For years Sunday mornings have been a time for locally produced music programming — often classical but also bluegrass, gospel, folk, and other forms. Many station managers believed that when their listeners got up on Sundays, they wanted a day of rest from NPR talk.

Furthermore, aside from the original senior producer of the program, Kitty Ferguson, the rest of the *WESUN* staff was relatively inexperienced in the ways of producing the long arts pieces Susan wanted to do. Nor was everyone comfortable with the entire program being on tape. *Weekend Sunday*'s first few months were a bit rocky.

Then, before the show was a year old, Kitty announced that she was leaving NPR. At that point, Joe Gwathmey, in one of his last acts at NPR, strongly suggested to Susan that one of the most experienced arts producers from the early days of the network be brought back to solidify the program: and so Bob Malesky returned to NPR on an interim basis, to help smooth out the kinks in *WESUN*.

By talent, temperament, and experience, Bob Malesky might be appropriately viewed as a *paterfamilias* — if not actually a patriarch — of arts and cultural features at National Public Radio. His career presents an interesting counterpoint to that of Jay Kernis. Just two years older than Jay, Bob grew up in Norwalk, Connecticut, where he listened to radio stations from New York City, played music in rock 'n' roll bands, and spent a good deal of time on his high school newspaper. His work on the paper led to his winning a scholarship, in the summer of 1966, to attend a journalism seminar for teenagers at Catholic University in Washington, D.C. He liked the college and eventually enrolled there, in the fall of 1967, planning to be an English major. After a year, he dropped out, returned to Connecticut, worked in a rock band, and eventually married a young woman from Brooklyn. In 1969 Bob and Kee Malesky returned to Washington to study at C.U. This time Bob was a psychology major.

Bob graduated in 1973 and while waiting for Kee to finish up, he looked for a temporary job. "Kee and I had started a free library when we were in college," Bob explains, "so I could do librarian stuff, and we'd also both worked for this film group, so I was actually looking for some kind of film librarian's job. Well, the Career Services Department at C.U. said, no, they couldn't find *that* kind of position, but NPR was looking for a radio librarian. So I applied and got the job. This was when the Watergate hearings were going on, right? So my first job at NPR was logging the Watergate hearings."[3]

In those early days, the NPR Library was located near Robert Montiegel and the NPR Arts and Performances Department. Bob got to know the arts staff and started teaching himself the basics of tape editing. After three months in the library, he moved across the hall and became a production assistant under Montiegel. "The first PA job that opened up happened to be in that part of NPR," Bob explains. "If it

---

[3] The librarian tradition continues in the Malesky family. Kee has been one of NPR's research librarians for many years.

had been in news, I might have ended up in news. But Montiegel hired me and the first thing I began producing was something called the 'Five-Minute Art Package' — which was a collection of commentaries that we would send out each week."

A few months later, in the spring of 1974, Montiegel started up the hour-long arts magazine *Voices in the Wind* and Bob Malesky became production assistant for the new show. Round about this same time, young Jay Kernis arrived at NPR and began working in the promotional department, turning out minute-long spots advertising upcoming programs. Within a couple of years, Montiegel had moved on from *Voices* to pursue special documentary projects and Bob Malesky had taken over producing the weekly arts program. One of the first people he added to his staff was Jay Kernis. It was Jay's first job on an NPR show.

By the late seventies, the game of musical chairs had shifted once more: Malesky joined Montiegel as a producer of special documentary programs (both were involved in *A Question of Place*), while Jay took over *Voices in the Wind*. Then, when Jay began producing *Morning Edition*, he asked his former boss, Bob Malesky, to join the staff as arts producer. Bob worked on *Morning Edition* for two months to help the show get started but afterward went back to producing documentaries. He just didn't like the daily pressure. "I still don't," Bob says. "It's just not my style. Also I had been enjoying doing the documentaries so much that I didn't want to give them up and I didn't feel that they were going to die anytime soon." Bob smiles ruefully. Long-form radio on NPR was to become extinct far quicker than he had imagined.

As NPR continued its tilt toward hard news, Bob found the opportunities for documentary production drying up. So like many other radio producers of his temperament and sensibility, Bob had decided by 1982 that he would rather leave NPR and become a freelancer than fight over the dwindling arts budget. The passionate and driven Jay Kernis continued the struggle to shape and perhaps to contain aspects of the hard-news juggernaut. Bob Malesky's quiet, reflective personality was ill suited to such battles, and for five years he withdrew from the field.

But now in September 1987, Bob was back on NPR's staff, at least for a while. "*Weekend Edition Sunday* was in a little bit of trouble at that point," Bob recalls, speaking slowly and with some reluctance. "They had a lot of rookie producers — a lot of new people — and I was able to walk in there with — again — the old style NPR production. I could do things in an afternoon that others on the staff were taking three or four days to pull together. So Susan was very happy to keep me on board. At first I was supposed to fill in for one month, then I wound up staying two and then three months. And when the job of senior producer formally opened up, I thought long and hard about whether I should apply.

"I could have stayed a freelancer and made a living at it. I probably would be doing books on tape and things like that by now — this is where I was heading. But I also learned that I needed structure. I didn't hustle very well, I find it hard to sell myself to someone. And also I hated to get locked into doing similar stories, two or three a day, every day, in order to make money, which is what freelancers have to do. You gain experience doing a wide variety of things, but you also wind up doing a lot of horrible, boring work, too, just to get by.

"For her part, Susan respected my production abilities a great deal, but I think she had serious qualms about whether I'd be able to oversee the *news* side of the show — she knew the program needed some of that. But I think she finally realized that, when it came right down to it, *Weekend Sunday* was not a hard-news show and that with my background, I was able to bring more of what the show needed at the time."

So Bob was appointed senior producer of *Weekend Sunday* and began to work on developing the unusual mix of arts features and news that would come to characterize the youngest of NPR's magazine programs.

The most difficult part of Bob's first couple of years on *Weekend Edition, Sunday* turned out not to be his inexperience with news but the fact that Susan Stamberg remained wedded to her plan that she not do the program live. "I mean, the fact that she didn't want to go live would have been a perfectly suitable idea — perfectly fine — in any other slot *except* a news slot," Bob explains. "But the fact was that when people tuned in to *Weekend Sunday*, they were tuning in to what was, on every other day, an NPR *news*magazine. We didn't have to be as *hard*-news oriented as the other shows, but I think the audience found it disconcerting to tune in to the top of the Sunday program and get what sounded like a stale, older piece — taped a couple of days earlier — instead of discussion of something current, perhaps something that had just broken Saturday night or Sunday morning.

"What Susan wanted was a nice salon show: a staff pianist, with a variety of guests, mostly authors, who'd drop in and chat. And I still think that's a valid format — it could make a wonderful show — and

Susan could make it work beautifully. But it would have to be on the air Saturday evening or some time like that. *Not* in a *Morning Edition* time slot."

Bob found himself in a delicate balancing act as he worked to make *Weekend Sunday* a successful program. "Not having a live host," Bob explains, "meant that everyone at NPR felt that we were producing a features show. That did not make it easy to get *newsier* pieces from reporters — they never thought of us. Furthermore, I was perceived by many people at NPR as an old arts dinosaur in the news department, so it was sometimes difficult to get support from the editorial desks.

"The minute we started going live, it turned everything around."

In November 1989 Susan Stamberg left *Weekend Edition, Sunday* to become NPR's senior arts reporter and a frequent substitute host for daily *Morning Edition.* Liane Hansen — a ten-year veteran of public radio — took over the *WESUN* hosting chores. The show would now be broadcast live and thus fall in line with all the other newsmagazine programs NPR produced.

In an odd twist of history, at the very moment when the "old dinosaur" and arts patriarch Bob Malesky was coming back to NPR and quietly building a niche for himself on the Sunday program, the *wunderkind* of public radio, Jay Kernis, unexpectedly announced his departure from the medium to which he had devoted so much creative energy. In November 1987, Jay moved to New York City and started a new career at CBS Television; his first assignment would be to design yet another morning program, only this time for TV.

Jay had been a nagging, articulate conscience at NPR for a decade, urging always the best in sound, the best in production, the best in *radio.* His talents and contributions to the network were as famous and as hotly debated as his equally legendary temper tantrums. Jay was not the first — nor would he be the last — highly talented NPR person to abandon radio for television. But Jay had had such a profound effect on so many people in public radio that his departure was deeply shocking to many at NPR. An inspiration, as well as an old colleague and friend, was leaving. One of the staunchest advocates of radio as aural art would no longer be battling for his particular vision of the sound medium in the offices and corridors of the network. Meanwhile, the movement away from aural reporting continued to gain momentum due to the fuller development of the editorial desks and the general push toward harder news coverage. The departure of Jay Kernis from

NPR symbolized, as much as anything did during the late eighties, the new path that the network was choosing to follow.

Still, Jay left a powerful institutional legacy at NPR in both *Morning Edition* and the two *Weekend Edition* programs. His strong influence remained, as well, in the sensibilities of dozens of NPR staff members who worked under him and identified themselves as being touched or influenced by him, whether consciously or unconsciously.

The woman chosen to succeed Jay as producer of *Weekend Edition, Saturday* had learned the craft of radio while working under him at both the daily and the weekend shows. Something of a *wunderkind* in her own right, Cindy Carpien was not yet thirty when she took over the reins of *WESAT.* Though Cindy is viewed by many at NPR as a Kernis "protégé," that word oversimplifies the complex web of creativity that Jay spun around the staff members who worked with him; it also tends to downplay Cindy's own innate talents for radio production, which are considerable.

"With Jay, you kind of learned through osmosis," Cindy explains. "I worked for six years on the *Morning Edition* overnight shift and hardly ever saw him — most of the time I was there, he worked days. So he never taught me how to mix pieces or any of that stuff. But then nobody taught me how to white-line tape, how to insert breaths, and things like that — I mean, I just made it all up — we *all* made it up. You picked up these techniques on your own.

"But one thing Jay did was to *inspire.* He taught you — through example as much as anything — to really *care* about what you're doing in radio and to really love it. And as far as being a producer, I think what I learned from him was the importance of encouraging people to want to do well for you — and to be their best.

"Jay had this ability to make things feel *magical* somehow. His enthusiasm for radio: you felt it, and it made you feel different.

"I mean, I've always said that when I directed *Morning Edition,* I directed it 'for Jay.' Because I knew he was listening and I knew he would respond if I chose just the right piece of music to follow a particular story. And it's true: he'd call in after the show and say, 'That was really incredible the way you used so-and-so.' And on *Weekend Edition* we used to say — I mean, sometimes it was a bit of a joke — 'Will Jay like it? Let's do it for Jay.' And it was true that sometimes we'd do something because it would make Jay happy. But I mean, that kind of thinking may be one way to bring out the best in radio production, or anything else for that matter: to think about *one* person who is really listening, who is really paying attention, who really cares. If you think about trying to impress two or three million people . . . I mean, how can you do that? How are you going to be able to make a decision? There are so many different tastes out there. But if you think about *one* person, it probably helps bring out your own individual creative judgment."

Cindy Carpien has helped *Weekend Edition, Saturday* air much radio magic since she became senior producer. Though the weekend programs at NPR continue to exist in a kind of institutional backwater, with more glamour, prestige, and resources being funneled into the daily programs, Cindy has developed a singular reputation among her colleagues at NPR as being "the finest show producer" and possessing "the best ears" in the organization. The fact that Cindy may be more frequently singled out than Bob Malesky is partly a product of the fact that for the first seven years of its existence, *Weekend Edition, Sunday* was not carried by either of Washington's two public radio stations. Bob's work is seldom heard by his colleagues. Furthermore, for all that *WESUN* has evolved and changed from the days when it broadcast almost exclusively arts features, its image and its reputation within NPR remain softer — less distinct and vivid — than the image and reputation of *WESAT.*

But it must also be noted that *Weekend Saturday* grows out of the dynamic magic initially woven by Jay Kernis, now refined and developed by his successors; *Weekend Sunday* is being guided by a gentler, quieter, though no less creative sensibility, which preserves some of the oldest and, in some respects, most overlooked traditions of public radio. Both producers, both shows, both program staffs sustain and nourish in their different ways many of the creative possibilities of the sound medium, which these days other parts of NPR seem to be handling with less care and less interest.

Comings and Goings

While the new weekend morning programs were evolving their styles and developing their audiences, *Weekend All Things Considered* followed along its own separate history. With its flexible format and tradition of perpetual innovation, *WATC*'s tone and shape were significantly affected by the particular hosts and producers who were in place at any given moment. Some of the most interesting shows ever done on

Weekend ATC were broadcast in the late eighties during the time that Alex Chadwick and Lynn Neary cohosted the program. Two fine writers, with excellent ears for the radio feature, Alex and Lynn went on various trips around the country and filed a fascinating mix of stories — sometimes offbeat, often touching, always informative.

When Alex tired of the weekend shift, Lynn became the solo host; then, in 1992, Lynn took a break herself from the weekends in order to help out with hosting chores on daily *All Things Considered* — freeing up Linda Wertheimer to cover the election campaign. Lynn's "break" turned into an extended leave of absence, and her "temporary" substitute host, Katie Davis, an experienced reporter and producer with an excellent sense of radio, wound up holding down the host's chair for an entire year. Katie worked hard to master the art of hosting, and as one of the nicest and most popular individuals at NPR, she had the best wishes of almost everyone in the organization. But a quiet discussion continued at NPR throughout Katie's tenure as to whether or not she would "make it" as a host. Her voice, which was fine for a reporter, sometimes sounded rather young and overeager for a host. While some liked the nontraditional quality of Katie's presentation, others felt that she lacked that intangible sense of authority that is so important in someone who anchors a program.

Katie took over the hosting chores at *WATC* at a particularly vulnerable time in the program's history. Within the space of a couple of months, several longtime key staff members left the program, including the producer, the associate producer, and the director. Jane Greenhalgh, a young Englishwoman who had been working at NPR for only a short time, was tapped to become the show's new producer. She quickly assembled a group of young staffers, who joined veteran editor Robert Rand, and in the space of a couple of months, the relatively inexperienced team began turning out some fascinating pieces and unusual programs. Katie and production assistant Sara Sarasohn shared a love of poetry, and suddenly *WATC* was bringing poems and poets to the weekend afternoon airwaves, including a memorable, sound-filled interview with New Mexico poet Jimmy Santiago Baca, who taught himself to write while in prison. (Katie's fluency in Spanish led her to do a number of reports on Hispanic Americans.)

Yet as long as Lynn remained in the wings, Hamlet-like, the future of Katie Davis and *WATC* hung in limbo. The long-term direction of the program would not be resolved finally until the winter of 1994.

· · ·

Lynn Neary was not the only weekend host to take a leave of absence from her show in 1992–93. In July of 1992, public radio was again rocked with news of another defection to television — only this time it was Mr. Radio himself who was making the switch.

When Scott Simon announced that he was moving to NBC-TV to cohost the new *Weekend Today* program, his colleagues at NPR were as shocked and upset as his *WESAT* audience. Many older staff members wondered if public radio was going to hold on to *any* of its brightest, most sound-oriented reporters and producers. Scott was certainly one of the most idealistic, least materialistic members of NPR. A highly principled man, a vegetarian, a Quaker, even something of a happy-go-lucky ascetic . . . if *Scott* could be lured away from radio (in part by the promise of a six-figure television salary), would *anyone* be able to resist the call of the one-eyed monster?

In his final essay written for *WESAT* listeners before his departure, Scott composed an expression both of thanks and of principle. The top line of the copy is slugged, simply, "bye SSIMON." It bears the date "Sat 25-JUL-92" and carries a time mark of 02:56 . . . which is to say it was completed at three o'clock in the morning. Scott is one of the most famous procrastinators on the NPR staff (another eccentricity in a medium of absolute deadlines), and he often worked on his essays and scripts late into the night before a broadcast.

Scott always punctuates his scripts with large ellipses, and occasionally uses italics and boldface to help him read more clearly:

> As you may have read . . . or heard . . . next week . . . NBC News begins a new Weekend Today Show . . . and I'm going to be on it . . .
>
> I'm taking a leave-of-absence to try this because . . . at the age of forty . . . I'd like to see if I can learn to *do something* creative . . . challenging . . . and fulfilling . . . in what's become the medium of our times . . .

After thus acknowledging the overarching power of the visual medium, Scott went on to praise the sound medium in which he had worked for so long:

> Ten years ago . . . when I was working for this network in El Salvador . . . we kept a set of wooden . . . souvineer [sic] shop initials . . . **NPR** . . . in the window of one of our rooms . . .

Other reporters . . . would walk by and hail us . . . *"Hey . . . NPR folks . . . how you doin'?"* . . . And it was then I began to grasp how those initials . . . had become enduringly *fastened* to the front of my name . . . *NPR's Scott Simon* . . .

Frankly . . . at thirty . . . I didn't much like . . . so much of *my life* . . . being signified by *any* three initials . . . But now . . . at forty . . . I am only *proud* . . .

Over the past fifteen years . . . it has been my privilege . . . and I do believe . . . *a blessing* . . . to have been a part of a group of people who have created one of the most cherished institutions of American life . . . For millions of Americans . . . those initials . . . **NPR** . . . have come to signify civility . . . and conviction . . . protected from sanctimony . . . by *a sense of humor* . . .

Sometimes . . . past midnight on a Saturday morning . . . when I'm strolling these hallways looking for words . . . I'll turn a corner . . . *and begin to hear voices* . . . from an open door . . . One of our staff members . . . editing a tape . . . or listening back to an interview . . . their faces intent . . . exhausted . . . and alert . . .

I think that to **care** about the work you give to others . . . so deeply that you feel only *the best* within you is good enough to be received . . . reveals something sacred in human beings . . . And on so many mornings . . . I have turned that corner . . . to see Cindi [sic] and Neva . . . Rich or Marta . . . Laura . . . Smokey . . . Steve . . . Ken . . . Doug . . . Cecilia . . . Brooke . . . Mandalit . . . Ina . . . Jay . . . or Maria . . . and felt **lifted up** . . . by their example . . .

To have had these years with them . . . and with you . . . is a gift that I will keep . . . in the core of my heart.

Thank you . . . And now . . . Rich . . . it's summer . . . The streets are scorching . . . I think I know the song we want to hear . . .

And the script indicates that at this point the song "Dancin' in the Streets" should be brought up.

(Scott's short weekly essays on *Weekend Saturday* came to be called the "Music Cue," or "Music Q," by the staff because the commentaries would inevitably lead into a piece of music that reflected in some way upon what Scott had just said — most often a subtle, witty response but sometimes, as in this case, an aural underscoring of the mood established by his words. Neva Grant originally developed the form with Scott; Cindy Carpien has now assumed responsibility for the Music Cue, and the work takes her back to her early days as director of *Morning Edition* when she would search for just the right aural bridge between stories. The music that followed Scott's farewell "Music Cue" was meant to inspire bittersweet smiles. It thus evoked, in typical Scott Simon fashion, the old vaudeville tradition of "leavin' 'em with a smile and a song.")

Everyone in public radio who was familiar with Scott Simon — who knew the kind of person he was and the sensibility he brought to his work — wondered whether this talented, caring, and committed young writer and reporter could survive commercial television, could come out of the experience, not to put too fine a point on it, with his soul intact.

Yet Saturday morning, August 1, 1992, arrived, and there was Scott, staring amiably, if a little wistfully, into the NBC television camera on the fake living room set of *Weekend Today* . . . while over at NPR in Washington, Neal Conan — the first of many substitute hosts — was reading the opening to the *Weekend Edition Saturday* program . . . Scott's program. The famous Scott Simon voice had jumped to television, and it now had a face to go with it — handsome, square, with big, brown puppy-dog eyes and his dark hair combed up and back, with a slight tousle on top where a part used to be.

From August 1992 to August 1993, the future of Scott Simon and NBC remained a hot topic of discussion at NPR. Scott kept in regular touch with all his old colleagues. Indeed, he held on to his apartment in Washington and spent several days a week there. He even wrote a few essays for *WESAT* and hosted the program a couple of times. It was clear that there was a great deal about television that Scott enjoyed, and there was a great deal that appalled him. In one respect, he was staging a return to his earliest days of broadcasting: NBC allowed him to produce weekly essays, some of which he illustrated with still photographs . . . While some people at NPR expressed complete confidence that Scott would return to radio, others were equally convinced that NBC would make him offers he would not be able to refuse. In fact, no one, not even Scott, knew what the outcome would be.

The issue remained in doubt until the moment that Scott's contract with NBC expired in the summer of 1993 — and a little bit longer.

Following a Different Drummer

Even though two of the three NPR weekend programs originated as vehicles for particular hosts, one salient fact about *Weekend Saturday, Weekend Sunday,* and *Weekend ATC* remains: whoever happens to be hosting each program at any particular time, the shows, taken as a whole, broadcast a fundamentally different kind of radio from NPR's daily fare. The weekend producers still envision their job as creating "radio programs," not turning out a radio service. They spend far more time worrying about and working on the *sound* of individual pieces. They actively consider subtle issues of program *flow* and *rhythm*, points that casual listeners may not notice consciously, but which do affect everyone in the audience, however subliminally. The weekend programs are less news-driven, on the whole, than the daily shows, though they are far from being solely purveyors of soft-focused features. If major stories break over the weekend, *WESAT, WESUN,* and *WATC* will work hard to bring the news to listeners thoroughly and intelligently.

Weekend Saturday and *Weekend Sunday* retain the segmented format of *Morning Edition* even though the structure has been modified and spread out. A residue of the "service" identity thus remains affixed to these programs — and every so often a station will "cover" (that is, replace) a story from the network or an entire eighteen-minute segment with a feature of its own, usually a locally produced arts piece. No matter: Cindy Carpien and Bob Malesky continue to design their shows with the entire two-hour shape in mind. Both remain convinced of the importance of *thinking* of their programs as a whole, whatever the listening habits of some audience members might be and however much individual stations might tinker with the show once it is sent up to the satellite.

In general, the younger staff members on the weekend shows are more comfortable with the two-track thinking in which you work to create a complete program, but accept that some stations may fiddle around with what you send out. Some of the older NPR hands have not adjusted as well to the new realities. Once when Susan Stamberg was hosting *Weekend Saturday,* a local Washington station substituted its own feature about a rock band for an interview that Susan had done with a women's a cappella singing group. Susan was extremely upset. "Are they within their rights to do that?" asked the former host of *All Things Considered,* where such practices were never allowed. When someone explained that they were, Susan was not mollified. "We should *scream* about that," she said. "I mean, it's as if a conductor played three movements of a Beethoven symphony and then decided, 'That's enough Beethoven for now' — and finished off the concert playing a movement from someone else."

There are few producers left at NPR who would think to compare their work with a symphony, but there was a time when Susan's sentiments would have been shared by a large number of her Washington colleagues. And it's also fair to say that even in those days, many local station program directors would have been quite offended by such an attitude, thinking that it demonstrated the typical arrogance and high-handedness on the part of folks "at the center." The debate over the content and shape of public radio programs has had a long history.

The weekend shows are looked upon as slightly different animals by the network as a whole and also by the rest of the NPR organization in Washington. It's no accident that in the old NPR offices at 2025 M Street, the three programs occupied the same wing of the second floor, literally at the opposite end of the building from *All Things Considered* and *Morning Edition*. The schedule of the weekenders differs, of course, from that of everyone else at NPR. Since staff members come to work on Saturday and/or Sunday, their days off occur during everyone else's normal work week. People on *WESAT* stay home Mondays. *WATC* and *WESUN* define their weekend as Monday and Tuesday. These slightly different work schedules suggest that there are different rhythms of production among the three programs and, indeed, the weekend shows do present distinct personalities to their listeners. There is nothing monolithic about "creative radio." A wide range of options is available to any producer who wishes to engage the medium of sound on its own terms and to fathom its strengths and possibilities.

Not that NPR's weekend programs are *always* fountainheads of stimulating, groundbreaking radio. They operate with significantly smaller staffs and smaller budgets than the weekday programs, and upon occasion — even with a week to put together a program — they must fill up their shows with admittedly second-drawer material. Not every freelance producer is a radio artist, not every backup reporter is a Tom Gjelten or Nina Totenberg in training. Nor is every listener in NPR's expanding audience going to have the patience — and the ears — to slow down and take in the more leisurely pace offered by the weekend shows. But these qualifications used to be applicable to *all* of the programs broadcast by National Public Radio; the current weekend programs can be seen as participating in some of the oldest traditions of the network. Whether these traditions should be preserved — or discarded — remains a continuing question facing NPR . . . *and* its audience.

The great divide between daily and weekly shows emerges in the process of production, when the weekend programs are being designed and assembled. During these days of creation, staff members make their way through labyrinths of aural possibility, tracing the threads of sound and story with ears that have developed a particularly acute, even obsessive, sensibility to rhythm, pacing, texture, nuance . . . The special intensity with which weekenders *listen* separates them from the rest of public radio, and this aural culture makes their shows resonate in unique ways.

"And on the Fifth Day . . ."

Monday is supposed to be a day of rest for all the weekend programs, and so the corridors, offices, and cubicles on the far side of NPR remain deserted for the most part until the *Weekend Saturday* staff returns on Tuesday. But, surprisingly enough, by nine-thirty Monday morning, a light is usually burning in one office, in the remotest part of the weekend maze. Senior producer Cindy Carpien, a dark-haired, pale-skinned woman of modest height and slender build, sits alone amid the stillness of *WESAT*, attending to paperwork, making phone calls, and leafing through piles of newspapers and magazines. (When reading, she frequently pauses to cut out a story with a razor blade or scissors and puts it in a pile to pass on to one staff member or another.) Cindy originally kept to the same slightly skewed schedule as other weekenders, but when she had her first child in 1990, she decided to stop coming in to NPR on Saturday mornings and instead to work a Monday to Friday week. She had sufficient confidence in her production staff to assign one of its members to be line producer on the day of the program. Cindy believes that the arrangement has been beneficial to everyone. Cindy herself can become a member of the audience when *WESAT* is broadcast, which helps sharpen her own ears about how the show is working. Meanwhile, staff members are given added responsibility and experience. (They are also provided with that "single person" in the audience who they know is listening intently to everything they do.) Finally, the schedule allows Cindy to catch up on a lot of administrative chores on Monday, as well as affording her some quiet time to reflect upon the program.

Cindy's office is part of a little suite that clusters around a common area, whose large windows overlook the swimming pool attached to the adjoining apartment building. A rectangular table, narrow end to the wall, stretches out from the center column between the windows and serves as a kind of analogue for the *All Things Considered* horseshoe or the *Morning Edition* desk. Staff members will come sit at the table, with their backs to the pool, and stare at the big white storyboard on the wall opposite the window. Beneath the board sit two soft, purple sectional chairs, forming a kind of couch. Cindy has to stand on these unsteady surfaces when she wants to fill in the tops of the A segments, high up on the board.

Five small rooms open out onto the common area. Cindy's office and that of the host face the swimming pool. The program editor, Steve Tripoli, and the new producer for special projects, Peter Breslow, have inner offices, with no windows. The show director — Doug Mitchell — inhabits a slightly larger room that is, appropriately, right behind the board.[4]

Along the corridor leading to *WESAT* sits assistant producer Ken Hom, a quiet, intense young man with a quick smile and a dry, soft-spoken wit. In just a couple of years on *WESAT,* Ken has earned Cindy's respect and trust to the extent that he is usually the one who puts the show on the air Saturday mornings. Ken's wry sense of humor propagates in all directions, including back on himself. He tells so many stories about his age and his "life before NPR" that few people know exactly where he is from or how old he is. In fact, though his dark hair is just beginning to show some fringes of gray, friends report that Ken is in his thirties and that he's been in public radio almost a decade.

A few feet from Ken's desk, on the wall of the corridor closest to the common area, hangs a long white board filled with dates and names written in different colors. This is the *WESAT* "Weeks Ahead" and "Futures" board. It outlines upcoming programs and their guest hosts and lists pending interviews, proposed pieces, and possible host trips. In order for *Weekend Saturday* to maintain its unique mixture of news

---

[4] The game of musical chairs continues at NPR, as Doug moved over to *WATC* during 1993, in part so he could "sleep a little later" on Saturday mornings, in part, also, so he might do more producing.

and features, Cindy and her small staff must plan far ahead. Shortly, Susan Stamberg will fly to Arkansas for a couple of days with Ken Hom; Peter Breslow will be heading out to the Rocky Mountains with Alex Chadwick, who will guest-host in six weeks; later Peter will go to New York City to do three stories with Lynn Neary, another future host.

The walls of *WESAT* — along with its doors, shelves, and window-sills — are covered with far more than lists, charts, and notices. The complex and quirky personality of the program spills out like a rich sound mix into a splattering of decoration and display . . . layers of bric-a-brac accumulated over the years. At the entrance to the common office area, next to the Futures board, hang three large rubber masks — a pig, a monkey, and a white cat. The masks partly cover a collection of snapshots, apparently taken at various parties (and at least one wedding) over the years. In one photo, resonant with NPR history, Neal Conan, Noah Adams, Smokey Baer, and Jay Kernis cluster round a smiling Scott Simon. A newer picture shows Cindy's baby girl, Jessie, leaning over to kiss an equally young Christopher Tripoli, son of the show's editor.

Meanwhile, an artifact with a more ancient history balances pre-cariously on the thin upper edge of the Futures board: three separate, carved wooden letters, about six inches high, decorated with fading but still vivid patterns of color. The letters spell out "N P R." The leg of the "R" has broken off and has been glued back on repeatedly, if ineffectually. These are the letters from Central America that Scott Simon eulogized in his farewell to *Weekend Saturday* several months ago.

The founding host of *Weekend Saturday* may be currently spending part of his weekend mornings exchanging pleasantries across a sofa with his stereotypically pretty TV coanchor. But here in the backrooms of NPR, memories . . . echoes . . . take a long time to fade. The door to Scott's former office remains covered by a large green and white street sign: "DIVISION ST.," a Chicago landmark. Beside the door, on top of a tall bookshelf, next to three large and rather awkward plants, a small golden staff points upward and outward at an odd angle. Tipped with a gaudy blue star, which has a small electric light in the center, the staff resembles a kitschy magic wand, such as some old vaudeville clown could have used. It might be taken as a symbol of Scott's continuing legacy at *WESAT.* The wand, held by an unseen hand, seems raised in midair and frozen in midspell.

Indeed, the *Weekend Saturday* common room appears to be framed by both magic spirits and frozen time — like an endless loop of tape continually playing. On the other side of the room, right outside the door of Cindy's office, near a hard-rubber caricature of Ronald Reagan and a color photo of public television's "Mister Rogers," a Xeroxed article from *Variety* conjures up another of *WESAT*'s "dearly departed": stark paragraphs announce the resignation of Jay Kernis from NPR. The clipping — copied onto thick white paper — looks extraordinarily fresh, and the words reverberate with as much power now as they did when they first appeared, in part because whoever copied the original article managed to exclude any *date*. So Jay Kernis continually "prepares to leave" NPR, even though he has been gone since 1987.

Thus the moods, the interests, and the fancies of the *WESAT* staff — past and present — intermingle and interplay to create the physical and the creative space out of which unique radio programs are born.

Weekend Edition, Saturday — along with all the other weekend programs — has a considerably longer gestation period than either *Morning Edition* or *All Things Considered*. Yet the staff does not experience the extra time as a luxury. "Going slow" in the context of radio production does not necessarily mean "taking it easy." The work on the weekend shows can be every bit as intense as that which takes place on the daily shows, but the intensity is of a vastly different kind. In place of the adrenaline rush that propels *Morning Edition* and *ATC*, *WESAT* and its fellow programs substitute an obsessive attention to detail, which can be equally grueling and exhausting.

"I definitely think we're under a lot of pressure to *be* creative," says Cindy Carpien. "Since we have all week to work, people expect us to come up with more clever and fun ideas. It's an interesting contradiction. On the one hand, because we *don't* have the largest audience, the weekend shows have always been sort of left to their own devices. We don't get the support from the editorial desks that the daily programs do. I mean, the desks were actually told, at the beginning, that they would not have to worry about supplying *WESAT* with reporters. We struggled to change that early on — and the desks do help us these days — but I still get that argument thrown back in my face from time to time.

"So partly, in a sense, we've been *forced* to be creative because we have to come up with so much of our own material. In general, my show is seventy percent host. And that gives us a good deal of freedom to be creative. It's also a big responsibility, especially as so many people now really *do* care about the show."

During the first months of Scott Simon's absence from *Weekend Saturday*, the program went through a minor crisis of identity: *WESAT* had been so inseparable from Scott's unique personality that everyone involved worried what might happen without him. "I've never had such a challenge to my career," says Cindy candidly, her pale oval face flickering with the remembered worries. It's the middle of winter 1993, and by now "life without Scott" has taken on a certain routine. "Would we keep it going — keep people wanting to listen? Because even though the staff came up with a lot of creative stuff ourselves, it was *Scott* who was doing it. Would the audience appreciate *other* people doing the same kinds of things? So it became a time of testing for the staff: we had to demonstrate that *Weekend Saturday* is a *show* in its own right."

Cindy's dark eyes glimmer, and her face breaks into a smile. "To be honest, I didn't really expect the show to be as good as when Scott was here. But in fact, I think we've been doing fine. I mean, it's sad not to have Scott — he's absolutely wonderful at what he does. There's nobody like him. But I wanted us to prove that *Weekend Saturday* could *still* be many people's favorite show, even without him. I don't know if that's true now, but it's been many months since he's gone, and I think the show has been succeeding. We're giving it our best shot, and I'm very proud of it — I'm very proud of our staff and I'm very glad about what we've done. I know that people miss Scott, but the show's ratings seem to have remained consistent, even right after he left. Here in Washington, WAMU in a recent Saturday fund drive raised more money this year than last — I mean, you expect a slight increase each year, but it's nice to think that having Neal as host that week and not Scott didn't seem to phase the audience."

Scott's departure from NPR has allowed a range of some of the best NPR hosts to cycle through *WESAT* for a few weeks at a time — Alex Chadwick, Lynn Neary, Neal Conan, and Susan Stamberg, chief among them. Cindy admires them all, though every host requires slightly different handling: "I mean, I had to nudge Scott a hundred percent — but that's just the way he is. He procrastinates; everyone knows that about Scott. But he's so much fun to be around, he's genuinely so entertaining . . . and when the work is finished, well, I mean there's nothing more incredible than a Scott Simon script, and the way he reads it. But with the other hosts, you handle things differently as you try to help them bring out their best.

"So with Susan, for example, no nudging! She doesn't forget anything! Every so often I'll gently mention something to her, just to make sure we're all headed in the same direction. And Susan has an *incredible* ear. I can't believe it. I've never heard anybody who could so quickly listen to a piece of tape and say, 'You can switch that around, condense that, move that . . .' I've really been impressed! It's been great working with Susan.

"But I have to say that I've enjoyed each person that's come to host. I think they all have a real respect for the program, which is nice to feel, and they all bring something a little different with them — something special."

Shaping the Show

From Tuesdays through Fridays, *WESAT* staff members usually arrive at the office between nine and nine-thirty. Likely as not, Cindy is already sitting at the main table drinking her coffee and going through *The New York Times*, *The Washington Post*, or *USA Today*. A couple of staffers will start reading magazines as well as newspapers, looking for interesting stories in the features sections. While everyone on the program likes to keep abreast of the news, the principal challenge facing *Weekend Saturday* is coming up with interesting *host* pieces, finding those slightly out-of-the-way story ideas that the main news desks at NPR are going to overlook.

The one person on the *WESAT* staff charged with keeping a sharp eye on the hard-news side of the program, editor Steve Tripoli, usually begins his morning scanning the wire services on the computer terminal in his office, a cup of pot-brewed tea in his hand. Steve comes from a solidly print background. A tall, thin, bespectacled man in his late thirties, he tends to dress more formally than the rest of the *WESAT* staff, often wearing particularly shiny leather shoes. He sometimes plays the role of the "nay" man when story ideas are discussed, as suits a *news* reporter who is working in an environment that specializes in radio variety. But Steve possesses a wry sense of humor that Cindy says has emerged increasingly in the scripts he writes for the show. And during his three years at NPR, he has learned a great deal about radio, a medium for which he has developed a particular affection.

The host of the show often arrives between nine-thirty and ten, then spends time going through E-mail messages and catching up on the list of stories already sketched in for this week's show. At some point either Cindy will walk into the host's office or the host will come out and join the small group gathered in the common area. A conversation will start up, often reviewing some points about the previous program and then going on to discuss potential two-ways for the coming week.

During the midwinter of 1993, Susan Stamberg hosted *Weekend Saturday* for several weeks. While most of the programs produced after Scott Simon left continued to demonstrate the familiar *WESAT* qualities of care and creativity, the shows with Susan in the host's chair exuded a special kind of sparkle. Cindy had never teamed up with Susan before, and some staff members wondered how well these two strong-willed women would work together. The results were extraordinarily satisfying for all concerned, staff members and listeners.

In appearance, Susan and Cindy present quite a contrast. Where Cindy is small and sharply energetic, Susan is a large woman with a volcanic kind of drive. Tall, with a broadly boned face, Susan enters a room with the same authoritative swagger she uses on the air. Her smile, her voice, her quick wit, her hearty laugh — all command attention. Yet her longtime star status at NPR has not diminished her ethic of hard work nor lessened her pursuit of perfection. She remains deeply passionate about her work and may be her own sharpest critic. ("I often don't like what I hear myself do on the air," she says at one point, after listening to a piece of an old broadcast. "I can almost always think of a dozen other things I should have done or could have done.")

On this particular Tuesday morning, Susan arrives in a thick overcoat carrying a large paper bag that contains a big cup of coffee for herself and a box of pastries for the staff. She puts the bag on the table, and Cindy begins to extract its contents while Susan takes off her coat.

"What did you bring us, Susan?" asks Cindy, in her lightest, almost childlike voice. "Danish? Scott used to bring us Danish every day."

Susan laughs as she hangs up her coat, then she takes her coffee and one muffin into her office, explaining that she has to make a couple of phone calls.

As the staff parcels out the goodies, Susan's voice suddenly erupts from her office. She's speaking on the phone, with tremendous warmth and enthusiasm, to pianist/composer William Bolcom. "*Wonderful* to *hear* you!" she exclaims. Then her tone shifts in the space of a breath, and she almost purrs with sincere, but grandly gestured, dismay. "Are you really only here for today?" After a pause, one of the famous Stamberg laughs explodes like a skyrocket. In short, Susan Stamberg talks on the telephone the same way she talks on the air, the same way she talks in ordinary conversation. Susan's voice *is* her personality, and she uses her instrument like a virtuoso, except that a great deal of the time her "performance" is spontaneous and unrehearsed. With Susan — as with so many of the older broadcasters on NPR — what you *hear* is what you get.

A few minutes later, Susan comes out of her office, smiling broadly and sipping her coffee. Standing, she discusses with Cindy the idea she has had for the Music Cue. Justice Thurgood Marshall, who died on Sunday, will be lying in state tomorrow at the Supreme Court, and Susan would like to record some of the sounds of the event, and to talk with some of the people filing by. Cindy nods her head and says that's a wonderful idea but suggests that they check with Nina Totenberg first to make sure *WESAT* doesn't duplicate anything that she might be doing for the daily programs. Susan hears Cindy's objection but dismisses it. "I'll do something very different — just a quick little essay, a vignette, about the scene." She already has a shape in her mind. Cindy agrees but says she'll check in with Nina anyway.

Susan then moves to the *WESAT* board and picks up a marker. She's about to write in "Marshall" at the end of A2, the location of Music Cues, but she stops herself in midmovement. "Do you mind?" Susan says to Cindy, still learning the traditions and procedures at *Weekend Saturday*.

"No — not at all," says Cindy brightly, then adds, "Just put your initials up so if I have any questions I know who to ask."

Susan speaks as she writes. "I asked because I know some producers go *nuts* if anyone else writes on the board."

Susan walks over to the desk and takes a seat while Cindy opens up a manila folder and starts going over possible story ideas with Susan. "How about a cut-away on this guy's story?" Cindy asks, handing over a clipping from a sports magazine about a study that shows little or no difference in performance when athletes have sex before they compete. Susan laughs as she reads the article.

"A cut-away? A two-way, don't you think?" says Susan, with some enthusiasm. (A cut-away lasts less than three minutes. A two-way can continue considerably longer.)

"You think it's a worthy topic of discussion?" Cindy replies, laughing.

Susan grins and rethinks her first reaction. "Yeah. Cut-away might be plenty." Then her face breaks into a wide smile. "Oh, I think it'd make a very *funny* cut-away!"

Cut-aways consume a surprising amount of attention from the

WESAT staff, especially if you consider that many local stations do not carry these short pieces, which conclude the B segments. But in the context of the longer rhythms of most *Weekend Saturday* features, these short, often playful stories provide a nice change of pace. Cindy, in particular, thinks that good cut-aways can add a lot to the overall flow of the program. Furthermore, cut-aways give *WESAT* producers welcome flexibility. Some conversations that would not be successful as long pieces will function quite effectively in short form.

Dean Olsher, a freelance reporter and producer who is currently on temporary assignment to *WESAT* as a production assistant, now brings up the possibility of doing an interview with actor Judd Hirsch, who is about to conclude a long run on Broadway in the play *Conversations with My Father.* Dean says that Hirsch is famous in the theater for never having missed a performance since he first went on stage many years ago.

Dean is a young man in his late twenties who looks as if he just stepped out of a time warp from the 1960s. His long black hair is pulled back in a small ponytail, a short scruffy beard rims his face, and he wears gold-rimmed granny glasses. A musician, Dean attended Simon's Rock of Bard College in Massachusetts and then went on to the University of North Carolina, Chapel Hill, where he studied ethnomusicology.

Susan and Cindy both love the idea of interviewing Judd Hirsch. Cindy immediately starts imagining that the two-way would end with the theme from *Taxi,* in which Hirsch played Alex, his most famous TV role. "And best of all, look, it'll fit perfectly with Iva!" Cindy goes to the board and points to a piece tentatively marked into the C1 segment: a special eleven-minute story that Susan did with independent producer David Isay in New York City. Iva Pekarkova is a Czech immigrant who drives a cab nights while writing novels. Her second book has just been published. Above "SS/Iva: 11:00," Cindy adds the slug "SS/Judd Hirsch."

Cindy then walks over to the clipboard on the wall and looks over the rundown of Susan's schedule for today. The host has a number of two-ways scheduled, including an interview with an anthropologist, Katherine Milton, of Berkeley, who has investigated a strange South American ritual in which secretions are taken from live frogs and then ingested as some kind of hallucinogen. Further medical research suggests that a new peptide found in the frog liquid might help treat victims of strokes or Alzheimer's disease. Susan says the story sounds *very* bizarre and interesting. She wants to be sure she sees a copy of the original article before the two-way.

The conversation around the table winds down. Susan goes back to her office. Cindy leans on her elbows and stares at the board, the merest sketch of what it will eventually become. Cindy already has possibilities to think about, stories to hear in her head as she begins to imagine the upcoming program.

It's a little after ten o'clock. The previous half-hour of conversation — with staff wandering in and out — represents the closest thing *WE-SAT* ever has to a morning meeting. Alone among NPR programs, *WESAT* has no regularly scheduled staff get-togethers. In fact Cindy occasionally teases the *Weekend All Things Considered* staff — just down the corridor from *WESAT* — because it seems to Cindy that their show is *always* having meetings. "What's there to meet *about?*" she will say to the *WATC* producer, Jane Greenhalgh. Jane smiles and talks about constant "exchanges of ideas." Cindy shakes her head.

WESAT and *WATC* are following established traditions for their particular programs. *WATC* has long been produced in a highly cooperative and collaborative spirit. Jane, in particular, comports herself as a *prima inter pares*, actively involving all of her young staff in program decisions. Cindy is following some of the traditions established by Jay Kernis when he produced the show. In particular, Cindy holds a tight rein on every step of the production process — she will listen to every story before it goes on the air and frequently recut pieces that her staff submits to her. Like Jay, Cindy is a perfectionist, and everything from the simplest two-way to the most complicated produced piece comes under her intense scrutiny and is subjected to her quick razor blade.

On the other hand, Cindy is not a despotic "absolute ruler" of the *WESAT* domain. One reason *WESAT* never has formal meetings is that Cindy spends her days in *constant* conversation with staff members . . . at the main table, at the storyboard, in the show's various offices and cubicles. Ideas for stories are continually being tossed around, and the staff is constantly checking in with Cindy to keep her apprised of the progress of their various pieces. If they do not seek her out, Cindy more than likely will track them down to make sure there are no problems.

In the absence of formal conclaves — or printed lists of upcoming story ideas, suggestions, and the like — the main board takes on an added significance as the one public declaration of the "show idea" that is taking shape, ultimately, in the mind of the producer. The physical layout of the *Weekend Saturday* storyboard reflects the unusual approach to structure that seems to be a part of *WESAT* culture. The board begins as something approaching a tabla rasa — a large, white rectangle with only a few divisions taped on it (such as a long dividing line between the first and second hours) . . . nothing like the vivid grid structure of *Morning Edition*. Each hour is divided into three main parts, segments A, B, and C. And between each B and C section, CUT1 and CUT2 will eventually be filled in. But most of the lines on the board are drawn by Cindy herself, as stories are proposed, come in, and are moved around.

Weekend ATC's board is the most unrestricted in the building — four blank panels, not even divided into columns until the producer starts wielding her marker. Yet *WESAT*'s board approaches *WATC*'s openness of form in spite of the fact that its show is more rigidly structured. The relative absence of permanently inscribed divisions on the *Weekend Saturday* board suggests Jay Kernis's challenge to producers that they transcend the constrictions of format. The casual layout may be seen as a metaphor expressing the desire — perhaps it's better called an ideal — that an underlying wholeness unify the *WESAT* radio experience for listeners. Cindy Carpien continues to pursue this ideal.

The very top of the board usually remains blank until late in the week. The A segment in the first hour (A1) always contains late news stories. It may also include the Daniel Schorr three-way interview, which has become one of the traditions of the program. Each week, Dan conducts a conversation with two experts on some current topic. He often does these interviews "to time," though some discussions require editing. Dan appears again in the A2 segment (the second hour), reviewing the news of the week with the host. This segment was originally done on tape, but a few years ago, Dan was encouraged to go live. While much of the back-and-forth conversation is written out ahead of time by Dan (after consultation with the host and the show editor), there's a good deal of spontaneity in and around the script. Also, Dan is a master at reading his copy and making it sound as though he were "just talking." "WIR" (Week in Review) is always followed by the Music Cue.

The C segments usually hold the longest pieces of the program, and since these are often highly produced pieces, they are usually known well in advance. At the moment, though, only the Czech cab driver, Iva, is listed in C1.

Otherwise, "Frogs" (the interview about the Amazonian drug) has already been placed in the B2 segment. B1 is slugged: "Kaufman, 8:00." This story has come from the national desk. One of NPR's Los Angeles correspondents, Wendy Kaufman, will profile the upcoming civil rights trial of the police officers originally charged, and acquitted, in the beating of Rodney King. Ahead of Wendy's piece, Cindy tentatively adds the slug "Urban Crisis," which refers to an interview Susan Stamberg is doing today with a former mayor of Albuquerque, David Rusk, who has innovative ideas about how to save American cities. (Eventually, this two-way will be held over for another week, when it will be paired with a curious piece in which Susan plays the computer game SimCity while talking over the phone with a hacker who is an expert at this simulation of urban planning. The attempt to convey the contours of a computer game over the radio is not entirely successful — the fact that the hacker is recovering from laryngitis doesn't help much. But the piece represents a typical *WESAT* attempt to be creative and to have some fun.)

The board is filled with holes and will change many times before the Saturday show. But even at this early stage, Cindy is trying to put pieces together that make some kind of thematic sense and that flow gracefully into one another.

Though the talk around the board this morning centered on feature pieces, *Weekend Saturday* devotes a good deal of its airtime to harder news stories. For example, one of Susan Stamberg's tasks this week is to move forward with assistant producer and show director Doug Mitchell on a story that they covered during a trip to Nashville, Tennessee, several days ago. The piece concerns the closing of a hospital that has been serving the black community for generations. The report poses, in vivid fashion, some of the dilemmas facing health care providers as they try to balance community needs with economics. Doug traveled to Nashville with Susan and an engineer. Once back at NPR, Doug logged all the tape, that is, he made notes about what they had recorded. He then went over the notes with Susan, and they decided which pieces of tape seemed the most promising. Today Doug will finish "pulling the tape," dubbing the selected excerpts from both analogue cassette and DAT tape. Susan will have this rough-cut reel by late morning, and she will then start composing the story, "writing to the tape" as the expression goes. Then Steve Tripoli will edit the story before Susan records her talk tracks. Finally, Doug will work with an engineer in-studio to mix the story together. Following Cindy's final approval, the story is scheduled to be aired on next week's *Weekend Saturday* in one of the C segments. Originally conceived of as a thirteen-minute piece, Doug currently thinks the report may run longer since it looks as if they have a lot of good tape.

Host trips on *Weekend Saturday* usually result in at least one hard piece and one softer story. While in Nashville, Susan and Doug also collected tape during "Open Mike Night" at the Bluebird Café, a local country and western nightclub. Susan talked backstage with aspiring country and western singers and then sat in the audience with a record producer, soliciting his comments on each act. This promises to be a funny, poignant story, filled with sound and atmosphere. Susan has already sketched an outline for the piece; indeed, she conceived her narrative framework almost from the moment they left the café. With a touch of amazement in his voice, Doug explains that as he was driving their rental car away from the nightclub, Susan immediately began writing on a small piece of paper some notes about how the story might be culled from all the tape they had recorded. She then read her ideas to Doug, who said they sounded great. While Susan is working on her script for the hospital story this week, Doug will begin pulling the Bluebird tape.

Susan's two-way schedule for Tuesday winds up being light enough that she gets a good start writing the Nashville hospital piece. Her interview about the South American frog ritual proves intriguing and will make a good five-minute two-way, when Ken edits it down tomorrow. Other staff members research other upcoming interviews, make phone calls, and do bits and pieces of tape editing.

On Wednesday, the pace of the program noticeably picks up. A little before noon, Susan leaves for the Supreme Court to observe Justice Thurgood Marshall lying in state. She is wearing a black blouse and a flowing, dark red skirt and puts her old Sony 5000 monaural cassette recorder into her shoulder bag. Dean Olsher goes with her as field producer. They spend two hours inside the Court and with the crowd lining the street outside. They collect about a half hour of tape that Susan will condense down into a three-minute Music Cue.

Meanwhile, legal affairs correspondent Nina Totenberg has already covered the same event; her report will appear on tomorrow's *Morning Edition*. Nina drops by *WESAT* for a visit while Susan is off at the Supreme Court.

"Oh, you're hot pink!" Cindy exclaims as Nina walks down the corridor in her familiar, confident stride. Nina is wearing a gray skirt, black shoes, and an attractive pink jacket. The two women start discussing Nina's large pin, which is threatening to put a hole in the jacket. Cindy comes up with the idea of using Scotch tape — or even splicing tape — to stave off the hole. She grabs a razor blade from a nearby tape recorder to help make the adjustment in Nina's accessories.

As Cindy works on the pin, Nina recalls her morning visit to the hall of the Supreme Court. "It's really very touching," Nina says. "Normally, only chief justices lie in state. Douglas did not lie in state. A lot of people are going to want to come by and pay last respects."

Cindy takes a step backwards after finishing her work on the pin. "You can't even see the tape," she says.

"But I can feel it," says Nina, smiling. "It's good. Thanks."

Cindy leans against the table and repeats the story she's read that Marshall told about himself. When a boy, he was often so unruly that he was forced to stay after school and read the Constitution. He got attached to the document and that was why he became a lawyer.

Nina nods. The scene at the Court comes back to her mind and she says quietly yet matter-of-factly, "I cried." She smiles wanly. "I was fine till I saw his son, Goody, and went up to pay my respects. I gave him a hug, and the minute I did, I began crying. After that, it seemed like a lot of reporters started weeping."

"You had to do that, you had to," says Cindy with understanding.

"So much for my image as a tough reporter," says Nina with a little laugh. Then her face grows more serious. "I saw [Justice] Souter helping [Justice] Brennan up from his wheelchair and holding his hand as they walked around the casket. I found that very touching."

On Thursday, *Morning Edition* will broadcast a short piece from Nina about Justice Marshall lying in state. The *WESAT* staff will discuss the spot and will conclude that even though Nina mentions the moment when Justice Souter helps Justice Brennan pay his respects, the report, overall, contains surprisingly little emotion. A brief setup by Nina is followed by two minutes of "vox" — that is, interviews with people who came to pay their respects. "Maybe Nina just didn't respond emotionally," someone suggests. Cindy shakes her head and tells of Nina's visit to *WESAT*. "It's the program," someone else says. "They just don't think about doing deeply emotional pieces on the morning show. They don't think it's what people want to hear as they're waking up." Cindy shrugs, noncommitally.

The short piece that Susan Stamberg will put together for the Saturday program will work in a slightly different way from Nina's report. Conceived as a personal essay, Susan's slightly longer story includes comments from mourners waiting in line outside the Court and a few brief reflections from Susan. But the emotional high-point occurs when listeners move into the hall of the Court itself. The somber scene is evoked in a few whispered words from Susan and the echoing rustle of clothes, the clicking of shoes, as people walk past Marshall's casket. This portion of the Music Cue lingers in the mind, bringing a lump to the throat, a small shiver down the spine.

The Art of the Two-Way

As invariably happens, Wednesday afternoon on *Weekend Saturday* sees a number of possible two-ways start falling through. When Susan returns from the Supreme Court, she hears from Cindy that Judd Hirsch has not yet confirmed an interview, but that one of the staff members has suggested talking with his understudy instead. What is it like to be the backup for someone who never gets sick? Susan does not like the idea. She'd rather have Judd. Cindy nudges. "Well, look, we can always use Judd if he comes and then only use a small cut from the understudy." Susan wants to hold out for Judd.

Meanwhile, production assistant Franc Contreras has tracked down the author of the report on sexual activity and athletic performance. (Franc is in his final couple of weeks on *WESAT*, having zigzagged back and forth between *ATC* and the weekend program since he pulled up roots in New Mexico and arrived back in Washington a couple of months ago.) Franc has some bad news. The sex report is six years old. The researcher wonders why the media still remains interested. Franc assumes this kills the story. Cindy at first can't believe her ears. The article in *Runners Magazine* clearly states, "in a *new* study." But then she shifts her perspective on the two-way. Now the story becomes: why does the press keep pestering this researcher about his old study? Susan agrees with Cindy . . . and then they remember the scene from the movie *Rocky* in which Burgess Meredith counsels Sylvester Stallone to abstain from sex before a fight. "Women ruin legs," Meredith says.

Susan, Cindy, and Franc all laugh and agree that this clip from the movie will make a perfect end to the cut-away. Cindy tells Franc to go ahead and schedule the interview.

Once again a story decision on *WESAT* is made not simply on the basis of "news value" but within the *ears* of the producer, who *hears* the way a particular topic might be handled.

By Thursday the pace on *WESAT* production has picked up considerably. The staff is in a sprint from now till Saturday morning, when the show goes on the air. Susan conducts a couple of two-ways in the morning. The first does not go well, and will be deferred till next week, or dropped; but the conversation with the sex researcher works out all right and will make an amusing cut-away. By midafternoon, Susan writes her Marshall Music Cue, much to Cindy's amazement (Scott Simon often finished his essay late Friday evening).

Meanwhile, editor Steve Tripoli has been perusing the board and, as is his wont, he complains mildly about the lack of harder news stories. "I feel comfortable with the B's," he says. "I'm not that happy with the C's. I'd feel better if we start plugging up all the remaining holes with news pieces." At the moment the B segments are anchored by two substantial pieces, Wendy Kaufman's pretrial report from Los Angeles and an interview — slugged "State of the World" — held over from last week, in which a sociologist assesses current economic and social conditions in the nonindustrialized world. The C1 contains the Isay feature with Iva, the novelist/cab driver. Cindy is about to audition the piece currently in C2 marked "Egypt." This is a report Susan has assembled from an interview she did with photographer Robert Lyons, who has published a book of pictures he took during a year traveling in Egypt. Steve notes that at the moment, the show's two hours are ending with pieces about books, even though neither feature is a traditional "author two-way."

Cindy acknowledges Steve's concern about a lack of news. She is counting on harder pieces to come out of the news desks today and tomorrow to fill out the A and the B segments. The exchange between producer and editor is a familiar one and forms part of the dynamic tension within the production staff that helps keep the appropriate balance between "the soft and the hard."

In fact, following the general editorial meeting at ten-thirty, *Weekend Saturday* winds up with a couple more news pieces, including a six-minute story that Alan Siporin, a freelance reporter from Oregon, will be sending about Senator Bob Packwood's return to his home state following the controversy over charges of sexual harassment. At the same time, Julie McCarthy, at the foreign desk, gives Cindy the first hints that Tom Gjelten may submit a feature from Sarajevo about a theater company that stages performances of the sixties musical *Hair* in the midst of the raging civil war. Cindy and Steve are excited by the prospect of Tom's report, though Julie won't know till Friday whether it will be ready in time for Saturday's show.

Sometime on Thursday, Cindy has a brainstorm about a piece that she's wanted to do for some time. Weeks ago, she saw a small news item mentioning that the separation of Czechoslovakia into the Czech Republic and Slovakia would also cause a division within the seventy-year-old Czechoslovakian national anthem. Apparently when Czechoslovakia was formed earlier this century, two previously existing nationalistic songs were joined into one. Now the tunes will be split apart again. Cindy immediately heard in her mind a bit of production in which the breakup of Czechoslovakia would be illustrated by playing the separate anthems. But she never found the appropriate moment to use this idea.

Earlier in the week Václav Havel was elected president of the new Czech Republic and Cindy thought again about using the music in the show — but how? The foreign desk was not offering a story on Havel's victory; by Saturday it would be old news. Susan already had a Music Cue written. But while Cindy listens to a CD sent over by the Czech Embassy, she suddenly thinks of the show's Open. Each hour of *WE-SAT* starts not with a billboard of the upcoming program but rather with a quick story (or stories) recollecting the day in history. Sometimes the host will describe an unusual piece of news from the previous week. Cindy imagines excerpts from the two new anthems playing behind Susan as she reads forty-five seconds of copy. She listens to the two parts of the Czechoslovakian anthem. In her mind's ear, she can hear the fade from one section of the music to the other. She's almost sure it will work. She mentions the possibility to Susan, who thinks it's a great idea. Cindy says she will supervise the mix, as it may take a while to get the cross-fade sounding just right. She beams happily in anticipation.

Late in the afternoon, Ken brings Cindy the results of his work editing the two-way with anthropologist Katherine Milton, about the frog-secretion hallucinogen. Cindy sits at her desk, listening to the tape, while Ken stands in the doorway. She looks out the window and alternately giggles and shivers as Milton tells the story of watching how villagers in the Amazon collect liquid from frogs:

> . . . [S]everal of the younger men ran off into the forest and came back with a big, leafy, green branch and on this branch was seated an absolutely gorgeous frog. They then pegged the frog out, with stakes. And then they began to harass the frog by poking it around the eyes and nostrils with a splinter. And I noticed that it just began to secrete copious quantities of a very clear substance — it actually was secreted in such a quantity that it ran down the legs of the frog and even, sort of, collected in a viscous pool around the ankles of the frog.

Cindy suddenly stops the tape, rewinds and replays the section. Something has caught her ear. She listens a second, then a third time. Her suspicions are confirmed. She turns to Ken and asks him if he thinks that the phrase "pegged the frogs out with stakes" is necessary. Ken looks surprised. He says it's one of the most vivid and important parts of Milton's story. Cindy agrees that it's vivid, but she wonders if it isn't *too* vivid. She thinks it may distract the listener's attention from what follows. "Let's just try it without the phrase," Cindy says, "and we can hear." She quickly makes the cut and puts the short piece of tape carefully to one side. She replays the segment — and the effect is stunning. Instantly, the entire passage becomes *aurally* much clearer than before. Milton's story sounds more powerful and effective. It's as though a layer of dust had been removed from a painting that seemed colorful enough until the cleaning. Milton now says, in part: "[S]everal of the younger men ran off into the forest and came back with a big, leafy, green branch and on this branch was seated an absolutely gorgeous frog. And then they began to harass the frog by poking it around the eyes and nostrils with a splinter . . ."

The change is difficult to convey on the printed page. But due to a curious mixture of vividness and vagueness, the phrase "pegged the frog out with stakes" *did* dilute the impact of Milton's story. The words are emotionally striking — something awful is being done to a little animal — but they do not define a clear image, paint a specific picture, and so our imaginations *stumble* over the phrase "pegged out" and we don't let go of the words. We take a couple of seconds to fill in the blanks, to make sense of the image. Meanwhile, Milton is continuing her story — but we are not focusing on what she says. By the time we reconnect with her, we've lost some of her story. By contrast, without the distraction of the "pegged out" phrase, each image that Milton speaks carries the correct amount of weight and clarity and her narrative builds, step by step, through more and more powerful pictures, culminating in the "viscous pool" forming around the legs of the frog. Nothing impedes the flowering image in our minds.

Cindy smiles broadly, pleased with her edit. Ken nods his head, appreciatively. "Cutting two-ways is a very undervalued art," Cindy says, with a laugh. "I don't think many people realize how much you can *do* with a two-way — how important pacing is . . . how a breath or a phrase can make a huge difference in how listeners will hear the piece."

Cindy continues through the rest of the two-way, tightening and pruning here and there. In all, she spends about an hour going over the five-minute piece.

At five-thirty, Susan and Cindy are sitting together in the common area. It has been a long day, but tomorrow, Friday, will be even longer. Susan has several two-ways scheduled, including the understudy to Judd Hirsch, as it's proved impossible to get the man himself. Cindy is taking a long look at the board. Suddenly she exclaims, "It's going to be a good show! We've got 'State of the World', we've got frogs, we've got sex . . ."

Susan laughs. "Looks good, Cin," she says.

Franc Contreras hangs around long after the rest of the staff has gone home. At six o'clock, he is down in the *WESAT* studio putting together the long piece about Senator Packwood. The report will run six minutes, and contain a mixture of acts and tracks, along with a bit of ambiance to "sweeten" the piece (sounds of a demonstration and street noises). As he directs the engineer through the various tape changes and cross-fades, Franc is constantly in motion — sometimes crouching, sometimes pacing, often waving his hand as though he were directing music. The mix has to start and stop from time to time, because the levels of the various pieces of tape don't always match perfectly and Franc does not always anticipate changes that have to be made. Also, he asks the engineer to redo a couple of the cross-fades. But all the work is completed in about twenty minutes.

Franc then retires to his edit booth where he works until eight o'clock, splicing together the various pieces of the mix. He also attempts to fix some parts of the report that still don't sound good to him. "The actualities from Portland, at the top of the spot, are just not right — they come too fast," Frank says. "I'm adding bits of ambiance to slow them down. Some of the pieces of tape I'm splicing in are only the size of my thumbnail."

Frank will not finish his work tonight. He will be back in the studio tomorrow morning, remixing the first few minutes of the story, trying to make it perfect.

Fridays are the most hectic day in the week for *Weekend Saturday*. Any questions that have been postponed must now be answered, pieces that have not been completed have to be finished off, the final shape of the show has to be decided. Cindy continues to come in at nine in the morning, but it is rare that she leaves the office before six o'clock. She attends to a myriad of little details throughout the day and has frequent conversations with the line producer Ken Hom, who will be in charge tomorrow morning. The meticulousness with which Cindy approaches every aspect of the show is almost less astonishing than the extent to which she is able to communicate her care and planning to *others* who will execute what she has in mind.

A little before noon, Cindy finally has a chance to listen to David Isay's piece with Iva Pekarkova, the Czech cab driver and novelist. She emerges from her office ecstatic. "It's wonderful, absolutely wonderful," Cindy exclaims to Susan. "It's vintage NPR. My only concern is the ending . . . it just sort of stops. We'll have to think of something to fade up — just the right piece of music. But it's just wonderful."

Susan is delighted that Cindy likes the piece so much. "David is just terrific," she says. "Great to work with."

Cindy laughs, then says, more seriously, "You work great with people — it brings out your best work."

"Well," says Susan with a big smile, "Irving Berlin and Gershwin did better when they were collaborating."

Cindy goes back to her office and starts looking through her CDs for the right music to use at the conclusion of the piece.

Susan immediately gets on the phone to call David Isay and let him know Cindy's response.

In the early afternoon, Cindy receives the Tom Gjelten tape from Julie McCarthy. After production, it should come in at about six minutes. Cindy gives Franc the tape to work with. The arrival of this tape allows Cindy to drop a weak national story of which she has not been particularly fond, though how to fit this powerful story of Sarajevo into the program will remain a challenge and a matter of discussion right up until the time of broadcast — and afterward.

Susan spends a good portion of Friday in the production studio doing several two-ways and rerecording some revised introductions and other continuity for the program. Working in the *WESAT* production studio can be a bit nostalgic for Susan: it's on the ground floor and is one of the original locations from which *All Things Considered* and all other NPR programs used to be broadcast during the 1970s.

All of the weekend programs use the old studios during the week to do their mixes and most of their two-ways. These three cavernous facilities were originally color-coded, the walls being soundproofed in different colored acoustic tile. *Weekend Saturday* does its production work in Studio Three, the "orange suite." The threadbare carpet and the faded colors on the walls and ceiling reveal the underlying age of the room. The cellarlike chill of the place (the air conditioning seems perpetually set too high) and the dim lighting (darker than the upstairs control rooms) contribute to the hoary, cavelike feeling. Yet there is a history of NPR sound trapped somewhere in these deadening walls: resonances of the early days, when the orange, red, and blue caves often became wombs of creativity in which NPR staff members rediscovered the lost magic of radio.

Cindy Carpien attends many of the two-ways that her hosts record for *Weekend Saturday;* as editor of the show, Steve Tripoli tries to sit in on every interview. Normally, weekend programs record slightly longer two-ways than do weekday shows: weekend hosts may work with their guests a bit more, probing, prodding, encouraging . . . However, the goal remains to keep the interview as short as possible, to make the job of tape editing easier.

The art of interviewing is so varied — and different hosts employ such different styles — that it is hard to give an example of "a typical" weekend interview. On this particular Friday afternoon, however, the conversation Susan Stamberg has with Judd Hirsch's understudy presents a vivid portrait of an experienced radio host at work. It also demonstrates the importance of expert editing in creating an effective piece of tape.

Susan is sitting in Studio Three, a scarf around her shoulders. She's wearing her headphones while waiting for Dean Olsher to reach the understudy, Ron Hunter. Steve and Cindy are standing in the back of the control room, continuing the endless discussion of how to order stories in the program. Susan's dark eyes look tired and she's leaning her face in her hands — it's a little before four o'clock, the end of a long day. Hunter will be her final two-way and Susan's job will be to get something under three minutes of good tape from him. Cindy has scheduled the understudy to fill one of the cut-aways.

Dean speaks to Susan over the intercom: Hunter is on the line. Susan sits upright in her chair and her face breaks into a warm smile.

"Hello?" says Susan.

"Hello," an extraordinarily rough, gravely voice answers.

"Hi, Mr. Hunter, it's Susan Stamberg calling from Washington. How are you?" Susan speaks with charm and graciousness.

"I'm great today," says Hunter. "How are you?" Though his voice is rough-edged, there's a pleasing lightness to his tone, along with that matter-of-fact directness which suggests that Hunter is a native New Yorker.

Cindy's ears prick up. She looks around the control room. "He sounds great!" she says.

"Very well, thank you," says Susan, with a big grin. Then, in typical Susan fashion, she bursts out, "You sound just like Judd Hirsch!" And she laughs.

Everyone in the control room laughs. Dean exclaims: "Oh! I wish we were rolling."

Hunter may be a bit too surprised to laugh out loud, but there's a smile in his voice as he answers in crisp syllables. "Well, after all, I am his understudy. " And then he chuckles.

Cindy says, "You know he does sound like Hirsch. It's positively creepy."

Susan turns to the technical business necessary before the interview starts. "Mr. Hunter? Could you talk to me a little bit, please? We need to hear your voice."

"Well, what would you like me to say?" says Hunter.

"Anything you like," Susan begins. "Tell us what you had . . ." But Hunter begins talking before Susan can finish suggesting that he talk about his lunch.

"You know," Hunter says, "it's very odd that we should be having this conversation right now because just a short time ago I got a call from Judd . . ."

"Oh no!" Dean exclaims. "Can we start rolling tape?"

But Dean need not worry. Susan jumps right in to interrupt Hunter. "Oh, Mr. Hunter, wait, wait a minute, wait, please wait . . ."

". . . and when I heard who it was, my heart dropped . . ."

Susan finally gets Hunter's attention. "Oh, wait. Don't tell me this until we start taping." And she laughs.

"Oh, all right," says Hunter.

"Tell me something that's completely unimportant. Tell me what the weather is like in New York — we just need a level."

As Hunter begins talking, Cindy looks at Dean and grins. Recalling Dean's struggles to reach Judd Hirsch, she wonders why Judd has had time to call his understudy but hasn't had time to talk with *WESAT.* Dean laughs.

Hunter is saying that the weather is chillier than Los Angeles, where he was last year.

"Okay," says Susan, "let me interrupt you. You sound very, very good, so let's begin. Now, we're making a tape and we'll talk for maybe ten minutes and then edit it down for broadcast tomorrow morning."

"Okay," says Hunter.

"And if you'll stand by," Susan continues, "I have a little introduction to put at the beginning here before I get you with the first question, okay? Here we go . . ."

"Fade down Hunter," says Dean to the engineer. As editor of the piece, Dean is also directing the two-way. It's safest when a host is reading an introduction to take the telephone line out of channel, preventing any breaths or coughs or telephone noises from interfering with the flow of the host's lead-in.

The tape is rolling, Cindy, Dean, and Steve are listening attentively, and Susan starts reading: "Next week, unless something awful happens, actor Judd Hirsch will end his run in Broadway's *Conversations with My Father* with a perfect record. In fact, since 1975 Judd Hirsch hasn't missed a single performance anywhere. Could there be anything worse then being Judd Hirsch's stand-in? Ron Hunter is on the phone with us from New York . . ."

"Bring him in," says Dean to the engineer.

"You're the stand-in," Susan continues. "What's the answer, Mr. Hunter?"

"Well, I think there are a lot of things worse than that," Hunter begins, his gravely voice speaking in short choppy phrases. "Like not being unemployed [*sic*]. Like not being affiliated or associated with a marvelous play like *Conversations* and like not having the opportunity to watch Judd perform every night. But there are a lot of much worse things than that. Being unemployed is also much worse."

"I bet it is," says Susan quickly, with a laugh. "Do you ever feel like the Maytag repairman, though, with a guy like that?" Susan laughs again. (This line sounds spontaneous, but in fact Dean has included the question in the script that Susan has in front of her.)

Hunter chuckles. "Well, um, perhaps, I haven't thought of it quite that way. I hope that I'm as essential as the Maytag repairman, after all he's great insurance. It gives you great peace of mind, although I wouldn't mind that job either."

Susan changes her tone of voice and asks a leading question: "Have you ever had a phone call from the theater, though, that maybe got your heart going?" Susan sounds as though she doesn't know the answer to the question, when, of course, she knows that Hunter has a tale to tell.

Hunter burbles a few words, his thick voice seeming to stick on itself, then his response clarifies. "It's very odd that you should say that because I think about an hour and twenty minutes ago I got a call from the theater, from the stage manager . . ."

There's a sudden click on the line — the call-waiting tone indicating that Hunter has an incoming call.

Hunter is a little confused. "Hello?" he says.

Susan picks up on the moment without missing a beat. "Wait! Maybe that's the stage manager again!" She laughs. Hunter chuckles. Then Susan says, "Go ahead."

"Right!" Hunter continues. "It could be another emergency call. But, uh, she was sorry to bother me, but she had just gotten a call from Judd, and accidentally he . . . and my heart dropped. It was like the first time that I was on a flight, we hit an air pocket and I left my heart at about two thousand feet above where I now was . . ."

People in the control room are laughing. Cindy is impressed. "He's describing just what it felt like," she says. "This is good."

"I was shocked . . . startled . . ." Hunter continues, speaking very slowly. Then he pauses.

Cindy is getting impatient. "So what did she *say?*" she asks aloud.

Hunter obliges Cindy. "But [she] then went on to tell me that it was just a message that he had received inadvertently for me, that he had taken with him."

Susan laughs. "Oh jeez!" she exclaims as Hunter talks.

"I tell you, it's relieving not to have to go on. It's not the kind of show that one wants to do without ever having rehearsed it . . ."

"Wait a minute," says Cindy as Susan smiles and nods in response to Hunter's story. "What was the end? What did he say?" Cindy feels that the punchline of Hunter's story has not been expressed clearly. She's a little surprised that Susan is letting Hunter continue.

Meanwhile, Susan is following Hunter's train of thought.

"You've never had a rehearsal?" she asks.

"Well, we've had run-throughs with the other understudies, but once you come into a show in the function that I'm in, you don't have the luxury of the rehearsals with the director. It's a difficult situation."

Cindy is getting impatient again. "I don't care about this. It's not very interesting," she exclaims. Dean murmurs in agreement.

Hunter continues: "I have certainly watched the show many times. And I certainly feel prepared to go on but not anxious to."

"You sound just like him, you know," Susan says again, sounding as though this is the first time she's expressed this thought.

"No, I didn't know that," says Hunter, not letting on that Susan is repeating something she said earlier. "I guess that's the reason I'm in the position I'm in."

Susan looks down at the list of possible questions that Dean has prepared. She moves the discussion over to another line of inquiry.

"There are, you know, these sort of legendary stories about people like you. Shirley MacLaine, didn't she get a huge big break one night when she was the understudy in *The Pajama Game?*"

While Susan asks her question, Dean is remembering that the story of the phone call was not done clearly enough. "She's not going to go back to the telephone," he says with disappointment.

Cindy nods. "Well, at the end she can ask him the question again, and then you can cut his answer back in to the top."

Susan is saying, "And others . . . do you know of any other sort of famous stand-in-to-star stories?"

"No, I don't," says Hunter very matter-of-factly. "I'm sure there are some. I think it's really a fantasy. Doing that is like being an actor in the first place. It's like trying to play the lottery. That isn't the reason why I took the job. It isn't why I do it. And there is some significant satisfaction, in and of itself, working with the people and being affiliated with the people who are involved in *Conversations*, it's a marvelous experience."

There are a few moans in the control room. Hunter is being a bit too predictable here and is giving rather dull, uninteresting answers.

Susan takes another tack. "Do you have to go to the theater every night?"

"Yes, I do."

"And what do you do?"

"Well, I sign in and check to see that Judd has also arrived." Hunter is speaking in the same rather flat matter-of-fact way, but Susan senses an opening, an opportunity to provoke good tape. To great laughter in the control room, Susan chuckles and says in a very teasing tone of voice, "I *bet* you do, Mr. Hunter!"

Hunter immediately picks up on Susan's tone and replies spiritedly. "I do! I do! In fact, when he's not there, I don't move! But once he's arrived . . . I mean, he's legendary. His work ethic and his commitment to his work. And, ah, I'm very relieved once he's there."

There are some dissatisfied murmurs in the control room: couldn't this guy be a little less *nice?* Dean and Cindy both had the image of a starstruck understudy who couldn't wait to fill the shoes of the famous actor. Hunter is coming across as an altogether reasonable, responsible — and therefore, in radio terms, slightly dull — person.

Hunter has moved on to discuss the complexity of the role as being one reason he is not anxious to try to fill in for Hirsch. "Because of the magnitude of this role, I mean this is a role like King Lear and Macbeth together: the character almost rarely leaves the stage. He moves the play, he's the focus of the play and has endless dialogue. In case an emergency were to arrive — an act of God — if Judd were to break his leg backstage, have an attack of appendicitis, something . . . I would have to be prepared and available to go on."

"But otherwise," says Susan, still probing for a more vivid picture of what Hunter's life is like backstage, "what do you do? Play cards? Read the newspaper?"

"No, I have actually only been involved with the company for a short period of time, about seven weeks now. So I still am in the ether . . . I'm still watching the show. I actually enjoy watching it."

"Well, you don't have to keep that in," Cindy says to Dean. "That's not the point."

Hunter goes on to qualify his previous remark. "I must admit I don't watch every second of it now, but . . . I'm around the theater."

Susan instinctively feels the time is ripe for another "assault" on Hunter's reasonableness. Can she get beneath the veneer of "good sportsmanship" to a deeper layer within this actor? She begins speaking with seriousness and understanding, then flips into an intimate, almost conspiratorial tone. "Mr. Hunter, I can hear your deep respect for Judd Hirsch, but is there not some *small* part of you" — and here, Susan's voice almost croons — "that wishes at least he'd *lose* his *voice . . . once?*"

"No," Hunter replies emphatically, though Susan's nudgey voice inspires a big laugh. "Not one part of me. Not right now." Susan laughs, too. And then Hunter continues in a more serious tone. "Certainly I would love to do the role, and I hope someday to do the role, but I don't want, I have *no* desire at this moment to go on and replace him. My job as a standby is to keep the show intact and do as much of what he's doing as possible, so that the other actors aren't thrown, so that the essence of the show as he's conceived it — as the director and the playwright and Judd have all conceived it — is preserved."

More moans in the control room. Dean says, "Yeah, yeah. He would *die* to go on!" But though staff members seem to be complaining because Susan is not getting the kind of vivid tape they expected, they are also finding Hunter quite likable — he's coming across as a very decent fellow. Good character does not always make for memorable radio, however.

"To do anything that would be more personal would be in violation of what my function is," Hunter is saying, "and that's fine. That's my understanding. I'm not trying to duplicate what he's doing but to present the essence of his concept."

After his initial response to Susan's question, Hunter's answer has become rambling and not entirely clear. At first Susan listens intently, looking for an opening to probe the actor again, but as he keeps talking, she begins just to nod and say an occasional "Uh-huh" while looking down at her script.

Cindy looks at Susan and wonders aloud. "Is she trying to think of a way out?" At the moment, there's no clear finish to the two-way; Cindy knows Susan must sense this, but wonders what she's going to do next.

Susan's next move catches the control room by surprise. She begins to close the two-way.

"Thank you very much," she says almost abruptly. Then she reads the close from the script. "Ron Hunter, who has lived the understudy's nightmare. He is the stand-in for Judd Hirsch, who has never missed a performance. Next week, Mr. Hirsch ends his run in *Conversations with My Father* on Broadway." Here the script ends, but Susan now begins a brilliant improvisation, sneaking up once more on Hunter's apparent lack of ambition. "Who's coming in, Mr. Hunter?" Susan asks, pulling the unusual stunt of adding a coda to the interview after she has formally closed it down.

"Uh, Jim Belushi," says Hunter, sounding a tad surprised to still be fielding questions.

"Do you stay on?" asks Susan warmly.

"Yes, I do."

"Well, listen," Susan coos conspiratorially. "Maybe Belushi will get a little case of laryngitis!"

The control room bursts into laughter. Someone even claps a couple of times.

"That's great!" Cindy exclaims.

Hunter laughs, perhaps charmed by Susan's dogged pursuit of this issue. But he also gives one of his most engaging responses. "Well, I wish him good health, I really do. But I certainly, at some point, would like to go on myself. I look forward to *only* an occasion when he is unavailable because he's got perhaps other more important things to do. But I certainly don't want to go on on the basis of some kind of personal tragedy."

"What a lovely guy," says Susan with genuine feeling. "You really have a good heart!"

Cindy takes a step forward, preparing to speak to Susan over the intercom, to ask her to circle back to the initial question. But Susan demonstrates that she is completely aware of what's worked, and what hasn't, in the interview.

"Listen," Susan continues to say to Hunter, assuming a congenial tone, "this was nice to talk to you. But you have to do *one* part again that wasn't clear to me, okay? So, tell me again the story about how you got the call. It wasn't clear what the phone call from the theater in fact was."

Dean and Cindy smile at each other. "She knows, she knows," says Dean.

Hunter begins answering. "Well, okay. You know, one never knows, uh, I mean, I check my answering machine regularly, and the other day I came in and I found that there were five messages, and I had been out for about an hour and there were five messages on the machine, and my heart jumped . . . I was startled, shocked, and anxious, only to find out it was the same person that tried to get me and it wasn't from the theater . . ."

"Wait a minute," says Cindy. "I thought he said he got a call from the stage manager."

Susan is on the same beam. She cuts in on Hunter. "No, I'm sorry, I have to interrupt. What you told us before was, an hour and a half ago today you got a call from the theater. So tell that story again, please, so that we understand what the mix-up there was."

"Okay!" says Hunter, now understanding what's required. "Well, I received a call about an hour ago, an hour and twenty minutes actually, from the stage manager of *Conversations*. She introduced herself, reminded me who she was and told me that she was from *Conversations* and that she had just gotten a call from Judd and that he had 'accidentally' . . . that's really all I heard for the next ten minutes!"

While Hunter is answering, Cindy is already talking to Dean about how to edit the story. "We have to figure out the best way to do this. This is not quite working out right."

Hunter is still talking. "Now, she had called to tell me that he [Judd] had inadvertently picked up a message for me and wanted to remind me that he had picked it up."

Cindy waves a hand in the air. "*That's* just the line we need. The rest he did better the first time." Dean agrees.

Hunter continues. "But all I heard was that he had 'accidentally' dot, dot, dot and thought that he'd broke his leg or uh . . . you know, accidentally left — I didn't know what."

"Whoa!" Cindy exclaims at once. "That's great! It's perfect! So you'll put this part at the top and then, at the end with Belushi, just kind of end it quickly."

But while Cindy is editing out loud, Hunter is amplifying his response, and his story is becoming increasingly vivid as he talks. "But the fear, the trauma, the anxiety, the pain, even some degree of exhilaration . . . these moments all passed through my mind. And I thought, 'Well, this is it. This is the moment!'"

In the studio, Susan has heard none of the control room discussion, but she knows that Hunter has now given the program a nice little cut-away. "Good, good, well, fine!" she says, adding with considerable enthusiasm, "It was *lovely* to talk to you. Thanks a *billion!*"

"Thank you."

"Best of luck! And I mean, not that I wish Belushi any harm, but I'm keeping my fingers crossed for ya!" And Susan laughs a big, full laugh.

"Well, I thank you. Thank you so much," says Ron Hunter.

"Good-bye!" says Susan.

"Bye." And the phone line goes dead.

In the control room, Cindy is very pleased. "See, now that was great to do the understudy; I think if it was Judd Hirsch it would have been a totally different thing."

Dean nods. "I'm completely proud that we did the understudy."

"It's a perfect cut-away," says Cindy. "If it was Judd, it would have been a longer piece."

Susan emerges from the studio as Cindy and Dean leave the control room, and the three walk upstairs together. Susan is looking tired again but happy. "That's a good piece! What a lovely guy," she says. She begins trying to remember where it will fit in the show. "And Iva comes right after him?"

"No," says Cindy, speaking slowly. "It's really the cut-away."

"This?" says Susan. "*This* is the cut-away?" She speaks in a high voice and sounds incredulous.

"If it were Judd it'd be one thing, but, yeah, that's all we wanted was two forty-five . . . There's not much more there."

Susan has been doing some quick rethinking as Cindy talks and changes her tone of voice. "He says the same thing over and over, doesn't he?"

"It was only a few moments which were very quotable," says Cindy.

Dean chimes in that those parts were really great.

Susan is going over her sense of the piece in her mind. "I think," she says in a high, slightly prodding voice, "there may be forty seconds more than a cut-away . . . don't you think?" Susan feels that the rhythm of the piece is three and a half minutes, which would be a short two-way rather than a punchy cut-away.

Cindy shakes her head. Then Susan concedes the point to Cindy's ears and to the needs of the overall show. "Okay," she says in a quieter tone. As they come to the top of the steps, she adds, "For a while you had him on the board as a two-way, didn't you? Right before Iva."

Cindy explains patiently. "We were going to do that *only* if we got Judd."

"Ohhhhh," Susan exclaims, remembering.

"*Then* we could get the *Taxi* connection with Iva," Cindy continues. "But if it's the understudy with Iva . . . that's so loose a connection, I think it's better not to try. Anyway, we have this piece on Packwood now, which will fit before Iva."

A story about the aftermath of sexual harassment charges against Senator Packwood might at first seem like a bit of a stretch to pair with a piece on a New York cab driver, but an underlying theme of both reports is the role and status of women in a male-dominated world . . . so similar kinds of emotions are touched within very different contexts.

"Of course, I suppose the Packwood might also go well with the sex researcher cut-away," says Cindy, and everyone laughs.

Susan is still resonating with the two-way, which she worked at quite hard. "So Belushi is going to have a run on Broadway," she says. "That's interesting."

Cindy says, "It was *good* that you pulled that out."

"Yeah," Dean adds enthusiastically.

"You really saved the ending with that," Cindy continues.

By now the group has arrived back at the *WESAT* offices to find Cindy's husband, Bob, and their three-year-old daughter, Jessie, waiting. People greet Bob, who asks how things are going.

"Fun show, *woohoo!*" replies Cindy, while reaching down to pick up Jessie.

In the general hubbub that follows, Susan recalls her comment that Hunter sounded just like Judd Hirsch. "I thought he might say back to me, 'You know, you sound just like Susan Stamberg!'" Everyone laughs.

The Art of the Edit

While Dean starts to cut the Ron Hunter interview, Cindy focuses on a series of last-minute decisions about tomorrow's show. In addition to auditioning various spots, she revises the board in consultation with Steve Tripoli. In the past few hours, a couple of new stories have been offered to the show. Mike Shuster is now back in Moscow after a visit to Armenia, where fighting still goes on between the Azerbaijanis and Armenians. The foreign desk has suggested a two-way on the subject for tomorrow morning. In addition, *Morning Edition* has sent over a story from Boston reporter David Barron: it describes a new thriller written by a scientist-novelist that imagines a future when damaged or diseased brains will be repaired by machine implants.

Tomorrow's A's are already filled. In A1, Dan Schorr's three-way discusses the admission of gays into the military. Brian Naylor will set up Dan's conversation with a report on the latest developments in the controversy. The A2 will consist of the usual "Week in Review" and Susan's Music Cue. Furthermore, the B2 segment has already been filled with two stories originating in Los Angeles: Wendy Kaufman's long report and Susan's chat about tomorrow's L.A. Super Bowl with regular commentators Ron Rappaport (sports) and Elvis Mitchell (entertainment). Therefore any new pieces must be placed in the B1 segment.

Four stories are vying for the fifteen-minute slot (before the cutaway) that has room for only three pieces: Shuster, Barron, the interview slugged "State of the World" . . . and "Frogs." In a decision typical of the spirit of all the weekend programs, Cindy is totally committed to using "Frogs" as the anchor of the sequence — the final story. The piece is unusual, amusing, and offbeat. As Cindy and Steve talk about their choice of reports, Cindy keeps asking herself what stories will lead best into "Frogs." Neither Azerbaijani politics nor problems of global development seem appropriate subjects to immediately precede a two-way about the hallucinogenic secretions of Amazonian amphibians. But Barron's spot about futuristic science might work nicely, so it gets locked in as the second story in the segment. "State of the World" in part "looks to the future," so it might make a good lead-off piece for the B1 — but now questions of news value enter the picture. Mike Shuster is offering a two-way about a continuing story from the former Soviet Union. "State of the World" is a background report that could easily be broadcast next week. So Cindy opts for the newsier piece to start off this B, though "State of the World" will be held in reserve in case there are any problems establishing connections with Moscow early tomorrow morning.

"Frogs" has an interesting influence on the sequence of stories for the rest of the program. Cindy loves the idea of following "Frogs" with the sex-study cut-away. She imagines the theme from *Rocky*, Burgess Meredith speaking his lines . . . and thinks the thematic flow from male rituals in South American jungles to male attitudes in North American sports will be extremely funny. But Cindy also believes it would be in terrible taste to follow all this amusement with Siporin's report on Bob Packwood's troubles regarding charges of sexual harassment. Packwood must lead one of the C's, but *not* the segment that follows the sex-study cut-away; therefore, Packwood must go into C2.

Earlier on, Cindy determined that "Iva," the story of the Czech cabbie/novelist, must be broadcast in the second hour of the program, and Susan's report on the Egyptian book in C1. The Open for the second hour of the show will include the story of the Czechoslovakian national anthem, and Cindy thinks it would sound very strange for David Isay's evocative piece on Iva to be followed (a couple of minutes later) by yet *another* Czech story — which is what would happen if "Iva" ended the first hour. On the other hand, having something Czech at the start and the finish of the *second* hour will add a nice feeling of interconnection and unity.

The evolving logic of the broadcast thus has dictated that Packwood be paired with Iva. But the recent arrival of Tom Gjelten's feature from Sarajevo has momentarily confused matters. Cindy and Steve must again review the C's. Shouldn't they try to put together the pieces about Eastern Europe (the Bosnian production of *Hair*, and "Iva")? Stated another way, how much sense does it make to go from the theater in Sarajevo to a book of pictures about Egypt? Gjelten's piece is liable to be very evocative and emotional; the interview with the photographer is interesting but not that intense.

Still, for the moment, Cindy can see no other possible sequence. At five o'clock, the board pairs Gjelten with "Egypt" at the end of the first hour, Packwood with "Iva" at the end of the second hour, and "Frogs" (with its accompanying stories) in B1. (C1 includes one more item: a short segment of letters from listeners is marked tentatively as the first piece. "Egypt" is considerably shorter than "Iva," and even with an additional six-minute piece, the C1 will run a couple of minutes short. The Letters feature can be written to fit whatever gap remains.)

In the late afternoon, Cindy goes over the upcoming show with the substitute director for tomorrow's program, Ned Wharton. Ned is the associate producer and director of *Weekend Sunday* and will be filling in tomorrow for the usual director, Doug Mitchell, who has some pressing family commitments. Cindy reviews a number of points with Ned — a highly experienced director, easygoing yet efficient. Before Doug leaves for home tonight, he will select much of the music to be played during the show, but Cindy specifically asks Ned to find something to use at the end of Susan's Music Cue, and she mentions some other stories as well. "It'd be nice to have someone else's taste, here," Cindy says. "We should make use of the fact we are using a different director."

Cindy mentions a few danger spots in the program, including the conclusion of "Iva," which ends in a dreamy, unfocused way. Cindy says the music that Ned will fade up during the final moments has to be handled just right. She urges Ned to listen to Isay's feature ahead of time. Cindy concludes her briefing by telling Ned to phone her at any time if any questions come up. "Don't hesitate for a *moment* to call me at home. Okay?" Cindy looks at Ned intently. "I don't think you'll have any problems — the show is in pretty good shape. But *call* me." Ned — a quiet, handsome young man — nods good-naturedly.

At ten minutes after six, Dean Olsher hands Cindy his final edit of the Ron Hunter cut-away along with his outtakes reel. Dean goes back into Peter Breslow's office to do some other work, but he keeps the door open so he can hear when Cindy starts listening to his tape. He doesn't have long to wait, as Cindy eagerly sits down at her desk, rewinds Dean's tape, and starts playing back his edit:

SUSAN: Next week, unless something awful happens, actor Judd Hirsch will end his run in Broadway's *Conversations with My Father* with a perfect record. In fact, since 1975 Judd Hirsch hasn't missed a single performance *anywhere.* Could there be anything worse than being Judd Hirsch's stand-in? Ron Hunter is on the phone with us from New York. You're the stand in, what's the answer, Mr. Hunter?

HUNTER: Well, I can think of a lot of things worse than that. Like not being affiliated or associated with a marvelous play like *Conversations.* Being unemployed is also much worse.

SUSAN: I bet it is. Have you ever had a phone call from the theater, though, that maybe got your heart going?

HUNTER: No, I don't know why — it's very odd that you should say that because I think about an hour and twenty minutes ago I got a call from the stage manager . . . [A noise indicates he's got call waiting.]

HUNTER: Uh, hello? Who said that ah . . .

SUSAN: Wait, maybe that's the stage manager again! Go ahead.

HUNTER: Right! It could be another emergency call. Okay, well, I had received a call from the stage manager . . . she had introduced herself — reminded me who she was, and that she had just gotten a call from *Judd* . . . and that he had *accidentally* . . .

SUSAN: [Laughs.]

HUNTER: . . . that's really all I heard for the next ten seconds. She'd called to tell me that he had inadvertently picked up a message for me and wanted to ah, to ah, remind me that he had picked it up — but I, all I heard was that he had "accidentally" dot, dot, dot . . . perhaps he had broken his leg or — I, I didn't know what. But the fear, the trauma, the anxiety, the pain, even some degree of exhilaration — all passed through my mind. And I thought, Well, this is it, this is the moment!

SUSAN: You sound just like him, you know.

HUNTER: No, I didn't know that.

SUSAN: [Big laugh.]

HUNTER: That's the reason I'm in the position I'm in. [Laughs.]

SUSAN: There are, you know, these sort of legendary stories about people like you. Shirley MacLaine, didn't she get a huge big break one night when she was the understudy in *Pajama Game* and . . .

HUNTER: That isn't the reason why I took the job. It isn't why I do it. And there is some . . . ah . . . significant satisfaction, in and of itself, ah, working with the people and being affiliated with the people who are involved in *Conversations*.

SUSAN: Do you have to go to the theater every night?

HUNTER: Yes, I do.

SUSAN: And what do you do?

HUNTER: Well, I sign in and check to see that Judd has also arrived . . .

SUSAN: I *bet* you do, Mr. Hunter!

HUNTER: I do! I do! In fact, when he's not there, I don't, I don't move!

SUSAN: Yeah. Uh-huh.

HUNTER: And ah . . . I'm very relieved once he's there.

SUSAN: Thank you very much. Ron Hunter, who has lived the understudy's nightmare. He is the stand-in for Judd Hirsch, who has never missed a performance. Next week, Mr. Hirsch ends his run in *Conversations with My Father* on Broadway. Who's coming in, Mr. Hunter?

HUNTER: Uh, Jim Belushi.

SUSAN: Do you stay on?

HUNTER: Yes, I do.

SUSAN: Well, listen, maybe Belushi will get a little case of laryngitis!

HUNTER: Well, I wish him good health, I really do. But, ah, ah, I certainly would, at some point, like to go on myself.

Within seconds of completing her audition, Cindy slaps the outtakes reel on her tape machine, rewinds it, and starts listening. Next door Dean hears what Cindy is doing and comes into her doorway.

"What are you listening for in the outs?" he asks, more curious than defensive.

Cindy stops her tape recorder and swivels round in her chair to address Dean. She speaks rapidly, often not finishing her sentences. "I'm just looking . . . I'm just thirsty for so much more — and I remember other stuff being there. The Shirley MacLaine understudy thing said nothing . . . I think we can lose it. And I think you should go right to . . . Well, I'm sort of trying to find other things." Cindy is flying by instinct at the moment — she's been moving in a lot of different directions in the couple of hours since the Ron Hunter two-way, so the specifics are not coming back to her. But she *feels* that she heard some things in the conversation that are not in the final version that Dean has presented to her.

"I mean, what you've done is fine — it's very close — but it just doesn't *quite* do everything I thought it would. I was expecting more — and I think you're sort of thinking the same thing. Aren't you?"

Dean nods. "Yeah, I had to lose a lot of stuff I didn't want to."

"Do you mind working on the first Fo Break while I'm doing this — just so we can save time?" Cindy asks. "I mean ordinarily I'd like you to sit here and we'd go through this together, but it's getting a bit late . . ."

"No, that's fine, that's fine," says Dean.

"I want you to hear whatever I wind up trying to do," says Cindy as Dean turns to go. "Let me just take a crack at this."

In the fragmentary outs (which are interspersed with ums, ahs, and all manner of disconnected phrases and sentences) Cindy comes across Hunter's phrase about Judd Hirsch. "Ah . . . and once he's arrived — he's legendary. His work ethic . . . his commitment to his work . . ."

"This is the part that I missed," Cindy exclaims. "Because this hearkens back to the fact that he's never missed a performance. That's the whole reason why we're talking. I mean, we never hear that again, except in the intro. And I almost forgot *why* I am talking to the understudy of Judd Hirsch."

The outtakes tumble into each other. "She told me from conversations . . . an hour and twenty minutes . . . trying to play the lottery . . . *like having the opportunity to watch Judd . . .*"

Cindy nods. "Yeah, that's another good line — about what's good about being an understudy." But as the outtakes whiz by, Cindy sits expectantly in her chair — she's waiting for something she knows is there, but she can't remember what it is. She's almost at the end of the reel and still hasn't heard what she's listening for. "Didn't he say something else about the fact that Judd hasn't missed a performance?" Cindy wonders aloud. "Is nothing else said?"

At that moment, Dean's last big cut appears on the reel. Susan asks, "Do you ever feel like the Maytag repairman, though?" And Hunter answers, "I hope I'm as essential."

Cindy laughs and exclaims: "I *like* that! It's great because it also refers back to Judd Hirsch as well — *he's* like the Maytag repairman, too!"

Dean hears Cindy's excitement and pops his head back into her office. "I tried to keep that question, but in the end I felt that the question was so much better than the answer."

Cindy hears the tape a little differently. "Well, I think the answer is good. I like his answer — it's sweet. 'I hope I'm as essential.' It also keeps us one step closer to Judd. Comparing him to the Maytag repairman was such a wonderful image."

"Then, you see," Cindy continues, speaking rapidly, "you drop the question about Shirley MacLaine and go right to 'What do you do when you get there?' Then the answer is, 'Well, I wait for Judd to come, I hold my breath.' And then you're totally centered on the subject." Cindy is starting to hear the entire piece reshaped, even before she can articulate it fully.

"Well," Dean says, "I was married to that question, but I thought his answer didn't go anywhere."

"No, it does go somewhere," Cindy replies with enthusiasm, "but it's really part of the first answer — it's not just *any* answer, it's part of the initial setup for the whole piece . . . Well, you'll see me put it together, and then we'll discuss it."

Cindy's reconstruction of the Ron Hunter cut-away takes a little less than an hour. She leaves most of Dean's work intact, but she drops the reference to Shirley MacLaine and along with it the somewhat tangential and distracting comment that Hunter sounds like Judd Hirsch. She puts back in the Maytag repairman and the question from Susan about Hunter secretly wishing Judd Hirsch would get sick, along with a few other phrases — all of which return some of Hunter's *personality* to the interview. By cutting some of the references to Hirsch, Dean had also cut out Hunter's *endearing* quality, which Susan had responded to so strongly at the end of the interview.

Cindy also does a brilliant bit of editing Hunter's still confusing story about the phone call from the theater. Dean had focused on taking out various *ums* and *ahs*, and while Cindy does quite a bit of that kind of cosmetic editing, she also hears through whole phrases that are unnecessary. The easiest decision is to drop the call-waiting interruption. "It's cute," Cindy says, "and I kind of like it, but it's really distracting. The piece stops moving. You want to get to the heart of the story quickly." Cindy also makes a few internal edits within Hunter's narration — the simplest being taking out a qualifying phrase attached to the stage manager (that "she had introduced herself — reminded me who she was"). As with the "Frogs" cut, the effect, aurally, is striking: the passage becomes suddenly sharp and clear. Once again Cindy has used her razor blade like an art restorer's tool.

Here is the broadcast version of the Hunter cut-away, beginning toward the end of Susan's introduction (the italics indicate passages that Cindy put back into Dean's cut):

SUSAN: . . . Could there be anything worse than being Judd Hirsch's stand-in? Ron Hunter is on the phone with us from New York. You're the stand-in, what's the answer, Mr. Hunter?"

HUNTER: Well, I can think of a lot of things worse than that. Like not being affiliated or associated with a marvelous play like *Conversations*. *And like not having the opportunity to watch Judd perform every night.*

SUSAN: *Ah.*

HUNTER: *But there's a lot of things much worse than that.* Being unemployed is also much worse.

SUSAN: I bet it is. *Do you ever feel like the Maytag repairman, though, with a guy like that?*

HUNTER: *Well, I hope I'm as essential as the Maytag repairman. After all, it gives you great peace of mind. I wouldn't mind that job either.*

SUSAN: Have you ever had a phone call from the theater, though, that maybe got your heart going?

HUNTER: No, I don't know why — it's very odd you should say that. Because I got a call from the stage manager, that she had just gotten a call from Judd. And that he had *accidentally* . . .

SUSAN: [Laughs.]

HUNTER: . . . that's really all I heard for the next ten seconds. She'd called to tell me that he had inadvertently picked up a message for me and wanted to, to remind me —

SUSAN: [Laughs.]

HUNTER: — that he picked it up — but I, all I heard was that he had "accidentally" dot, dot, dot . . . perhaps he had broken his leg, or — I, I didn't know what. But the fear, the trauma, the anxiety, the pain, even some degree of exhilaration passed through my mind.

SUSAN: Do you have to go to the theater every night?

HUNTER: Yes, I do.

SUSAN: And what do you do?

HUNTER: Well, I sign in and check to see that Judd has also arrived . . .

SUSAN: I *bet* you do, Mr. Hunter!

HUNTER: I do! I do! In fact when he's not there, I don't, I don't move!

SUSAN: Yeah.

HUNTER: *But once he's, once he's arrived . . . I mean, he is legendary. His work ethic and his commitment to his work . . . And* I'm very relieved once he's there.

SUSAN: *Mr. Hunter, I can hear your deep respect for Judd Hirsch, but is there not some small part of you that wishes at least he'd lose his voice once?*

HUNTER: *No, no, not one part of me. Not right now. Certainly, I would love to do the role. And I hope someday to do the role. But I don't want to, I, I have no desire at this moment to go on and replace him.*

SUSAN: Thank you very much. Ron Hunter, who has lived the understudy's nightmare. He is the stand-in for Judd Hirsch, who has never missed a performance. Next week, Mr. Hirsch ends his run in *Conversations with My Father* on Broadway. Who's coming in, Mr. Hunter?

HUNTER: Uh, Jim Belushi.

SUSAN: Do you stay on?
HUNTER: Yes, I do.
SUSAN: Well, listen, maybe Belushi will get a little case of laryngitis!
HUNTER: Well, I wish him good health.

In her final conversation with Dean about the cut-away, Cindy explains that the shape of his cut proceeded logically from the decisions he had made to keep the call-waiting episode and the question about understudies who had made it. But once these sections were removed, there was room for all the other good tape that Dean had been forced to cut. Dean understood exactly what Cindy had done and said she had definitely improved on his work.

It's twenty minutes to eight when Cindy finally adds the two-minute forty-one-second cut-away on the pile of reels now stacked up for the show. "I was supposed to have dinner this evening with my husband," she says ruefully, as she prepares to do one more major piece of production work before she can finally go home.

The Art of the Mix

Cindy walks quickly down the staircase to the ground-floor recording studio one final time. She has now been at work for almost twelve hours, but her energy level remains high, her drive for perfection undiminished. She carries a couple of tape reels and a CD under her arm and walks quickly to the door of Studio Three, her head hunched forward slightly, her face looking paler than usual in the quiet lighting of the hallway.

She talks a bit about what she's about to do. "It's one of these rare things, to prerecord an opening of the show the night before. It's such a little moment of the show — it's a thing that all the shows take for granted . . . like the billboard, this is what happened in the news today, first the news. We always do an 'on this date,' like *Morning Edition*, only ours are always more extended — usually we just cover one event, sometimes a couple. But now we're actually going to try a big production number. And it's all going to happen in fifty-nine seconds."

Renée Pringle, an experienced engineer, is sitting at the console reading a book when Cindy arrives. Cindy explains what's about to happen and carefully works Renée through the setup for the mix. Three different pieces of music must be wound around Susan's narration, which is already on tape: the opening *WESAT* theme, then a fragment of the Czech national anthem, then the concluding strains of the Slovakian anthem. Cindy has worked out in her mind how to do the mix. The beginning is simple enough: establish the usual theme (recorded on DAT), then fade the music under a short greeting from Susan; bring the theme back *up* briefly, then *under* again as Susan begins to read the copy about Czechoslovakia. The ending of the Open is also straightforward: Cindy wants the final chords of the Slovakian national anthem to fade up and over the conclusion of Susan's talk-tracks. In order for this to happen properly, Cindy decides that the simplest approach is to do a deadroll — that is, to cue up the CD of the Czechoslovakian anthem fifty-nine seconds from its conclusion (the last half of the anthem contains the Slovakian national music) and to start the CD, with the volume all the way down, at the same time as the *WESAT* theme music begins. Thus Renée will begin recording the Open with a simultaneous *live* roll (the show theme) and a *dead* roll (the CD).

The tricky part of the production occurs in the middle, when Susan introduces the two anthems. Cindy has already dubbed the Czech melody (the opening bars of the Czechoslovakian anthem) onto a piece of tape. This Czech theme must be cross-faded with the *WESAT* music behind Susan — ideally listeners won't even notice the shift — and then brought up into the clear for four seconds so listeners can hear the tune. Then, when Susan's narration continues with a description of the new Slovakian anthem, the engineer will perform another cross-fade behind the host (again, subtly enough that listeners won't quite hear it) from the Czech to the Slovakian melody — which will then have *its* few moments in the clear. The Slovakian anthem will continue behind the final words of Susan's opening, and the music will come up full on its final chords for a second or so after Susan finishes reading, if everything works right.

All this to-ing and fro-ing will take place in under a minute, leaving a second of silence before the news begins at one minute past the hour.

The setup for this mix takes almost half an hour. While Renée struggles with a recalcitrant CD player, Cindy places Susan's narration on Tape Recorder Number One, and the Czech anthem on Tape Two.

Then she listens for the precise segment of the Czech music that will fit smoothly into the four-second pause in Susan's narration — in the jargon of radio, she searches for a "post." (The expression is used as a verb — "you want to post that music at some point" — or as a noun — "look for your post.") Cindy finds her post several bars into the Czech anthem, a phrase where the theme swells slightly. This crescendo will make the fade-up sound natural to listeners, a part of the music's normal flow.

Cindy white-lines the post with the grease pencil that she's been holding in her teeth. She crouches by the tape machine and looks at the tape head as she plays the music in order to confirm that she's made the mark properly. Her line shows Renée at what point the music should be heard in the clear.

Then Cindy uses the electronic timer on the big Studer tape machine to back up the recording exactly twelve seconds from the start of the post. Afterward she goes to Tape One and fast forwards Susan's tracks to the first piece of white leader tape, exactly four seconds long, that's been inserted into her narration. This leader will play through the four-second pause during which the Czech music will post. Cindy now backs up Tape One the same twelve seconds and then presses the play button to hear what Susan is saying at that point. "Recently split from Slovakia" becomes the aural cue signaling that it's time to deadroll the Czech music. Cindy takes her grease pencil and white-lines this all-important section of Susan's talk-tracks.

Finally Cindy stretches her arms and starts Tapes One and Two simultaneously. She's checking to be sure that she's worked out everything correctly. Sure enough, when Susan finishes speaking, the Czech anthem swells smoothly into the four-second pause. Cindy smiles. She rewinds Susan's narration back to the beginning of the tape and cues up the Czech tape at the white line. This part of the mix is ready to go.

Meanwhile, Renée has been running into serious problems with both the CD player and the DAT machine. These products of digital technology are supposed to make production easier because of their ability to start and stop instantly at any point in a recording. But first the CD player and then the DAT player begin acting up, displaying inaccurate timings and not starting up immediately. Renée winds up dubbing both the anthem and the show theme onto old, reliable analogue tape . . . and the mix is ready to go. *Four* analogue tape recorders will now play into a fifth machine, which is set to record at fifteen inches per second, standard speed for major program elements like Opens, Returns, and Promos.[5]

This is the "simple" opening that Cindy and Renée are about to record.

TAPE FOUR: *Weekend Saturday theme up full, then fade slightly.*

TAPE ONE, SUSAN: From National Public Radio, in Washington, D.C., this is *Weekend Edition.*

TAPE FOUR: *Weekend theme up, then down behind Susan.*

TAPE ONE, SUSAN: I'm Susan Stamberg. This week Václav Havel was elected to a five-year term as president of the new Czech Republic, recently split from Slovakia. One problem between the two nations has been easily solved: what to do about the National Anthem. That was split in two, also. The first part goes to the Czech Republic, with its traditional stately tones.

Cross-fade has occurred behind Susan, from Tape Four (WESAT theme) to Tape Two, Czech anthem. Tape Two now posts for four seconds. Czech theme fades down behind Susan.

TAPE ONE, SUSAN: The second half, which sounds more like a happy folk dance, becomes the Slovakian national anthem.

Tape Two cross-fades behind Susan with Tape Three, the Slovakian theme. Tape Three posts for four seconds. Slovakian theme fades down behind Susan, but continues.

TAPE ONE, SUSAN: This split is actually poetic justice. The two halves of the anthem were joined earlier this century when Czechoslovakia was created. Coming up after the news, a dis-

---

[5] To preserve tape, most NPR programs and spots are recorded at seven and a half inches per second, even though fifteen ips gives better fidelity. By contrast, European radio programs are usually done at fifteen, and many European producers can't understand how Americans can even *edit* at seven and a half. (If your various vocal sounds are spread out over more tape, you have an easier time making certain kinds of fine edits.) American engineers defend their use of seven and a half by saying that American equipment is adjusted and tweaked to work just fine at the slower speed. Of course, the spread of digital recording should soon render this debate moot.

cussion of the week's top stories with Daniel Schorr. It's Saturday, January 30th, 1993.

Tape Three, Slovakian theme, comes up for about a second, after Susan's final words.

Since the mix is only fifty-nine seconds long, Cindy has no script for Renée to follow. She explains verbally what needs to be done and then directs Renée through the different stages of the mix. The tape recorders are arrayed to Renée's right and along the back wall, a few feet behind the mixing console. Cindy wanders around the area behind Renée but leaves the starting and stopping of all the machines to the engineer, via remote control buttons, though Cindy will help out by recueing the various elements after each take.

"Now we have to use the Favag," says Cindy, meaning that since the length of the Open must be *exactly* fifty-nine seconds, they will use the huge electronic clock on the front wall of the control room as their timer. To speed matters along when using the Favag, however, producers won't wait for the second hand to come round to the twelve each time but may declare that when the second hand hits the number three or six or nine . . . or whatever . . . that's when the mix will start. On the first take, Cindy says, "You want to do it on the five? Okay."

Cindy then gives instructions to Renée, naming each tape recorder by number. She speaks quickly and distinctly and tries to give Renée as much warning as she can for each switch, cross-fade, and so forth.

"Now, you're beginning with Four up, and Three dead," Cindy says, meaning the volume on Tape Four — the *WESAT* theme — will be up full and Tape Three — the Slovakian anthem — will start as a deadroll. The Favag second hand touches five. "Hit it," says Cindy. Then she continues with a slew of instructions, with only a couple of seconds' pause between each one. Her voice is barely audible over the sound of the various program elements. "Ready One. [Susan.] Under [the *WESAT* theme] and hit it [Susan]. Ready to bring up full [*WESAT* theme]. Up full. Ready to go back to Susan early. [Due to the tightness of the mix, Cindy has decided to play less of the *WESAT* theme than is usual at the beginning of the show.] Ready: under, now. [*WESAT* theme goes under Susan.] Ready to deadroll Two. [The Czech anthem. The white line comes up on Susan's tape, and Susan says the key words 'recently split from Slovakia.'] Hit it! Ready on the cross-fade [from *WESAT* theme to Czech anthem]. *Cross-fade!* [Cindy speaks sharply, clearly. The *WESAT* theme imperceptibly changes into the Czech national anthem.] Okay. Ready to bring it up full. [Susan says, 'with its traditional stately tones.'] *Up.* Let it roll through. [That is, let Susan's tape keep running — no need to start and stop it, the pause is leadered in. The Czech theme swells.] Cross-fade Two to Three! [Susan picks up her narration as Renée lowers the volume on the Czech theme and starts bringing in the Slovakian anthem, which has been deadrolling since the start of the mix.] Ready to bring it up full. [' . . . becomes the Slovakian national anthem,' says Susan.] Up full! Let it roll through . . . and . . . under . . . [Renée lowers the volume on the music as Susan's narration returns: 'This split is actually poetic justice . . . '] Ready to bring it up full under Susan. Watch the Favag! ['January 30th, 1993,' Susan concludes.] Up full!"

The Slovakian music ends a second later, precisely fifty-nine seconds after the mix began.

Cindy lets out a squeal of delight. She has been imagining a mix like this for several weeks, and though she detected a few problems during this first take, overall she thinks the Open is going to work just fine. She didn't know for certain, until this very moment, how well the idea she heard in her head would work in the real world. She now knows that it will be fine, with a few slight adjustments.

"Okay. Let's do it once more," Cindy says as she starts rewinding the tape on all the machines. "That was great, Renée. You're very good! That was nifty. But it would be great to have just a little more music at the end."

"Okay," says Renée, smiling. What's complex about the mix is the speed with which all these cross-fades have to be made, but it's a pleasing challenge for the engineer as well as the producer.

"Also," Cindy continues, "I think I'm going to have you bring Susan in a little earlier on the theme music . . . there's an earlier point, and I missed it. Let's just hear that back. Just to make sure we feel comfortable with all the cross-fades."

Renée replays the take, and Cindy is pleased all over again. "That's not bad at all. I'll save that one." Then Cindy checks out the *WESAT* theme, listening for just how much earlier she can start Susan's narration. She picks a spot a couple of beats earlier than usual. "But I really can't bring her in any sooner than that."

At around eight-thirty, Cindy and Renée start the second take of the mix. The cross-fades are gorgeous — the *WESAT* theme blends incredibly smoothly with the Czech national anthem — they seem to be in the same key and almost sound like the same piece of music. And the second cross-fade, from Czech to Slovak anthem, happens imperceptibly, magically. It's a perfect realization of Cindy's conception.

In the midst of her direction, Cindy has occasionally oohed and ahhed as the mix was proceeding. As the final notes die away, she again exclaims, "Oooh!" But this time it's a sigh of disappointment. "It's too tight!" she says.

She looks at Renée with a wan smile. "The music went right into a minute." She pauses, leaning her head against her hand. She wants to keep the take, but she knows some of the stations will scream about it. "They're going to get really mad at me, right?" she asks, sounding as though she wants Renée to contradict her. "They hate that, right? But that was fabulous."

She pauses again, but only for a moment. She knows her responsibilities. "No. I have to do it again. We'll keep that, too, because it was great. But we have to do it again."

The Open cannot run over fifty-nine seconds, and by the Favag, whose word is law, that mix ended at sixty seconds. Stations that pick up the newscast at one minute after the hour but are not carrying *WESAT* will sometimes tune into the network one second before the newscast starts, expecting NPR to be carrying silence. They do not want to hear the decaying sound of the Slovakian national anthem instead.

As so often happens with work as inherently obsessive as radio production, the second take of the Open was a moment of spontaneous inspiration — and good luck — when everything came together perfectly. For the next twenty minutes, Renée and Cindy struggle to recapture that clean and well-orchestrated mix. A timing glitch here, a volume level mistake there: all manner of small errors occur during the next *seven* takes. Most of all, though, the cross-fades behind Susan don't happen with the same ease and flow . . . with the magical sense that one continuous stream of music is manifesting itself in different disguises throughout the fifty-nine-second piece.

Before the eighth go-round, Cindy looks at the Favag and says, "Let's do it on the seven. Lucky Seven." Her words are prophetic. Fighting the gathering fatigue of the evening with skill, with stubbornness, and with the expertise born of repetition, Renée's hands move deftly across the various sliders and buttons while Cindy's voice entones the familiar cues. Sections of tape enter and fade away easily and right on target. The Favag hits fifty-nine seconds and Cindy says, simply, "Perfect! That was it."

Renée leans back in her chair. "Finally!" she exclaims.

Cindy collects the various elements of the mix, while thanking Renée profusely. "I mean, we obviously spent far too much time on this," she says, "but it was really *fun!*" And her voice rises into a surprisingly high, almost giggly enthusiasm.

It's well after nine o'clock when Cindy walks upstairs. Back in the *WESAT* office she runs into Ken Hom. And just when Cindy thinks she might be able to go home, she hears about a major problem with the rundown of the program. Instead of being six minutes long, Gjelten's piece has come in a minute and fifteen seconds shorter than expected. Ken and Cindy stare at the C's again, counting up the minutes and seconds. Finally Ken speaks, in his characteristically quiet voice. He suggests pairing the shorter Gjelten piece with "Iva" and moving Siporin's report on Packwood over with Susan's Egyptian book interview. "Iva" is long enough to cover Gjelten's short fall. But Cindy doesn't like putting Packwood and "Egypt" together. She thinks it will sound odd. Ken says, okay, separate them with Letters. Perfect, says Cindy. She reminds Ken that if Packwood moves over into the first hour, then the sex-study cut-away has to "flip" with the understudy, so as not to have sex and Packwood in the same hour. And this also means flipping the B's, so that "Frogs" will lead into sex study.

So now, in what proves to be the last major change in the road map, Ken rearranges the stories in C1 (Packwood, Letters, Egypt) and in C2 (Gjelten and "Iva" — the two Eastern European pieces will be paired after all) and draws arrows from B1 to B2 and from Cut-away 1 to Cut-away 2, indicating that these are to be swapped. "Frogs" and the sex study will now appear in the second hour, as will the Shuster two-way.

As happens so often in NPR magazine programs, this final — and significant — change in the *WESAT* schedule was inspired not by content but by *time.* Earlier in the day, Cindy had felt that Packwood went better with "Iva" than with "Egypt." Now she makes adjustments. Furthermore, though it seems to make sense for Gjelten to proceed "Iva," the piece from Sarajevo has come in so late that it's only just been mixed. Cindy won't hear it till it's on the air tomorrow. Whether she might have arranged the program differently if she *had* heard the piece will become a brief topic of retrospective conversation in the following week. But the fact remains that for all the flexibility and creativity that Cindy and her staff employ as they assemble their program, in the final analysis, the show retains the puzzlelike format of *Morning Edition*. Every so often, what goes on the air is determined by what *fits* the various time slots, and not by what the producer might prefer.

By ten o'clock, Cindy has left for home. Ken keeps editing tape and writing scripts till late into the night, as is his wont. (Quite often on Fridays, he does not go home but instead takes a cat nap on one of the sofas upstairs, before getting up at about three o'clock to start making final preparations for the morning's broadcast.)

Sometime around four o'clock, Ken prepares *WESAT* for its journey from the back offices, where the show is conceived and developed, into NPR's main workspace just outside the broadcast studios. The trek begins with a gesture of symbolic as well as practical significance. Ken copies the *WESAT* storyboard onto a much smaller traveling board, which he puts under his arm. He carries the board and the program tapes through NPR's deserted corridors down to the *Morning Edition* area. The little board fits neatly onto the shelf protruding from the bottom of *Morning Edition*'s big board. That board is already covered with notes and outlines for Monday morning's program, which is why the two weekend morning programs, *WESAT* and *WESUN*, must use their own portable storyboards.[6]

Ken then sits down in the producer's chair at the *Morning Edition* desk, and for the next few hours *Weekend Saturday* occupies center stage at National Public Radio.

Weekend Showtime

Like any performance art, a live radio broadcast always provokes anxieties and tensions. Still, the showtime pressures that afflict the staffs of the weekly programs seem different from those that bear down on the staffs of daily *ATC* and *Morning Edition*. The comparison may be strongest in the control room. Daily *ATC*'s directors enforce an atmos-

---

[6] *Weekend All Things Considered* does not labor under the same constraints and takes over the *ATC* horseshoe, and most of its board, for the entire weekend.

phere of focused, intense energy — even though director Bob Boilen says that it's part of his job to remain calm and good-natured, whatever chaos may be threatening. (Bob alternates directorial chores with Marika Partridge.) "What I can bring to the show is a steady, even temperament," explains Bob, a laid-back, friendly man who wears round glasses, baggy pants, and sandals. When he directs *ATC*, the control room remains fairly quiet, with occasional exchanges of banter to ease the tension. Even when a piece of tape is very late arriving in the studio and Bob picks up the red "Bat Phone," used only in emergencies to connect with the horseshoe, his voice remains calm. "The worst thing I could do is actually be excited," he says, "because if they heard *that* at the desk . . . well, the producers are already tense enough."

The culture of the *Morning Edition* control room seems noisier and more flippant than that of daily *All Things Considered*. Yet there remains an undercurrent of great tension, and some of the hijinks and joking seem analogous to doing a jig on the edge of a precipice.

While *Weekend ATC* can experience a touch of the news-deadline pressure — with a number of its reports coming in on the day of the broadcast — the bulk of the weekend *morning* programs have already been produced and thoroughly obsessed over long before airtime. So Saturday and Sunday mornings, on *WESAT* and *WESUN*, the producers and directors can focus their attention on making the various music bridges, tape segues, deadrolls, live readings to tape, and other components sound as clean and attractive as possible. There's an almost palpable feeling of delight percolating through the early-morning activities of *Weekend Saturday* and *Weekend Sunday* on the day of a broadcast, inspite of all the normal butterflies in the stomach that everyone is also experiencing.

When Scott Simon worked on *WESAT*, humor constantly bubbled outward from the host's chair. Scott is a showman and an entertainer in person as well as on air. But Scott's old Chicago colleague, Rich Rarey, technical director for both weekend morning programs, carries on the tradition of happy lunacy in the control room with or without his mentor on the other side of the studio window. A tall, round-faced, straight-nosed man with tortoiseshell glasses and short brown hair, Rich sustains an almost perpetual stream of banter and wisecracks before and during a broadcast. He also enjoys pulling aural stunts, such as causing a cued-up CD to make funny noises or fading in a few moments of rock 'n' roll music from somewhere or other right before a show goes on the air. Yet Rich also upholds another Chicago tradition of having extraordinarily sharp ears, and for all the pranks and tom-foolery, he treats the results of everyone's hard work, the radio pieces themselves, with utmost care and seriousness. Whatever might be happening in the control room, Rich never loses touch with the *sound* that's going out over the air. He will frequently catch a flub or a minor tape glitch that no one else has noticed. Or he will abruptly interrupt one of his own wise-aleck remarks to pass on a compliment to the host or a producer about a particularly nice moment that has just been broadcast.

Weekend Edition goes on the air at eight o'clock and members of the *WESAT* team show up at different hours on Saturday morning. Ken is already preparing scripts when Dean and Franc arrive a little before five. Steve comes in a bit later, while Susan and Ned, today's director, show up at six. Fifteen minutes later, Susan is in Studio Five conducting her two-way with Mike Shuster. She sounds remarkably fresh and awake and asks excellent questions about Mike's trip to Armenia. Steve listens in the control room and works with both "Mikey" (as he calls Shuster) and Susan, having them redo a couple of exchanges. He then gives instructions to Franc about how to cut the two-way and reduce twelve minutes of conversation to six.

During the two-way, Rich has left on the control room's small black and white TV set, though the sound is off. Cartoons are running. At one point Sylvester and another cat are fighting over Tweety Bird.

At the same time, in an edit booth, Dean is trimming the Dan Schorr three-way — recorded on Friday — that discusses whether gays should be allowed to serve in the military. Ken asked Dean to "clean up" the tape just a little, but Dean takes out so many *ums, ahs,* and the like that the original eight-minute piece is now seven minutes and five seconds. The tape editor emerges with a sheepish grin and apologizes to Ken and Steve. "I did my best, I tried — I left in everything I could."

"Don't worry about it," says Ken, very calm and understanding. But in fact, Steve will now have to write a little more copy to bridge between Brian Naylor's report and Dan's three-way: the A1 segment has become a bit short.

Steve razzes Dean about his "overcutting." "Goddamn razor-happy producer," Steve says, grinning. "Why don't you use the razor on your beard!"

"You're just jealous," says Dean, stroking his hairy chin and laughing.

"You know," says Steve, a bit more seriously, "sometimes I think it's better to let Dan's three-ways ride with their *ums* and *ahs*. It's sort of like live radio."

"Yeah," says Dean, "but I really felt they were slowing this piece down. I think it moves much better this way."

"Okay, okay," says Steve, and he goes off to write more copy.

A few minutes after seven, Susan enters the studio to record various short elements for the show: the Open for the first hour, the first Fo Break, a thirty-second promo broadcast between the A and B segments after the Fo Break, and so forth. Some time ago, *WESAT* staff members began a tradition of wearing sweatshirts the day of the broadcast, and Susan has a large gray one with the colorful logo "Radio Free Delmarva." She brings a bag of fruit into the studio with her and a liter bottle of Evian water. (Evian seems to be another tradition among some NPR hosts. You will often see people like Katie Davis or Liane Hansen walking down the corridor toward a recording studio swinging the distinctively shaped bottle.)

One slightly longer piece still needs to be committed to tape, three minutes of Letters from listeners. Steve has gone through last week's mail and has put together an initial draft. Susan sits in the studio, reading over the copy and making a few revisions. In particular, she sees some ways to add some humor to the segment, and writes down some notes to herself.

In the control room, Ned cues the familiar typewriter-and-music theme and Susan proceeds smoothly through a number of listener comments about the Zoë Baird affair (President Clinton's first attempt to nominate a woman to the post of attorney general). Then she comes to a witty letter: "Thomas Kahn of St. Louis," Susan reads, "took umbrage at our offhand remark, after an interview with the former cook in the Arkansas governor's mansion, that President Clinton probably ate Wonder Bread with his favorite dish — steak marinated in bottled salad dressing. 'Shame on you to criticize one of the great American foods, Wonder Bread,' writes Mr. Kahn. 'Frankly, I think it is delicious, light and airy, especially when fresh, and I'm tired of having to shop late at night or in other neighborhoods in order to avoid the mockery of friends.'" Susan's voice echoes the smile on her face as she reads the letter. Then she adds a comment of her own. "It's also great with Velveeta," she purrs, adding quickly, "No, Velveeta fans, stay away from the post office this week, please!"

The control room erupts with laughter. But Susan doesn't like the way she sounded with her Velveeta ad-lib. She pauses in her reading and, with the tape still rolling, retakes her Velveeta comment. She uses a slightly different inflection, which sounds more like an aside and is even funnier. She then goes on with the next letter — "a geographic observation" — in which a gentleman in Tucson explains that Patagonia is not a mythical place but a real town in Arizona. "Thank you for the clarification," Susan says; then she begins to read the final letter, in which a couple write that "Freedonia is not just a fictional kingdom" in a Marx Brothers movie . . . but Susan does not finish the letter. She's been keeping her eye on the clock, and her remarks about Velveeta have helped make the segment longer than it should be. It's time to wrap things up. "I'm not going to read that last letter," she announces to the folks in the control room and goes right on to the close. She waits for a couple of seconds in order to settle her voice and pick just the right tone. Then she begins reading quietly, in a manner that will cut perfectly with the end of the Tucson letter:

> Well, we welcome your thoughts, your geography lessons, whatever . . . send us Wonder Bread! Write to "Letters . . ." — *don't* send us Wonder Bread — ". . . *Weekend Edition, Saturday*, National Public Radio . . ."

Susan slips in "send us Wonder Bread" and then "don't send us Wonder Bread" in a unique vocal modulation — whimsical, chummy, *sotto voce* . . . a kind of phrasing that Susan has made famous and that only she can pull off. The staff in the control room again dissolves in laughter. The Letters segment will have considerable pizzazz this week.

When she concludes, Susan apologizes to Ken for all the edits he'll have to do. But Ken doesn't mind: he knows the tape will cut perfectly. Susan has hit her various tones so well that there's no question of needing any retakes. Ken also doesn't worry about the time. In spite of her starts and stops, Susan has an intuitive sense of pacing: Letters will last no longer than its allotted three minutes.

Then it's on to the opening for the first hour and the various other elements. Ned is directing, fresh-faced and calm, with his neatly trimmed brown hair and a comfortably wrinkled blue-and-white-striped button-down shirt. Ned runs into some minor problems when he gives Susan cues, for though *Weekend Saturday* and *Weekend Sunday* use the same theme music, the *WESAT* version is upbeat and quick while the *WE-SUN* arrangement is quieter and more reflective. Susan knows when to come in, though, and smiles off Ned's apologies. All the connecting elements are recorded in one take. After they are done, Rich Rarey splices in the prerecorded open for the second hour that Cindy and Renée did the previous evening, and at seven-forty *WESAT* is just about all set to go on the air.

Susan is sitting behind the microphone at eight o'clock when the pretaped opening of *Weekend Saturday* begins. She wears her headphones like a headband, back from her ears and around her thick, curly hair, when she's not broadcasting live. Ken brings in a bunch of scripts for her to look over. Newscasts over the weekends are only five minutes long, so by five minutes and thirty seconds after the hour, Susan is readying herself for her first live announcement of the day. She does not sit quietly in her chair waiting for the cue but stretches her arms over her head and from side to side in dancelike gestures. She leans back in her chair and bends her neck, then, with a few seconds to go, settles her headphone around her ears and positions herself properly in front of her microphone. "This is *Weekend Edition*. I'm Susan Stamberg . . ." *WESAT* is now fully under way.

Susan listens closely to most of the program as it is broadcast. After the first Fo Break she buzzes Ken on the intercom and asks if he thinks she should redo it for the second feed — she worries that her voice, taped a short while before, didn't quite match what she heard in the surrounding pieces, recorded earlier in the week. Ken asks Ned what he thinks. The director doesn't hear any problems. Susan here is demonstrating her sensitivity to one of the trickiest parts of hosting a weekly show: maintaining vocal continuity through a series of recordings made on different days. Susan has such a wide range of deliveries — her vocal instrument is so varied — that she must be particularly sensitive to how she comes out of one kind of story and leads into another kind of story. She will often rerecord an introduction to a piece, for example, or choose to do it live, if the road map is rearranged and the flow of the segment changes sufficiently that she feels her original tone won't sound right. The end result of her concern is that listeners can almost never tell when Susan is reading live and when she's on tape. This is true of all the good hosts on NPR but it's easier to maintain that seamless feeling if your vocal technique is less virtuosic than Susan Stamberg's.

At twenty-six minutes to nine, just before the cut-away with Ron Hunter starts, Susan is rigorously doing her arm stretches while sitting at the host's desk. As the music leading to the break begins, Susan starts dancing her arms in rhythm. With her arms held out to either side of her, she leans toward the microphone, a big smile on her face, and says in a perfectly controlled voice, "You're listening to *Weekend Edition*." Then she continues her exercises as the cut-away starts playing.

The rest of the program flows onto the air smoothly. As Cindy said, it's a fun show with a number of unusual pieces in it. Then, as the second hour draws to a close, *WESAT* airs two pieces, back to back, which are memorable examples of the power of radio. Susan reads a news-oriented introduction to Tom Gjelten's story from Sarajevo. She describes the apparent failure of mediation efforts in Geneva yet reports that some of the participants are hopeful of a more positive response from the Bosnian Serbs. Then she sketches a portrait of Sarajevo before the civil war broke out. "It was a city of culture known for its artistic and intellectual life and its lively youth scene," she says, and adds that in spite of the devastation caused by the current siege, a group of musicians, actors, and dancers continues to stage a production of the rock musical *Hair*. She introduces Tom Gjelten. His five-minute report will become one of his most famous from the former Yugoslavia.

Musical clip from Hair.

GJELTEN: 'No home, no shoes, no money' — life in Sarajevo summed up in a song. Actually, the cast of *Hair* warn against making too much of the fit between the lyrics of the musical and the real-life reality of Sarajevo. That wasn't the reason for choosing this show, they say. As much as anything, it was the familiar music. But the antiwar theme of *Hair* and the musical's love-and-peace message are especially poignant when played out in a city struggling to survive.

More music from the production.

The Sarajevo producers of *Hair* shortened the musical and rewrote it around Bosnia's own war story. A Serbian boy is called up for service in the Yugoslav army. His friends try to talk him out of going, telling him it's wrong to fight against his neighbors. In another scene the players bow their heads and quietly pray that the war stops, that peace comes, that those who burn villages and rape children vanish from the earth. Then they turn to each other on stage and ask, 'What did you do when the country was overrun?'

Song: Easy to Be Hard

Tom Gjelten alternates his narration with music and interviews with cast members, who describe what it's like to work with no electricity, with no heat. The dancers hurt, they are tired, yet they continue on. Their comments are incredibly moving. The lead singer says that the hardships of life in Sarajevo actually help keep the cast in shape. "We are not spoiled stars," he says. "Every day we bring water to our house. We — you know, we walk, we don't drive anymore."

"We work under really hard conditions," says production manager Leila Samek. "You see, ballet dancers, they need lots of energy. We have no food, we have no pay."

Yet Samek has no intentions of closing down the production; indeed, she dreams of taking *Hair* on tour.

Gjelten's brief portrait concludes with a poignant exchange concerning why the cast perseveres. As Samek speaks, the singing of a strong, vibrant Sarajevo chorus fades up in the background:

GJELTEN (on the scene): Why is it important, do you think, for the people of Sarajevo to be able to come and see this?
SAMEK: It makes us happy because we are all sad. You can see sad faces around you. And we are all unhappy in this war.
Music fades up: "Let the Sunshine In." Established for several seconds.
GJELTEN (narration): The Sarajevo production of *Hair:* performed when conditions permit. I'm Tom Gjelten in Sarajevo.
Music continues, then fades down.

During the playing of the Gjelten piece, Susan listens intently, leaning her chin on her hand. She is deeply moved and shakes her head from time to time. "This is an extraordinary story," she says at one point. When "Let the Sunshine In" begins, she rubs her eyes. Anyone who first heard this song in the sixties will feel a particularly thrilling resonance as its hopeful cry emerges from the sadness and misery of Sarajevo. Even before Gjelten gives his SOC (standard outcue), Susan is on the intercom to the control room. "We should have ended the previous hour with *this*," she says emphatically. "This is an *extremely* powerful piece."

No one in the control room can respond, because at that moment, Ned and Ken are trying to work out how to move from Gjelten's report to "Iva." They come up with the idea of a long, slow fadeout of

"Let the Sunshine In" — a "Motown fade" Rich Rarey calls it — taking maybe nine seconds. Ned was originally thinking of something faster, but Ken has heard both pieces several times and in his quiet way he urges the use of a slower transition. Unfortunately in the quick discussion neither Ned nor Ken makes clear *when* the "nine seconds" is to begin — at the beginning of Gjelten's last talk track or at the beginning of his SOC or after he has signed off. Furthermore, the sense of pacing in a control room during a broadcast is seldom as leisurely as it is in an edit booth or in a producer's office: the adrenaline surge of being on the air mixes with the perpetual worry of a program going long — it is *always* better to be a little short than to go over your allotted time. So, in the event, the gentle nine-second fade from *Hair* to "Iva" turns into a rapid four- or five-second fade. Susan's introduction to "Iva" starts much too quickly after Gjelten's piece and disrupts the haunting mood created by the old rock song: "By day, Iva Pekarkova reads the Wolfes — Virginia and Thomas — also William Faulkner . . . and she writes. She's working on her fourth novel. By night, Iva Pekarkova drives a cab in New York City. She's one of just a handful of night-driving female cabbies in a town that teems with taxis . . ."

In a hurried conversation following the start of Iva, Ned worries about the transition having been too quick and regrets not having had time to listen to the Gjelten piece beforehand. Others say the transition sounded okay. But in fact, many listeners will miss the opening words of Susan's introduction because they will continue to reverberate with emotions conjured up by Gjelten's report. A few seconds of breathing space can make a big difference to the aural imagination.

But the eleven-minute portrait of the redoubtable Iva Pekarkova is a powerful and touching story in its own right, beautifully produced by the talented independent David Isay and poetically written and narrated by Susan. Listeners meet the Czech refugee, Iva, in a taxi garage, then go driving with her one evening. Susan talks with Iva and with some of her passengers and even manages to interweave quotations from Iva's first published novel, *Truck Stop Rainbows*. A vivid aural portrait emerges of a talented, individualistic, quirky young woman, living a life, as she admits, "close to the edge." As the piece draws to a close, Susan begins to evoke a fantasy future for Iva. Susan's voice merges with the purring of the nighttime cab and carries listeners along the final stretch of this evocative taxi ride of the imagination:

Sounds of the cab in the background.

SUSAN: Although she likes the money and the flexibility, days free, days off, if she chooses, Iva Pekarkova's cabbing may be nearing an end. She's writing another novel. Like *Truck Stop Rainbows* it has a travel motif.

PEKARKOVA: [She speaks with a thick accent.] I'm working on a book now which I hope I won't finish too soon because it's about taxi driving. And, I guess, when it's done, I'll stop liking it, probably, because there will be no point in doing it anymore.

Sounds of the cab fade up more strongly and continue.

SUSAN: [Slowly at first but with gathering momentum.] And, who knows? Maybe Iva won't have to do it anymore. Maybe after that book comes out, Meryl Streep will get in Yellow Cab number 9L85, and Iva will hand her *The Book of Iva*, and they'll get to talking, and she'll describe the new novel, and Streep will get interested, and then the book will be a major motion picture — and Iva Pekarkova will ride around Manhattan in the back of *someone else's* cab.

Sounds of the cab continue.

Cross-fade into "That's Entertainment" . . .

The conclusion of the Iva sound portrait weaves a spell — a strange, offbeat mood — which unfortunately is then broken almost as abruptly as was the conclusion of Gjelten's story. The difficulty Cindy foresaw last night befalls Ned. The C segment is running tight, and instead of playing "That's Entertainment" for thirty seconds, thus allowing listeners to both identify the music and to reflect upon what they've just heard, Ned fades down the song after about five or ten seconds, sustaining it beneath Susan's back-announce: "Our thrilling, chilling cabbie cruise was produced by the intrepid David Isay. This is NPR's *Weekend Edition*. I'm Susan Stamberg." Ned fades up the music briefly but then brings it down again for the transcript cart, which tells listeners how they can get transcripts or tapes of the preceding program. The cart ends, and Ned neatly brings up the final couple of seconds of "That's Entertainment." It's now fifty-eight minutes after the hour, time for the familiar twenty-nine-second funding credit. The program finishes on schedule.

The interweaving of voice and music during the final minute or so of the program occurs cleanly and with the familiar NPR panache. Unfortunately, Ned has left no time for listeners to savor the end of Iva's story . . . to let Susan's final words echo in the imagination, to let the playfulness of the music sink in.

Susan gets on the intercom as soon as the show is off the air and calmly, but firmly, states that the ending didn't work right. Listeners won't even have had time to identify the music as "That's Entertainment." Ned doesn't disagree, but he's not sure how else he could have managed the final moments given the time constraints. Dean agrees with Susan that there should have been more music in the clear. A small crowd now gathers in the control room and discusses how the ending could be made to sound less rushed. (Ken is notably absent from the group.) Susan reiterates her conviction that Gjelten would have worked much better as the conclusion of the first hour. Then she wonders if *something* could be trimmed from within the C segment to open up more time at the end for the music to be heard.

"I'm sure we can get five seconds out of Iva and five seconds out of Gjelten," says Susan. "That's all we'd need."

Ned feels that the only way for the music to work is for it to be heard in the clear for a full thirty seconds. Susan wonders aloud if the transcript cart has to be played. Ned laughs and says that's *always* an issue, but Ken, as line producer, would have to make that decision.

While all this discussion has been going on in the control room, out at the *Morning Edition* desk, Ken has already received a call from Cindy. She's been listening at home and says that the ending of the second hour was totally wrong. They both agree on the simplest solution to the problem. Ken transfers Cindy's call to Ned and the senior producer gives the substitute director permission to drop the transcript cart. Cindy says it's very important to let the ending of "Iva" breathe. Everyone agrees.

During the second feed of *WESAT,* between ten and noon, the portrait of Iva Pekarkova will conclude more gracefully. But no fix is made to the transition from Gjelten's piece to "Iva." That sequence remains as originally produced.

On Monday morning, Cindy reflects upon the Saturday program. In general she is very pleased with how the show sounded. There were a lot of interesting and unusual pieces. She disagrees with Susan about the placement of Gjelten. She sticks by the decisions she and Ken made on Friday night. She doesn't think that *Hair* would have worked well following the Egyptian photography story. Susan continues to feel that the story from Sarajevo would have been far more effective if placed at the end of the first hour. The difference in "ear" in this instance may also reflect a difference in generations. The music from *Hair* carries emotional weight for people of Susan's generation; Cindy, almost twenty years younger, may not respond in quite the same way to "Let the Sunshine In." However, with creative radio production, as with any art form, there are seldom "right" answers — there's never only *one* way to put a program together. The ultimate, unresolvable dilemma of this particular *Weekend Saturday* program might well be that there were three strong "end" pieces broadcast in a show that only had room for two.

The Ears of Another Generation

While Cindy Carpien seems perfectly at ease with the segmentation of *Weekend Saturday* — and even says that seventeen minutes is perhaps about as long as any radio piece should ever be — her counterpart on *Weekend Sunday*, Bob Malesky, grew up in a more leisurely tradition of radio, when documentary programs were regularly a full sixty minutes long, with no interruptions even for station breaks. Bob has adjusted to the demands of a faster-paced NPR and in recent years has achieved considerable success with the shorter forms of radio, both as an independent producer and as producer of *WESUN*. But having experienced long-form radio, he remembers in his bones the potential of that more measured, more stately pace. His imagination still reverberates with the range of possibility for aural evocation, practiced so dramatically in *A Question of Place* — especially in his remarkable contribution to that series, the profile of Michel Foucault.

Bob is thus ideally suited to produce the Sunday version of *Morning Edition*. The opening music of the show — a peaceful piano rendition of the *Weekend Edition* theme — and the low-key, pleasant voice of host Liane Hansen set the mood for a program that encourages members of the audience to sit back in their chairs and *listen*. The average story on *Weekend Sunday* is not significantly longer than those on other shows, but *WESUN* probably broadcasts more full-segment features in the final third of each hour than does *WESAT*. These C's tend to be profiles of musicians, writers, actors, or artists of all kinds. Musical selections, readings from books, excerpts from plays and movies — all are elements used in these features. *Weekend Sunday* plays *more* of the music in its arts reports than other shows do. "We used to get a lot of complaints after a music piece on [daily] *Morning Edition*," Bob recalls, "from listeners who said, 'You didn't let me hear enough!' Well, in some ways you *can't* because that's not the nature of an informational program. People set themselves up differently when they are going to listen to ideas or when they are going to listen to music. Say they've been listening to forty minutes of ideas and then suddenly you throw them a piece that has a full seven minutes of music in it: the audience will get confused, if only half-consciously. Or say a program constantly switches back and forth between idea and music pieces — this used to happen on the old *Performance Today* program. That kind of rhythm, too, can get *very* fatiguing subliminally. People actually get tired 'switching gears' from one kind of listening to another. So it's a continual problem when you are producing a show which has both news and the arts. You have to shape your hours carefully."

Bob's finely tuned ears extend to all aspects of *Weekend Sunday*'s production, even to such standard NPR fare as the teasers the show uses to give listeners a taste of an upcoming report. Alone among NPR show producers these days, Bob insists on *never* using an excerpt from the story to be broadcast. In the *WESUN* promos (which occur during the times that *WESAT* uses for Fo Breaks), Bob will have his staff pull a quotation from the *outtakes* of an upcoming piece. "This point used to be endlessly debated here," says Bob. He believes it's inherently less interesting — and even distracting — for listeners to hear the words in the teaser repeated when the story plays. Some in the audience may think, "Hmm . . . now where have I heard *this* before?" Also, teasers often contain punch lines, or at least strong pieces of tape. Bob feels that the impact of the story gets diminished if listeners have heard some of the most interesting sections beforehand. Meanwhile, producers over at *All Things Considered* remain convinced that if listeners *don't* hear the same words repeated later in the advertised story, they will fear they have *missed* something. Bob's approach seems inherently to address an audience that listens with care and with concentration. The other approach sacrifices some of the spontaneity of discovery and seems to assume more literal and more prosaic listening habits on the part of the audience. (Of course, most weekday afternoon listeners are surrounded by more distractions than the Sunday morning audience.)

WESUN is unusual in other respects: it's the one newsmagazine produced in stereo, and Bob and his staff try to make use of the added sound potential that technology provides. While the benefits of broadcasting *music* in stereo are obvious, the enhancements for news or documentary production may not be so apparent to audiences who have become used to monaural newsmagazines. But hearing the ambient sounds of a place in stereo — be it a city street, a farmyard, a forest, or even a quiet room — adds a layer of presence, of depth which can be quite astounding in its vividness and power. Conversations, laughter, crowd noises, even simple two-way or three-way discussions — all take on an added dimensionality, an added punch. It's far more difficult for a report which uses stereo sound creatively to be placed "in the background" by listeners, if only because even the most subtle sounds (a clock ticking, a river gurgling) tend to leap out at your imagination and focus your attention. It might even be argued that audiences may be more apt to *turn off* a stereo documentary if they are not prepared to pay attention than to have it play in the background, since the stereo sounds are so much more challenging, insistent, and difficult to ignore.

Stereo recording and stereo production are inherently more complicated, more time-consuming, and more expensive than monaural work, and while both daily and weekend versions of *All Things Considered* occasionally present special features in stereo, the art of stereo documentary production — so actively a part of NPR's life during the seventies and early eighties — is now pretty much confined to *WESUN* and a few specialized programs produced at the corners of National Public Radio, such as the series *Soundprint*. (Independent radio producers continue to work extensively in stereo.)

Weekend Sunday is produced with all the care and attention of *Weekend Saturday*, for Bob Malesky is as much of a perfectionist as Cindy Carpien. But his style as producer reflects the quieter, more laid-back tone of the Sunday-morning show as well as his mellow temperament, his age, and his long experience in the radio medium. Bob's apparently easy-going manner — emphasized these days by the slight, bearish thickening that middle age adds to his modest frame — can be as deceptive as his casual appearance (rimless glasses, droopy gold and brown mustache, a tendency toward jeans and sneakers). Beneath his gentleness lurks a powerful drive for excellence and a good deal of repressed tension, only partly alleviated by his ready laughter, his broad smile, and his long habit of smoking.

(The ritual of smoking helps break up the accumulating pressure of Bob's work, for it assures that several times during the day he will disappear from the office and retire to the roof or the front sidewalk, where lighting up a cigarette will provide him with a moment of private reverie and contemplation. Bob takes his identity as one of the last NPR smokers with his typically stylish good humor. On the door of his office hangs a poem in old French, "Puisque Je Suis Fumeux," with the following English translation:

> In between puffs, his thought:
> A smoker smokes through smoke.
>
> For smoking suits him very well
> As long as he keeps his intention.
> A smoker smokes through smoke —
> A smokey speculation
>
> — SOLAGE, 1380)

Bob speaks about the adjustments he has made as he's moved from the slow, patient craftsmanship of the old documentaries to the demands of a weekly magazine program. "Although I'd like to be more demanding at times," he explains, "I've also learned there's a diminishing point of returns when you have the number of pieces to produce every week as we do. You know, there are some times when my *staff* will want to go back to remix and rework things. And I completely understand their point of view — I can put myself in their shoes very easily — but I have to take a wider view and see the four or five other things that they could be working on rather than remixing this one piece for perfection's sake."

Just as it is easy to spend hours in an edit booth pruning and shaping tape till it sounds exactly as you'd like it, producers and engineers can spend extended periods of time in the studio, mixing and remixing, to get all the balances of voice, ambiance, music, and sound just right. In a sense, the relative simplicity of radio production — starting and stopping a series of tape recorders and fading volume levels up and down — makes it very easy to fall into an obsessive labor that consumes hours and hours.

While Bob Malesky must impose some restraints upon his staff, it's also true that, by current NPR standards, he allows his producers an unusual amount of time to develop their stories. In part this is because they do so many long arts pieces, in part because they work in stereo. Bob explains: "The way I've often looked at it is that I want to create a space where people can work creatively. So if there's drudge work to do, I often wind up doing it myself — freeing the staff to work on their longer projects. (I used to edit out all the *ums* from the car guys, the Magliozzi brothers, for example.[7] They *um* a lot you know.) The point is that I've had a lot of chances to be a creative, artistic producer and I want to be sure that others have the experience as well, so that there's another generation of radio producers who are comfortable with these longer-form features."

Part of the way Bob structures the *Weekend Sunday* production schedule grows out of his understanding of how people learn to work with sound. Simply put, he's not sure that you can be taught directly how to "use your ears." He sees no substitute for jumping into the process directly and learning by doing.

"That's how Bob Montiegel trained me," Bob recalls. "I spoke about this at his funeral last year, and what I said surprised a number of people. Bob never wanted me to produce like Bob Montiegel. He never guided me through cutting a piece, or showed me how he'd do a mix, or took me down to the studio and told me what he was doing. He did not what I call *micro-manage*. We'd talk about my pieces *after* they had aired — how I might have improved them. But I learned as much by doing as by being told what to do.[8]

"And I've found that this works best with my own staff as well. There's always more than one valid way to produce a piece, and I think it's very important to let individual producers find their own particular approach — to develop their own ears. I really don't have any desire to turn out 'Malesky clones' . . . even if I knew what that was or how to do it."

Bob's small staff — half a dozen including host — has nothing but admiration for its senior producer. They all speak of how much they have learned from him, through his gentle but perceptive critiques of their work, and his generous gift of the rarest commodity of all at NPR — *time*. So it happened that, when, in April 1993, after five years without doing a major piece of production himself, Bob asked his staff to take on a bit more work themselves so he could be freed up to spend three weeks working exclusively on a special feature, everyone pitched in enthusiastically. What Bob had in mind was to commemorate, with

---

[7] The hosts of *Car Talk* began their national exposure on *WESUN*.

[8] Robert Montiegel was killed, tragically, by muggers in Washington, D.C., in 1992. He was in his fifties when he died, and was only doing occasional pieces for an NPR that no longer had a place for his particular form of radio genius.

a major sound portrait, the twenty-fifth anniversary of the assassination of Martin Luther King.

The result of Bob's labors (in collaboration with assistant producer Walter Watson, host Liane Hansen, and technical director Rich Rarey) was broadcast on the first Sunday in April 1993 and immediately became the stuff of legend at NPR . . . an extraordinary eruption — an awakening, really — of the dormant power of the sound medium to stir the intellect, move the emotions, and elevate the spirit.

The idea of producing a special report on Martin Luther King grew out of the coincidence of dates. "Since the anniversary fell on a Sunday," Bob explains, "we started having long discussions among the staff, many months ago, about what we should do. We decided in the final analysis that we didn't want to do the *legacy* of Martin Luther King because that's what everyone was going to be doing. Instead, I really wanted to re-create as much as possible the *feeling* of the time, a sense of the *place*. I wanted to be able to take the listener there, in one way or another."

So the idea of an historical documentary took shape. *Weekend Sunday* would attempt to portray some aspects of King's final year and to evoke the feelings that surrounded the assassination. (*Weekend Sunday* frequently takes a "long view" of current events, as Bob feels the pace of the program suits that approach.)[9] Bob and Liane read extensively about King's life, considered the modest NPR travel budget available, and decided on one field trip, to Memphis, Tennessee. They would visit the Lorraine Motel, where the shooting had taken place, and record interviews at other locations in town that King had visited during his final days.

Though the *WESUN* staff began trying to set up interviews two months ahead of time with people like Andrew Young, Jesse Jackson, and Marion Wright Edelman, by the time Bob and his small production team set off for Memphis three weeks before the show would air, they had only been able to confirm a single conversation — with Reverend Billy Kyles, who had been standing next to King on the motel balcony

---

[9] Daniel Schorr's frequent essays on *WESUN*, for example, are generally more historically reflective than his commentaries on other programs, in large measure because Bob encourages him not to worry so much about pressing issues of the moment.

the moment he was shot. Liane would conduct the interviews with Kyles, who they hoped would accompany them around Memphis, talking about the final days of Martin Luther King.

As Bob began imagining the kind of piece he wanted to do, he realized that he would be operating on an extremely fast turnaround time. He knew he wanted to include a substantial excerpt from the final speech King delivered, at the Mason Temple, the evening before he was killed — one of his most eloquent and most moving, in which he appears to predict his coming death. Bob also wanted to present a portrait of King's final year — a troubled one in which he launched himself far beyond his original concerns with civil rights for blacks and began to address the war in Vietnam and the underlying economic inequalities in American society. And Bob imagined melding Liane's on-the-scene interviews in Memphis with natural sound recorded there, in order to bring the entire piece aurally alive. Three weeks seemed hardly enough time for all the editing, scripting, and mixing Bob had in mind.

During a strategy session a couple of days before the trip to Memphis, Rich Rarey made the key suggestion that they record all the interviews on a Nagra — a portable reel-to-reel tape recorder of outstanding quality — so that Bob would not have to spend precious time dubbing from DAT to analogue tape (which he would then be able to edit). The ambiant sounds, however, could be recorded on DAT. The Lorraine Motel had now been turned into a museum, which Bob said might present some interesting sound possibilities. Also, the museum had agreed to allow the *WESUN* team access to the balcony itself, usually closed to the public. "It could be very potent to stand on the balcony," said Bob quietly, and the team sitting around the table grew still.

Liane and Bob discussed the kinds of questions they would ask Kyles. "We want to get an image of King as a human being, not as a saint," Liane said.

Bob also reported that he'd been listening to a lot of music, trying to decide what to use in the report. "We'll have to use [the spiritual] 'Precious Lord' in there somewhere. That was King's favorite, and it was in some of the final words he spoke.

"Overall," continued Bob, "we're going to have to judge the length of this piece by the tape we collect in Memphis. I'm already thinking that seventeen minutes is dubious. Especially if we get people who are scintillating speakers."

"Will they let us break format?" Liane asked.

"We'll see . . ." said Bob.

"Breaking format" happens very rarely in the segmented world of *Morning Edition* and *Weekend Edition*. What it means, simply, is that one of the divisions between program segments is dispensed with and NPR takes back time normally given to stations. Over the weekend, this usually means segment B is allowed to run into segment C — and suddenly a continuous block of some thirty-eight minutes opens up. Local stations do not look kindly on breaking format. They do not like their local cut-aways and announcements tinkered with. When format is going to be broken, many messages must be sent out to stations, far in advance of the event. Even still, some board operator somewhere or other will be surprised and confused by the change in routine.

WESUN's two days in Memphis turned into a typical radio adventure in improvisation, which completely altered the shape of the piece Bob had planned to do. The first day it was raining so hard that Bob scrubbed the idea of traveling with the Reverend Kyles to the various sites in town. Instead, the production crew gathered in Kyles's office and Liane conducted what turned into an intense revelatory two-hour interview.

Afterward, Bob and Liane explained what happened. Bob began: "Kyles does tell the story of the assassination a good bit. He takes his idea of being a witness very seriously, and what Liane had to do was break through the regular story that he told and press for details, more and more details, and bring us back . . . back to the motel balcony."

Liane spoke quietly: "And by the time we got to the end of it, you could tell he was probing places in himself he hadn't probed before. He had told this story many, many times before, but you got the feeling he was behind a shield — you know, to protect himself. But there was a key moment in his story — I think it's one of the most powerful moments in the broadcast — where he lets out a sigh. And we could all feel it — something happening, something being let out that hadn't come out before, as he was describing the shot, and his reaction to it, and what he saw as he knelt by King . . ."

"We were all leaning in at that point," Bob continued, "you know, hanging on every word. And he was speaking so quietly . . ."

Liane added: "It was very difficult to just keep trying to remember my job at that point . . . to keep going after the objective questions."

"And Rich also did a *wonderful* job," Bob said. "By the end there was literally a half inch between Kyles's lips and the microphone. And, you know, there is *nothing* that draws your ear more then someone whispering. And I think much of the impact of Kyles's story on tape comes from that proximity — you simply cannot listen to anything else but Kyles's voice describing what he saw and felt. But if the mike hadn't been that close, a listener would have heard a little more room-sound and thus been, aurally, just a little more distant. Kyles's story wouldn't have had quite the same impact."

The remarkable intensity of Kyles's narrative developed in part because he was able to focus his attention entirely on Liane, in spite of the fact that there were three other people in the room (Bob, Rich, and Walter Watson). Bob explained: "If Kyles had decided to tell this story to *all* of us together, rather than just to Liane, he would have been turning his head, going off mike all the time, and his story would not have sounded as intimate."

"It wouldn't have sounded as if he was telling the story to *you*," added Liane. "But of course I used all the interviewing techniques I know to keep him focused on me. I try *never* to lose my eye contact with somebody I'm interviewing. Sometimes I'll memorize my first four questions so that I don't have to look down. And if I keep *looking* at someone intently, they're going to forget that there's a microphone here, and they're going to start talking directly *to* me.

"And another thing: there's *nothing* better than *silence* to draw someone out. People fall into a silence — they don't like it if there's silence . . . unless they're practiced at this art, like politicians, who are used to stonewalling, I guess." She smiled. "But mostly people will run right into that silence and keep going, if you can just refrain yourself from saying something. So some of the Kyles interview happened because I listened intently and sometimes *didn't* ask the question but let him flow deeper and deeper into his story."

The *WESUN* production team emerged from the interview with Billy Kyles profoundly moved and sensing immediately that *this* was to be the cornerstone of their report.

"After the interview," Bob explained, "we knew obviously we had at least a major C segment. But I still did want to bring the audience along to Memphis, I wanted the piece to have a strong sense of place, and since we couldn't bring Kyles to those spots, we decided to bring Liane and have her read script at various sites in Memphis. So we talked it over for a while, and then I locked myself in my hotel room — I had brought all my research material with me — and wrote three pieces of copy for Liane to read: at the Lorraine Motel, Beale Street, and the Mason Temple. She made some changes herself in the scripts the next morning, and then off we went."

At this point in Memphis, Bob did not yet know the precise length of each section of the story, but a clear sense of structure was beginning to form in his mind. He was able to write Liane's narration to weave through that outline. The report would end with Kyles's story. Before that would come a part of King's speech at the Mason Temple. Kyles described the scene surrounding that speech in entrancing detail, so Bob knew he would weave Kyles and King together here. The section would be set up with Liane speaking in the temple herself. Bob also had long envisioned beginning the entire piece with an historical overview that would describe the events leading up to King's Memphis trip. So the script would tell about the strike of garbage workers in Memphis which triggered King's presence. Crucial to this part of the story was a peaceful demonstration in the city that turned violent even while King was in attendance. Bob wrote some copy for Liane to read while standing on Beale Street, site of the near riot twenty-five years earlier.

The *WESUN* crew wanted to visit one more location: the balcony of the Lorraine Motel. Bob had originally thought Liane might interview Kyles here. Now another idea came to mind. The second hour of *Weekend Sunday* would open with Liane standing on the balcony telling about the upcoming documentary. Bob composed the following lines late at night in his Memphis hotel room, and the next day Liane tried her best to get the words out as she stood on the spot where Martin Luther King had been shot. Through several takes and after a few tears, she managed to speak her words with a calm yet intense dignity:

From National Public Radio in Washington, this is *Weekend Edition*. I'm Liane Hansen. This hour we travel south to commemorate a special anniversary. It was sunny in Memphis, Tennessee, twenty-five years ago today. The thunderstorms of the previous night had abated, but there was still electricity in the air. Dr. Martin Luther King, Jr., stood where I am standing now on the balcony of the Lorraine Motel. He was about to go to dinner with some friends, then suddenly, his career, his hopes, his fears, his life ended. Today is Sunday, April fourth.

Coming up on *Weekend Edition*, we remember the assassination of Dr. Martin Luther King, Jr. First, this news.

In addition to Liane's tracks, Rich recorded ambient sounds at each location, including part of the guided tour through the museum section of the Lorraine Motel.

When Bob returned to Washington, he was pretty sure he needed to break format in order to do everything that he felt the Martin Luther King feature deserved. But he waited until he had cut the Kyle interview (it came in at ten minutes) and had chosen the sections of King's Mountaintop speech (nine minutes) before he went to his executive producer, Bob Ferrante, and then to the head of the news division, Bill Buzenberg, to get permission to go long. "At that point," Bob Malesky said, "I just didn't feel I could cut anything more from either segment without severely damaging their impact." Bob Ferrante was less enthusiastic than Bill Buzenberg about the proposal, but *WESUN*'s request was approved. And now Bob had his work cut out for him: how to fill out, and sustain, thirty-eight minutes of NPR air with a single story.

For the next two and a half weeks, Bob spent a good deal of time at his own home, editing tape on an old Otari machine. He was left undisturbed to smoke his cigarettes and drink his coffee. "Sometimes I could even stay in my pajamas," Bob explained with a smile. He worked on the piece backward, honing the Kyle interview and then assembling the section in the Mason Temple. After allowing space at the opening of the feature for a short but impressive commentary from regular *WESUN* contributor (and Chicago newspaper columnist) Clarence Page, Bob wound up with five minutes to devote to the opening section on the historical background. Liane's narration here would be enhanced with excerpts from radio reports of the period uncovered by Walter Watson, who also tracked down some wild sound of the street disturbances in Memphis from TV films made in 1968. (Liane's tracks would include the short pieces she recorded on the scene in Memphis, though the bulk of her narration would be committed to tape at NPR.)

Four days before the piece was to air, Bob was ready to begin mixing. He had found a piece of music to act as his continuity from section to section, an explosive modern work entitled "New Mourning for the World–Daybreak of Freedom," composed by Joseph Schwantner in King's memory. And Bob had an emotional ace up his producer's sleeve: he already knew the magical moment at which he would introduce Mahalia Jackson singing "Precious Lord."

While parts of Bob's documentary wound up sounding deceptively simple and uncomplicated, an extraordinary amount of time and effort went into assembling the entire thirty-eight minutes. An outline that Bob wrote for one half-hour of the feature contained eighty-seven different cue markings: to start and stop tapes, to fade music in and out, to add a touch of reverb here and there that would expand the texture of sound . . . Rich Rarey was Bob's frequent partner in these mixes, which took place in NPR's most modern recording facility — Studio Two, the digital studio, home of what remains of NPR arts and performance recording and of *Weekend Sunday*.[10] Overall, Bob spent about eight hours mixing — a great deal of time by contemporary NPR standards, though far shorter than he might have indulged in fifteen years ago. Bob directed each mix with his calm professionalism and his unerring ear. Rich was a perfect in-studio partner, making all manner of subtle adjustments in volume and balance as he glided smoothly from tape to tape, sometimes having to merge five or six elements into the final result. Occasionally Bob might alert Rich to a particular "bump" in a sound bed that had to be flattened out so it wouldn't clash with the narration on top; often Rich could sense the impending difficulty and adjust for it without a word from Bob.

"You get the *feel* of these mixes — literally in your fingers — when things are going well," Rich said afterward. "The better [mixing] consoles are great for that because the faders have very smooth action and you can stroke rather than grind them. And that creates a sensation that's more like playing the piano. You can nurse the keys — you can strike them as delicately as you want, when you mix. That's when sound designing becomes an art. It's a palette on which to work. The coordination of starting and stopping tape machines and watching for white lines and listening for aural cues . . . you can get quite swept up in it when everything is going right. The 'artful' is the goal, and the 'mechanical' is merely the tools and methods we use to get to it."

On Sunday morning, April 4, 1993, *Weekend Sunday* broke format and broadcast a two-segment documentary on the assassination of Martin Luther King. It might well be argued that the feature Bob Malesky produced is not so much an exercise in old-fashioned, long-form radio

---

[10] Studio Two is one of NPR's ground-floor facilities; unlike *WESAT*'s studio, however, Two has had a complete facelift and looks nothing like it did fifteen or twenty years ago.

as a cleverly arranged sequence of short-form pieces, integrated in content and bridged by fanfares from "New Mourning for the World." The sections are brilliantly constructed, using a series of different radio techniques and styles, in order to capture, and then rivet, the attention of listeners. Following Clarence Page's introduction, listeners are taken to the Martin Luther King museum at the Lorraine Motel, where, through a montage of sounds and narration, they go on an aural tour of the facility and are introduced to the world of civil rights protests in the 1960s. Afterward, a kind of radio newsreel begins: excerpts from some Martin Luther King speeches weave in and out of on-the-scene accounts of the garbage workers' strike in Memphis and other protests. The Reverend Billy Kyles appears for the first time.

These complex, interwoven mixes attract listeners with their dense texture and compelling narrative line. They move along at a pace familiar to NPR audiences. The opening several minutes of the King documentary are immediately accessible and quickly engaging. Step by step, through a tapestry of sound and story, listeners are drawn into the events leading up to Martin Luther King's final, fateful trip to Memphis.

Bob Malesky also introduces a brilliant bit of foreshadowing, when Liane describes the motel room in which King was staying when he was shot. That room has remained untouched since that fateful day — the same newspaper, with coverage of the Vietnam War, remains open on the bed — and as crowds of visitors walk up and look through the glass window walling off the room, Mahalia Jackson is heard dimly through a loudspeaker, quietly singing the spiritual "Precious Lord." Here, the song forms part of the jumbled, aural background of the museum: later the music will emerge in all its loveliness to enhance the emotional climax of the radio commemoration.

Toward the end of the "newsreel" section, Bob starts varying the rhythm of the documentary. The changes are imperceptible at first, but by the time the scene shifts to the Mason Temple, the quick pace of the early montages has been replaced by a clearly more leisurely cadence: large sections of King's speech alternate with passionate, personal recollections of the event from Kyles. Yet few listeners may notice the slowdown, because by this point the documentary has woven a subtle web that inexorably holds their attention. The scene in the temple on that final night pulls the audience closer and closer to King — and to the impending tragedy.

The exploding refrain from "New Mourning for the World" offers a momentary respite from the intensity of King's final speech, and then the documentary slides into its final nine minutes, which consist almost entirely of a breathtaking story, told by Billy Kyles. Occasionally Liane asks a question, but at one point Kyles talks for a full *five minutes* without interruption . . . without another sound. Yet the audience hangs on every word. Because of all that has come before, listeners are fully open to the magic of Kyles's voice, as it conjures up the images, the feelings, the textures of a moment in history. Complex mixes are irrelevant; so is the stopwatch. Listeners are spellbound and time is frozen. Kyles speaks in the dry, quiet ambiance of his office — a witness manifesting himself in half whispers and sharply recollected details:

> He was leaning over the rail, talking to Jesse [Jackson]. And so, only as I turned to walk away — when I walked away I got four or five steps. I heard the shot, and I didn't realize it was a shot. I looked over the railing, and people were ducking. And I looked back, and he was lying, mortally wounded. And I ran to him and saw this huge hole in his face, and it knocked one of his shoes off. And he had this crushed cigarette in his hand. And the tie I noticed, because the impact severed the tie and turned the knot upside-down. And he was just lying there. He was bleeding profusely. It was one of those dum-dum bullets. It went in there, but it created a big hole that we couldn't even see. But he was speaking at Jesse — speaking to Jesse at the impact of the bullet, 'cause he was still talking.
>
> And then, people started running up on the balcony. I went in to call the ambulance, and I picked up the phone and the phone required an operator assistance. I couldn't get anybody, and I was beating on the wall, saying, answer the phone, answer the so-and-so phone, answer the phone. And no one ever answered.

Kyles's voice is mesmerizing in its clarity, its intimacy. Little details are springing to life — there's a freshness to his memories, an aching quality, the hush and stillness of tragedy and death. And the radio lets Kyles speak on and on . . .

> We finally got someone on the switchboard, call Coretta and tell her what had happened. It appeared to me by the time the ambulance got there (the police had come and secured the balcony, nobody else could come on or off) his *color* had changed. And I remember seeing my father, in his deathbed, and *his*

color had changed. And I said, "Oh, my goodness." The ambulance finally got there, and then we made the calls that we
needed to make. I called the house and told my wife, and I
said, "Looks like it's fatal. Martin's been shot." And, of course,
the house just — they just went into . . . into fits. And it was
just — it was almost unbelievable. During the whole thing, I
was shaking my head, like you have a nightmare, and you think
you're going to wake up. But I couldn't wake up, I mean, I just
kept shaking my head. But I didn't wake up.

So, they finally took him away. And then, about an hour
or so later, they called and said that he'd been pronounced
dead.

I — I must tell you that . . . and I do . . . because of all the
places in the world I could have been and he could have been,
I had to wonder a long time, *Why was I there? Why was I there?*
You know, why — *why was I not someplace else?* And I had to deal
with that. And what do I do? We were like in shock, we were
angry. You know, if you do this to a nonviolent person, what
will you do — what's the point?

And so, I think it was really only my Christian faith and
belief that kept me going. But God unfolded to me, little by
little, that I was there to be a witness. And here I am, twenty-
five years later, with some degree of clarity, telling the story.
And that's — you know, events like that have to have witnesses.
Events like that have to have witnesses. I just tell what I saw.

And in the midst of this stillness, this sadness, this quiet faith, Bob
Malesky plays a masterstroke of radio art. Every so often in creative
radio production, as in any art form, an opportunity magically arises to
present the audience with a moment of such beauty, power, and intensity that an ordinary aural gesture becomes transformed into an experience of transcendent meaning and resonance. In painting, the trans-
figuring moment may be provoked by the juxtaposition of certain colors
or the flow of certain lines. In literature or poetry, a collection of
well-chosen words or phrases may create the perfect image, the vibrant
metaphor. In the art of radio, the instrument of transformation may be
a particular sound — the sigh of a mother upon giving birth, the
bellowing of a steer being slaughtered — or the transcendent moment
may be evoked by the unexpected, yet perfectly chosen, introduction
of music, working together with the voices or sounds that have come

before. In his documentary on Foucault, Bob Malesky had used a merciless drumroll and the crash of a guillotine to create an unforgettable aural metaphor about madness and history. In this moment of quiet, intimate revelation from the Reverend Billy Kyles, Bob fades up, with exquisite poignancy, Martin Luther King's favorite spiritual, which we have heard dimly in the background early on. But now the full impact of Mahalia Jackson's incredibly slow, mellifluous voice spreads out and envelops us with the most mournful tenderness, the most soulful sorrow, and the most profound prayer. The power, the meaning, the glory of this moment can occur *only in the medium for which it was created.* It is radio that brings forth our tears, which mingle with those shed by Billy Kyles and the millions of others who wept on that day in April so long ago.

> Precious Lord, take my hand
> Lead me on, let me stand.
> I am tired, I am weak,
> Lead me home . . .

But simple grief is not where Bob wishes to leave those listeners who have entered upon this journey in sound and space and time. The moment of transcendence has only just begun, and with Mahalia's prayer continuing, oh, so beautifully, in the background, Liane gently asks a final question in tones that seem to echo perfectly the spirit within Mahalia's voice — even though when Liane spoke these words in Kyles's office she had no idea what kind of aural magic Bob would weave to enhance, and to elevate, the conclusion of these extraordinary, spoken intimacies.

HANSEN: We know a man died on that balcony, at the Lorraine Motel. [Long pause.] What was born . . . that day . . . if anything?

KYLES: I guess his blood watered the earth, and what has grown from that is all this that we see. We see, you know, all the positive things that have happened, for this nation and our race. He died, but another kind of movement was born — that said, you know, it's not going to be — you're not going to be able to shoot one of us anymore and stop the movement.

[Mahalia Jackson's singing continues throughout.]

But I look — I look at an African-American mayor in Memphis, Tennessee. I look at a Doug Wilder, I look at a Jesse

Jackson making a meaningful run for the presidency of the United States. That blood that watered that soil — I mean, a serious run. His Rainbow Coalition is a follow-through of Martin's Poor People's Campaign, bringing people together. And when you touch people on common ground, I mean, you get past the racial thing. And Andy Young, Carol Moseley Braun — I can't even name all the congresspersons — it's wonderful — of African-American descent. Isn't that great? I can't even name them. I've got a book for it, I'll have to go look in the book, not because they're so new, but because there's so many. You see, it's like going back to the bus. We didn't grow any new arms or new legs when we stopped going to the back. We had a change of mind.

And so, a man dies on a balcony, but new life springs up from the blood that waters the soil.

[Mahalia Jackson's singing continues.]

> Guide my feet, hold my hand,
> Take my hand, precious Lord
> And lead me home.

The soundless words on the page cannot begin to convey the emotions conjured up by the final few minutes of Bob Malesky's radio production. Mahalia Jackson's singing has never seemed so slow — so beautiful — so painful. And the tone of Billy Kyles's voice is mesmerizing when he moves from the almost joyful "Isn't that great?" to his rhapsodic yet bittersweet conclusion: "And so, a man dies on a balcony, but new life springs up from the blood that waters the soil." There were many other commemorations of the assassination of Martin Luther King in 1993: many were moving in their own ways. But NPR's aural memorial had a force of unequaled intimacy and immediacy. Kyles appeared on a public television documentary that same night, but he did not speak with the same power or to the same effect. The armor, which Liane had sensed in Memphis, was back in place.

When the Martin Luther King piece was played at a special NPR listening session some weeks later, the force of Mahalia Jackson's song was too much for many people in the room. They found themselves embarrassed and fighting the emotions that swelled up inside, because they were not alone. Afterwards many said that Bob's documentary was too powerful to be listened to by a large group of people — better just a couple of friends, or even just lone individuals. When these NPR colleagues — many from the editorial desks and daily news shows — acknowledged this truth about the intimacy of radio, they were facing directly the latent power of the medium, which they themselves, for a variety of reasons, so often had to overlook.

At some point during the Sunday morning of the broadcast . . . after the congratulatory phone call from Bill Buzenberg (who listened to the program in Kansas City and called in immediately, deeply moved, saying it was the finest piece of radio he had heard in years) . . . after the tepid champagne passed around by the staff (who said, individually and collectively, that it was moments such as this that made their work at NPR worthwhile and that they were proud to have been associated with such a wonderful piece of radio) . . . after the heartfelt thanks to his staff for allowing him the time to pursue this project . . . following the big hug from his wife, Kee ("Once every five years this organization lets this man do the work he's capable of!"), and, then, their quiet walk together, alone, down the empty halls of NPR . . . it's certain that Bob Malesky took one more private moment for himself and, riding the elevator up to the roof of NPR, smoked a quiet, reflective, celebratory cigarette. The old "arts dinosaur" had roared, and a good number of people had listened. But a dinosaur who smokes is not just a dinosaur: he is, in fact, an archetype for a dragon. And Bob Malesky must be considered one of the great hidden dragons of creative radio, lurking, still, in the darker corners of NPR.

Epilogue:
Goings and Comings

And for this evening, that's All Things Considered . . .
I'm Daniel Zwerdling.
— *Weekend All Things Considered,* 1994

In the fall of 1993, Scott Simon came home to radio. He had had mixed experiences at *NBC Weekend Today.* The network wound up taking quite a liking to him, even though it disagreed with most of his values and contradicted a great deal of his fundamental principles. NBC enjoyed his sweet curmudgeonliness. It thought there was a future for at least one "oddball personality," especially if he did well in the ratings.

But Scott was never really content at NBC. He did some work that pleased him: some photo essays, some commentaries, some interviews. But in the end his love of NPR — and his joy at doing his old show — remained undiminished. He left his cozy sofa and his six-figure income and returned to his aural family.

Meanwhile, in the winter of 1994, at the other end of weekend programming, Lynn Neary, host-on-leave from *Weekend All Things Considered*, decided not to rejoin her old show. She was enjoying her role as special correspondent to the arts and cultural desk, with occasional substitute host stints on *Morning Edition*, a position similar to that occupied by Susan Stamberg. When Lynn's departure from *WATC* became official, the management at NPR decided to return Katie Davis to her previous role as reporter and to bring in a quite different personality to host the show.

Daniel Zwerdling had been attracting attention at NPR for some years, as a reporter and an occasional fill-in host. (He first joined the organization in 1980.) During 1993, he was reporting from all over Africa, with the help of a foundation grant, and his stories had gotten rave reviews from many at NPR, both those oriented toward news and those interested in radio production. Danny's pieces were rich with sound and were solid pieces of journalism. His work was often compared to that of Scott Simon, and, indeed, when Danny started broadcasting on *Weekend ATC* in the spring of 1994, it was instantly clear that another engaging sensibility was now appearing regularly as an NPR host. His voice was distinctive — slightly nasal and slightly throaty simultaneously, not at all a traditional radio instrument. Danny was a superb storyteller. He wrote with a touch of Scott Simon's flair, but pursued a more laid-back and easygoing style. In general, Danny was less in-your-face quirky than Scott. His wit ran right on the surface of his copy — you could hear an almost audible gurgle as he spoke — and his humor was gentler, less boffo, than some of Scott's vaudevillian playfulness.

Daniel Zwerdling's arrival at *Weekend ATC* suggested that another chapter in that program's history had begun. The exact nature of the program's new sound would await the fuller development of Zwerdling as a host.

•   •   •

Also during the winter of 1994, Cindy Carpien went on maternity leave for the second time. Peter Breslow — usually resistant to becoming a show producer — took over the reins of the only program he says he would ever consider producing on a permanent basis. There was some minor speculation that Cindy, now a mother twice over, might leave *Weekend Saturday*, but by the summer of 1994 she was back in harness, occupying brand-new offices in NPR's new building, with her old partner Scott Simon again in the host's chair.

A final perspective on the weekend programs: for all the interesting radio these shows produce, their share of the NPR audience remains quite small. With *Morning Edition* approaching seven million listeners, and *All Things Considered* climbing through the low six millions, *Weekend Saturday* was reaching two million listeners by the middle of 1994. *Weekend Sunday* put on a growth spurt and was now heard by an audience of one point three million (up 13 percent from the fall of 1993). Listenership for *Weekend ATC* remained well under one million — the shift from Lynn to Katie did not affect the numbers much. (NPR executives obviously hope that Danny can help increase the audience.) For most NPR listeners the weekend programs remain an undiscovered country. Yet for the audience that knows the way — and for the hosts, producers, and staffs who live in these less-frequented regions of NPR — the weekend radio programs form a magical electronic kingdom, filled with unexpected aural treasure . . . much of which has yet to be mined.

BREAK THREE

The Art of Radio Reporting

The Blind Messenger and
the One-eyed Monster

Daniel Schorr, a stalwart presence at CBS News for two decades, one of the first big names to join Ted Turner's Cable News Network, and now the white-haired senior commentator on NPR, remembers the days when television news was a joke and the only serious reporting occurred on the radio.

"I started at CBS in 1953, when television news was in its infancy," Dan recalls. "I was assigned to the Washington bureau, theoretically available to radio and television. But in fact, I didn't do very much television.

"There was a great deal of skepticism about television, grounded in the idea that it was a toy and an entertainment thing — it was not as serious a medium as radio for transmitting news. When TV came in, it started out with little comedy shows and cartoons and so on. I mean, Doug Edwards became the first anchorperson for *CBS Evening News* mainly because no one else wanted to do it. It was not taken seriously. Television was kid stuff. It was playing around with a studio, with lights and so forth — it was like doing a high school play or something."

Much of TV news consisted of still pictures with wire service copy read over it, though occasionally some newsreel-like footage would get on the air. "Radio was free to cover things in ways that television wasn't in those days," Dan explains. "TV was really far behind radio as a medium for covering news. The technology worked against it — it was all very experimental. And the budgets worked against it. There was a time in '53 where people were really not sure if TV would last at all. There was nothing inevitable about it. Television was marvelous for entertainment, Jack Benny and so on. But we really weren't sure that television would ever amount to anything. It seemed possible that it would wind up being an experiment that would collapse of its own weight, and we'd all go back to doing radio."

Dan's own view of the new medium changed entirely in September 1955, when he was sent to open a CBS bureau in Moscow. "The Russians were not very good about letting camera crews in," Dan remembers, "but they did let us do some filming for a while. We raced all over town, shooting everything that we could shoot. People had not really seen Russia before. It was so exciting! So we put a camera up and filmed faces of people passing by, and we'd film what buildings looked like — we filmed the simplest things. And we'd get reports back from New York saying, 'This stuff is thrilling!' And, remember, these were just black and white films of ordinary street scenes in Russia. We put together half-hour specials and hour specials — "Moscow Today," just showing what Russia looked like. They had tremendous impact back home. And that was the first time that I began to realize television's potential. And so from then on I began to take television more seriously."

A good deal has changed in the intervening years, and Dan Schorr's career has traced both the rising dominance of television news, the hard times that began to befall the networks' news divisions during the eighties, and the unexpected reemergence of serious radio news on NPR.

"I must confess," says Dan, "that I am amazed at what is happening with NPR. I had never expected anything like this. When I left CNN in 1985 and decided to get involved in two or three different programs over here, I really thought I was going into semiretirement. I thought that very few people would ever know what I was doing — that people would meet me and say, 'Hi, what are you up to these days?' And I am amazed that people stop me in the street and say, 'You are on NPR. We listen to NPR all the time.' It is, to me, quite astonishing."

While Dan still believes that television, properly handled, can be a powerful vehicle for delivering the news, he does not miss the medium, at least, not the way it is being run these days. "My memory of television is that you cover some event — a hearing on the Hill — you come back and the producer says, 'Okay. We looked at the tape. Here's the spot sheet that tells you what you got. We need voice-over the first twenty seconds, which shows you this and this happening, and somebody walking in. You will see him at thirteen seconds, so at thirteen seconds hit his name. Then we go to a sound bite. Coming out of the sound bite you have about fifteen more seconds to set up the next thing that happens.' And so, you are sitting there trying to write your report to a sheet that tells you that your deathless prose has to be constrained within these seconds and moments . . . and tells you *where* you must mechanically hit certain things at certain times. The picture dictates what you do. And that to me is a symbol of what television news has become: you work for a producer, and both of you work for some pictures. You both are the servant to those pictures.

"Let me tell you how I am very happy, on the whole, with radio. I spend more time thinking and less time moving than I used to. And that's very nice. Sometimes I'll come up with an idea that hasn't occurred to a lot of people, and it wouldn't have occurred to *me* unless I had the repose to think about it. Sometimes people compliment me on original ideas. Well, whatever original ideas I have come to me (a) because I'm old [Dan is in his late seventies] — I have a lot of historical experience, a lot of history to fall back on, and (b) because it has worked out so that I have ample time to think."

Having worked extensively in both electronic media (he's also had a career as a newspaper columnist), Dan has experienced firsthand the different ways that people respond to what they see on television and what they hear on the radio. His anecdotes echo common experiences among many reporters. "When I was working for CBS in the days during Watergate," Dan says, "I received a great deal of exposure and was pretty well known. A typical encounter with a stranger might run like this:

"'Gee, you're Daniel Schorr, aren't you? I saw you on television yesterday.'

"'Right,' I'd reply, and then, just to test out a theory I had, I would press the person a bit. 'Which report did you see? I did one thing on the morning news, had a piece on the evening news about Watergate, and then there was that special we did. Which piece did you happen to catch?'

"'Uh . . . well . . . I see you all the time.'

"'Right . . . and . . . ?'

"'Well, you look pretty good!'

"Now a typical encounter in the past five years with somebody who has heard me on radio is:

"'I remember you from TV. You're Dan Schorr, aren't you? I'd know your voice anywhere. Listen . . . what you said about Russia last Saturday was very interesting, but I'm not sure that I agree with you.'"

Dan smiles. "Radio listeners go *immediately* to the substance. People who see you on television almost immediately go to appearance. And you're not even sure that they heard what you said. They're impressed with the fact that your identity is established by the fact that you are on television. That means that you are very important. It doesn't *matter* what you say. And it really is *astonishing* the way in which I'll get remarks about 'I liked your tie' or 'Listen, you've got to get a different barber.' I'm not exaggerating. Whereas with the radio audience, it really is very flattering. People who hear you on the radio take you seriously." Dan's voice drops to a half whisper. "They *take what you say seriously*. You get a little mail — not a whole lot of mail, but some mail. And it is agree, disagree . . . but *whatever* it is, boy! they were *glued* to that set and they *heard* it.

"I think what it all means is that unlike television, where people are part of your *audience*, with radio, people are part of your *community*."

Scott Simon's odyssey to and from NBC TV collapsed into a single year Dan Schorr's lifelong circuit from radio, through television, back to radio. These days when Dan meets former colleagues from CBS News, he is invariably told that he left the network "just in time" — that morale is low, that standards are dropping, and that it's all too depressing to talk about. But for the younger generation of reporters at NPR, the lure of television is often irresistible. It is the medium, after all, that many grew up with; it is the dominant disseminator of mass culture; its financial resources — though diminishing — are awe-inspiring when contrasted with the budgetary constraints of public radio.

For Scott, however, the attractions of TV were far outweighed by its disadvantages and by the inherent strengths of radio — or at least radio as it is practiced at NPR. Before formally announcing his departure from NBC, Scott speaks about his perspectives on radio and television while sitting in the large yet pleasantly cluttered living room of a surprisingly upscale condominium apartment he has recently bought in Washington (partly on the strength of his TV earnings): "I've always been uncomfortable with people who talk about radio as a medium, as if there's something generalizable about it, everywhere and for all times. I mean, most of the radio done today is quite unendurable. I don't spend a lot of time listening to the radio, except for the local NPR station, wherever I happen to be. I mean, I'm not trying to be a snob about it, but most radio is done with ads in mind, not an audience. The strengths of radio don't just happen automatically whenever you turn on a radio dial or get behind a microphone. You have to consciously make *use* of those strengths.

"I do think that the way NPR in particular uses radio, you will find a quality of engagement with the mind, an extra depth, a level of dimension in there that you do not have in television. I speak from some experience at this point. Forgive me, but with some exceptions, I think that even the *best* television will *not* have that level of commitment that the best radio can have. The best television that Edward R. Murrow did, something like *Harvest of Shame*, still doesn't have the same level of *commitment* in terms of *reaching out* to an audience that something like his radio dispatches did when he was with the troops in Buchenwald and he talked about survivors clapping . . . he said the sound was like 'the hand clapping of babies' because they were so weak.

"I think radio combines the immediacy that broadcasting can offer — the sensation of actually being there — with a level of depth and perspective that print can offer . . . the interiorization of the mind. It's a storyteller's medium. It's a way of opening people up to hearing something — and it brings something *inside*, I think, much more deeply than other media can.

"It's almost as if seeing something on the *surface* of the television screen *keeps* it on the surface at some level. Which doesn't mean it's not possible to occasionally penetrate below. But, that being said, one thing I've noticed is that people who work in television tend to think that everybody in the audience absorbs *everything* that they can see on the screen. Hold up a camera in front of the explosion at Waco, Texas, and the audience takes it all in. Now in radio, we would point out what could be seen burning, we would describe details for the mind's eye — and so focus the listener's attention. In television, they believe in this nonsense that a picture's worth a thousand words. And it's not. Not even close."

Scott feels the "surface" metaphor percolating through many aspects of TV journalism. "All through television, from sitcoms to news programs," Scott explains, "the emphasis is on the conclusion . . . coming to some kind of resolution. I mean, particularly the plethora of television newsmagazines that they have now: they're always looking for the switch that will throw an issue to one side or another. They're not comfortable living with ambivalence. Whereas, I think, interestingly enough, that's where radio can really shine. You can present the ambivalences we all live with. I mean, 'ambivalence' isn't just a matter of 'on the one hand this, on the other hand that.' I'm talking about something far more complex than that. Life is filled with ambivalence — life is filled with reservations, which sometimes make us very uncomfortable. And I think radio's just a much subtler medium that allows us to explore those ambivalences . . . without necessarily trying to resolve them. Television seems to want to simplify, to come up with answers. Before the next commercial break."

During his time at NBC, Scott has found the surface quality of the medium further exaggerated by many behind-the-scenes practices and procedures. He's been shocked to find that focus groups are used, in part, to determine what stories news programs cover. A report might not be aired on Haiti, for example, because a number of viewers (representing the target audience for a particular news program) told researchers that they weren't interested in the story. Scott equates this kind of thinking with the attitude that might prompt a producer to air a shocking, sensational story. "By making these decisions — constantly thinking about your audience — you may get people to tune in to your program," says Scott, "but you won't necessarily get them to *believe* you. Lots of people watch late-night wrestling. They enjoy it, but they know it's fraudulent. I think one of the reasons why the press is such an unpopular institution in this country is that we can get people to tune us in, but if they don't trust us, then what have we accomplished?"

The financial disparity between NPR salaries and those that even local television stations can offer have meant that, over the years, far more reporters have moved from public radio to commercial television than the other way around. Along with Daniel Schorr (and now Scott Simon), the only major television network news correspondent to move from in front of the camera to behind the microphone is Harvard-educated Russian scholar Anne Garrels, who worked in TV for a decade — a good portion of that time at ABC News — before coming to NPR in 1988. She took a sizable cut in her paycheck when she made the switch — but she has never been happier, or felt more fulfilled, in her work.

"This isn't like any other kind of radio you've ever heard on the air," Anne (whom everyone calls "Annie") explains, while sitting in her small cubicle of an office. She leans back in her chair, her long legs stretched out and propped up by the edge of a bookcase. "And if you haven't heard it, you can't even imagine what it is *until* you've heard it. And for many years, *I'd* never listened to NPR. I grew up overseas, then I lived in New York, and after college and whatnot, I finally started to work for ABC in New York — this was in the seventies. Then I was sent abroad again, and it was only when I finally came back in the early eighties that I began to listen to NPR. My now husband said to me, 'I'm sorry, I don't know who you are, because I don't watch television.' And so, I said, 'Well, if you don't watch television, what do you listen to?' He said, 'I listen to public radio.' And so I started listening. And then, very quickly, I said I really don't want to work for ABC — I'd *really* rather do this . . . but I didn't know how to make the change."

Within a few years, though, after a tour in El Salvador, Annie's frustration with television — and the appeal of NPR — finally pushed her to switch. "I realized that the values in TV news were not my values," she says. The problems Annie encountered are part of a familiar litany, experienced by more and more network correspondents: a shrinking amount of airtime devoted to foreign news, increasing difficulty in getting stories on the air, and a sharpening of the show-biz orientation of television — which in Annie's case prompted occasional critiques of how she "looked" on the air (a curious fact because in person Annie is an attractive woman, with short brown hair and widely spaced hazel eyes).

"I had grown up being taught that the work you did was more important than how you looked," says Annie. "And here I was working in an environment in which producers and executives were obsessed with 'appearance.' Never mind how good my stories were. It was all messed up."

Annie also became increasingly troubled by the kinds of stories she was allowed to do and the brevity that was enforced. "I was horrified at the idea of writing these short, pithy news pieces for the rest of my life. A minute and a half of copy: that was the standard length for an evening news piece. Frankly, I don't see how people understand what they're hearing half the time, the stories are so short. I might have tried to get on one of the magazine programs. And, indeed, some good pieces are done on there. But often it's got to be the truck that kills, the disease that kills . . . the programs are fairly formulaic.

"But the main thing was I felt that my mind was beginning to shut down in a way. You knew you only had a minute and a half of copy to write, and God forbid you should want to include more information than would fit into that space of time. So I began to not pay attention to certain things because it was more than I needed to know — a *lot* more than I needed to know. And it was just going to clutter up the works."

Once Annie came to NPR, everything changed. "There's no question, it's a magical place to be. You have incredible freedom. You have the time to *explain* the world — you don't have to oversimplify and only write about extremes. You can tell wonderful stories, you can use wonderful sound, you can be funny, you can be satirical — you have far more latitude in the tone in which you tell stories than you were allowed at the commercial networks.

"You can change your voice — you don't always have to be the same person. You're allowed to be frivolous one day and serious the next. I don't always take advantage of these possibilities, but they are there when I want them. And I think of the fun of it — my God! — all these opportunities that I can play with." Annie's eyes sparkle and bracelets on her wrists jingle as she gestures enthusiastically. "I write about foreign policy, I write about Russians — I can even write about their confusion — the morass of the Russian soul. And I can play around with how to do this. Once I took a tape recorder into the baths in Moscow. You could never have taken cameras into a Russian bath without telling everybody to go quickly wrap themselves up in towels.

"I feel incredibly lucky. It's a joy to do the kind of work I do now. You know, when you're on television, people feel like they know every part of you. Diane Sawyer is a package — because you know what she looks like, you know whether she got her hair cut lately. And that's limiting in a way. But now, on the radio, who am *I* to people? They don't know what I look like, they don't know how old I am. And I think it allows there to be much more of a *communion*. You're just doing it with your voice and with the other sound that you have. So it's much more demanding: you have to hug people with much less."

Annie lowers her legs and leans forward, waving her hands slightly for emphasis. "I'm not sure I'm explaining myself very well. People always say to me, 'Don't you miss the pictures of television?' I have to say, no, most of the time I don't. I find it much more innovative to use a tape recorder. I found pictures far more restricting for most things.

Most of the time you are fighting to get the pictures and they dictate the way the story goes. I think you can tell a better story on radio. "*I* paint the pictures now."

Even as Daniel Schorr, Scott Simon, and Annie Garrels eloquently describe their reasons for leaving television, a steady flow of NPR reporters keeps heading toward the visual medium. The more senior correspondents, such as Nina Totenberg and Cokie Roberts, strike deals that allow them to keep more or less of a presence on public radio. Cokie appears once a week with Bob Edwards on *Morning Edition*. Nina has slowly added more TV work to her schedule, beginning as a "pundit" on a Sunday program, doing some work on public television, and most recently becoming a part-time special correspondent for ABC News. ABC, in fact, is the most assiduous wooer of NPR talent, in part because many producers and correspondents there, including anchors Ted Koppel and Peter Jennings, are tremendous fans of National Public Radio.

When younger NPR reporters decide to do TV work, they tend to leave radio altogether. Deborah Wong was courted by ABC News after her standout reporting from the Gulf War and from Somalia. She was offered what seemed like the plum post of Beijing correspondent. Everyone at NPR was upset when Deb left. One experienced foreign editor shook his head and echoed the general sentiment that Deb did not know what she was getting herself in for. The danger was great that she would "disappear" into the belly of a commercial television news organization and rarely be heard from again. (This disappearing act has happened more often than not to ex-NPR people, including once major voices on public radio like Jackie Judd, David Ensore, and Robert Krulwich. In recent years, Jackie has begun to be used more often on *Nightline*, but the fact remains that competition is keen for airtime on the commercial networks and the amount of time available to correspondents continues to shrink.)

For her part, Deb simply could not resist the lure of a new opportunity, even though she approached the job with some trepidation. "It was not a conscious decision," she explains shortly after her departure from NPR but before her move to China. "It just sort of happened. I've been in public broadcasting all my professional life, and so for all the obvious reasons I'm a little bit worried about this move. I do still feel tremendously guilty about leaving NPR because they gave me a shot to do reporting from abroad, which I never had before."

On the other hand, like many newer NPR staffers, Deb views herself as a *reporter* first and a *radio* person second. "I think I'm a good reporter," she says, "and I worked well at NPR because I think and write like an NPR reporter. But in my perception, there is a division between people who really developed as radio producers, like Peter Breslow and Deborah Amos, and people who are just reporters. I love NPR, but I'm not sure I love it because it's radio. I think I would love NPR if it was television, if it was possible to translate what NPR does into a visual medium."

Though Deborah Wong did not consciously approach NPR as a stepping-stone to television, Scott Simon expresses the worry that the very notoriety NPR is now receiving — and its current hiring practices — may lead to that kind of syndrome for the network. "I think inevitably with NPR's success, we're going to get people who really want to be in television," Scott says, "who want to be stars that way. And they're going to see NPR as a place where they can learn a lot — which they certainly can — and then make the leap. I think we have to worry about that."

Reporting with Your Ears

Though the flickering images of television will continue to lure some talent away from National Public Radio, many reporters and producers who remain in the sound medium continue to invoke the magic and the poetry of radio as a central reward that keeps them wedded to their microphones and their mixing consoles.

"I think radio is like a Picasso sketch," says reporter Ted Clark. "You know those line sketches that Picasso would do that just suggest a figure and allow the viewer to fill in the rest. And it takes just very little sound on the radio to do that. The sound of the wind blowing through the trees can be evocative enough. So I think radio journalism is more vivid than print journalism for that reason. And it's more fun to listen to than television is to watch because you're part of the creative process."

Producer Margaret Low Smith broke into radio under Jay Kernis at *Morning Edition* and then moved over to *All Things Considered*, where, like Art Silverman, she produces special host features. She's also in charge of *ATC*'s commentaries. (Margaret's husband is Greg Smith; they met while both were on the *Morning Edition* team.)

"This medium requires you to go out and see the world and encapsulate it into a sort of pearl essence of voices and sounds," Margaret says, her face lighting up with a gentle smile. "There probably isn't a word for what you need — a combination of both an eye and an ear for what is interesting, for what draws people into a story. When you go out to produce a piece with a reporter, you have this intense experience, but then when you're thinking about it afterwards and start planning the scenes, the tape you are going to use, the experience is even more intensified. You have to encapsulate all your experiences into a few minutes of sound and give it what I call a cinematic quality. I believe in the cinematic quality of radio, whether it's news, feature, or whatever.

"There is something very transporting about sound, especially subtle sound. That's something I've developed over the years. I'm much more responsive to the smaller sounds now than I used to be. I think it draws out the imagination of listeners more."

"I'm a storyteller," says Neal Conan. "I get to tell stories on the radio. And whether I'll introduce you to this fascinating person, and here's the story of his life, or something really important happened in the Persian Gulf today, and here's what it was — it's still, essentially, 'Gather round and I'll tell you a story.'

"I've always liked Peter Jay's line that on radio we have 'a mission to explain.'"

Neal has been in radio since 1966, when he was sixteen years old. He started as a volunteer engineer at WBAI, Pacifica Radio's station in New York, even before NPR was created. After dropping out of college, he eventually dropped into freelance work for NPR and then was hired as producer of *Weekend ATC*. His hosts were Noah Adams and Jackie Judd, his director was Deborah Amos. Since then Neal has moved through countless positions, from production to management, from hosting to reporting. Through it all, he has retained his boyish yet articulate enthusiasm for the medium in which he works.

"We should never forget that every report we do on the air is a narrative," Neal says, his blue eyes flashing above his bright red beard. "They're not abstract essays. They need to have a beginning, a middle, and an end. Your writing is all-important — good writing can transform bad tape into a good piece, and it can take good tape and really make it *sing*. But it's your use of *sound* that makes your story special, that . . . well, makes it *radio*.

"You should be constantly aware of the sound environment when you are reporting for radio," Neal explains. "I remember working in London with a friend who is now on *The New York Times*. He was consistently fascinated by the stuff that I would go do, that he, as a newspaper reporter, would *never* do. I remember we were both preparing stories about the coal strike. It was around Christmastime, and I stopped off at a department store to get the sound of the Santa exhibit — or Father Christmas, as they would have said. And my friend said that would just never have occurred to him.

"But sound gathering is second nature for me — I really don't think about it. Though I guess I can imagine how it must look to someone who doesn't know what the heck you are doing. 'Why is this person doing a Statue of Liberty imitation?' There's that picture of me up on the wall behind my desk — I'm holding a microphone up in the air in front of a burning cross. Well, of course, I'm miking the fire. I was trying to get the crackle, crackle, crackle of the burning cross. [This was at a Ku Klux Klan rally in Connecticut that Neal was covering — one of his more famous assignments.] You know, you can look pretty silly sometimes.

"But I *never* take a camera on a gig, not even just to take snapshots. Because if I'm thinking about pictures — *any* kind of pictures — I'm not thinking about sound. People have said, 'Gee, you've missed a lot of great pictures — in Europe, in the Gulf.' Yeah, but I don't think I missed any of the sound."

Sound-gathering can not only look silly or incomprehensible in a world where people think more about *seeing* than about *listening*, sometimes it can look downright suspicious. Sylvia Poggioli, NPR's Rome-based correspondent, once found herself covering a G-7 economic summit conference in Venice when Ronald Reagan was president. Sylvia came to NPR through print and is not an especially sound-oriented reporter. But after she filed a report on the conference, her editors in New York asked her to collect some sounds that they could add to her piece to give more of a sense that she was in Venice. "The sounds had nothing to do with what I was talking about in the report," Sylvia recalls during a brief visit to the U.S. to receive a Polk Award for her reports from the former Yugoslavia. "I think the piece was about China having sold Silkworm missiles to Iraq or Iran. But we were using a high-quality line back to the States, and people here at the shows wanted more of a *feel* that I was actually in Venice, and not in some anonymous studio somewhere.

"Well, the summit was taking place on this small island called San Giorgio, and the security was incredible — I mean Jim Angle and I actually did a funny story about that.[1] 'Can you imagine secret service agents in gondolas?' — something along those lines. Anyway, there was tremendous, tremendous security on this island every time we came — dogs sniffing, metal detectors, all our bags opened up. So, anyway, I noticed that there was a little jetty down by the water, and I thought I would get the sounds of the water lapping the island of San Giorgio. There was nobody around, so I walked to the jetty, sat down, and stuck my mike down close to the water.

"Within ten seconds I had seven secret police people of four nationalities surrounding me with their hands on their guns. They probably thought I was placing a bomb on this little pier.

"The top guy was an Italian, and I said to him, 'I know you're not going to believe this, but I work for this radio network in the States that kind of likes sounds.'" Sylvia laughs a deep laugh, consistent with her low voice, though quite inconsistent with her small, thin appearance. "I showed him all my credentials, I showed them it was just a mike — I played the tape for them. And they said, 'Well, that's just water lapping,' and I said, 'Yeah. It's just water lapping.' But of course it was *Venetian* water lapping, right?

"Well, he thought it was sort of funny and weird and let me go about my business. Except that he never let me live it down. Every time he saw me come by he would say, 'Ah! Here comes the weird American who likes to tape sounds!'"

Many NPR reporters have stories about some of their favorite sound pieces. Scott Simon frames his discussion in the wider context of how sound works on the radio. "Sound is very important in helping to bring the audience along with you into your story," Scott explains. "As a reporter, you need to offer people some of the same set of sensations that made you think and respond the way you did when you were in a particular place at a particular time, and sound is a major part of those

---

[1] Jim Angle is a former NPR newscaster and White House reporter who first moved to American Public Radio's *Marketplace* program, and then jumped to ABC News as economics correspondent.

sensations. What you hope is that the sounds you use can help listeners procreate in their mind at least a little bit of what you saw and felt — and at the least that the sounds make everything a lot more vivid than otherwise.

"I remember writing something on the Gulf, in fact, it's probably one of the lines that gets quoted back to me the most. I was with some paratroopers from the Eighty-second Airborne, and the soldiers were all *incredibly* young. So what do I see when I stumble out of my bunker one Saturday morning? The soldiers are all sitting on sandbags eating *Froot Loops*. And they're laughing in a kind of disconnected way, the way young men their age do. And, I mean — what an image! It reminded me all over again of how *young* these soldiers were: here they were fortifying their bodies twelve different ways to kill people.

"So I had the line in my script describing them eating Froot Loops, and I had the sound of their laughter, which underscored their youth and cued me, stimulated my own memory of the scene . . . and then, hopefully, my audience would also be stimulated to enter into the scene. Even though that particular sound wasn't especially distinguished, the laughter was part of an overall scene that was indelibly etched in my mind, and so I used it to try to communicate a little bit of something I saw and what I reacted to."

Reporter Tom Gjelten painted vivid aural scenes from the war in the former Yugoslavia for a number of years before taking a nine-month sabbatical from NPR in the middle of 1993 to write a book about a newspaper in Sarajevo. Tom's use of sound had been exemplary, especially because he so often fed his stories over telephone lines and rarely had the full-fidelity sound that radio documentaries employ. A very tall, large-boned man in his late forties with broad Nordic features and dark blond hair ("Gjelten" is a Norwegian name), Tom discusses his style of radio reporting during a brief visit to Washington when he, too, receives a broadcasting award. "One thing that I've learned being overseas is that you approach using sound completely differently. I listen to pieces over here, and I hear a lot of ambiance sound. But when you send pieces over phone lines, ambiance sound often just adds static or noise. So you have to look for very particular sounds that are on the one hand evocative and really add something to the piece and give a sort of visual sense of what's going on . . . but on the other hand, sounds that are so precise and identifiable that they can come over a phone line and not lose their meaning."

In one of Tom's most famous reports, he profiled how life had deteriorated for a middle-class family in Sarajevo during the long siege of the city. The father had been a professional man before the war and had seldom worked with his hands. Tom described the depravation in which the family now lived — they had burned a lot of their furniture to stay warm, for example. And as Tom spoke his narration (which was interspersed with poignant words from members of the family), in the background, like a faint, yet distinct ostinato, came the slow, repetitive sound of someone chopping wood.

Toward the end of the piece, Tom took his microphone out into the courtyard and described that, all this time, the father had been working to chop down some trees that he had planted a few years ago, before the war had started. The man had never wielded an axe before and his labor was hard and painful.

The chopping noises flowed through Tom's piece with great power and meaning. On the simplest level, they helped build an image of an educated, middle-class man, with soft hands, using all his strength to save his family. On a more symbolic level, the sound gave voice to the steady destruction of a way of life; it suggested an aural motif of fate, grimly cutting through the lives of people in Sarajevo.

While Tom believes that television pictures can have a certain dramatic impact with which radio cannot compete, TV reporters have been at a disadvantage in covering the war in Bosnia because of their difficulty in getting pictures. "The great thing about radio," Tom explains, "is that you are far more mobile and can get around. At the various checkpoints they usually are looking for cameras, which, of course, I don't have.

"And I like to think," Tom continues, "that I have a closer, more direct, and more personal relationship with my listeners than the TV reporter has with his viewers or a print reporter has with his readers. I just think it's the nature of radio — and NPR in particular. I was with somebody recently coming back on the plane, and she was saying how NPR sounds kind of like a family. I mean, if I feel a personal relationship with my listeners, you can just imagine how much more of a relationship someone like Noah Adams has — who's been on the air so much longer and has been hosting a show and so forth. But the audience also knows me, so when they hear Noah interviewing me, let's say, or Noah interviewing Sylvia [Poggioli] or Deborah [Amos] or when Bob Edwards talks to Cokie Roberts . . . you do sort of have the sense of this being a family. You can hear the familiarity and the affection —

the good feelings between us. I think that comes through on the air in a much greater way than on television. People can hear that. So it's not just an intimacy between the listener and the individual NPR person. It's sort of a feeling that you are connecting with a family."

Having lived abroad for several years, Tom Gjelten has not viewed much American television lately. It's interesting to consider how many TV news programs these days are trying *to look* like happy families . . . from the living room interiors of the morning shows, to the congenial bonhomie that's drifted up from local news programs to the network anchor desks themselves (epitomized most dramatically when Dan Rather *held Connie Chung's hand* at the conclusion of their first joint appearance as anchors on the *CBS Evening News* in 1993). The "family values" displayed on TV shows represent a different order of experience from those inner connections that the medium of radio weaves between practitioners and audience — and, in certain circumstances, among the practitioners themselves. But then, throughout history, aural communication has woven people together, into families, extended families, communities, nations. From stories of clan mythology told round camp fires, to the poetry of Homer sung in royal courtyards, to the lays of traveling minstrels performed in medieval villages, to the dramas of Shakespeare staged in Elizabethan (and contemporary) theaters — voices have often been used to bring people together in common understandings, common identities. Modern radio technology has added taped sounds and voices to the basic narrative tools of aural evocation. But the subtle web of *story*, which can build special and profound relationships among people, remains always a potential, buried in the heart of creative radio.

For all Tom Gjelten's instinctive sensitivity to the art of radio, when it comes to the internal NPR debate between newshounds and sound producers, Tom allies himself firmly with those who wish to make NPR into a primary source of news for listeners. "I should say in the first place that I wholeheartedly support that transition," Tom says. "I think that our self-image should be that of a serious professional news organization, that we should provide everything that the listener needs so that he doesn't have to read *The New York Times* to get the whole picture. On the other hand, I think that I have the kind of radio values that are in many ways associated with the old NPR. And I *have* seen a decline in the production quality of NPR over the years, particularly as someone overseas who sends my pieces in to be produced. I'm sure people would be offended if they heard this, but I just have to say it: in the old days there were show producers who were real radio artists. And maybe it's just inevitable that that loss of production refinement takes place. But it's regrettable."

Tom agrees that some of the changes he perceives at NPR are a function of more people being hired who have no background in radio. "But that, too, is a trend that I support," he explains, "because unfortunately there isn't a real serious journalism background in the radio world, either at the level of local public radio stations, unfortunately, or commercial radio. And so if you have as your top priority journalistic integrity and then try and balance that against radio experience, the pool that you have is going to be so small that I think there has been a decision that it's easier to teach radio production to a good journalist than it is to teach journalism to some radio producer. And I think that's true.

"I think that the skills of radio production are fairly simple skills. They can be acquired. I mean it's a craft. And that's something you learn on the job, with a guiding hand, with somebody who really knows how to do it. It's more mechanical, it's a craft. Journalism is something that requires a lot more judgment, experience. The lessons that go into making a really good dependable journalist are just more profound than those that go into teaching radio.

"Now I think probably that some people who care more about aesthetic value would probably disagree with me, but I think in the end if there is to be a mistake made on NPR's air, I would rather that the mistake be made on sound not used perfectly as opposed to the journalistic. I mean I would vastly prefer that we consciously hire for both people. Hire radio artists, and hire journalists, and then try to get them to work together as much as possible. But if we must choose, I think nowadays we must choose the experienced journalist over the radio artist."

Tom explains that he has not always seen the issue in this way. In the past, he was much less concerned about being first with the breaking story. "But now I really get annoyed when we're *always* late on stories," Tom says, a note of frustration entering his voice. "Listener interest in a story is at its peak at the *beginning* of the story. And I think that we should try as much as we can to meet that interest. I remember, for example, when there was a coup in the Philippines. It happened early one Saturday morning, and I was going to be sent in. But NPR couldn't decide until *Monday* to send me in because they didn't have the bureaucracy around over the weekend. By the time we got there we'd missed a good portion of the story. NPR is much better now than it used to be, but it still is not able to move as quickly as it should. You sort of have to sit and *think* about it a little bit. And as a result we have generally been too late with stories."

Tom Gjelten's perspective on news coverage reveals that not all the pressures encouraging NPR to focus on hard news come from outside the organization, nor are they exclusively the result of newly hired newspaper and magazine journalists on the staff. Tom began working for NPR in 1980 and quickly fell in love with radio, especially with its potential to bring the stories of hitherto unheard voices to a wider audience. (His first pieces were from coal-mining towns in Appalachia.) Before that, he had been a freelance writer on education, with a particular interest in rural communities. He had majored in anthropology at the University of Minnesota.

He went abroad for NPR for the first time in 1986, and has worked a great deal as a foreign correspondent ever since. It would appear that as Tom started to cover more important, breaking news stories, his impatience grew with those very qualities of quirky, nonmainstream radio production which, at one point, he had found intriguing and appealing.

But can it be at all surprising that someone who has literally been on the front line of a war in the former Yugoslavia, who is perhaps more responsible than any other single American journalist for bringing the horrors of that conflict vividly to life for American audiences . . . is it surprising that such a reporter should become dissatisfied with NPR's older, slower ways of getting stories on the air?

It's understandable that the fires of reportorial ambition should drive such a committed, articulate, and intelligent journalist as Tom Gjelten. But it may be harder to explain why someone as clearly touched with an instinctive appreciation for the art of radio should so readily diminish the importance of that art, or the significance of his own gifts, by referring to the medium as a "craft," whose skills "are fairly simple" to teach and to learn. Why also would Tom refer to the sound production in his work as "aesthetics," implying in his tone of voice that these aesthetics are less important in the final analysis than the journalism, the story, the hard facts that NPR must be sure it gets onto the air? Why this division between two elements that seem equally vital to the radio medium — the *story* and the *sound?* Why should either be privileged over the other?

Yet Tom's perspectives are common at NPR. Many reporters and editors there use even stronger language when talking about "hard news" versus "pretty radio," "straight-ahead journalism" versus "self-indulgent fluff." And it must be said that even someone who practices, so brilliantly and unequivocally, some of the older traditions of NPR production, Bob Malesky, winces at the phrase "radio art" and, like Tom Gjelten, prefers to think of what he does as a craft. "I know a lot of independent producers who take strong objection to this point of view," says Bob. "But I do not think of myself as a radio artist. I just can't look at my work that way. I exercise as fine *craftsmanship* as I can in what I do. But I do not think of myself as an artist — though, as I say, I know a lot of people who get quite offended when I say that."

Be it art or craft, the role and importance of *sound* to the kind of journalism that NPR broadcasts remains a hot and unresolved topic of discussion and debate among everyone who works in the medium. That such a question should continue to prompt controversy more than twenty years after the creation of public radio begins to suggest the extent to which NPR is fighting against many of the most powerful trends in contemporary culture . . . trends that value reflexiveness over reflection, speed over care, disengagement over involvement, pictures over words. People who work at NPR know that they offer the public an alternative to commercial broadcast news options. But in the struggles to define what that alternative is to *sound* like, definitions, language, and strategies are used that often divide those who need to work together if they are to stand up to the cultural juggernaut that is assaulting every other form of American mass communications.

Broadcasting on the Edge

Neal Conan has had a lot of demanding yet rewarding jobs at NPR. He organized coverage of the Gulf War in 1989. He produced *All Things Considered* during one of its Golden Ages, right before *Morning Edition* was created — when NPR was being carried forward on a wave of Frank Mankiewicz' visionary energy and almost all its news resources were focused on the afternoon program. Yet for all Neal's wide range of experience in public radio, he still gets the most enjoyment, the biggest kick, out of one of the most straightforward forms of radio: the live broadcast.

"I *love* doing stuff live," Neal says, brushing his red hair away from his eyes in a characteristic gesture. "I just love it. I like pushing the envelope, I like being on the edge.

"I think broadcasting something live — being host of a show or of a special event — is inherently better than doing something on tape. It's more interesting. Mostly because *I'm* more interested, I think. 'Cause I'm up there, you know. If you're taping it, you know that there's a safety net. If you're live, everything's hanging out — just *do* it. It puts enormous strain on your wit, on any number of skills. And they're not production skills, they're not 'use of sound'-type skills. They are other kinds of skills: poise, experience, ability to come up with coherent phrases on the spot, ability to ad-lib . . . and to bring it out to time. All that stuff really makes me focus — it really makes me concentrate. And, like I say, it's adrenaline. I love adrenaline. If you're not nervous, if it's not scary in some respect, it's not fun. It gets boring.

"And I know the audience responds to the excitement and the interest in your voice, in your presence . . ." Neal pauses for a moment. He is speaking outside NPR on a warm day in May and glances briefly at the crowds walking by on the sidewalk before continuing. "Of course, it's not really *the audience*, you know. People listen to radio one person at a time. You're addressing a million people, *one* at a time. How do I listen to the radio? In the car . . . washing the dishes . . . alone. That's the way people use radio these days; it's not the family gathering around the wireless. It's not Jack Benny. So as a host, you don't address 'an audience.' You have a conversation with one person." A noisy truck passes by and Neal raises his voice momentarily. "My tone of voice — now, my inflections — other than when that garbage truck is going by — should be pretty much the same as they are on the radio. Obviously, I'm focused a lot more when I'm on radio. But it's a conversation. It's a conversation with a friend.

"I think that we were lucky at NPR that we were an FM network because it was much easier to develop that conversational style, that sense of intimacy, because the FM sound quality is so good. You know, the BBC World Service mikes people very differently from the way we do. The mike is placed two and a half feet away from the announcer. So that one *addresses* the microphone. We like the microphone right here" — Neal holds his hand three or four inches from his face — "so that you're talking very close. The BBC likes the acoustic space — the sound of the radio space — to be a room. The announcer is in *one* room, and the audience is listening in *another* room. We like it that we are right *inside* the loudspeaker of the radio the audience listens to: that's our space."

Neal has often imagined tinkering with the acoustic space from which NPR hosts broadcast. "When I was executive producer of *All Things Considered*," Neal explains, "I used to talk about wanting the hosts to sound distinctive. I imagined making subtle changes in Studio Five so that it would have a special sound — be ever so slightly different in tone, not just the same anonymous, blank background as every other radio studio. So that when a guest would 'join us now in the studio,' they would move into that distinctive sound environment. But it turns out that we don't have enough control over the technology — over the engineering aspects of it — to do that properly. I'd even like to see a studio that had an *open wall*. So that you might occasionally let natural sound come in. Though you'd have to design it carefully, because you don't want garbage trucks." Neal smiles, then continues:

"My point, though, is to work against the 'taped' quality that magazine shows can sometimes develop. I mean, you wouldn't avoid it completely — part of what makes NPR distinctive are the highly produced pieces of tape, which somehow *don't* sound like they're taped. Cindy does an amazing job of making *WESAT* sound live and spontaneous. But I think the more live radio we can do, the better for everyone — audience as well as hosts and reporters. And certainly, I'm hooked on the adrenaline rush of going live. As I'm sure you've heard, adrenaline is the most dangerous drug of all. Definitely the most addictive." And Neal grins broadly, his red beard sparkling in the clear spring sunlight.

One of the most experienced NPR reporters, who is equally at home going live or doing taped reports, is also, probably, the most famous (or infamous) correspondent for public radio, her notoriety extending even to people who never listen to the network. In twenty years of covering the Supreme Court, Nina Totenberg has carved out a unique niche for herself, both at NPR and in the wider community of Washington journalists.

Nina has one of the sharpest intellects — as well as one of the quickest wits — at NPR. She also possesses the necessary drive, ambition, and savvy that any reporter needs who is trying to become established on a beat in the highly competitive atmosphere of Washington. Though she had no formal legal training ("I'm pleased to say that even justices on the Supreme Court have been surprised when they found out that I didn't go to law school," Nina says with a bright laugh), Nina used her native intelligence and curiosity to build up, over the years, a thorough understanding about the law and the American legal system.[2] Nina explains, "In a way, the best part of not being a lawyer is that when I start writing a story about a court decision, I have to make it understandable to *me*. And I figure if *I* can understand it, then so can my listeners.

"Now it's true I've covered the stuff a long time, and I think by now I have a pretty good sophisticated knowledge of constitutional law, better than most practicing lawyers probably; but on the other hand, I was pretty good at it when I was very young, and that was because I was not afraid to ask questions. I would ask anybody anything. In fact, I was much less afraid of asking questions back then than I am now because for me to admit *now* that I don't know something is quite different than for me to have admitted that when I was starting out!" Nina laughs. "But I remember when I was a quite young reporter — this was in the early seventies — I was once going through the cases that were being reviewed, and one of them argued that women were covered by the Fourteenth Amendment. And I said to myself, 'Self, how can this be?' The Fourteenth Amendment was passed after the Civil War. It had to do with slavery. How come it covered women? So I looked up the name on the brief, and it was by a young law professor teaching at Rutgers whose name was Ruth Bader Ginsburg. I called her up, and she spent an hour on the phone explaining her reasoning to me. And she wasn't the only person to do that, many people did that. And many of them became my friends — I mean, I've met wonderful people that way. I met Judge John Minor Wisdom from New Orleans that way. I was reading some lower court opinion of his on some civil rights case and I didn't understand it, and I called him up and he explained it to me. I was about twenty-six years old. I was too young and stupid to know how outrageous that was!" Nina smiles broadly. "And many years later, Judge Minor Wisdom performed my wedding ceremony.

"It would be a lie to tell you it wasn't sometimes a help to be a young woman," Nina says, her broad, pleasant face growing more serious. "It was a great disadvantage in nine out of ten ways. I was always getting shuttled aside and not included in things, like the small

---

[2] Not only didn't Nina go to law school, she dropped out of college, like Neal Conan.

briefings that various people gave, because I wasn't important and I was female and I wasn't from *The New York Times* or *The Washington Post*. And I felt that very acutely. So I felt very strongly that I had to try to compensate for it and to meet as many people as I could and to ask as many questions as I could so I could get smarter and smarter about what I was doing. And, fortunately, I was reasonably tough. I mean, I don't *think* of myself as tough, but I guess I had to be, up to a point, to put up with all the nonsense as I was trying to establish myself."

At this point in her career, Nina knows personally most Supreme Court members and quite a number of other judges and members of the bar, and this not only adds a breadth of understanding to the reports she can make about the law, it also leads frequently to exclusive stories that Nina breaks before anyone else. No one keeps a scorecard on these matters, but it's apparent to everyone at NPR that the one reporter on staff who has consistently been able to scoop the major newspapers and the commercial TV networks is Nina Totenberg. She's done this by a lot of hard work and networking through her legal and political beats over the years.

"If there's a trick here it's to know people when they're not terribly, wildly, insanely important," Nina explains. "And to have them be your friends — and to keep in touch."

At first glance, much of what makes Nina a good inside-Washington reporter seems to be unconnected with her role as a *radio* reporter. All reporters in all media develop their special contacts and use these relationships as they pursue their stories. Yet Nina's connection with NPR made her distinctive and unusual among the correspondents covering the Supreme Court. Once her work crossed a minimum threshold of visibility, she would become (much like Sylvia Poggioli in the eyes of the Italian security police) the bright young woman who worked for the strange organization that devoted large chunks of time to oral storytelling about the Supreme Court. Also, her *voice* became famous around Washington. In radio's heyday, fifty years ago, this would have been a familiar occurrence, but during the seventies and eighties it was quirky and unusual to be known only by your voice. Nina tells the story of going up to a newly sworn-in Supreme Court justice, extending her hand and saying, "Hello, I'm . . ." and the justice saying, immediately, "Oh I know you, you're Nina Totenberg. I hear you on NPR all the time." (This was in the days before Nina had done enough television for her face to become recognizable.) While Nina likely would have become a topflight reporter in whatever medium she worked, radio may have helped her develop the peculiarly special position she enjoys today among the Washington press corps.

Nina had done no broadcasting before she joined NPR. She did come from a highly musical family, however. Her father, Roman, was a concert violinist and teacher, and she herself has a wonderful singing voice.

"I probably had an easier time learning to *write* for radio," Nina says. "It turned out that my writing always had a sort of radio style. Short sentences, very direct . . . I abandoned the pyramid style used in print very easily.

"Of course, the key to good radio writing is having a strong narrative. I may write a lead for the host that's general, but for me, by and large, there may be an overview paragraph, but it's always very factual at the top so that people have a particular idea of what the issues are in terms of *human beings* and *concrete situations.*"

In addition to her strong narrative sense and her inimitable voice, Nina's reporting is probably best known for her extensive use of quotations from lawyers' arguments or witnesses' testimony, excerpts from courtroom transcripts she must read herself since in most cases neither cameras nor tape recorders are allowed in courtrooms. "One thing I do that most people in radio don't is dialogue," Nina explains. "I cover this beat which most of the time doesn't produce any tape. If you cover an argument before the Supreme Court, you don't have tape except outside with the lawyers putting a spin on what happened inside. And I'll usually throw in a little piece of that just for cosmetic purposes as much as anything. But the *meat* of the story happens in the courtroom with no cameras and no tape recorders. And so to compensate for that — and because I have the luxury of a rather significant amount of time as opposed to a one-minute spot — I do my best to sort of *re-create* the discussion, the back-and-forth, in the court.

"I remember one day recently I did a very long voicer [a report in which there is no tape, just the reporter reading copy], like a five- or six-minute voicer, which most people can't do. I was working with a young producer, and I said to him, 'This is an *awful* long voicer,' and he said to me, 'That's all right, it's not really a voicer.'" Nina laughs. "And I know what he means. It isn't. *I'm* substituting for the characters involved — for the tape I don't have. I'm play-acting. Now it has to be well written. It has to be smooshed together and made very tight, and it's not quite as good as the real thing. Though, of course, sometimes it is better than the real thing." And Nina laughs again.

For all her star status in the Washington press corps these days —

and her increasing forays into television — Nina remains firmly committed to National Public Radio as her base of operations and as her first loyalty. She explains: "I've said 'no' to a number of jobs in TV that I didn't want to have for a variety of reasons. All you have to do is look at the way TV is now and you know that you're part of a big corporate entity. You don't own your own life. They may pay you rather well for a year or two and then just spit you out dead. Increasingly, I only want to do television if I can do it on my terms rather than on their terms. If I'm going to do something for television, I want to do something that has my stamp on it. And it's been clear to me for some time that most TV shows don't have an appetite for the kind of reporting which I want to do."

During Susan Stamberg's final years with *All Things Considered*, Nina became a frequent substitute host on the program. She has never wanted to be a permanent host of a magazine program, however. "It's not a reporter's job," she says. "Also, quite frankly, I have terrible eyesight, and reading is difficult. I can *extemporize* forever, but my reading is often less than perfect." Though Nina may have some qualms hosting scripted shows, she has no such reluctance these days about anchoring live events — in particular congressional hearings, a kind of broadcast that has played a key role in NPR's history. It was National Public Radio's live and continuous coverage of the Watergate hearings in 1973 that first drew significant attention to the young network. Ever since then, NPR has been quick to go to the Hill and broadcast sessions of any important committees.

So it was, early one morning in the spring of 1993, that Nina Totenberg traveled to the Dirksen Senate Office Building to attend the confirmation hearings of President Clinton's third nominee for attorney general, Janet Reno. The outcome of the meeting was a foregone conclusion. Still, the appointment represented one of the most important members of the cabinet, and, when confirmed, Reno would be the first woman ever to run the Justice Department.

Whenever NPR moves out of its studios to broadcast an event live, some of that adrenaline to which Neal Conan alluded energizes the entire experience. But more subtle forces are at work as well, which emanate from the aural magic of the medium of sound. The visual wizardry of live television — which has "taken us" to the moon, to wars abroad, and to catastrophes at home — may have desensitized us to some of the quieter miracles of live radio. But then, it can be argued that television has not stimulated our sense of wonder — enhanced our capacity to "witness" events — so much as it has inured us to the marvels and horrors at which we stare, so passively, on the surface of the cool and colorful tube. Be that as it may, close observation of what happens when National Public Radio's special events unit goes live reveals some mysteries that probe layers of the imagination never penetrated by the visual razzle-dazzle of television.

Nina and the Empty Space

Nina is wearing a salmon-colored suit today for the hearings. (In part because she spends so much time out of the office, Nina tends to dress well: she's usually turned out in nicely tailored suits and shoes with heels.) She walks briskly, with confidence and authority, through the gathering crowds of the hearing room. The hint of a smile plays around the corners of her mouth. Sometimes it dissolves into an ironic glance, more often it widens into a warm greeting for a friend or acquaintance. Her light brown hair, cut at medium length, frames a face whose large features and smallish eyes suggest both sweetness and a strong will. In fact, Nina mixes sophistication with street smarts, charm with tenaciousness. She throws herself with complete commitment into any work she does. Nina strides toward the witness table, where she sees a number of people she knows, and exchanges some amiable words with several others, whom she refers to as "handlers," who have been working with Janet Reno, preparing her for the committee's questions. A few moments later, Janet Reno herself enters the hearing room. Tall, broad-shouldered, and wearing a green dress, she's clearly visible above most heads in the crowd. A smattering of applause greets her, and then TV lights switch on as she follows the route Nina took through the crowd, though she takes a long time to make it down to the witness table. Nina does not wait around to attempt a chat with the attorney general designate. One of the handlers introduces the reporter to Reno's aunt and uncle. Nina learns that they have journeyed down to Washington from Bangor, Maine. Then she leaves the enlarging coterie of staff members and well-wishers and walks over to where her NPR colleagues have set up their gear for the remote broadcast.

The hearing room of the Senate Judiciary Committee forms a large and cavernous rectangle with suitably ponderous wooden paneling halfway up the walls — connoting (in terms of the Washington architectural idiom) seriousness of purpose if not exactly "dignity." The thick wooden horseshoe, behind which the senators place themselves, extends across one narrow end of the room. The witness table — covered with the *de rigueur* green baize cloth — faces the horseshoe, and behind that table stretch many rows of foldable chairs where sit members of the public, friends of the nominee, friends of the senators, and various members of the press who choose *not* to position themselves at the huge table set up for them beneath the curtained windows along the outside wall of the room.

Members of the broadcast media and photographers tend to cluster toward the horseshoe end of this table. NPR has four chairs reserved for it about a third of the way down, within close proximity to the various telephone and electronic connections that will send audio from the hearing room back to NPR headquarters and then up to the network's satellite.

A few TV cameras are installed at their appropriate spots around the room, but their limited range of vision and the flat, two-dimensionality of their pictures will give viewers at home very little true sense of the size of the audience or the sheer *volume* of the room. The cameras will, of course, supply close-ups of the principles involved in today's hearings — Janet Reno and whatever senator happens to be posing her questions. An occasional wide shot will show a small portion of Reno's entourage sitting behind her or reveal a few empty senatorial seats to one side or another of the current interlocutor. But neither the senators nor the audience (who actually sit *behind* Reno) will ever see the nominee in as close detail as the TV camera with the zoom lens; for her part, due to the muted white glare of television arc lights and the significant distances between tables, Reno will never see her senatorial questioners as sharply as will the audience at home.

Meanwhile, at any given moment, only a handful of senators may be sitting in their seats behind the horseshoe. The lawmakers come and go through their private entrance behind their table, following cues from a hidden script that seems entirely disconnected from the proceedings taking place in the chamber. The members of the audience stare from the relative darkness into the relative brightness of the horseshoe and can barely see the faces of the senators sitting low in their chairs.

All of which raises two apparently simple yet in fact rather subtle questions: *what* is really going on, and *where* is it happening? The most cynical answers are (1) that the hearing is being held "for the record" so that the Judiciary Committee will leave a written account of questions asked and answers given as Janet Reno's nomination made its way toward the Senate floor and (2) that it is taking place in a space designed to make good television pictures. For indeed, the pictures that C-SPAN will carry all day and the brief snippets of testimony that will appear on the network evening news shows tonight *will* convey clear images of a committee having met and a nominee having been asked questions. But by collapsing the rather large and amorphous "ritual space" defined by the various tables, the sizable audience, and the vast hall into a series of back-and-forth close-up shots (with an occasional medium-distance view for variety), television completely changes the physical event of the hearing into what might be considered a visual counterpart of the *Congressional Record.*

Yet it would be inaccurate to say television *distorts the reality* of the hearing simply because someone inside the hearing room has a totally different experience from that witnessed by a viewer at home. The most surreal quality of the Judiciary Committee meeting is *precisely* the ephemeral quality of the physical environment in which it takes place. The hearing room is not in fact the stage upon which a drama is enacted: 90 percent of the space defines an offstage area. The audience is sitting *behind the scenery,* amid the discarded props and dangling backstage ropes and pulleys. The various senators who are not asking questions are standing in the wings, close to the action but not participants in the drama until the TV cameras turn on them and they start speaking. Janet Reno appears to define center stage when she's answering a question and the red light of the TV camera facing her goes on. But, of course, in another sense she is not center stage at all, not in the old Shakespearean meaning of that term. Reno and the senators are participating in a TV drama . . . and this great hall of government, wherein deliberate the elected leaders of the republic, has been turned into nothing more nor less than a television studio.

While TV coverage of the Reno hearings doesn't distort the event, it must be said that Congress, television, and the public have yet to come to grips with what it means to turn the halls of government into sets for television shows. It can be argued that this lack of candor about TV's role — the blithe acceptance with which viewers look at reports of the Reno hearings, for example, and think they are eavesdropping on government in action instead of watching a made-for-TV soap opera — has been having a powerful and deleterious effect on politics in this country over the past twenty-five years.

Radio provides a somewhat different perspective on the curious spectacle in the hearing room of the Judiciary Committee. With no pictures to misrepresent anything about the physical setup of the hall, listeners will hear only the words exchanged, plus a bit of color and commentary added by Nina and her cohost for the morning, *Los Angeles Times* correspondent Ron Ostrow. Members of the audience will create their own pictures of the hearing, until they see images on television, which will change forever their internal imaginings. Of course, radio cannot, by itself, do anything to alter the impact that television has had on government, and of all stories broadcast on public radio, coverage of political events like congressional hearings come closest to reducing the proud medium of sound to a status of being "only television without pictures." (What else could radio possibly be if it starts broadcasting from within a TV studio?) How many listeners to congressional hearings on NPR rush to their television sets the first chance they get to *see* the faces of the people to whom they have been listening?

Yet having said all this, radio coverage of even so TV-minded an event as a congressional hearing continues to exercise a powerful, and even magical, effect on listeners — as an aural experience in itself, quite divorced from television. That effect is vividly demonstrated by considering what occurs "behind the microphones" when Nina Totenberg begins her live broadcast.

Nina reaches the NPR area of the press table at about nine-thirty. The broadcast will begin at ten o'clock, the scheduled starting time for the hearings. It's expected that Nina and her guest host, Ron, will have to do some extemporaneous talking for several minutes before Senator Joseph Biden gavels the proceedings to order. The technical director for the broadcast, Michael Cullen, has already been at work for an hour or so, setting up the remote mixer, arranging the microphones for Nina and Ron, making sure the official audio feed of the hearing is working properly, and checking the broadcast-quality telephone lines back to NPR. Producer John Ogulnik — an athletic young man with dark hair and a quick yet easygoing manner — has also been around for a while, and he's already begun scouting the crowd, looking for potential interviewees should there be an unexpected break in the proceedings. He's been in contact with the NPR offices, making all kinds of minor and major decisions about the upcoming broadcast. He has also synchronized his digital wristwatch to NPR's official Favag time.

The most remarkable feature of NPR's broadcast setup is its unremarkable appearance. The mixing board (in essence, the portable studio) looks almost like a toy or some simple piece of gadgetry you might pick up from Radio Shack. It's a small black box, eighteen inches long, twelve inches wide, and two inches thick, with various small plastic knobs and buttons on it. In reality, the Sonosax Remote Board costs thirteen thousand dollars and the quality of its sound and its mixing flexibility rivals the big studio consoles back at NPR. A few short cables lead from the Sonosax to three simple, directional microphones — no Neumann U-87s here — two for the hosts and one for any guest who happens by. The mikes are set into small adjustable table stands, about four inches tall. Two of the mikes are placed in front of opposing chairs. Nina takes the seat with her back to the window; Ron Ostrow sits across from her on the other side of the narrow table. A cheap, grungy-looking, one-piece telephone connects John Ogulnik with NPR headquarters. Three pairs of headphones will allow Nina, Ron, and Michael Cullen to hear what is going out over the air.

Amid the forest of video cameras, the arrays of lights, and the maze of thick cables draping the edges of the committee room . . . in the confusion of senatorial staffers, White House staffers, scores of reporters with notepads, cassette recorders, and still cameras — the small island of public radio, with its minimalist equipment, is easily overlooked. Indeed, in the general noise and hubbub Nina and Ron can just about hear each other as they chat casually about some of the things they might say during the upcoming broadcast. A few minutes before ten o'clock, they speak directly into their microphones so Michael can set levels. Then Nina stands up and tries to get a sense of what's going on in the room. But with everyone else standing, it's difficult to see anything but a lot of backs and anonymous heads.

"Two and a half minutes to air," says John. Then he stands on his tiptoes. He has more success at reconnoitering. A small crowd has gathered near a corner of the senators' table. "It looks like just [Senator Ted] Kennedy and [Senator Howard] Metzenbaum." But he decides to make his way forward and check out the situation.

Before John leaves, Michael asks: "We going to play the credits at the top of the hour?" Michael is referring to an NPR underwriting announcement that he's brought with him on cassette.

"Yeah," says John. "Plan to." If there is any sign that the committee will start up exactly on time, John will not waste thirty seconds with the funding credit but will go directly to Nina. But chances are good the committee will start late. John starts walking away. "If I'm not back in time . . ." he says over his shoulder.

"I know what to do," says Michael, evenly.

"We'll start without him," says Nina, in the same matter-of-fact tone. Then she turns around and starts joking with a reporter friend who has dropped by to say hello.

In less than two minutes, NPR's live broadcast will begin, yet the crew is treating the event with utmost calm. Only Ron Ostrow, the print journalist who has done several stints as guest commentator on NPR, shows the slightest bit of the nervousness one might normally expect in such circumstances.

John returns in less than a minute, walking unhurriedly, and confirms there's nothing happening up front.

"It's just 'nice-nice'?" asks Nina, and John nods. Then he looks at his watch. "We've got about a minute." John makes the formal decision to start with the credits, which means Nina will go live at thirty seconds after ten o'clock.

Ron has been listening to the sound of the committee room through his headphones, but the noises through the small earpieces suddenly stop. He looks up in surprise. Michael explains that he has killed all the sound feeds to NPR. "We do this a minute before broadcast," he explains. The dead air — the silence — alerts everyone that a broadcast is about to begin.

John has handed Nina his digital watch. "Can you read that okay?" he asks. "I don't have it, so I can't tell you how long to air."

"You want to cue me?" says Nina in her high, musical voice. "You cue me if it makes you feel good." She smiles broadly.

"Whatever," says John, and he reaches over to retrieve his watch.

"We're playing the credits, right?" says Michael, double-checking.

"Yeah, we're going to credits first," says John. "So . . . thirty seconds to credits. Fifteen . . . stand by."

During this countdown, Ron and Nina have fallen silent, while all around them the committee room has grown noisier. More people seem to be crowding into the audience seats. Nina has a yellow pad on the table in front of her and a pen beside it. The pad is blank. Ron has a smaller notebook in which he's been writing. He also leafs through some newspaper clippings. Nina idly watches the crowd milling around.

"Hit it," says John Ogulnik to Michael Cullen, clearly, calmly. The cassette with the funding credit starts playing, but though the words of the funder are audible to Michael, Ron, and Nina through their headphones, no one else in the committee room has any idea that NPR has gone on the air.

Nina looks down at her blank yellow pad as the credits play through. She will do her Open with no script and no notes. Her face is taking on a focused, preoccupied look. But otherwise she sits calmly in her salmon suit, her hands crossed in front of her on the table.

John speaks up for the last time before going live. "All right. We're about ten or fifteen seconds from you, Nina." The noisy babble of voices in the committee room continues to ebb and flow like surf against the shore: out of the incomprehensible wash, a few distinct words take shape . . . only to disappear into other sentence fragments, less clearly heard . . . and then these groups of voices jostle against each other for a while, until suddenly another wave of phrases, from an entirely different direction, rushes in and washes away understanding. The undulations of voices — intermixed with the punctuation of laughter — continues in its amorphous way, until a moment when, quite subtly and close at hand, some quiet yet distinct words rise out of the confusion, words that remain audible enough to become sentences and then paragraphs. One — then two — clear voices emerge from the background babble of the hearing room in the same way that sometimes, in the midst of a crowded dinner party, a particular conversation will catch your ear. You're not sure why the voices have become suddenly so distinct — they seem to be carried toward you on a random breath of wind. But you begin to focus — to pay attention — and within a short time you cannot hear anything else. Something has compelled you to eavesdrop on this conversation between strangers.

"From Washington, D.C., National Public Radio brings you live coverage of hearings before the Senate Judiciary Committee on the nomination of Janet Reno to be the next attorney general of the United States. Good morning. I'm Nina Totenberg, and with me for this broadcast is Ron Ostrow from the *Los Angeles Times*. Good morning, Ron."

"Good morning, Nina."

"Well, it's déjà vu all over again, as Yogi Berra said at one time. Just a few weeks ago, we were in this very hearing room in the Dirksen Senate Office Building listening to testimony from Zoë Baird, who, as we all know, within two days withdrew her nomination for attorney general."

Were it not for the key phrase "From Washington, D.C., National

Public Radio brings you . . ." it would be difficult to tell that Nina had suddenly gone on the air. Within the noise and confusion of the committee room, it's hard to hear any significant change in Nina's tone of voice, her inflection, or her vocal mannerisms since the last time she spoke, when she was exchanging words with John Ogulnik about who was to have the digital watch. Nina *seems* to be talking now the same way she did five minutes ago. Yet something has changed. Though she occasionally looks across the table at Ron, as she did before, and seems to address him — to the extent that he nods his head in response to what she says — in fact, a part of Nina is looking past Ron, beyond John and Michael, over the heads of the audience and the senators. She is speaking, now, on some gut level, to the faceless, unseen NPR audience, quite distant from this Washington committee room. And as she talks to this audience, her words begin to conjure up a startlingly new and different space within the hearing room itself. Nina's voice — and then Nina's and Ron's voices — define an aural environment separate from everything else around them; it is a protected place allowing for focused, good-humored conversation and discussion, along with evocative description. Nina and Ron begin the construction of this "arena of the mind" by speaking to one another across their microphones. The arena is completed in the separate imaginations of those people who are listening to the NPR broadcast, all across the country.

What do listeners *see* in their mind's eye when they hear Nina's voice and behind her the hubbub of the committee room? What pictures form before the chairman gavels the session to order and a series of images lifted from the television screen can obscure the magic of the aural incantation? Probably the images are not very distinct, though perhaps some listeners may picture a little studio overhanging the room, or a raised dais somewhere that resembles the radio broadcast booths in baseball parks. It's more than likely that whatever vague pictures come into the minds of listeners, the dominant *sensations* they feel involve weight, significance, and excitement. *Something of importance* is happening right now in the presence of Nina Totenberg. Listening to her broadcast means, to some measure or other, sharing a moment of history.

If you listen to Nina's voice on the radio anchoring a live congressional hearing, you will hear distinctly her aura of authority, the clarity of her thought, the power of her narrative abilities. She speaks with wit and humor, she sounds spontaneous and unrehearsed. She seems at once accessible and slightly imposing. She is believable, she is informative — she is enjoyable to listen to.

These same qualities are apparent if you listen to a *tape* made, not from over the air, but within the Judiciary Committee hearing room during the live broadcast. But curiously enough, if you happen to be sitting near but not *next* to Nina around the time NPR goes on the air with its coverage, you will hear something a little different. When overheard amid the noise and confusion and hoopla of the hearing room, Nina appears to be talking, rather matter-of-factly, with her colleague Ron Ostrow. Nina's voice commands attention in the way her articulate, good-humored conversation always does. But the magic and the authority apparent over the radio does not emanate very far outside the charmed circle created by the NPR production crew. You must listen very closely to what is going into NPR's microphones in order to begin to imagine the communicative power that is coming out on the other side.

But then, the stage on which radio works is always small-scale and intimate. The great British director Peter Brook once wrote, "I can take any empty space and turn it into a stage." The key to the transfiguration was ritual and imagination. The "space" occupied by this particular live radio broadcast is, in a sense, as small as the diaphragms inside the microphones that are capturing the words spoken by Nina and Ron. The microphones intensify the hosts' voices by extracting them from the other noises in the room and then transporting them on an incredible electronic journey — to NPR's M Street headquarters, then up to the satellite, then down to about a hundred local stations, and finally out into the radio sets and speakers of hundreds of thousands of listeners. The images that Nina's voice inspires in the minds of those who hear her bear little resemblance to the physical presence of the hearing room itself. Even if some in the radio audience rely in some way on television images they have seen, they will still not have an accurate image of the great cavern of a hall. Certainly few NPR listeners could possibly imagine the tiny Sonosax mixer, the simple microphones, the Walkman-style headphones that Ron is wearing. Yet the physical presence of the NPR remote unit is as irrelevant to the evocative power of the live broadcast as is the physical "reality" of one of Peter Brook's "empty spaces." The conjurer — the alchemist — is judged not by the tools used but by the extraordinary transformations created.

CLOSE

An NPR Family Portrait

Studio Five: Saturday Morning

Neal Conan sits behind the Neumann U-87 microphone and holds his
script in front of him with his left hand. He's wearing his headphones
over his New York Yankees baseball cap. The time is ten minutes after
eight. *Weekend Saturday* has been on the air since the top of the hour,
but Neal is now going live for the first time this morning. Two big
digital clocks are counting down on either side of the glass window
leading to the control room. Through the glass Neal can see the
director and the producer sitting on their high chairs.

With about ten seconds left on the clock before he reads a live
introduction to a Dan Schorr three-way, Neal suddenly bends over at
the waist, puts his face parallel to the floor, takes a deep breath, shakes
himself a little, then stretches himself out, emerging with a big smile.
Neal sometimes uses techniques like this to add wake-up vitality to his
voice. The speaker that's been carrying the sound of the broadcast cuts
out. The MIC light turns white, and Neal begins reading. In the
extraordinary deadness of the broadcast studio, his voice sounds very
loud. Neal is one of those hosts who projects his words with some gusto
into the microphone; yet by the time his voice reaches the home radio
speaker, he sounds considerably more laid-back.

The atmosphere within a studio that has just gone live is difficult to describe. The heavy soundproofing normally lends the space an eerie feeling of weight and density, even in as large a room as Studio Five. But when the studio's speaker cuts off and the white light goes on, it's almost as though you were sitting alone in a pressurized diving bell that has suddenly dropped full fathom five. You are sealed off and isolated physically from every other person, your only connection the electronic audio line that terminates in the microphone suspended in the air before you. Yet while you are so perfectly alone, you are also perfectly on view — like a glassed-in animal in a zoo. Your voice is about to be heard by a vast audience (in the case of *WESAT,* more than two million people). If you sneeze, if your teeth click, if you drop your pencil on the desk, if you swat a fly . . . if you, God forbid, burp or start hiccuping . . . you will seriously harm the continuity of the broadcast. More than that, you may make a fool of yourself.

There used to be times when radio personalities would broadcast from restaurants or from their homes — when they would speak to their listeners, that is to say, from within real-world, recognizable sound environments. For many reasons having to do with the shape and flow of the magazine format, NPR hosts most often speak to their listeners from within the completely artificial environment of a broadcast studio. Through experience and training they learn to forget or at least ignore the strange space in which they do so much of their work. But an observer of a live broadcast, who has not been acclimatized to the anaerobiclike chamber, may well feel that when Neal opens his mouth to speak, he is teetering on the edge of a precipice, a watery chasm whose bottom is yet another five or even fifty fathoms below.

With his black headphones squishing the top of his cap and his Irish blue eyes shining, Neal seems oblivious to the odd regions beyond space and time that he has just entered. His voice hits the walls of the studio like a wad of gum, but it travels smoothly, pleasantly, with a friendly, wake-up brightness, through the microphone and out toward the millions of listening ears. Neal wags his finger in the air as he reads over his copy — he's directing himself through some of his sentences. He has said that he loves live broadcasting because of the adrenaline rush it creates, and while there's no outward sign of nerves or jitteriness in the way he presents himself to the microphone, there does seem to be a certain *energy* moving through him. Or maybe it's just that his brilliant red beard, in the bright light of the studio, seems to quiver a bit as he speaks.

When Neal finishes reading his introduction, the digital clocks change their numbers, the white light goes out, and sounds again are heard through the studio speaker. The atmosphere within the sound-proof chamber returns to something approaching normalcy. Neal looks into the control room. He can see a lot of heads turning and mouths moving. As Rich Rarey is at the control board, Neal might assume there's considerable joking around and horseplay on the other side of the glass. But the host is completely cut off from what's happening and watches the pantomime for a moment as he might a silent movie.

Neal leans back in his chair, stretches himself slightly, clears his nose. He begins reading over upcoming scripts, holding a pen in his hand. Within the control room, the strangely silent play winds down as the program prepares to move to another segment.

At the conclusion of *WESAT*'s first hour — during which Neal has gone live a half-dozen times — the door to the studio swings open and in walks Daniel Schorr. He moves slowly, bending forward slightly from the waist, his shock of white hair combed upward and looking a bit disheveled. Dan carries his script in one hand, and with the other he taps Neal a couple of times on the shoulder as he walks by. He takes a seat at a microphone a few feet away. Dan is dressed for sports. He has on a turquoise tennis shirt, white shorts, and sneakers. Right after his live broadcast with Neal, he'll be heading out for a tennis game. Rich Rarey comes in and moves Dan's microphone a little closer to him.

During the newscast, Neal and Dan exchange a few pleasantries, but mostly they look over their respective scripts. When the MIC light next goes on and the digital clocks repeat their inevitable countdown, the isolated radio chamber no longer feels quite so oppressively lonely. There are two people sitting on the edge, reading and talking to each other. They represent two different generations of broadcasters. Dan began in radio when *all* news programs were done live, and here he is, forty years later, still facing that open microphone, still floating inside that strange anaerobic bubble. Dan seems totally relaxed — at home — reading his words in his familiar chopped-up diction. Neal eases up his delivery ever so slightly in Dan's presence. Though Dan reads most of his comments, he looks up at Neal after each section, and Neal smiles at Dan as he asks the next question, half scripted, half ad-libbed. Dan sits with his legs crossed, his headphones slightly off his right ear, looking every inch the curmudgeonly, deeply respected grandfather.

During the last forty-five seconds of the segment, Dan looks up at the clock frequently as he reads. He finishes a little early, which was part of his plan, and before Neal can sign off, Dan ad-libs a comment about how much he has enjoyed spending these past several weekends with Neal, who is about to yield the host's chair for a while. Dan's tone sounds affectionate and genuine as he refers to Neal's "sheer professionalism." Neal seems touched and surprised by Dan's remarks, but focuses his attention on closing out the segment on time.

When the MIC light goes off, Dan does not add much more to what he has already said on the air. He asks what Neal will be up to next. Neal mentions work on the foreign desk and then . . . who knows? Dan takes off his headphones, stands up slowly, pats Neal on the shoulder again, and goes off to his tennis game.

Some forty-five minutes later, *Weekend Saturday* is in its closing moments. About this time of day — nearing ten o'clock — the *Weekend Sunday* crew has arrived in its offices and is making its final push towards tomorrow's broadcast. Liane Hansen and Neal sustain one of NPR's longer-running marriages. Liane has brought their two children — son Connor and daughter Casey — to work with her so Neal can take them to a baseball game when he finishes broadcasting.

Casey — a round-faced girl of ten with long dark reddish hair — comes into the studio during the final story. She plays for a little bit in a corner of the room until Neal calls to her. She climbs into the chair right next to Neal and puts on a pair of headphones, like her father. She's wearing a blue T-shirt and glasses and she grins at Neal as he keeps an eye on the digital timers, counting down. Neal is holding the closing credits in his hand. He stretches his neck to loosen himself, and Casey laughs. Neal smiles at her and puts his finger to his nose. Then he turns back to watch the clocks. The white MIC light goes on for the last time. Casey joins Neal silently as the diving bell descends to the edge of the precipice. But she doesn't seem to feel anything strange in the atmosphere of the radio chamber. She has a large grin on her face as her father reads the final credits.

"This is NPR's *Weekend Edition* . . ."

Neal has a long script to get through, as the program ends with an unusual plug for next week's special show about Texas. He completes his reading and the white light goes off. Neal and Casey stare at each other for a moment, both wearing their black headphones. The digital clock reads 00:00:00.

So the generations meet on the edge of live radio, and their voices and their laughter mingle within the curiously creative stillness that surrounds them.

Sightless Courier
of the Air

"Oh, Brave New World . . ."

When I returned to National Public Radio in the winter of 1993, after a ten-year absence, several staff members said to me that I had arrived at an important moment in NPR history. "There's a struggle going on for the heart and soul of NPR News," they said, adding that the results of the struggle would affect the direction the organization would take for some years to come.

During my stay at NPR, I seemed to perceive at least two separate "media cultures," coexisting in sometimes uneasy and unexamined partnership. The divisions have already been described in this book in a variety of ways, but essentially the split centers on different conceptions of the medium of radio and different opinions about the proper relationship of NPR *to* radio. The following questions oversimplify and dichotomize the issues, but I think they frame the underlying terms of the debate fairly:

- Is radio primarily a medium of language or a medium of sound?
- Should radio journalism be regarded as an outgrowth of newspapers and magazines, or should its roots be traced back to traditions of oral storytelling (and aural performance)?
- Should NPR strive to be a primary news source for its audience or

should it provide a range of insights and experiences for listeners that they cannot get through television or in print?

- Should public radio build the largest possible audience by catering to current American listening habits, or should public radio offer alternative programming that may be unfamiliar and challenging to many listeners?

While everyone I spoke with at NPR would argue that the answers to these questions lie somewhere in the *middle* of these extremes, people tend to cluster along one side or the other of the continuum, and tensions between the different perspectives have smoldered within the organization for years. At one fascinating moment toward the end of my research, the differences of opinion within the newsroom bubbled out into the open in a series of unusual meetings during which staffers confronted each other about the nature of the work they did and about the direction in which NPR was headed.

Two separate events sparked this ferment. One was a documentary, *Ghetto Life 101*, broadcast in early June on *All Things Considered*. The feature brought to the surface many tensions between minority and nonminority staff members. Some of the issues raised were specific to radio, others related more generally to concerns found throughout American society. A little before *Ghetto 101* was aired, an organization called the Self-Help Group (SHG) began convening a series of lunchtime meetings to discuss the content of NPR's "editorial policy." A wide cross-section of staff members — from managers to production assistants — participated in these large and sometimes heated conversations. (Ironically enough, the SHG itself was established originally by several minority staffers who wanted a forum within which to discuss a variety of issues concerning radio and NPR.)

Why did staff members at NPR feel the need in the spring of 1993 to discuss the future of their organization? Perhaps it was the mood of uncertainty and change which hung in the air, almost palpably, in the corridors of 2025 M Street. After almost a decade as president, Doug Bennet had recently resigned and his successor was still being sought. NPR would soon move to its new offices in an entirely different part of town. And — not to be underestimated — the local stations had just entered into a brand-new financial relationship with NPR: during a five-year experimental period, the cost of NPR programs would be set at a *fixed percentage of station revenues*. Thus the budget for NPR would rise and fall according to the financial health of its members. (In the past, NPR News created its annual budget in conjunction with the NPR board of directors, and would then negotiate with stations over the fairest way to pass the costs along. Local stations fought to keep membership fees down; NPR News struggled to keep its budget from expanding.)

Bill Buzenberg, NPR's vice president in charge of news, spoke glowingly of the new arrangement — it heralded a promising new partnership between the center and the periphery. But some staffers in the newsroom worried about what the new system might mean in times of economic recession. Would the already tight budget face additional, unforeseeable squeezes?

The controversy generated by *Ghetto Life 101* and the discussions at the SHG meetings on editorial policy vividly brought to light fault lines and tensions within NPR. An examination of these forces might serve as a fitting coda to this portrait of NPR, suggesting problems and possibilities that lurk in public radio's future.

NPR and Diversity

Ghetto Life 101 represented another astonishing piece of radio produced by the talented independent David Isay. He had given tape recorders to a couple of African-American teenagers who lived in and around a housing project on Chicago's south side. Isay worked with the kids as they assembled an "audio journal" of their lives, interviewing friends and family and making an aural journey through their neighborhood. The kids narrated the piece themselves and wrote most of what they read. Just about everyone who auditioned the documentary before it aired thought it was tremendously powerful radio. Just about everyone who auditioned the piece was white. *All Things Considered* broke format in order to carry *Ghetto Life 101* as a full, twenty-seven-minute feature (the five-thirty newscast was dropped). But after the broadcast, it quickly became apparent that the documentary had hurt and offended a great many of NPR's African-American staffers. They felt that *Ghetto Life 101* presented a series of unmitigated, unflattering stereotypes. "I thought the piece was one-dimensional, one-sided, overwhelmingly negative," explained foreign desk editor Joyce Davis, an energetic woman with a charming smile and flashing brown eyes. "I grew up in a very poor community and I can tell you, what that program broadcast is *not* the whole story."

As mentioned previously, NPR seems to have a pretty good record when it comes to staff diversity. A little more than half the organization is female, one quarter is minority. African-Americans, Hispanics, Asian-Americans, and other groups are represented throughout the news staff: from producers and directors on various shows, to the editorial desks, to the engineering staff (a surprisingly mixed group, in terms of gender, culture, and ethnicity). To mention only those people who have appeared in this book: African-Americans on the production side include Audrey Wynn, Greg Peppers, Doug Mitchell, Akili Tyson, David Rector, and Walter Watson; and on the engineering side, Renée Pringle, who worked with Cindy Carpien on the Czechoslovakian mix; Asian-Americans on the production and reportorial side include Ken Hom and Deborah Wong. Furthermore, there have always been a handful of regular NPR reporters and newscasters who were minorities; their numbers are larger today than ever before, ranging from African-American to Hispanic to Asian-American to (Asian) Indian. Minorities have appeared from time to time as hosts of NPR programs, though as of the spring of 1993, only Ray Suarez held that position on a permanent basis: he was host of *Talk of the Nation*.[1]

But the *presence* of minorities on NPR's staff does not by any means assure that minority perspectives are well integrated into NPR's editorial or executive decision-making process. Multicultural harmony, respect, and sensitivity requires more than a numbers game. So it was that *Ghetto Life 101* — a terrific piece of creative radio — struck many people at NPR as insensitive, one-sided, clichéd . . . bad sociology and bad journalism. Some African-Americans on staff said they were most upset that their white colleagues should be *surprised* by their response.

American radio documentaries, however creatively produced, remain as susceptible to unintended bias and distortion as any other products of our complex society. But upon reflection, it is possible that one important aspect of *Ghetto Life 101* may have been overlooked in the pain and controversy following its broadcast. It seems to me that

---

[1] Traditionally, cultural pluralism at NPR has not always percolated as high up the chain of power and responsibility as it might — with some notable exceptions. In the fall of 1993, NPR chose as its next president Del Lewis, an African-American who is an expert in the field of emergent communications technologies, with which NPR will have to get involved if the organization is to survive into the next century (when, many predict, radio in its current form [stations, networks] will cease to exist).

placing a microphone and tape recorder into the hands of teenagers living on the south side of Chicago could have powerful and wide-ranging significance. If creative radio affects people differently from television or film, it's possible to imagine that *aural documentaries* produced from, by, and for the inner city could help shape a new set of images and self-images, redefining a portion of our society so excluded and stereotyped by the dominant, preternaturally visual culture. I wonder whether radio, properly pursued as a mode of expression and communication (and not, as Scott Simon says, as just another way to sell soap), could be used to help reconstitute communities . . . could suggest new verbal and oral possibilities for a variety of subcultures. Homer helped define Hellenistic identity, West African Griots expressed a shared history and culture for many of their societies. What would happen if latter-day electronic Homers and Griots were encouraged to develop in America's cities? Liberated from the narrowing tyrannies of video, what compelling mixtures of sound and story might they create? What kinds of radio might emerge that connected with the deepest imaginative potential of people struggling to survive in our neglected urban landscapes — from the projects of Chicago to the barrios of Los Angeles?

The Two Cultures

The tensions and divisions within the NPR staff that came to the surface over *Ghetto Life 101* are not unique to public radio; but the wide-ranging discussions about editorial policy organized by the Self-Help Group brought out a number of conflicts specific to NPR. What was said publicly echoed much of what many people had said to me in private conversations: yet now "print" people and "radio" people were squaring off, face to face, in the crucible of the executive conference room. Their comments crystallized the long-standing debate.

The meetings were moderated by Joyce Davis, one of the founders of the SHG. (A former freelance reporter based overseas, Joyce had been editing an op-ed column in foreign affairs at *The Times-Picayune* in New Orleans, before coming to NPR in 1990 as a foreign editor.) Early on, Joyce articulated a view, shared by many, that a particular tension existed at NPR between "those people who are journalists" and others whom she called "radio artists." The journalists were primarily concerned with the coverage of breaking news, the artists with producing radio pieces that sounded wonderful.

Almost immediately, Lynn Neary objected to the phrase "radio artist." Used in this context, she said, the term denigrated the work of serious radio journalists. "It *shouldn't* be that we have 'radio artists' and we have 'journalists.'" Lynn said, forcefully. "We have *radio journalists* who understand how to use the medium of radio creatively."

But Joyce (and others) insisted that there was a different perspective between a hard-news orientation toward journalism and what another producer began calling "pretty radio." Joyce gave a practical example. Say a story is breaking in Cairo, but the reporter on the scene is unable to collect actuality or sound: does NPR wait a week till some other reporter can get tape? "The report is going to sound pretty if we wait," said Joyce, "but by then every newspaper in the country will have already done the story. That's the dilemma we have. What is more important: getting the information out there, or getting it done in this wonderful radio fashion that NPR does well?"

Ira Glass thought that Joyce was presenting a false dilemma. He recalled when he was producing for Daniel Zwerdling at the *Exxon Valdez* oil spill: he and Danny were constantly using what Ira called the "strengths of radio as a storytelling medium" as they covered the hard-news story. "But the reporter has to be thinking in radio terms, and *the editor* has to be thinking that way," Ira said.

Liane Hansen seconded Ira's remarks, saying that hard news done without sound, without the techniques of radio storytelling, was often boring. "You tune right out after one minute because it's so poorly written and bad in its [aural] presentation."

Susan Stamberg argued strongly against making a dichotomy between hard news and radio production. "I really object to a term like 'pretty radio,'" she said. "That puts us on a shelf and talks about the use of sound as some little addition afterward — like you put a bow in your hair. The *advantage* we have as a medium is that we *do sound*. And to me, *not* using sound is like printing a newspaper without bold headlines. It does exactly the same thing. It pulls the listener in, it grabs them, to get that information to them that they need to have."

While conceding that sound had some importance, Joyce returned to the logistical problems an editor faced when trying to find good reporters who also do good radio. She admitted that occasionally she offered "mediocre" radio pieces to shows in order that the news be covered. "I find myself saying that the *news* is more important than the medium — what else can I do?" Joyce asked. "What it really boils down to is that if I'm going to put the best product on NPR's air, then I don't deal with certain reporters, and there are parts of the world we do not get news from. Is that what we want?"

So the familiar debate continued . . . And yet viewed from a certain angle (admittedly, the point of view of an outsider), the discussion seemed a little surreal. Why should a medium of *sound* be debating within itself the *importance* of sound? Does anyone in television ever question the importance of pictures to TV news? Does any newspaper staff seriously discuss whether they should *not* rely on words to tell their stories? (Though, of course, in recent years, what I call the tyranny of the visual has spread so far through our culture that some newspapers *do* seem to be downplaying language: witness what passes for "writing" in *USA Today* and the increasing importance of color photography in most newspapers.)

If television has no pictures from a certain part of the world, then that part of the world does not get on the Evening News — except for late-breaking events, sometimes reported over the telephone. Why should there be any question about putting people on the radio who do not have a sense of radio as a medium of sound? And yet there are many NPR staff members these days who consider "sound" a separate issue — a luxury — something which is not as important, in the final analysis, as the news.

What becomes of news on the radio if it has no sound? That is, if the genius of the medium is not engaged? Doesn't radio then turn into an oral teletype spewing out words? Doesn't it start acting like a second-class medium — a substitute vehicle that carries *another* medium to its listeners, in the way that a dry gourd carries water?

Furthermore — and more subtly — what has happened to public radio when editors and producers and managers start referring to reports — or programs — as *products?* Why should *this* bit of vocabulary from commercial broadcasting enter the public broadcasting newsroom? Is this a continuation of the process that starts when local stations want more breaks "to do business" and when local managers start obsessing about "audience share," "market penetration," and "high-skewing demographics?"

The final SHG session was organized as a conversation with the top manager of the news division, Bill Buzenberg. Bill is a tall man, in his late forties, with a big frame but a somewhat small face. His short blond hair, blue eyes, and youthfully pitched voice combine with a sometimes shambling demeanor to create an almost boyish aura. Yet Bill is very much a leader and has done a great deal to build up morale in the news department in the three years that he's been in charge. His handling of the SHG discussions demonstrated his approach to his job, which is at once to promote excellence and to build consensus — as much as possible, to get people at NPR News *working together*. Bill played down the divisions between ex-print people and sound-oriented people. "I really agree with Lynn Neary that this is a false dichotomy," Bill said. "We come from many different perspectives but we're here to do radio journalism. It takes all of us to do it. We don't want everybody from print. We don't want everybody who's just a great recording artist. We need this mixture of people and ideas and thinking. We *are* this mixture."

Bill recalled conversations with Bill Siemering, one of NPR's earliest visionaries, in which Siemering reported that from the very first, National Public Radio had been imagined as an organization that would "not concede today's news to anybody." The desire had always been present to have high standards of journalism, while also pursuing high standards of radio production. Bill Buzenberg agreed that there was a danger of becoming so hard-news driven that "we lose sight of the value of production." But he insisted that NPR would continue trying to achieve a balance between these approaches. "Clearly we want big produced pieces and small produced sound portraits," Bill said. "We need stories that create more scenes and wonderful moments." He envisioned that if *All Things Considered* became a two-hour show, the extra half-hour might become a showcase for what he called "path-breaking" work. But NPR also had an obligation to cover the news. "When this mix [of stories and approaches] is right," Bill concluded, "and when you hear it in a program, it's wonderful. It's difficult to achieve. Our resources do not match our ambitions, yet. But though we can't do everything all the time, we should keep our focus on what we do best — which is *great radio*."

Bill's call for NPR to "do it all" presented a mission statement with which everyone in the room could agree. Out of Bill's dry but compelling words emerged an image of public radio programming that retained its creativity yet also served its audience's hunger for news, that broadcast artful pieces pushing the envelope of radio but also included meat-and-potatoes reports about breaking events. Bill spoke practically, directly, but his voice echoed with some of the idealism upon which the network had been originally founded.

Financial Constraints

In the aftermath of the Self-Help Group meetings, staff members responded cautiously to Bill Buzenberg's articulation of purpose and vision. "Talk is easy," more than one person said. "We'll see what happens." Many circled back to the hard economic realities that severely limit the amount of time and resources that can be devoted to non–hard news production.

One of the first great tests of Bill's inclusive approach began to take shape during 1994, after NPR moved to its new headquarters and installed its new president. In late 1994, NPR decided to expand the oldest of its magazine programs, *All Things Considered*, from ninety minutes to two hours. The new show will eventually start at four o'clock and the new format will debut sometime during 1995. The decision resulted in part from the continued lobbying of local stations (prime afternoon drive time is four to five, not five to six); in part from pressures within NPR (most managers had long wanted a two-hour *ATC*); but also in part because Public Radio International began talking about launching its own four o'clock afternoon news program. If PRI "went prime time," how could NPR hold back?

The decision to enlarge *ATC* was announced publicly in late 1994 and the logistics for the new show were still being worked out as this book was going to press. The expansion was expected to cost an additional $1 million, but audience researchers suggested that *ATC*'s listenership would increase significantly, perhaps even surpassing *Morning Edition*'s. With *ATC* starting at four o'clock, and its rollovers going to ten o'clock, the show's staff will grow substantially. The most significant decision, though, was still being debated by a committee that was soliciting suggestions from local stations as well as from NPR staffers: to what extent would the revised program retain its freewheeling format and to what extent would it borrow a segmented structure from *Morning Edition?* By the late fall of 1994, it seemed probable that the new *ATC* would add further cut-aways, allowing local stations to conduct more business ("making the show more user-friendly," is how John Dinges put it). The tricky question was how *ATC* could maintain some of its traditional variety of pacing and style, and also sustain its ability to broadcast the creative, longer-form pieces which Bill Buzenberg spoke about at the SHG meeting in 1993. The four o'clock starting time appeared to impose certain rigidities of format: for example, the program would need to "refresh" the main news stories each hour, since many would be developing during the course of the show. This in itself might alter the feeling of *All Things Considered*, making it sound far more like a news service than a magazine program. To what extent would *ATC* producers try to balance and transcend these structural constrictions with moments of challenging, creative, and unusual radio? Much would depend upon the spirit brought to the new *All Things Considered* by its staff — along with the expectations of local stations and listeners.

Bill Buzenberg, former peace corps volunteer in Bolivia, one time newspaper reporter, former state department and foreign correspondent for National Public Radio, constantly juggles the bottommost line of NPR News with the pressures of local stations, the demands of the news bureaucracy which he has helped build, and the high-minded ideals with which NPR was originally founded.

"I can't stress this enough that we are enormously underbudgeted for what our ambition is," Bill explained, in a rare quiet moment in his office, late one afternoon in the spring of 1993, many months before the decision to expand *ATC*. "We now have stations in every state of the country and cover eighty-six percent of the population with news. That's big. NPR now has four hundred and seventy-seven member stations, well over four hundred of which are carrying our news. When I first came on in 1978, we had two hundred and twenty. When NPR began, there were ninety. We do this with a total — including eleven part-time people — of one-hundred and seventy-six people here in this building: that's including receptionists, tape cutters . . . everybody. We have fifty full-time or contract reporters around the country and around the world. Fifty. We also have probably twenty-five stringers at any given moment, and we may use twenty-five reporters from local stations, from time to time.

"We are trying to meet incredibly high expectations with severely limited resources," Bill said, and then reeled off a string of figures. In 1993, NPR's total budget — covering its technical facilities, arts and cultural programming, development services, and so forth — was around $40 million. Of that, under $16 million went to the news division. Sixty percent of NPR's operating budget came from stations (whose dues totaled 5 percent of their annual revenue if they took a single program, 10 percent if they aired all of NPR's news shows, and 2 percent on top of that if they used the network's cultural programs). A quarter of

NPR's budget derived from foundation and corporate grants, including a small amount, 2.5 percent, directly from the Corporation for Public Broadcasting. (Estimates in 1993 showed that local stations relied on CPB grants for 16 percent of their operating expenses.)

In the world of American mass media, NPR redefines the cliché of operating on a shoestring. "The most we ever spent on a two-months running story was in Somalia, last year," Bill explained. "We had a satellite phone, an engineer, a couple of correspondents and producers, rotating in and out. We spent two hundred thousand dollars. One of the networks I know spent five million dollars on the same story.

"Let's face it," Bill said, shaking his head. "We have a very hobbled system that is not funded very well at all. I would love it, quite frankly, if we had a system like the British do — a license fee. Everybody contributes. We would be in fat city. I would like it if we had a one percent tax on the sale of commercial broadcast licenses. One percent tax? It would pay for all of public broadcasting, TV and radio — no problem. We wouldn't have to accept any funds from anybody else. But of course one of the reasons it hasn't been done is that the idea is fought hugely by commercial broadcasters."

And certainly the new Congress, elected in 1994, is liable to take an entirely different approach to NPR and may vote to eliminate all federal subsidies, even money going to local stations. After the elections, the man expected to become the next Speaker of the House, Newt Gingrich, reaffirmed his conviction that the National Endowment for the Arts, the National Endowment for the Humanities, and the Corporation for Public Broadcasting should all be "privatized."

So while the ambitions of Bill Buzenberg remain high, the future of public broadcasting — and its desire to remain a thing quite different from commercial broadcasting — seemed threatened once again, at the start of 1995, with some new financial hurdles and impediments.

A Noncommercial Future?

This book has focused on the historic center of the public radio system in this country — National Public Radio in Washington. But in reality, NPR supplies only a small portion of the programming which appears daily on almost five hundred local stations around the country. It is one thing to listen to the ideals of old-timers at NPR like Lynn Neary, Scott Simon, and Alex Chadwick or to witness Bob Malesky's brilliant production about Martin Luther King. It is quite another experience to tune to any number of local public radio stations and hear what the average day *sounds* like.

For a listener who has not become inured to it, the proliferation of business on public airwaves is astounding. The station call letters are repeated over and over — almost as frequently as on commercial outlets. Underwriting credits may pop up as frequently as every ten minutes, though sometimes they may sound like community service announcements. The "commercialization" can be subtle. For example, if an upcoming concert at a nearby location will be featuring two Brahms string quartets, the local public radio station might broadcast a recording of one of the quartets, after which listeners might hear the following:

Music Ends.

ANNOUNCER: WXXX has brought you a performance of the Brahms Quartet Number Two, with the Tokyo String Quartet. From an RCA CD.

The Brahms Quartets Numbers Two and Three will be performed this weekend by the Schlemmerhorn Quartet at the Green Briar concerts, Stonedale Farms, on Route 5, in South Norwalk, at five P.M. For tickets, call 555-5555.

You are listening to WXXX. Later this afternoon we'll be hearing two symphonies by Mozart and some piano sonatas by Beethoven and Schubert. A reminder that all music played on WXXX can be purchased through the Public Radio Music Source — your one place for all classical CDs and tapes. Call 1-800-555-5555 for the Public Radio Music Source.

Afternoon Symphony on WXXX is brought to you in part by Whole in the Wall Books — browsing, special orders, and collector's items. 101 Main Street, Culver City. 444-4444.

Our music continues now on listener-supported WXXX with a Sonata for Flute by Handel, performed by Frans Brüggen.

Music Starts.

A few years ago, classical announcers on fine arts stations would regularly talk about the music to be presented and they often programmed their shows on the basis of some theme, an underlying idea they wished to present or discuss. No longer. Most stations have severely reduced the amount of commentary and have stopped playing certain works, like the longer Mahler symphonies, because they consume too large a block of programming. Other guidelines suggest avoiding vocal music, because most listeners have neither a taste nor a tolerance for such works, according to audience research.

Local stations, obsessed with the need to convert listeners into members, follow more and more formulas in what their announcers play and what they say. Stations also try to work in more and more underwriting credits. Further, in the scramble to get corporate funding, certain standards once enforced by the FCC have been relaxed. Time was when a local brokerage firm would not be allowed to underwrite a financial news show, or when newspapers would not be permitted to help pay for *Morning Edition.* Such subtleties as wishing to avoid the appearance of "conflict of interest" have disappeared. Deregulation has allowed stations more latitude in their pursuit of contributions from businesses, even as the lines between underwriting credits and advertisements have gotten increasingly blurry. The most infamous example of this latter tendency is probably Public Radio International's daily business program, *Marketplace,* whose theme music concludes with the familiar tune from General Electric's corporate jingle. (The notes accompany the lyrics "We bring good things to life.") Talk about subliminal advertising and creeping commercialism!

The result of all this clambering for money and for ratings is that more and more minutes of local public radio are filled with lifeless air: time when audiences listen with half an ear. In a word, public radio is sounding increasingly like low-key commercial radio.

I have hinted already at some of the reasons for what I call this drift toward commercialism — and what others would call a necessary infusion of practicality into the business of public broadcasting due to severe cutbacks in government support. One of the most influential voices encouraging changes in the practices of public radio stations is himself an old NPR hand, an enthusiast for all kinds of radio, and a professional pollster and opinion researcher. For years, David Giovannoni has been arguing that public radio needed to be more aware of the behaviors and tastes of its audience, and he has unabashedly supported the segmentation of formats, the move toward hard news, the shift from a *program* to a *service* mentality among public radio managers.

"NPR is here as a public service," David explained to me over a cup of coffee at the 1993 Public Radio Conference in Washington. "Public service is defined — at least in part — by the number of people listening to it, right? By definition, if nobody hears it, there's no service. So the more people who listen, the better the service, in my definition."

David insisted that he wants public radio to maintain a qualitative difference from commercial radio, and he said that his definition of "public service" includes the *importance* of a program to its audience. (Surveys usually find that commercial programs — even ones with high ratings — measure out as being less important to their listeners.) Yet he explained that his research asks the same questions of public radio's audience as do surveys commissioned by commercial broadcasters. How are people using the medium? What do they *want* to hear? As a result of David's polling, he has concluded that many of the older forms of public radio programming are *inappropriate* for how the medium is used by most listeners. He compared broadcasting long-form programs on the radio — like half-hour documentaries — to publishing a novel in a newspaper. The message did not fit the medium. "These days, radio is typically a secondary activity," David said. "I'm driving my car, I turn the radio on. Okay? I'm doing some work that doesn't require great concentration, I turn the radio on. What you're demanding with long-form is that radio become a primary activity. And that's something that we don't do with radio, typically."

Ironically, David Giovannoni expressed a profound personal love for sound (he's an avid collector of early phonograph records) and he recalled with great affection many of the longer radio documentaries of the past — programs like Father Cares and A Question of Place. But he insisted that these shows are no longer "radio programs." Cassettes and CDs were now the proper vehicles for distributing these aural experiences. "Good audio may not be good radio," David concluded succinctly.

(The idea of putting long-form radio programs on tape and CD may seem like a good idea. But in fact, such a format changes the relationship of listener to program in a fundamental way. Part of the wonder of radio, the magic of the medium, is the lack of control that a listener exercises . . . the chance that something unexpected, something unintended, will float into consciousness. Giving up on long-form radio means inherently limiting the element of joyful and serendipitous discovery that has long been a part of NPR's underlying philosophy.)

David Giovannoni argues that the listening habits of American audiences are *immutable,* and he credits increases in the size of NPR's audience to adjustments the network has made to those facts of broadcasting life. If Giovannoni is right — or if a majority of public stations continue to believe that he is right — then a certain part of what I have been calling "the noble experiment of public radio" will have failed in its mission. Listeners will increasingly be pandered to instead of challenged and their use of public radio as a "secondary activity" will continue to grow. NPR will be in grave danger reverting to the same status as commercial radio — audio wallpaper for the backgrounds of our lives.

But not everyone in the public radio system buys into David Giovannoni's central premise that audience habits cannot be changed. Between the time that Doug Bennet resigned as president of NPR and Del Lewis was chosen as his successor, Joe Dembo served as acting president. A longtime NPR board member who worked for CBS Radio News for several decades, Joe now teaches at Fordham and Yale. A self-described "radio baby," Joe became hooked on the medium of the sound and the story when he was a teenager and went on to write and produce for some of the great CBS radio correspondents in the fifties and sixties. He resigned from a CBS executive post in 1988, after receiving many prestigious awards for his radio documentary work.

Joe does not see any immutable law of nature behind the diminution of the attention span of the average American listener. "I *cannot* believe that this mad rush toward brevity is due to popular demand," Joe explained, while sitting in the NPR presidential office. "I don't think that this was an outgrowth of a popular movement that knocked on the doors of the station managers and said, 'We can't stand your stuff cause it's too long.' I think it came from the front offices of the network's affiliated stations. I think it's due to the *greed* of the managers, who, when they saw something that ran two minutes, wanted it cut to one minute so they could shove in still another commercial. And I think the American people have been dragged into this stampede toward brevity. So that now everybody seems to have the attention of a bumblebee. And as a result, we live in a blur. Nothing stands out. There's no substance on commercial radio. It's really tragic. *We* have forced them to become used to it. *We* have trained them. And now people are no longer upset by it, because they've all become used to it. We are in the age of the sound bite. And that's pathetic." Joe looked down at the shiny tabletop of his large desk and shook his head. His small fingers tapped gently against the arms of his chair.

"So NPR is an oasis," Joe resumed, looking up with a quiet smile on his gray, lined face. "And I hope it always will be. And as long as we have people like Bill Buzenberg and others, who are the watchdogs, this kind of rush toward brevity will not happen here. You avoid it first by becoming convinced that it's *evil*. And if you are convinced that it's evil — that it's a disservice to democracy and everything we hold dear — then it's a little bit easier to avoid it."

As I have said, in the context of what's happening "on the ground" at local public radio stations, the debates occurring within NPR about the future of creative radio production may seem arcane and even irrelevant. Yet I would argue that a potential saving grace for the older ideals of public radio remains the medium's relatively low cost and small size. Unlike the vast corporate entities behind commercial radio and television, public radio is still run by a handful of people — in Washington and at the local level — and therefore it does not take very many individuals, nor a massive influx of cash, to make changes in the system.

Indeed, the membership of most public radio stations is small enough that individual listeners *can* make a big difference in what a station broadcasts. If enough listeners — either nationally or locally — were to suddenly start sending money to support certain kinds of programs, and made it clear they did not like other kinds, station managers would have incentive to change their offerings. If *Weekend All Things Considered*, for example, ever raised more money from its audience than *Morning Edition*, word would get around. If a large enough audience made a fuss over certain creative radio pieces and expressed less satisfaction with more straight-ahead radio forms, producers up and down the line would hear the message.

Frank Mankiewicz once said that NPR was the best kept secret in American broadcasting. I believe that the creative potential of public radio still remains hidden from some of the most ardent supporters of the medium. Public radio producers have been talking *among themselves* for years, arguing about what directions programming should take. The public has participated very little in this conversation, except when caught up by mindless and distracting controversies about political bias. If this book has helped suggest some of the creative possibilities of public radio as a form of expression — as a form of art — and triggered some imaginative expectations within the ears of public radio listeners, then it will have served a useful purpose.

Through the Aural Mirror

In some of his original goals for National Public Radio and its flagship program, *All Things Considered*, Bill Siemering envisioned a form of radio that would hold up a mirror to the country and reflect back to Americans "what they were" today. Siemering developed his ideas at a simpler time in American culture, when we did not have to struggle against some of the basic distortions of perception that have recently entered our field of vision. Simply put, we Americans today, on the whole, are not exercising our *independent imaginations* to the extent that we once did. Increasingly, we are becoming passive receptors of external imagery and we are focusing increasingly inward, upon our narrowed selves, for understanding and empathy. When we watch more television than we read books; when we would rather go to movies than sit around and talk with our families; when we become more comfortable with the rapidly changing images on the screen than with the fixed permanence of paintings or photographs whose movements occur in our minds and emotions; and when even our experience of music is overlaid with external images (such as those on MTV) that abort the growth and development of the private picture-making processes of our minds . . . in a civilization such as I describe, nothing less than our fundamental capacities as *imaginative beings* are challenged and diminished . . . and perhaps even threatened with extinction.

In this age of "digital numerology," where scientific measurements are supposed to give us the confidence and security that used to be afforded by more subtle senses (inner faith, belief in the power of one's own judgment), our private imaginations are assaulted on all sides and we lose touch with our innate ability to perceive our surroundings and locate ourselves — with compassion, and humility, and grace — within a world that both confuses and sustains us.

Radio, the long forgotten and much maligned electronic medium, offers us echoes of our former, more confident, more independent selves . . . and allows us to experience the best of what it means to be sensitive, aware human beings. Scott Simon spoke eloquently about people working in television: "They are not comfortable living with ambivalence. Whereas that's where radio can really shine." And by "ambivalence," Scott did not mean crude mechanical balancing acts — "on the one hand this, on the one hand that." Scott was talking about one of the essential qualities of human existence: that we are complex and contradictory creatures who live our lives caught in unresolvable paradoxes. To take one simple example: our consciousness both separates us from the natural world out of which we have come, and yet gives us a yearning to reconnect with Nature. Our fullest lives are spent living in the tension of those unresolvable opposites, finding temporary resolutions — which are only momentary — before we collapse again into our ambivalent condition. (Robert Frost called these brief insights "momentary stays against confusion," and he said that one role of poetry was to supply such moments; I believe that radio, creatively produced, can fulfill the same function.)

Unlike television, unlike movies, radio is a medium which can encapsulate and present back to us, pristine and undiluted, some of the central ambiguities of the human condition. The medium functions *through* ambiguity, after all: we *hear* but we do not *see*. Our understanding comes about when we combine the subtle suggestions of external sound and story with the vividness of our own private, internal imagery. The resulting ideas, pictures, thoughts, feelings are all the more intense and compelling because they mix the outer and the inner. They are all the more satisfying because we know, however unconsciously, that *we* are the ultimate arbiters of the awareness that flowers within our mind's eye . . . Radio, that is to say, humanizes our connection to the world around us. It encourages us to *pay attention* using capacities we may have forgotten that we possess. It rewards us with questions that fathom the depths of our inner resources and that measure the compass of our dreams.

Put simply, in the midst of this tyrannically visual age, this age of cynicism and loneliness and abbreviated attention span, creative radio retains at its very core the ability to make us catch our breaths — and, in that momentary *silence*, to place us, as Fitzgerald writes, face to face with something "commensurate to [our] capacity for wonder."

National Public Radio needs its listeners and supporters to help keep the institution alive; but we, the listeners — the members of this culture, this republic, this civilization — need NPR (or something like it) even more . . . if we are to persevere as humane individuals in a world that otherwise seems to drain nuance, meaning, and compassion from our lives, supplying in its place the cold, colorful comforts that emanate from the cathode ray tube gone mad. The sightless courier of the air may carry some of the antidote for the plague of our time — the atrophying of our private imaginations. Will enough of us see the promise and potential of creative radio to assure its survival as a vibrant, enriching part of our national life? Or is it inevitable that, to paraphrase a lesser poet, the harpies of the shore shall pluck our blind eagle from the air?